The Fundamentals of
Legal Drafting

The Fundamentals of Legal Drafting

Reed Dickerson
Professor of Law Emeritus, Indiana University

Second Edition
(incorporating "Legislative Drafting")

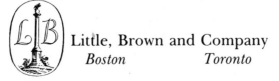

Little, Brown and Company
Boston   Toronto

Library of Congress Catalog Card No. 85-82034

ISBN 0-316-18397-0

HAL

Published simultaneously in Canada
by Little, Brown & Company (Canada) Limited

Printed in the United States of America

To
> W. Barton Leach, who struck
> the first spark
>
> David F. Cavers and Rudolf
> Flesch, who opened the
> first doors
>
> Kurt F. Pantzer, who believed
>
> Jane M. Dickerson, who
> unfailingly supported

. . . language is something more than a tool of thought. It is a part of the process of thinking.

—Arthur Littleton The Importance of Effective Legal Writing in Law Practice, 9 Student Lawyer 6 (1963)

Summary of Contents

Summary of Contents

Contents

Contents

V

The Architecture of Legal Instruments   79

VI

Substantive Clarity: Avoiding Ambiguity   101

Contents

VII

Substantive Clarity: Definitions   137

VIII

General Factors Affecting Readability: Simplification   153

Contents

IX

Miscellaneous Suggestions on Specific Wording   207

Contents

X

Verbal Sexism   221

XI

Amendments; Redesignation   241

Contents

XII

Computers and Other Scientific Aids   257

XIII

Problems Peculiar to Statutes   279

XIV

Some Specific Results   301

Contents

Postscript

Appendix A

Appendix B

Appendix C

Appendix D

Appendix E

Contents

Appendix F
On Teaching Legal Writing, Particularly Legal Drafting

Preface to the Second Edition

Although the art of legal drafting improves slowly, the past 21 years have yielded significant developments. We have seen, for example, the explosion of the consumer movement and the consequent "plain English" movement. Computers and symbolic logic have become important factors. The feminists' drive against discrimination has added a strong incentive to remove verbal "sexism" from legal instruments.

Some progress was made through the efforts of the American Bar Association's now defunct Standing Committee on Legislative Drafting. During the 1970s, the Committee tried to persuade the great bulk of the federal executive agencies, as the source of most legislative proposals, to professionalize their drafting operations by adopting the "legislative counsel" approach. Despite the unanimous support of the ABA's House of Delegates and the blessing of the Attorney General, the Committee's proposal for an executive order to establish the necessary machinery slowly bled to death at the hands of a federal bureaucracy still dominated by legislative ignorance and bureaucratic timidity.[1] Even so, a proposed program worthy of further consideration has survived.[2]

In the meantime, the Committee perceived that the legal profession needed to be educated in the basic principles of legal

[1]R. Dickerson, Materials on Legal Drafting, 381-385 (1981).
[2]R. Dickerson (ed.), Professionalizing Legislative Drafting — The Federal Experience (1973). See also Dickerson, note 1 supra, at 375-385.

drafting and, after reviewing the capabilities of continuing legal education, concluded that the only potentially effective instrument was the law schools. The next problem was to educate the law schools.

The process began in 1974, when the Committee persuaded the ABA's Special Committee for a Study of Legal Education to recommend that the American Bar Foundation undertake a study of what the law schools were doing in the field of legal drafting. The result was Professor Bernard Lammers's report,[3] published in 1977. His answer of "not much" confirmed the earlier impressions of the Committee. In 1975, the Committee (by then the Standing Committee on *Legal* Drafting) co-sponsored an international seminar and workshop on the teaching of legal drafting, which left a useful record of its deliberations.[4] In the early 1980s, the Committee established effective liaison with the Section on Legal Research and Writing of the Association of American Law Schools. Some of the educational fruits of these efforts are reflected in appendix F.

The continuing movement to simplify legal language had in the meantime become a major concern of such organizations as the Document Design Center of Carnegie-Mellon University, the Document Design Center of the American Institutes of Research, and Siegel and Gale, a commercial firm. Some organizations, such as Plain Talk, Inc., have come and unfortunately gone. Also unfortunately, a wholesome concern for legal drafting has been badly diluted whenever it has been absorbed into a broader concern for legal writing generally.

These and other developments are reflected in this new edition. The most significant changes from the first edition appear as new segments on a broadened drafting perspective, the ethics of drafting, an improved drafting strategy, language for sharpening Hohfeldian distinctions, "plain English" laws, verbal "sexism," amendments, computer aids, and legal education. Interspersed are more modest enhancements and updatings.

[3]Lammers, Legislative Process and Drafting in U.S. Law Schools (American Bar Foundation 1977).
[4]Dickerson (ed.), Proceedings of the International Seminar and Workshop on the Teaching of Legal Drafting (1977).

Also included and updated are most of the materials from my earlier book, Legislative Drafting, that were not included or otherwise covered in the first edition of The Fundamentals of Legal Drafting. Thus the current book is a modest second edition also of Legislative Drafting.

The reader will perhaps forgive me for continuing to include a disproportionate number of examples from the output of the Department of Defense and that of World War II's Office of Price Administration. Because good examples are often hard to come by, I have selected those from my own experience whenever to have done otherwise would have produced examples that were less apt or less reliable. In some instances, too, there has been no alternative. To this extent aesthetic balance has yielded to aptness.

The book's approach continues to be oriented away from matters of form and style toward a balanced aggregate of substantive policy, architecture, clarity, and style, in the hope that a wholesome perspective will help to elevate legal drafting from the subordinate position that it has traditionally occupied. Legal educators and members of the bar can hardly be criticized for putting a relatively low evaluation of something that has almost always been put forth as format or legal packaging.

This attempt to ground legal drafting on something more substantial than form and style is the main justification for the first three chapters and the other parts of the book that are meant to be read through rather than merely referred to. Important in their own right, these materials do not lessen the book's usefulness as a reference work on form and style.

The book also continues to be oriented away from mere legislative drafting toward drafting in general. The dangers in venturing into less familiar territory are unavoidable, because the total domain of legal draftsmanship is so large that no one can be personally experienced in all of it. But, although this may be ground for professional humility and even reluctance, the need to consolidate and extend common drafting principles is well worth the risk of an occasional lapse. To avoid the more obvious toe-stubbing, I have relied partly on the fragmentary literature now available in particular fields and partly on the suggestions of drafting specialists prominent in private practice. If I have succeeded in avoiding a lopsided book and the more obvious blunders of personal unfamiliarity, much of the credit is theirs. If I have not, the fault is mine.

Because the audiences for this book are not necessarily the same as those to which specific legal instruments are addressed, I have not felt as circumscribed in form or style as I would have had I been drafting a statute or consumer instrument. That is why, for reasons of clarity, I have felt free to use language that I might be uncomfortable with in a legal instrument directed to a lay audience. (Even this may not head off accusations that I do not practice what I preach!) On the other hand, because clarity is as important here as it is in any legal instrument, I have not exploited my greater freedom of expression to the point of using emerging forms that, however socially desirable, have yet to attain general acceptance. Respecting gender, the reader will note that I have at least been able to make substantial use of the second person without in any wise compromising clarity or impairing tone.

A few words about chapter 10 (Verbal Sexism): Some perceptive readers will wonder whether it isn't too long, too detailed, and unnecessarily provocative. That may well be the case. The problem it deals with not only is extremely complicated but tends to fray the nerves of both impatient feminists and the persons who zealously guard the interests of people seeking a clear understanding of what the law expects of them. The latter need is especially acute where legislative instruments are concerned.[5] A workable reconciliation not having been otherwise effected within the accepted standards of modern communication, I made a strong attempt here, handicapped only by a generous fund of fallibility. In extenuation, I can only add that the chapter went through 22 drafts, during the course of which it was exposed to the close secrutiny of legislative draftsmen, ar-

---

[5]"Do not forget . . . that [when drafting] . . . your overriding objective is to express an idea as clearly and simply as you can, not to pursue a social ideology, no matter how lofty. Certainty of meaning largely depends upon the draftsman's unbendingly conservative use of language." Hirsch, Drafting Federal Law 31 (Dept. of Health and Human Services 1980).

dent feminists, teachers of English composition, and a sprinkling of "ordinary" people.

It is hard to remember all the people who, in one way or another during the intervening 21 years, have educated me further in the drafting art and its supporting disciplines or otherwise supported my efforts.

In this country, my most prolific sources of help have been James B. Minor, Edward O. Craft, Maurice B. Kirk, Seth S. Searcy III, and Professors Layman E. Allen, B. Kent Dickerson, Frank P. Grad, and David Mellinkoff. I am also much indebted to Judge Eugene A. Burdick, Frank H. Edwards, the late Jerome A. Levinson, the late George S. Workinger, Richard G. Moser, Frederic P. Houston, Fred J. Emery, Charles B. Nutting, Duncan A. McDonald, Judge Shirley S. Abrahamson, Sidney A. Saperstein, Theodore Ellenbogan, Judge Paul H. Buchanan, Jr., the late Judge Harold Leventhal, the late Judge Robert C. Finley, John E. Molitor, John S. Dickerson, Martin Mayer, John K. Silk, Paul D. Newnum, Jane M. Hamblin, Jane M. Harper, Mark K. Stuann, the late Judge James K. Groves, Judge William H. Erickson, Arthur H. Peterson, the late James Craig Peacock, Diana S. Dowling, Homer Clay Buchanan, and Professors Mary Ellen Caldwell, Keith E. Morrison, Joseph D. Brodley, Bernard Lammers, Michael D. Carrico, Harry Pratter, F. Thomas Schornhorst, Michael B. W. Sinclair, Irvin C. Rutter, Hector-Neri Castanada, Henry B. Veatch, Thomas A. Sebeok, and Daniel Maki. Ralph F. Gaebler, graduating senior, provided valuable last-minute research.

Frank W. Daykin, Elizabeth S. Hogue, and Professors Julia Lamber, W. Edson Richmond, and Marilyn Sternglass helped guide me through the thickets of verbal "sexism."

On the readability of consumer documents, I benefitted from the experience of Francis X. Hayes, Janice C. Redish, Veda R. Charrow, Robert R. Charrow, Carl Felsenfeld, Alan Siegel, Robert L. Geltzer, and George H. Hathaway.

In bringing me up to date on computer technology, Robert P. Bigelow, Roy N. Freed, William A. Chatterton, Albert L. Moses, and Professor James K. Sprowl have been most helpful.

For moral, financial, or other support, I owe much to

Preface to the Second Edition

Professors David F. Cavers and Roger Cramton, Chief Judge Edward D. Re, the late William B. Spann, Jr., James D. Fellers, Robert W. Meserve, Justin A. Stanley, the late Leon Jaworski, Lee Loevinger, Milton M. Carrow, Frederick R. Franklin, Peter Sullivan, Daniel James, Earl W. Kintner, the late Kurt F. Pantzer, Ronald J. Foulis, Michael H. Carodozo, Deans Douglas G. Boshkoff, Sheldon J. Plager, and Maurice J. Holland, and the late Dean Dan Hopson.

Among my valued Canadian contributors have been Elmer A. Driedger, Robert C. Dick, Glenn Acorn, Arthur N. Stone, James W. Ryan, and Gérard Bertrand, all Queen's Counsel.

In England, I owe a special debt to Lord Renton and the late Sir Noel Hutton. Also very helpful were Lord Scarman, Sir Henry P. Rowe, Sir John Fiennes, Godfrey Carter, Terence and Sandra Skemp, the late Frank C. S. Bayliss, Sir William Dale, Judge Kutlu T. Fuad (now of Hong Kong), Jeremy D. Pope, and Professor R. W. M. Dias.

In North Ireland, William H. Leitch enriched my repertoire of drafting exercises.

In Australia, Professor E. K. Braybrooke and J. Q. Ewens, C.B.E., filled me in on drafting practices "down under."

In Japan, Professor Takeo Hayakawa helped dispel deep confusion by explaining some of the idiosyncracies of Japanese law language.

I thank Spencer L. Kimball and the American Bar Foundation for sponsoring the Lammers Report and for the Foundation's generosity in relinquishing any financial interest in the second edition that it might otherwise have had as a result of its welcome sponsorship of the first.

I am especially grateful to Roger F. Noreen and West Publishing Company for permission to include original materials from my Materials on Legal Drafting (1981) and its Teacher's Manual.

For guiding me through the mazes of modern legal research, I am grateful to Betty Lebus, the late Jurij Fednyskyj, Colleen J. Pauwels, Byron D. Cooper, Linda Farris, Keith Buckley, Helena Warburg, and others of the Law School's library staff and Elizabeth S. Kelly, recent librarian at Southern Illinois University and now law librarian at the University of Pennsylvania.

Preface to the Second Edition

Rachel Myers, as always, was indispensable on the typewriter, while Cindy Ellard, Cindy Flynn, Lisa Grogan, and Loretta Higgins performed admirably on various word processors. Mary Knuau added some important finishing touches.

Finally, thanks are owing to the following publishers for their generous permission to draw on the materials named:

ABA Journal — Dickerson, The Difficult Choice Between "And" and "Or," 46 A.B.A.J. 310 (1960).

Harvard Journal on Legislation — Dickerson, The Diseases of Legislative Language, 1 Harv. J. Leg. 5 (1964).

Idaho Law Review — Dickerson, Teaching Legal Writing in the Law School (With A Special Nod to Legal Drafting), 16 Idaho L. Rev. 85 (1979).

Journal of Legal Education — Dickerson, Legal Drafting: Writing as Thinking, or, Talk-back from Your Draft and How to Exploit It, 29 J. of Leg. Educ. 373 (1978).

McGill Law Journal — Driedger, Are Statutes Written for Men Only? 22 McGill L.J. 666 (1976).

Notre Dame Lawyer — Dickerson, How to Write a Law, 31 Notre Dame Law. 14 (1955).

The Poynter Center — Dickerson, Should Plain English Be Legislated?, from Plain English in a Complex Society (1980).

To all these, and any whom I may have overlooked, my warm thanks.

Reed Dickerson

Bloomington, Indiana
February 12, 1986

Special Notice
"MLD"?

Readers who are inclined to explore footnotes may be mystified (if they skip this page) by frequent references to "MLD." This is an acronym for Materials on Legal Drafting (West 1981), edited by the author of the present book. "Materials" is a compilation of items relating to legal drafting that, although intended to serve primarily as a course book, is useful here as a source. In some instances, it contains materials that are unavailable elsewhere. In others, it contains materials that would be hard to locate elsewhere. The rest, while available elsewhere (see the respective footnotes), can be sampled more conveniently at one alternative location. Otherwise, there is no greater need to turn to MLD than any other source that has been cited.

The Fundamentals of
Legal Drafting

I

An Introduction to Legal Drafting

§1.1. THE PROBLEM

At a meeting in London in January 1973, the Law Ministers of the British Commonwealth noted "the widespread shortage of expert legislative and legal draftsmen and the importance of taking early steps to overcome this shortage."[1] Additional evidence from Australia, Canada, and the United States indicates that this shortage is world-wide. Worse, the shortage extends beyond legislative drafting to legal drafting generally. Despite recent progress, the problem persists.[2]

The need is all the more striking when one realizes that, whereas only a minority of lawyers now participate in litigation, other kinds of lawyers are called on to prepare definitive legal instruments almost daily. No legal discipline is more pervasive.

Superior drafting requires a special kind of temperament and, even among the many lawyers who have it, there is a general lack of training. In the United States, there is little training in draftsmanship; of that, little is being provided by the law schools. This is especially unfortunate, because today's overbur-

§1.1. [1]Scheme for the Training of Legislative Drafting under the Commonwealth Fund for Technical Co-operation 1 (Commonwealth Secretariat, December 1973).

[2]11 Commonwealth L. Bull. 226-230 (1985). "The problem has been exacerbated by the degree of 'wastage' caused by the loss of trained draftsmen to other[,] more lucrative branches of the legal profession."

dening of the courts might be significantly alleviated by spending more professional effort to reduce the judicial input generated by substandard legal instruments than in merely lubricating judicial procedure.

This book tries to explain the basic principles and most commonly met problems of legal drafting. It deals, of course, with form and style. More important, it deals with general attitudes and approaches that differ widely from those of the traditional litigation-oriented lawyer. Those who may find this book useful include not only legislative draftsmen but private practitioners who are dissatisfied with the confusions, turgidities, circumlocutions, and expressions of downright gobbledygook that infect so many definitive legal instruments. Law professors also may find it useful.[3]

Unfortunately, many lawyers have tended not only to downgrade important aspects of drafting but to think of themselves as individually accomplished in this respect. It is hard to sell people new clothes if they consider themselves already well accoutered.

Even those who are interested in improving the drafting standards of the bar have tended to confirm the suspicions of the skeptical by treating legal drafting as if it were a mere literary exercise.[4] So long as drafting is considered solely a search for the accurate and felicitous phrase, many a vigorously practical lawyer will continue to think of it as the kind of exercise that can safely be minimized when the going gets tough.

One purpose of this book, therefore, is to put the matter in better perspective, in particular by showing the more important respects in which the drafting process goes beyond the consideration of specific language and improves substantive policy itself.

[3]Although many law schools now recognize the importance of legal drafting, their experiments in trying to teach it have produced, at best, only spotty results. For one approach to the baffling problems involved, see appendix F.

[4]Notable exceptions are J. Johnson, A Draftsman's Handbook for Wills and Trust Agreements 6-15 (1951); K. Pantzer & R. Deer, The Drafting of Corporate Charters and By-Laws (2d. ed. 1968); T. Shaffer, The Planning and Drafting of Wills and Trusts 32-39 (1972).

§1.2. WHAT IS "LEGAL DRAFTING"?

Legal drafting is the crystallization and expression in definitive form of a legal right, privilege, function, duty, status, or disposition. It is the development and preparation of legal instruments such as constitutions, statutes, regulations, ordinances, contracts, wills, conveyances, indentures, trusts, and leases.

Although to some lawyers it may seem arbitrary to group apparently disparate instruments such as statutes and ordinances, on the one hand, and private instruments such as wills, leases, and contracts, on the other, reflection should make clear that the similarity between (in most instances the identity of) specific drafting problems is more than coincidence. Charles P. Curtis, for one, has noted the close similarity between statutes and other kinds of instruments:

> Where two or three, or more, are gathered together in contract, they set up a small momentary sovereignty of their own. There is nothing fanciful about this. A contract is a little code for a special occasion. A lease is a little statute for your tenancy of a house you have neither built nor bought. Partnership articles or the charter and by-laws of a corporation are quite an elaborate code of law for those who are concerned. A corporate mortgage is a piece of legislation for a large and shifting population of bondholders, affecting, it is true, only a part of their lives, but affecting that part as completely as experienced and foresighted lawyers working late into the urban night can make it.[1]

The similarity between public and private instruments rests not only on closely similar objectives but on common tools of thought and language. The main difference is that the former are devoted almost entirely to regulating conduct or fixing a legal status, whereas many of the latter, such as wills and conveyances, besides occasionally regulating conduct, are mainly dispositive.[2] However, the fact that dispositive provisions operate

§1.2. [1]It's Your Law 42 (1954). See also Cavers, Legal Education and Lawyer-Made Law, 54 W. Va. L. Rev. 177, 178 (1952).

[2]There are two other important differences. One is a matter of degree. Generally speaking, the legislative draftsman has to think of a vastly greater number of contingencies. The other is that the likelihood that other draftsmen

3

at specific times instead of having continuing force affects only minimally the way in which they are written.

Besides the core principles common to legal drafting generally, each field has subordinate tools for dealing with problems peculiar to it. Savings clauses, for example, deal with a problem peculiar to statutes; attestation clauses with a problem peculiar to wills. The expression of reciprocal relationships is peculiar to instruments such as contracts and leases, in contrast to instruments such as statutes and conveyances.

Because the art of drafting is still relatively primitive in many fields, it is doubtful that any single volume could at this time reach beyond the common-core problems to do justice to the problems peculiar to each field. The need for a comprehensive coverage of special fields has been partly met by a bibliography (see appendix A). Unfortunately, the materials cited there are not always adequate guides to verbalization.

How does legal drafting differ from the preparation of documents such as briefs and pleadings? First, it seeks a degree of precision and internal coherence rarely met outside the language of formal logic or mathematics. Second, it is almost exclusively nonemotive;[3] that is, it contains almost no "sales talk."

The reader might well ask how language so full of imperatives can be classed with pure exposition.[4] Although all definitive legal instruments are intended ultimately to influence conduct, they do not ordinarily serve (outside special "inducement-giving" clauses such as penalty provisions) as their own instruments of persuasion.[5] As an example of an "instrument of

---

will later be tinkering with a statute makes it necessary "to employ a generality of expression, and to give his framework an elasticity of construction, which would shock the conveyancer." C. Ilbert, The Mechanics of Law Making 109-110 (1914).

[3]"The style of good legal composition . . . is free from all colour, from all emotion, from all rhetoric." Mackay, Introduction to an Essay on the Art of Legal Composition Commonly Called Drafting, 3 L.Q. Rev. 326 (1887).

[4]According to Williams, statutes are almost completely emotive, because they are intended to influence conduct. Language and the Law (pt. 5), 62 L.Q. Rev. 387, 396 (1946).

[5]Bentham may well have been the first to recognize the difference, in this respect, between commands of the state and commands of the head of a family. The former require "subsidiary or inducement-giving laws, laws defining the reward to be given or the evil to be inflicted as inducements." On the other

persuasion," when a young man writes a young woman to say that he wants to marry her, the letter not only conveys information but seeks to persuade. On the other hand, it is rare that a contract, will, lease, or statute materially relies on the form of the document itself to persuade the parties affected to comply with its terms. The usual legal instrument is like the warden who merely points out to the new inmate where the prison barriers are located.[6] Despite its form, it remains almost entirely a source of information. Accordingly, many aspects of general legal semantics, such as those discussed by F. A. Philbrick and others,[7] have no place in this discussion. They are not unimportant; they are merely irrelevant.

To understand the drafting process, the draftsman must realize that it operates on two planes: the conceptual and the verbal. Besides seeking the right words, he seeks the right concepts. Because a concept is usually grasped verbally, the two planes are easily confused.

Part of the draftsman's concern for concepts is with ascer-

---

hand, family commands such as "Set the loaf on the table" do not require these specific inducements, because of the "integrality of their character." C. Ilbert, The Mechanics of Law Making 93 (1914). "[W]e first tell someone what he is to do, and then, if he is not disposed to do what we say, we may start on the wholly different process of trying to get him to do it." R. Hare, The Logic of Morals 13 (1952).

[6]"A legal document is . . . not intended to move someone to take a particular course of action on his own initiative, but an operative instrument in itself, which those to whom it is addressed will be compelled to obey whether they like it or not. To this extent its draftsman has a captive audience, to whom he can express himself as he pleases since they are bound to listen." J. Johnson, A Draftsman's Handbook for Wills and Trust Agreements 6 (1961).

Although it is true, as Williams has said (Language and the Law (pt. 5), 62 L.Q. Rev. 387, 396 (1946)) that every legal proposition is reducible to the affirmation or denial of an "ought," the converse is equally true. Legal prescriptions, which are usually stated as commands ("Every person shall . . ."), are legally and tactically as effective when stated as factual propositions about the existence of specific duties ("Every person is responsible for . . ." or "Every person has a duty to . . ."). Thus, any bloodless command such as appears in a lease or will can be translated into an equally bloodless proposition. (Whether it is desirable to do so need not concern us here.)

[7]F. Philbrick, Language and the Law: The Semantics of Forensic English (1949). See also The Language of Law, A Symposium, 9 W. Res. L. Rev. 115 (1958).

taining and perfecting the substantive policies of his client, and part is with selecting the most appropriate means for carrying out those policies. Both parts underlie the attempts at verbalization usually identified with drafting. Drafting, therefore, is first thinking and second composing. "Thinking" does not mean making policy in any sense that invades the prerogatives of the client; nor is it implied that thinking and composing can be functionally divorced.[8]

To understand the drafting process it is necessary to have general attitudes or approaches that cannot be acquired by merely memorizing specific language techniques. Although the latter are important, they are not sufficient. The proper general attitudes and approaches are considered in succeeding chapters.

§1.3. LEGAL DRAFTING AND THE DIALECTIC OF PREVENTIVE LAW

Despite their increasing sensitivity to social issues and moral considerations, and their better grasp of sociology, economics, and some of the rigorous disciplines of science, such as symbolic logic, and, most recently, computer technology, lawyers have adjusted inadequately to the world of nonjudicial law making: the world of statutes, administrative rule making, and private ordering through consensual arrangements. This is unfortunate, in view of the profound shift in professional challenges from a preoccupation with litigation to an enormous involvement with public or private planning. Sound planning is the core of preventive law, which in implementing client programs tries to head off controversy, rather than mediate it. Yet most legal planning rests with lawyers who have been inadequately trained in the relevant conceptual and architectural disciplines or is being done by laymen.

Law's preoccupation with litigation and its accompanying

---

[8]In conversation on February 11, 1962, two days before his death, Karl N. Llewellyn remarked that "the management of judgment goes hand in hand with the management of information."

rhetoric has fostered not only a congeries of biased values but an insensitivity to a number of obstacles to rationality. Most of these are fallacies about language. Some involve the mishandling of concepts. Accordingly, to match its impressive achievements in the art of persuasion, the law needs a heavy dose of legal dialectic[1] by which lawyers are trained to develop and communicate useful ideas couched in legal form that is free of concessions to persuasion and free of fallacies attributable to a misunderstanding of the workings of language in its interaction with thought. A wholesome legal dialectic must also reject some of the standard language tools, such as euphemisms and the circumlocutions that H. W. Fowler called "periphrasis,"[2] upon which the successful advocate often relies. Even metaphors must be handled cautiously.[3]

Legal dialectic draws on many disciplines, including semantics, syntactics, and pragmatics (which coalesce into the now fashionable and burgeoning field of semiotics) and relevant aspects of epistemology, psycholinguistics, lexicography, and

---

§1.3. [1]"Dialectic" is used here in its classical sense of the art of ascertaining "truth" (or "the good"), which Plato differentiated from "rhetoric" (the art of persuasion), but only as a severable tool of it. The Phaedrus 260, 265, 266, 277 in the Dialogues of Plato (Jowett transl., 3rd ed.), as reprinted at p.233 of vol. 1 of the Random House edition, 1937; the page numbers first referred to are those in the margins. Dialectic apparently includes generalization, definition, and "division into species." For a short summary, see R. Weaver, The Ethics of Rhetoric 15 et seq. (1953).

The sensitive accommodation of rhetoric to dialectic is well discussed by Peter Goodrich in Rhetoric as Jurisprudence: An Introduction to the Politics of Legal Language, 4 Oxford J. Leg. Stud. 88 (1984). Rhetoric draws on dialectic, but only so far as it helps to persuade.

For the draftsman, "truth" (or "the good") means a clear-eyed understanding of what substantive results are needed and what elements in the process of concept selection or formation and the use of language are best adapted to shaping and articulating those results.

A greatly expanded version of this section is Dickerson, Toward a Legal Dialectic, 61 Ind. L. J. 311 (1986).

[2]H. Fowler, A Dictionary of Modern English Usage 445 (2d ed. Gowers 1965).

[3]Respecting the "mists of metaphor," Judge Cardozo once wrote, "Metaphors in law are to be narrowly watched, for starting as devices to liberate thought, they end often by enslaving it." Berkey v. Third Ave. Ry. Co., 244 N.Y. 84, 94, 155 N.E. 58, 61 (1926). Note: It took two metaphors to say so!

other areas with which the law has been adequately interdisciplinary.

Our immediate mission points toward three domains: The domain of language, the domain of concepts, and the domain of the so-called real world. However much these domains are functionally interrelated, they can, and indeed must, be intellectually separated to avoid confusion.

Although this book is not concerned with the full sweep of preventive law, legal drafting lies at its core. We cannot fully appreciate this without some familiarity with the ways in which legal dialectic can enhance the substance of legal drafting and the conceptualization that lies behind it. Many of the critical principles are discussed in this book.[4]

---

[4]They are more fully represented in Dickerson, note 1 *supra.*

II

Drafting and Substantive Policy

§2.1. THE DRAFTSMAN'S DIRECT CONCERN WITH SUBSTANTIVE POLICY

The legal draftsman has a strong interest in substantive policy and can even help to mold it, but how he approaches the matter is crucial. The draftsman's functions begin with the substantive ideas that he is called on to express;[1] ideas that more often than not are imperfectly formed when he first encounters them. Briefly, the draftsman's job is to help his client put in legal form what the client wants in substance, and to help him accomplish it as smoothly and effectively as possible.

Like the architect and the engineer, the legal draftsman must be brought into the particular problem long before he picks up his pencil.[2] He must find out as much as possible about what the client is trying to accomplish and about the factual environment in which the matter arises. A legal draftsman who allows himself to be less than fully informed on both the underlying policies to be expressed and their background is not discharging his central responsibility.

---

§2.1. [1]E. Piesse, The Elements of Drafting 1 (5th ed. Aitken 1976).

[2]"No stranger to a plant relationship or particular collective-bargaining negotiation can do an effective or even adequate drafting job. Calling in a lawyer to 'look over' an agreement about to be signed makes sense only if syntax is deemed more important than effect." Wirtz, Lawyers in Industrial Relations, 39 Fortune 153 (April, 1949), reprinted in R. Cook, Legal Drafting 536 (rev. ed. 1951).

How far beyond this is the legal draftsman legitimately concerned with substantive policy? He does not make substantive policy in the sense of having responsibility for its wisdom or of making final decisions on what is to be done and its desirability. On the other hand, in the drafting of many kinds of legal instruments the draftsman's advice on policy is often earnestly sought and properly given. The practical problem is to discharge this duty without encroaching on the prerogatives of the client. Discharging it takes a wholesome point of view and some sophistication. It also takes tact and diplomacy.

A draftsman who has earned the confidence of his client can have a profound and beneficial influence on the formulation of policy. The approach, training, and practical experience of a lawyer are such that he is likely to discover fundamental aspects of a proposed instrument that the client has overlooked. If he is diplomatic and the client shows no unwillingness, the draftsman can volunteer affirmative policy suggestions, based on his knowledge and experience, that may prove highly valuable. If in some respects he leads the client, he leads him in the direction in which the client wants to go.[3]

On the other hand, if he tries to impose his own substantive views against the wishes of his client, he is usurping a function that belongs to another. The draftsman of statutes is in an especially sensitive position. His client, a legislator, a legislative committee, or an administrative official, is presumably knowledgeable in matters of policy; indeed, policy-determining authority has been officially conferred on him. A legislative draftsman, although entitled to point out policy considerations involved in the draft, must take every precaution against the unwelcome injection of his own views into the policy features of the bill. To emphasize the vicarious position of the legislative

---

[3]Of course, even a skilled draftsman can't anticipate everything. On the other hand, leaving all such problems to the courts has little to commend it in an era when courts are swamped with litigation. Maurice B. Kirk recommends including appropriate "decision-making processes . . . for the resolution of unprovided-for changes in circumstance[s]." Elements of Legal Drafting, Part I(E) (mimeo, undated) (MLD 79, 83). This is easier said than done, but it is worth exploring.

draftsman, Middleton Beaman, late Legislative Counsel of the House of Representatives, once exaggerated the point by remarking that the draftsman must be an "intellectual eunuch."[4] He must also be an emotional oyster. However deeply he may feel about the wisdom of the policy he is called on to express, he must submerge his own feelings and act with scrupulous objectivity. Within the bounds of legality and professional morality, he should do his utmost to carry out his client's purpose even when he strongly disagrees with it.

The same considerations apply when the client is a private citizen for whom the draftsman is preparing a lease, an indenture, a contract, or a will. In this case, however, the draftsman is more likely to be engaged not only to use his drafting expertise but to give advice on policy, and even to participate in the policy decision. As with the legislative client, the less the private citizen knows about the relevant policy considerations the more likely it is that he will rely on the draftsman for policy advice. Even in these circumstances the draftsman should go no farther than the client wishes.

The key to success in this sensitive relationship consists not in knowing specific rules but in having a wholesome attitude of service. With such an attitude, the draftsman will find out how far he can appropriately go with the particular client in the particular case. Without it, even the otherwise able draftsman becomes officious and is often bypassed.

Maurice B. Kirk points out that, although the lawyer should have a sharp nose for trouble, it should not lead him to adopting more precautions than the client wants.[5] That the draftsman should sniff out every potential source of trouble does not necessarily mean that he should deal with it in the document. The draftsman sometimes concludes, for example, that the refinements of policy desired by his client are likely to produce administrative problems of which the client is generally unaware. The draftsman should bring this probability to the client's atten-

[4]Hearings on H.R. Con. Res. 18, Joint Committee on the Organization of Congress, 79th Cong., 1st Sess. 413, 416 (1945).
[5]Kirk, Elements of Legal Drafting, Part I(E) (mimeo, undated), (MLD 79, 84).

11

tion. In some cases the matter is insignificant. In others, the draftsman should hold back if his client does not want to push other parties to the deal as far as the law permits.

Lawyers tend to defend their clients to the hilt, even to the point that clients are occasionally shocked or disappointed to find that more has been done on their behalf than they needed or wanted done. If the client insists on putting legally sanctioned screws on another party, that's his legal right, but his lawyer should not take this for granted. Indeed, pushing other parties too far risks raising questions of illegality.[6]

One of the most significant principles here is that of un-conscionability. This is a ground for overturning private arrangements in which there is a lack of needed candor or a serious imbalance of bargaining power. The principle frowns on the indecent exploitation of people who are relatively unsophisticated or whose economic leverage is weak. This was the basis for throwing out the standard automobile disclaimer.[7] The draftsman must be especially careful when he is drafting a product warranty or other consumer instrument for a commercial enterprise. The key evils are oppression and unfair surprise. Although the doctrine is not new, the first statutory step against unconscionability in mercantile matters was taken in the Uniform Commercial Code, sections 2-302 and 2-719.

There are indications that the principle just discussed is expanding or being applied under the terminology of "reasonable expectations."[8] This development seems confined largely to standardized forms (especially insurance policies) prepared by enterprises that enjoy an unfair bargaining advantage over "consumers" who lack a decent opportunity to find and understand limitations of low visibility or who lack a feasible alternative. So far as the weaker party's reasonable expectations

---

[6]*Id.* Pantzer and Deer call this the "Equitable Sanction." K. Pantzer & R. Deer, The Drafting of Corporate Charters and By-Laws 14 (2d ed. 1968).

[7]*Henningsen v. Bloomfield Motors,* 32 N.J. 358, 405, 161 A.2d 69, 95 (1960).

[8]See, e.g., Slawson, The New Meaning of Contract: The Transformation of Contract Law by Standard Forms, 46 U. Pitt. L. Rev. 21 (1984). Slawson claims that this development warrants redefining "contracts" in terms of expectations.

determine the specifics of contract, the draftsman's problem is to determine whether and how the instrument can appropriately and effectively shape those expectations.

This opens up the broad field of morality in drafting. Aldous Huxley, citing religious authority, asserts that language carries great moral responsibilities.[9] Deceit is an easy case. Uncertainty often causes trouble, and even idle talk has been frowned on,[10] a proscription hard to evaluate. Much of this is supportable, if we define "morality" as embracing all matters that improve or weaken the human condition. Indeed, it is plausible to assert that even the languages of mathematics are founded on a pervasive moral principle, that of noncontradiction.

In any event, the matter should be clear in the case of law. Language is a basic tool of society. If we misuse it, we create trouble for ourselves and ultimately for society as a whole.

There are ethical problems peculiar to legal drafting. When I was drafting laws for the Pentagon, a high-level lawyer from the National Security Agency asked me to "fuzz up" a draft bill so that, when the particular provision came back to NSA to be administered, they could interpret it to mean what they wanted to have subtly hidden in it. Although such an action would certainly not have been unprecedented, I indicated that I would not participate in any scheme that put blinders on Congress. When we move from public documents to private ones, the professional strictures against lack of candor may be less severe, at least where the parties deal on a generally equal footing.

How far may a draftsman give vent to his own social values when shaping deals for his client? The answer is "not very far." If he cannot remain functionally loyal to his client's views, he should withdraw from the relationship.[11]

On the other hand, a draftsman who is deferential, decently

[9]Words and Their Meanings 35-36 (1940), reprinted in The Importance of Language (Black, ed. (1962) 2, 11-12 (MLD 84-85).

[10]*Id.*

[11]For a fuller discussion, see Dickerson, Statement of the Problem, MLD 88.

13

reticent, candid, and diplomatic can usually make much policy in the service of his client.

§2.2. THE DRAFTSMAN'S INDIRECT CONCERN WITH SUBSTANTIVE POLICY

Like happiness, important policy considerations are not always found by direct search. Seasoned draftsmen know this, but the fact can be fully appreciated only through firsthand experience.

Many lawyers do not seem to know that the application of sound principles of arrangement and expression can have a beneficial effect on policy quite apart from the substantive knowledge and experience of the particular draftsman. A draftsman who knows no more about the substance of his task than what he learns from his client can, as a by-product of orderly draftsmanship, make a substantial contribution to policy. The systematic application of basic drafting principles almost inevitably brings to light substantive discrepancies or policy considerations that would otherwise have been obscured. This happens with such regularity that it can be accepted as a standard bonus.

The intimate relationship between thought and its verbalization is not always grasped. As C. S. Peirce has told us, "the woof and warp of all thought and all research is symbols, and the life of thought and science is the life inherent in symbols; so that it is wrong to say that a good language is *important* to good thought, merely; for it is of the essence of it."[1] Language is functionally inseparable from the patterns of thought that help

§2.2 [1]Collected Papers, 129 (1932). "[L]anguage is something more than a tool of thought. It is a part of the process of thinking. Our ideas are clarified in the very attempt to express them." Littleton, The Importance of Effective Legal Writing in Law Practice, 9 Student Law. 6 (1963). "[W]riting is a way of coming to know as well as a way of communicating what is known." H. Martin & R. Ohmann, The Logic and Rhetoric of Exposition 5 (rev. ed. 1963). See also J. MacKaye, The Logic of Language 92 (1939); Morris, Foundations of the Theory of Signs, 1 International Encyclopedia of Unified Science No. 2, at 1 (1938); L. Stebbing, A Modern Introduction to Logic 11 (7th ed. 1950); Williams, Language and the Law (pt. 1), 61 L.Q. Rev. 71 (1945); and §4.14 *infra*.

to shape the relevant culture.[2] Every language thus presupposes a conceptual "grid" or "map" through which all experience is received. To adjust the one is inevitably to affect the other.[3]

§2.3. THE DRAFTSMAN'S MAIN TOOLS FOR IMPROVING SUBSTANTIVE POLICY

Although application of any formal principle (such as care in selecting particular words) tends to improve substantive policy, experience shows that the following three techniques pay especially high dividends. They do this not by handing the reader a neatly packaged improvement but by exposing the basic lack or inadequacy to the draftsman's view. Whether the opportunity is exploited depends on the perceptiveness of the particular draftsman. Needless to say, an experienced draftsman develops a sharp eye for the ambiguities, contradictions, omissions, and other discrepancies that these devices help expose.

§2.3.1. Consistency

Probably the most important formal technique for uncovering hidden inadequacies is to strive for complete internal consistency of terminology, expression, and arrangement.

In this operation, the competent draftsman makes sure that each recurring word or term has been used consistently. He carefully avoids using the same word or term in more than one sense, a verbal sin that C. K. Ogden and I. A. Richards called "utraquistic subterfuge."[1] Conversely, he carefully avoids using different words to denote the same idea, which H. W. Fowler

[2]B. Whorf, Language, Thought, and Reality 134-159 (1956). "Language and our thought-grooves are inextricably interrelated, are, in a sense, one and the same." E. Sapir, Language 217 (1921). "The real power of word symbols results . . . from the indispensable function of symbols in the process of conceptualization." E. Nida, Message and Mission 3 (1960). See also S. Ullman, Language and Style, ch. 10 (1964).

[3]Nida, *supra* note 2, at 70-71.

§2.3. [1]The Meaning of Meaning 134 (10th ed. 1956).

called "elegant variation."[2] In brief, he always expresses the same idea in the same way and always expresses different ideas differently. Insofar as he can, the draftsman applies the principles of consistency also to phrases, sentences, paragraphs, arrangement, and format. If two paragraphs or sections are similar in substance, he arranges them similarly. Consistency of expression has appropriately become the "Golden Rule" of drafting.[3]

A draftsman who follows these practices is certain to be rewarded. He may discover, for example, that in some treatments of a recurring idea important elements have been overlooked. These practices are effective because they facilitate comparison and recognition. Nothing will do more to improve the accuracy of a draft than following them, and nothing will do more to obscure its inadequacies than ignoring them.

§2.3.2. Sound arrangement

The second major formal technique for ridding a legal instrument of many of its substantive inadequacies is to arrange it rigorously and systematically. Although, like complete consistency, the best possible arrangement is hardly to be achieved in the first draft, continuing and thoroughgoing attention to the architecture of the instrument will do much to improve the substantive policies that it is intended to serve. The reason is simply that good architecture directs attention to the nature and relative position of each element in the hierarchy of the client's ideas.[4] Being logical, it contributes greatly to the equality of treatment that most legal instruments are intended to achieve.

The main advantage of severely hierarchical arrangement is that it helps produce the most significant juxtapositions of func-

[2]H. Fowler, A Dictionary of Modern English Usage 148 (2d ed. Gowers 1965).

[3]E. Piesse, The Elements of Drafting 43 (5th ed. Aitken 1976).

[4]"If the draftsman makes the effort to express his thoughts in a logical order, such that an outline could readily be made of the result, the very process of doing so will have sharpened and clarified his thinking, and the proper relationships will be much more likely to emerge." J. Johnson, A Draftsman's Handbook for Wills and Trust Agreements 7 (1961).

tionally related ideas. These, in turn, facilitate the most significant comparisons. We are talking here about the fundamentals of architecture. (The parallel with conventional architecture is strikingly close.)

"Architecture" is used here in its broadest sense, ranging from the general contours of the instrument through the design of particular sections and paragraphs. Because general arrangement is covered in chapter 5 and the arrangement of sections and paragraphs in chapters 6 and 8, further discussion will be deferred.

§2.3.3. Normal usage

The third major formal technique for uncovering hidden inadequacies is to make sure that the words and phrases of the instrument have been used in their normal general senses. There is no surer trap for the unwary reader, and even for the wary draftsman, than to use a term in a sense significantly different from that normally attributed to it by the audience to whom the instrument is addressed. Ridding an instrument of significantly abnormal uses will make its basic inadequacies more apparent, simply by clarifying what the instrument says. Although Lewis Carroll's Humpty Dumpty was undoubtedly correct in asserting his freedom to make words stand for whatever he pleased (in the sense that words have no inherently proper meanings),[5] it is psychologically impossible for a reader, even when fully and explicitly warned, abruptly to shift from an established meaning to a radically new one. Draftsmen often forget that this is true not only for the reader but for themselves. The perils of Humpty Dumptyism are examined more fully in chapter 7.

Because the conscientious draftsman can usually eliminate Humpty Dumptyisms at the outset, the technique of ridding an instrument of such usages to expose its substantive inadequacies to view is most useful when the instrument has been pre-

---

[5]Through the Looking-Glass, ch. 6, in Alice in Wonderland 163-164 (Gray ed. 1971).

pared by another and presumably less competent draftsman.

These three principles are the most important in legal drafting, because they not only contribute greater clarity and readability but, in so doing, tend to improve the document as an instrument of substantive change.

The rest of the drafting process is to apply the familiar array of specific principles and rules of semantics, grammar, and syntax. Important as they are, they need to be put in better perspective in the dynamics of drafting. At the same time, although many improvements have a lower potential, anything that increases clarity may uncover desirable changes in substance.

§2.4.   CONCEPTUAL PROBLEMS

Conceptual clarity is necessary to good drafting, both for the development of sound substantive policy and for its communication. Because the typical client goes to the draftsman with no more than a set of general objectives, the draftsman must first help to refine them and then develop a practical means for carrying them out. In the domain of ideas, this involves selecting the most appropriate classes and entities for the job.

In many cases, the draftsman can use established concepts. The problem is one of selection, guided largely by the immediate objectives. Not only should he avoid selecting a concept that is too narrow or too broad, but he should, as James P. Johnson has urged, try to reduce each congeries of specific concepts to its lowest common denominator.[1] Johnson points out, for example, that setting up cross remainders between trusts for three or more children is a highly intricate matter if they are treated as individuals, but is greatly simplified if they are treated as members of a single class.[2]

§2.4.   [1] J. Johnson, A Draftsman's Handbook for Wills and Trust Agreements 12 (1961). The first person to develop this idea was apparently Bentham. "Lists of species, once given, form a generic term, which afterwards substitute." Quoted in C. Ilbert, The Mechanics of Law Making 98 (1914).
[2] Johnson, *supra* at 10-11.

In his search for the right concepts, the draftsman does not search for objective fact or "truth." As with Euclidean geometry or modern quantum mechanics, he asks not whether the underlying concepts are "real" or "true" but whether, for the purposes at hand, they are the most useful. Utility and clarity depend largely on the conceptual simplicity inherent in an economy of ideas. This economy depends, in turn, on achieving the greatest degree of generality consistent with the objectives to be expressed.[3]

Finding the lowest common denominator involves looking at each enumeration of particulars to see whether in the aggregate they form or tend to form a class.[4] If the former, reference to the class merely avoids over-particularity. It is better, for example, to refer generally to "vehicles" than to name each kind of vehicle. If the enumeration of particulars only tends to form a class when the purpose of the instrument calls for dealing with the entire class, a significant omission has been disclosed. In the sentence, "If either trustee is at any time unable to act *by reason of death, disability or absence from the country* the other shall act alone,"[5] there is no reference to the contingency of resignation, which it would normally be desirable to include. This omission

[3]"To take an example from science, consider the Ptolemaic and Copernican descriptions of the solar system. It would be a mistake to say that the difference between these two descriptions is that one is correct while the other is incorrect, if by correct we mean something about whether or not the facts are correctly accounted for. All of the facts of the movements and positions of the planets can be accounted for with the earth taken as the center of the solar system as in the Ptolemaic model. These two accounts of the solar system are (or can be) equal in effective information. What makes the Copernican description much more attractive, insightful, and informative is simply that it is more simple. It takes less surface information to present the Copernican description. Here we may also note the generality that goes hand in hand with the simplification. The Copernican system is more general in that it ascribes the same basic patterns of motion to all of the planets, including the earth. . . ." Lamb, Stratificational Linguistics as a Basis for Mechanical Translation, Makkai & Lockwood (eds.), Readings in Stratificational Linguistics 34, 35-36 (1973).

[4]On the nature and reality of classes, see M. Cohen and E. Nagel, An Introduction to Logic and Scientific Method 223 (1934); Williams, Language and the Law (pt. 2), 61 L. Q. Rev. 179, 189 (1945).

[5]J. Johnson, A Draftsman's Handbook for Wills and Trust Agreements 13 (1961).

is easily repaired (by striking the italicized words) when the client confirms the draftsman's suspicion that the cause of inability is a matter of indifference and the whole range of inabilities should be covered.

Not only must the draftsman select among alternative concepts, but often he must change or refine them. A good example is the concept of food "processor" as developed by the Office of Price Administration (OPA) during World War II. The concept of a processor as simply one who "processes" (what constitutes "processing" did not create a significant problem) would not serve, because some persons process only part of the food they sell. Because OPA was forced to price commodities and items individually, it was ultimately driven to classify most processors not by their over-all operations but by what they did to the particular kind and brand of food product they sold. Accordingly, after a year and a half of development, a more clearly articulated definition emerged: " 'Processor' means a person who processes any part of what he sells of the kind and brand of product being priced."[6] Thus, the same person could be a "processor" of Ajax brand peanut butter, but a "primary distributor" of Wonder brand pickles. Underlying this verbalization was the refinement of a concept.[7]

Sometimes a draftsman uses a concept that is wholly unnecessary. In a recently proposed zoning ordinance, the draftsman set up a special class of uses called "contingent uses," and included a definition of the term. Because nothing depended on whether a use was "contingent," the concept served only to complicate the ordinance. In the redraft it was stricken.

The draftsman's system of concepts should also be internally consistent. In the zoning ordinance just mentioned, the draftsman divided the county into a series of mutually exclusive districts, one of which consisted of shopping centers. He also provided for special exceptions, by which an otherwise unauthorized use, including shopping centers, could be carried on in

---

[6]Food Products Regulation No. 1, §1.2, 9 Fed. Reg. 6711 (1944). See appendix C.

[7]R. Robinson, Definition 149 (1954).

a particular district once the Board of Zoning Appeals had approved it. Unfortunately, this approach bastardized the draftsman's family of concepts, because treating a shopping center as constituting a district in a series of mutually exclusive districts was inconsistent with treating it as a use that was to be permitted, by special exception, within a preexisting district. In this case the draftsman was trying merely to make the creation of this special kind of district contingent on the same kind of proceeding that applied to special exceptions. Upon revision the same result was reached, but with less confusion, by treating the shopping center as a district rather than a use, and by expressly extending the procedure for special exceptions to include the creation of shopping center districts.

Translating the client's desires into the most appropriate conceptual terms may involve not only problems of classes but problems of entities.[8] For example, the draftsman must sometimes decide whether a corporation is to be treated as a separate entity; if not, the decision entails "piercing the corporate veil." This is not the only occasion in the law when the draftsman is faced with the question of whether it is desirable to treat an aggregate of things as constituting an identifiable entity or merely an unintegrated aggregate.

The problem was vividly presented to OPA in its attempt to deal with tie-in sales. In a tie-in sale, the buyer is allowed to buy an article that he wants only if he also buys one that he does not want. Such a condition normally resulted in a price higher than the ceiling price for the wanted article, thus violating the applicable regulation. The main problem was what to do about situations in which the two articles, taken together, constituted a third article. Items that are sold only in pairs or sets, such as shoes and cups and saucers, created no problem. The result was different for combinations of items that are also regularly sold separately, such as gift baskets of fruit and silver place settings. For these, OPA adopted the standard of the market place. If it was customary to sell the items also in combination, OPA

---

[8]On the nature and reality of entities, see Williams, Language and the Law (pt. 3), 61 L. Q. Rev. 293, 298, 299 (1945). See also MLD 71-74.

treated the transaction as a single sale of the combination rather than as an aggregate of sales of the separate parts. The object might even be a single entity for one purpose and an aggregate of entities for another. Thus, a country shipper of produce might violate the law if he insisted that the wholesaler take one-half car of carrots to get one-half car of lettuce, whereas, if a combination car were already rolling, a carlot distributor would not violate the applicable regulation if he insisted that a buyer take the whole carload. (Carlot distributors deal only in whole cars loaded by others.)

Most, if not all, of such matters affect the clarity of the underlying ideas that the final legal instrument is intended to express. Their clarity in turn affects their substantive soundness.

Other conceptual problems are considered in sections 5.4 and 5.5.

§2.5. A CONCLUDING OBSERVATION ON CONCEPT FORMATION AND REFORMATION

Some draftsmen may feel uncomfortable with an approach that assumes that the legal draftsman is free, where it serves his mission, to rework firmly established concepts. Such reticence may be rooted in the widespread assumption that human beings should stay with the concepts that correspond with the "real world"[1] as revealed by the physical or social sciences. Such an assumption could seriously limit his effectiveness.

More intellectually liberating is a developing consensus among many modern thinkers, including physical scientists, that our concepts are a function not only of the real world but of the structure of the human observer and the kind of problem he is addressing. If this consensus is valid and if our knowledge is shaped by concepts, the possibility of unvarying hardcore knowledge is limited to situations in which the three aspects remain relatively constant. In a universe of apparently unlimited

§2.5. [1]Whatever is "out there."

diversity, such a contingency is possible only so far as the perceivable differences remain, for the purpose at hand, insignificant or uncritical. All-purpose conceptual structure is, at best, rare.

One "structuralist" contends that:

> [E]very perceiver's *method* of perceiving can be shown to contain an inherent bias which affects what is perceived to a significant degree. A wholly objective perception of individual entities is therefore not possible: Any observer is bound to *create* something of what he observes.[2]

This does not say that the creative observer creates, to any major extent, the real world. It says only that he participates in creating models of actuality, giving immediate shape to his indirect knowledge of it.[3] His "bias" consists of his relevant values

[2]T. Hawkes, Structuralism and Semiotics 17 (1977). Emphasis in original.

> [D]espite appearances to the contrary the world does not consist of independently existing objects, whose concrete features can be perceived clearly and individually, and whose nature can be classified accordingly. *Id.*

Another version of this notion is found in R. Jones, Physics as Metaphor 5-6 (1982): "[T]he failure to recognize the central role of consciousness in reality and thus to treat the physical world as an independent, external, and alien object has been a chronic problem throughout the modern era of scientific discovery." Jones (at p.4) defines "metaphor" as an agreement between author and recipient to a tacit "as if," that is, a fiction.

Still another version appears in F. Merrell, Semiotic Foundations, Steps in an Epistemology of Written Texts 3 (1982).

> [K]nowing is a process believed ultimately to rest in some precognitive, and hence nonconscious, level of experience. . . . [E]ach human being internalizes a hypothesis concerning what the world is — must be — like, and he constantly attempts to correlate his highly selective empirical world with it. This internalized hypothesis allows him to make discriminations in his field of experience. . . . [T]he content of these discriminations is determined chiefly by his particular environment-bound social and psychological needs.

[3]A crude metaphor may help: Look at external existence as a sort of infinitely complex cookie batter. Look on the human mind as the designer of cookie cutters, by which it divides the batter into consumable cookies, the only external world that it can directly know. Although designing cookies does not necesssarily include making batter, it is "creation" in a significant sense. (No one creates even batter in any absolute sense.)

On concepts generally, see P. Henle, Lanugage, Thought and Culture ch.

and the requirements of the problems he is trying to solve.[4]

In such a world view, it seems only natural for draftsmen to adapt or create concepts to reflect the varying needs that legal instruments confront. The problem then becomes one of alerting the audience to any conceptual shifts from the usual by making an adroit shift in language or an appropriate stipulative redefinition.[5] This approach illumines such practical drafting problems as determining how matters or things should be classified,[6] what should be treated as "entities,"[7] the principles of hierarchy needed to build useful legal taxonomies,[8] and the principles of definition.[9]

It is valuable because it allows the legal draftsman needed conceptual leeway. Fortunately, its practical validation does not depend on an exhaustive examination of the many competing theories of knowledge. That the approach works well in this field should be enough for present purposes.[10]

---

2 (1958) and other authorities cited in R. Dickerson, The Interpretation and Application of Statutes 105 n.8 (1975).

[4]This is the basis for Robert M. Pirsig's notion that human value shapes the abstractions out of which we build knowledge. Because mankind can cope with a world of infinite diversity only by reducing it to convenient abstractions, which include even facts, knowledge can legitimately vary among observers facing different problems even in respects that the "real world" does not. Even "pure science" is not immune. R. Pirsig, Zen and the Art of Motorcycle Maintenance 305 (1974).

[5]See §7.4 *infra*. Although Pirsig is not an accredited philosopher, I found his concept of the mental birth of facts a challenging insight.

[6]See §5.5 *infra*.

[7]See §2.4 *supra*.

[8]See §5.3 *infra*.

[9]See chapter 7 *infra*.

[10]But see §5.5 note 1 *infra*.

III

Drafting and Communication

§3.1. THE LEGAL INSTRUMENT AS A COMMUNICATION

Many draftsmen apparently do not realize that a legal instrument is both (1) a crystallization and declaration of rights, privileges, duties, and legal relationships and (2) a communication. In its latter role, it is subject to the principles of communication. Too many lawyers draft as if they were preparing an instrument solely for their own reference. Apparently, they assume that if they have the substance of the instrument clear in their own heads and reflect it in symbols intelligible to themselves they have fully discharged their drafting responsibility.[1] By doing this they often fail to convey the substance of their client's message.

That a legal instrument is a communication is seen most clearly in statutes, ordinances, and regulations, and such dispositive instruments as wills. In these, the client plainly addresses instructions to others. To be effective according to the client's intent, such an instrument must carry the same meaning to those who will execute it as to the draftsman. This also seems

---

§3.1. [1]"[I]t is not the subjective intention of the parties which governs in the construction of a contract, but the intention expressed or fairly to be implied from the wording found in the contract." L. Mandel, The Preparation of Commercial Agreements 8 (1955). See also E. Piesse, The Elements of Drafting 11 (5th ed. Aitken 1976); Holmes, The Theory of Legal Interpretation, 12 Harv. L. Rev. 417 (1899).

to be true of bilateral and multilateral instruments such as contracts. For all these instruments the ultimate audience includes the courts and other agencies that may be called on to enforce them. Accordingly, the parties are held to standards of meaning that transcend any purely private language. The draftsman, therefore, should respect the principles of communication.

§3.2.   BASIC ELEMENTS OF COMMUNICATION

The principles of communication are not a matter of legal fiat, to be changed at the will of the draftsman. Common to all human effort, they exist independently of the law. Communication is based on the language habits of particular speech communities.[1] Language is founded on usage[2] and, although in particular cases usage can be violated or changed, to dispense with it altogether would make communication impossible.[3] The core of sound communication, therefore, is general adherence to the existing conventions of language. This neither freezes nor sanctifies particular conventions.

In the written communication process there are four main elements: (1) the author, (2) the audience, (3) the written utterance, and (4) the relevant context or environment. The first

§3.2. [1]M. Black, Language and Philosophy 28 (1949). "A symbol incorporates a habit. . . ." C. S. Peirce, quoted in C. Ogden and I. Richards, The Meaning of Meaning 283 n.1 (4th ed. 1936). "[A] Usage is only Good for a given universe of discourse. . . ." *Id.* at 221.

> Specific context . . . always relates to a particular audience in a particular culture or subculture identified by a particular speech community. A speech community or relevant language system is usually defined, not by a group of specific people, but by kinds of activities or fields of interests. This is true both of major speech communities and languages identified with radically differing cultures and of secondary speech communities and special languages and technical dialects that exist in highly complicated cultures such as our own. The same person may participate in more than one speech community or be the user of more than one language. For example, a botanist may call a tomato a "fruit" when talking with a colleague but a "vegetable" when talking to his grocer.

R. Dickerson, The Interpretation and Application of Statutes 117 (1975).

[2]C. Cherry, On Human Communication 69, 71 (2d ed. 1966); B. Berenson, Seeing and Knowing 7-12 (1953).

[3]Cherry, *supra* note 2 at 13, 19, 67; Berenson, *supra* note 2 at 11-12.

element raises no significant problem, beyond the fact that the draftsman normally operates on his client's behalf rather than his own.

For present purposes the second element is more important. Every communication is addressed to one or more audiences, each of which defines or is part of an established speech community. A draftsman neglects this fact at the peril of failing to communicate. The nature of the audiences for whom he is writing helps to determine the concepts he chooses, his basic arrangement, and the specific language he uses. It determines also how much he can leave unsaid, as taken for granted. With a will, the primary audience is the executor and the probate judge, who are intended to distribute the property or, often in the case of real estate, to give effect to its distribution. The testator should make the will intelligible also to the secondary audience, the beneficiaries, who may want to press their claims. With a contract, lease, or similar instrument, the primary audience consists of the immediate parties, who are normally those responsible for its execution, and those whose rights or privileges depend on it. The secondary audience is the court, which may be called on to enforce the instrument in case there is a dispute or noncompliance.

With statutes and regulations, the audiences may be more varied. A statute addressed primarily to government officials may need to be written differently from one addressed to a segment of the public, and a statute addressed to a highly specialized segment of the public, such as the tobacco industry, may need to be written differently from one addressed to the public at large. Unfortunately, the concept of a particular legal audience and the broader concept of the "users of the language"[4] are complicated by the irregularity with which usages, assumptions, and values tend to be shared even within the same speech community.[5]

In analyzing the audience to which a consumer instrument

[4]M. Black, Language and Philosophy 29, 49 (1949).

[5]"We remain unconscious of the prodigious diversity of all the everyday language-games because the clothing of our language makes everything alike." L. Wittgenstein, Philosophical Investigations 224 (1953).

is addressed, Carl Felsenfeld and Alan Siegel suggest asking questions such as the following:

Who are the primary and secondary readers?

For example, the primary readers of an insurance policy are the policyholders; the secondary readers are the insurance agents.

What are their levels of education?

The instrument should focus on the lowest general level concerned.

How will they use the instrument?

For example, will they use it only for occasional reference, read it through at one sitting, or use it only with the help of a lawyer?

What do they already know?

Answering this tells the draftsman what he can safely omit and what context needs to be added.

What misconceptions, if any, do they have?

These can be corrected by adding appropriate context.

The concepts of legal audience and users of the language are further complicated because some legal instruments are not normally read or intended to be read by the persons to whom they directly apply. This is more likely to be true of statutes than of private legal instruments. Perhaps the best example is the federal income tax laws. Although these laws affect almost everyone, few laymen become acquainted with their terms through direct reading. Most tax information is delivered by word of mouth or through official instructions of the Internal Revenue

[6]C. Felsenfeld & A. Siegel, Writing Contracts in Plain English 81-90 (1981).

Service, private periodicals or services, or private legal or accounting advice. Because this is entirely appropriate, such laws need not be couched in a form appropriate to easy reading by the public at large, nor do their factual presuppositions need to be made obvious to the public. It is enough that they are understood by the general government or private lawyers and accountants in this field on whom it is customary for the general public to rely. It is desirable, of course, also to make such laws as intelligible as feasible to the general public.

Because their appropriate interpretative attitude is professional empathy with the typical member of the intended audience, the courts may ordinarily be disregarded as an independent audience, except where, as in the case of insurance policies, the draftsman needs to adjust to a judicial bias in favor of a class of participants, in this case the policy holders.

The role of the third element in any written communication, the written instrument itself, is reasonably plain. As the key factor in directing, orienting, and organizing the total message, it is the element to which the draftsman gives his primary attention. Here, the draftsman's main tools are the express meanings of particular words and phrases and the internal context, including syntax, that he creates within the instrument.

The fourth element in any written communication, including a legal instrument, is the part of the surrounding environment or external context that the written instrument takes into account. External context refers to the social, economic, and cultural setting in which the instrument is to operate.[7] The context in which an instrument operates is significant because it is highly improbable that any document, taken entirely apart from the relevant environment that it presupposes, can convey meaning, except in another environment that shares some of the same elements. It is the essence of a language to reflect and express, and even to affect, the patterns of established ideas and values that help to shape the culture to which it belongs.

---

[7]"A word is essentially contained in a context and the full effect of the word is felt only when it appears in context." C. Cherry, On Human Communication 72 (2d ed. 1966).

External environment consists of two elements: (1) the established patterns of ideas and values immediately underlying the language; and (2) the relevant collateral and usually tacit assumptions that are shared and taken account of by most of the speech community to which both the draftsman and his audience belong. The first of these two elements gives language its primary meanings. The second conditions or colors the primary meanings and provides the basis for the meanings known as implications. Implication, constituting, as it does, what Edward T. Hall has called the "silent language,"[8] thus furnishes a necessary part of the total message. A telephone call at 3 A.M., for example, carries emergency implications missing from a similar telephone call at 3 P.M.[9] So speaks the silent language of time.[10]

That no legal message is ever fully contained within the instrument or utterance that constitutes its express elements can be simply illustrated. If a draftsman prepares a trust instrument requiring the trustee to separate income from principal, the psychological response habits shared by the draftsman and his audience that give meaning to individual terms such as "income," "principal," and "compute" are examples of the first element of external environment. The second element is exemplified by the generally accepted assumption, usually left to implication, that fractions of one-half cent or more are to be rounded off to the next higher cent. As part of the relevant context, the second element conditions primary meaning, because, unless a different rule is expressly adopted, the normal reader will assume as a matter of course that fractions are intended to be treated according to the custom of that speech community. Like internal context, external context also is a powerful tool for resolving uncertainties, limiting otherwise over-general language, and even overriding typographical errors.

The first element of external context or environment is important to the draftsman, because it tells him how to select

----

[8]E. Hall, The Silent Language (1959).
[9]*Id.* at 16.
[10]*Id.* chs. 1, 9.

particular language. He must put himself in the shoes of his intended audience by becoming thoroughly acquainted with the language habits of the particular speech community or communities in which the audience operates. The second element is important because it tells the draftsman which information he must include in his message and which he can safely omit[11] (the latter includes the tacit assumptions of which courts are willing to take judicial notice). Omitting such information avoids what L. Susan Stebbing calls "intolerable prolixity" and allows the draftsman to concentrate his fire on the critical aspects of his message.

Conversely, needed context can be supplied by including appropriate information in the instrument or by referring to other documentation. A good example of the former is the introductory statement in paragraph A of the contract in section 14.8, below. In the case of a statute, legislative history is not an appropriate device for this purpose.[12]

From this discussion it is clear that for the purposes of communication it is not enough that draftsman and audience share the legal instrument. They must also share the relevant elements of the same general cultural environment and, within that environment, the same relevant knowledge, values, and purposes. Attending to these matters is the essence of developing the necessary editorial point of view.

§3.3. THE MAJOR DISEASES OF LANGUAGE: IN GENERAL

The importance of clarity to the substance of the client's wishes has been discussed.[1] Clarity is important also to a legal instrument as a means of transmission. Such an instrument is a com-

---

[11]H. Martin & R. Ohmann, The Logic and Rhetoric of Exposition 64-65 (rev. ed. 1963).

[12]R. Dickerson, The Interpretation and Application of Statutes, ch. 10; Dickerson, Statutory Interpretation: Dipping into Legislative History, 11 Hofstra L. Rev. 1125 (1983).

§3.3. [1]See §§2.2-2.4 *supra.*

munication and thus subject to the limitations inherent in language. What are the chances of achieving clarity? The inadequacies of language are cause for misgivings, but hardly for general despair.

Unfortunately, the courts' and litigants' normal preoccupation with sick or uncertain language leads easily to the belief that all language is as inherently weak and inadequate as the particular fragments of legal language that are scrutinized in legal opinions.[2] While even momentary reflection should dispel such a belief, the preoccupation has contributed to an undesirable depreciation of what language can be made to accomplish. The professional draftsman knows better. Despite what the courts have done with and to the language of legal instruments,[3] he knows that it is worth his and his client's while to exert every reasonable effort to make the legal message clear. At the same time, the job of writing a clear legal instrument remains formidable. This is due for the most part to several important, and largely curable, diseases of language.

§3.4.   THE DISEASE OF AMBIGUITY

Perhaps the most serious disease of language is ambiguity in the traditional sense of equivocation (see the reversing figure below, well known as the "Necker Cube").[1] Language is equivo-

[2]E.g., "an inexact, clumsy tool." Miller, Statutory Language and the Purposive Use of Ambiguity, 42 Va. L. Rev. 23 (1956).

[3]"Words in legal documents . . . mean, in the first instance, what the person to whom they are addressed makes them mean." C. Curtis, It's Your Law 65 (1954). "[A]fter all, it is only words that the legislature utters; it is for the courts to say what those words mean . . . all the law is judge-made law. . . . The courts put life into the dead words of the statute." J. Gray, The Nature and Sources of Law 124, 125 (2d ed. 1921). Who puts life into the dead words of the court?

§3.4.   [1]Louis Albert Necker first observed perspective reversal, or two ways of seeing in line drawings of rhomboid crystals in 1832. The same phenomenon occurs in line drawings of transparent cubes, best seen from the perspective exemplified by the figure in the text. Hence, the term "Necker cube" was born. Attneave, Multistability in Perception. Sci. Am., Dec. 1921, at 63, 67.

Ambiguity

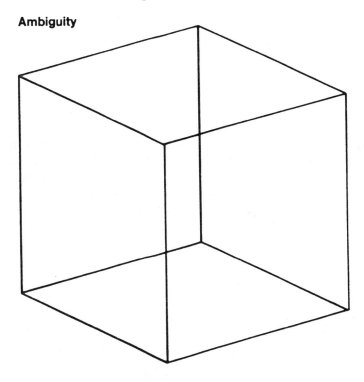

cal when it has "different significations equally appropriate" or is "capable of double interpretation,"[2] that is, has two or more competing thrusts. A good example is the word "residence," which, unless particular context resolves the doubt, can refer equally to the place where a person has his abode for an extended period or to the place the law considers to be his permanent home, whether or not it is his place of abode.

To avoid the so-called one-word-one-meaning fallacy, it is commonly assumed that all words are ambiguous in the equivocation sense because almost every word is used in various senses and thus has more than one meaning.[3] Does the existence of multiple dictionary meanings make a word equivocal and there-

[2] 3 Oxford English Dictionary E263 (1933).
[3] E.g., Frank, Words and Music: Some Remarks on Statutory Interpretation, 47 Colum. L. Rev. 1259, 1263 (1947); F. Waismann, Language Strata, in Essays on Logic and Language, 2d ser. (Flew ed. 1953).

fore ambiguous? The answer lies in the difference between an ambiguous word and a group of homonyms.

Groups of homonyms are easily confused with ambiguous words, because both have multiple thrusts of meaning, but the two are not the same.[4] On the one hand, the intended sense of a word designating a group of homonyms is almost inevitably revealed in use, whatever the peculiarities of context. The homonym's capacity for sense sifting is built in and automatic. Examples of these multipurpose words abound: "If he can, the buyer shall return the empty can." "If the bear causes damage, the owner shall bear the cost." This kind of multiplicity of meanings, often considered a defect of language, may actually be a benefit. At least, it makes possible an economy of symbols.

With the ambiguous word, on the other hand, the uncertainties of alternative reference are not resolved merely by use in context. In the statement, "His rights depend on his residence," it is not clear whether they depend on place of abode or on legal home. That, clothed in its broadest context, the uncertainty may in fact be resolved (as when the word "residence" appears in a divorce statute in which for jurisdictional reasons it seems probable that the legislature intended to refer to legal home) does not turn an otherwise ambiguous word into an innocuous cluster of homonyms. Intermediate are families of use patterns that, while related, are individually identifiable (e.g., "sanguine" and "sanguinary").

Whereas homonyms present no significant danger, the ambiguous word carries the threat, in specific use, of competitive thrusts of meaning that are almost never desirable or justifiable. Because of its potential for deception or confusion, an ambiguous word should not be used by the draftsman in a context that does not clearly resolve the ambiguity. Indeed, he should avoid the ambiguous word (e.g., "residence") whenever his intended meaning (e.g., legal home) may be adequately expressed by an unambiguous word (e.g., "domicile"). References to the "purposive use of ambiguity," sometimes found in legal literature,

[4]On this difference, see L. Stebbing, A Modern Introduction to Logic 21 (6th ed. 1948).

are usually directed to the purposive use of vagueness or generality, discussed below.[5]

[5]In the first edition of Legislative Drafting 15-16 (1954), my attack on intentionally "fuzzy or misleading language" and my plea for the greatest possible clarity provoked a charge by Judge Frank C. Newman that these views failed to recognize the value of "deliberate ambiguity" as "a device for a delegating authority to administrators and judges." F. Newman, A Legal Look at Congress and the State Legislatures, in Legal Institutions Today and Tomorrow 75-76 (Paulsen ed. 1959). In the field of judicial lawmaking in relation to statutes, if we make the elementary distinction between "ambiguity" and "vagueness," and if we can also assume that Newman meant "vagueness" when he said "ambiguity," most of the apparent disagreement between us disappears. Although there is little good in ambiguity, vagueness (in company with generality) is a proper device for delegating lawmaking power to the courts or to an administrative agency. If, on the other hand, he intended "ambiguity" to include its traditional sense of equivocation, our disagreement runs deep.

Layman E. Allen, too, has reservations about my unrelenting antipathy to ambiguity, including syntactic ambiguity. Just as the uncertainties of vagueness are not all bad, he urges that it should not be "unethical to deliberately incorporate uncertainty into a message by way of ambiguity in the logical syntax." Allen & Saxon, One Use of Computerized Instructional Gaming in Legal Education: To Better Understand the Strict Logical Structure of Legal Rules and Improve Legal Writing, 19 U. Mich. J.L. Reform 383, 385 (1985).

There is disagreement here, but I suggest that it concerns, not drafting ethics, but terminology. Although Allen's deep devotion to disclosing syntactic ambiguity is admirable, the examples he and his co-author rely on in some instances to justify uncertainty suggest that they are confusing the conscious uncertainties of omission with those of syntax. Take this example:

> A child shall not be admitted to the Apollo theatre unless the child is accompanied by an adult.

Allen and Saxon say that this is "structurally ambiguous," because we cannot tell from the express language, taken alone, whether the negation implies a positive permission or requirement (the converse of negative implication) for children accompanied by adults. My view is that, if such an uncertainty exists, it results, not from defective internal structure, but from the absence of information about the range of relevant tacit assumptions that are operating here. That we can guess at many of them is not enough. I believe that, until we know more, it is safe to assume that a simple prohibition was intended and thus that nothing is implied "about what happens when an adult does accompany a child." A conscious decision to leave collateral matters for other communications and understandings is certainly no drafting impropriety, nor does it in any way involve internal structure.

On the other hand, we do have enough relevant and reliable tacit assumptions in this instance to rule out the plausibility of an implied *requirement* of admission, at least an unqualified one. More specifically, I see no implication

Because the line between homonyms and ambiguity depends on their respective potentials for deception and confusion in use, differences in degree sometimes make it hard to tell on which side of the line a particular word falls. However, mere identification is not important; what is important is that the draftsman determine whether, in the particular context, there is likely to be a significant uncertainty of meaning. If there is, he should resolve it by using another word or by taking the precaution of adjusting the context or adding explanatory language.

The ambiguities just discussed are called "semantic ambiguities."[6] The uncertainty of their meanings, not inevitably resolved by context, is traceable to the multiplicities of dictionary definitions, which exist independent of context. That their evils are felt, nevertheless, only in specific context makes it desirable to distinguish them from a second kind of ambiguity.

By far the most prevalent kind of ambiguity is syntactic ambiguity. Syntactic ambiguities are uncertainties of modification or reference within the particular instrument.[7] Simple examples include squinting modifiers ("The trustee shall require him promptly to repay the loan")[8] and modifiers preceding or following a series ("charitable corporations or institutions per-

---

that the presence of an adult would guarantee admission to a child who wore roller skates, had grease all over his hands, or had a dog on a leash. (Freedom-loving Americans would, of course, put the burden of persuasion on the ticket-taker to justify exclusion.) The uncertainties of borderline cases involve only routine questions of vagueness.

Unmoved by these collateral considerations, I remain persuaded that ambiguity, semantic or syntactic, should be assiduously avoided. And if what I have just condoned can be appropriately classed as *"contextual* ambiguity" (which I doubt), so be it. Allen's and Saxon's example precludes judgment by necessarily omitting the kind of collateral information that would normally be available in a real-life situation. It is always worthwhile, of course, to consider potential uncertainties that might cause trouble in a specific context.

[6]On the detection and resolution of semantic ambiguities, see J. MacKaye, The Logic of Language, ch. 5 (1939).

[7]On the detection and resolution of syntactic ambiguities, see Allen, Symbolic Logic: A Razor-Edged Tool for Drafting and Interpreting Legal Documents, 66 Yale L. J. 833 (1957); Allen, Interpretation of California Pimping Statute, 60S M.U.L.L. 114 (1960); Montrose, Mock Turtle: A Problem in Adjectival Ambiguity, 59D M.U.L.L. 28 (1959). And see §6.3 *infra*, note 11.

[8]Does "promptly" modify "require" or "repay"?

forming educational functions").[9] These are usually ambiguities in the original etymological sense of alternatives limited to two.

Another and likewise prevalent kind of ambiguity is contextual ambiguity. Even when the words and syntax of a statute are unequivocal, it may still be uncertain which of two or more alternatives was intended. An internal contextual ambiguity may result, for example, from an internal inconsistency. When one provision plainly contradicts another, it is often not clear which is intended to prevail. Contextual ambiguities may also be external. Thus, an instrument may bear a similarly ambiguous relationship to another instrument with which it is inconsistent.

In a will, there may be a contextual ambiguity as to the time as of which heirs are to be determined. For example, in a gift to the testator's daughter for life and then to the testator's heirs, it is sometimes uncertain whether the daughter is to be included as an "heir."

Perhaps the most troublesome contextual ambiguity, and one of the most frequent, is the uncertainty of whether a particular implication arises.[10] This is often true of "negative" or "reverse" implications, covered by the maxim *expressio unius est exclusio alterius* (the expression of one thing implies the exclusion of another thing).[11] Sometimes the maxim applies and sometimes it does not, depending largely on context, which tends to show what tacit assumptions are being made and taken account of. Unfortunately, context tends in its particulars to be unique, and therefore does not always supply a clear answer. Even so, a person who has watched the currents and eddies of usage

---

[9]Does "charitable" modify "institutions"? (Or, does "performing educational functions" modify "corporations"?)

[10]Robert M. Benjamin (in a letter to the author, Feb. 26, 1964) gives an example: If a testator directs that estate and other death taxes be apportioned, it may be uncertain whether the context implicitly limits this to taxes on property passing under the will or allows it to apply also to property passing independently of it (e.g., life insurance). The ambiguity, he suggests, is easily disposed of by adding a few words ("with respect to all property in my gross estate for the purposes of such taxation").

[11]This is also called "coimplication." Allen, Symbolic Logic: A Razor-Edged Tool for Drafting and Interpreting Legal Documents, 66 Yale L.J. 840 (1957). See also §3.9 *infra*.

develops an eye for these things. The ascertainment of implied meaning, like that of express meaning, is largely the recognition of familiar language patterns and use situations.

For semantic and syntactic ambiguities, it is important to remember that their characterization as such normally depends on their demonstrated potentiality for giving trouble in particular uses rather than on their producing an actual ambiguity in a particular instance. As with some unesteemed kinds of people, classification is by established reputation rather than by specific performance. Thus, the word "residence," taken in isolation, is properly classed as "ambiguous," even though in a particular context the notion of domicile clearly emerges. Similarly, a squinting modifier may be syntactically ambiguous in the isolation of a particular phrase or sentence, but unambiguous in its broadest context. Because the typical reader usually sees the details of a legal instrument before he feels its total impact, what first appears to be an ambiguity may disappear on a more careful, comprehensive reading. If so, the ambiguity is apparent rather than actual. If not, the ambiguity is actual and can be resolved only by agreement or by judicial fiat, that is, by an act of judicial lawmaking.

The difference between apparent ambiguity and actual ambiguity is important. The draftsman's highest responsibility is to see that the final text, when read in its proper context,[12] contains no unresolved ambiguity.[13] It is also highly desirable, though not so critical, that he see that the effectiveness of the instrument is not impaired by unnecessary uncertainties of reference

---

[12]In view of the common practice of relying on even the shabbiest aspects of internal legislative history to condition or supplement express statutory meaning, it should be emphasized that under general communication principles context properly includes only those aspects of total environment that are available to both legislature and legislative audience. R. Dickerson, The Interpretation and Application of Statutes 116-120 (1975).

[13]"A technical writer, whether he be a literary critic or a nuclear engineer, may feel free to use ambiguous terms without taking the precaution of providing stipulative definitions simply because he knows that the audience for which he writes will understand the specialized meanings which he intends." H. Martin, The Logic and Rhetoric of Exposition 23 (1958). This statement was omitted from the revised edition.

that, although resolvable, risk misreading at the hands of unperceptive courts or, at best, require time and effort to untangle. It is also desirable that he avoid the needless use of terms and configurations of syntax that, whatever their immediate impact, are known to carry the general risk of real or apparent ambiguity. Fortunately, once an actual, apparent, or potential ambiguity has been recognized, it can almost always be avoided or minimized.

§3.5. THE DISEASES OF OVER-VAGUENESS AND OVER-PRECISION

It is unfortunate that many lawyers persist in using the word "ambiguity" to include vagueness.[1] To subsume both concepts under the same classification tends to imply that there is no difference between them or that their differences are legally unimportant. Ambiguity is a disease of language, whereas vagueness, which is sometimes a disease, is often a benefit.[2] Because of this significant difference between the two concepts, it is helpful to refer to them by different names.

Whereas "ambiguity" in its classical sense refers to equivocation, "vagueness" refers to the degree to which, independent of equivocation, language is uncertain in its respective applications to a number of particulars.[3] The uncertainty of ambiguity

§3.5. [1]E.g., Jones, Extrinsic Aids in the Federal Courts, 25 Iowa L. Rev. 737, 739 (1940). Cf. Christie, Vagueness in Language, 48 Minn. L. Rev. 885, 886 (1964).

[2]C. Curtis, It's Your Law 59-67 (1954); N. Dalkey, The Limits of Meaning, 4 Philosophy & Phenomenological Research 401, 409 (1944); Dickerson, Some Jurisprudential Implications of Electronic Data Processing, 28 Law & Contemp. Prob. 53, 62, (1963). In assigning benefits, however, Christie seems at one point to confuse vagueness with context. Christie, *supra* note 1, at 885, 886.

[3]On a color spectrum, notice how red shades into yellow. On the differences between vagueness and ambiguity, see M. Cohen and E. Nagel, An Introduction to Logic and Scientific Method 224-225 (1934); L. Stebbing, A Modern Introduction to Logic 19-21 (7th ed. 1950). For the interesting development of a "vagueness profile," see M. Black, Language and Philosophy 25-58 (1949).

is central, with an "either-or" challenge, while the uncertainty of vagueness lies in marginal questions of degree. The uncertainty of vagueness is said to result from the "open texture of concepts."[4]

Language can be ambiguous without being vague. If in a mortgage, for example, it is not clear whether the word "he" in a particular provision refers to the mortgagor or the mortgagee, the reference is ambiguous without being in the slightest degree vague or imprecise. Conversely, language can be vague without being ambiguous. An example is the written word "red."

Most words that denote classes or categories (these words include most of the words of which legal instruments are composed) have elements of vagueness. Terms such as "near" and "intentional" have wide margins of uncertainty, whereas terms such as "male" and "illegitimate child" have narrow ones. A few terms of general reference, such as "the first day of the calendar month," have no significant margins of uncertainty. Most non-vague terms, on the other hand, are terms of unique reference, such as "the current President of the United States."

As with ambiguity, vagueness may be semantic in that it attaches by uncertain usage to particular words and phrases, as in the examples just given, or it may be contextual. Contextual vagueness, which likewise is either internal or external, arises, for example, when one relevant provision prevails generally over another but the extent of prevalence remains uncertain. Similarly, when it is clear from context that an express grant of authority is intended to be exclusive and thus to carry a negative implication, it is likely to remain uncertain how far the implied withholding of authority to act extends beyond the express coverage of the instrument.

Unlike ambiguity, which is always bad, vagueness is often desirable.[5] How desirable it may be in a particular instance depends on the extent to which the client intends to leave the

---

[4]F. Waismann, Verifiability, in Essays on Logic and Language 117-120 (Flew ed. 1951).

[5]See note 2 *supra.*

resolution of uncertainties to those who will administer and enforce the instrument. (This is apparently what the advocates of "purposive ambiguity" have been trying, inartistically, to say.)[6] Fortunately, through his choice of terms and definitions and a partial control of context, the draftsman has wide control over the areas and degrees of vagueness. Even though he may be unable to avoid vagueness altogether, he can usually reduce it to the point where the residual uncertainties are no longer significant for the client's purpose.

Leaving more uncertainties (and the discretion to resolve them) than the client intends, that is, creating more vagueness than the substantive policies of the client call for, is the language disease of over-vagueness. What about an instrument that is *less* vague than those policies call for? This is the disease of under-vagueness, more conventionally known as "over-precision."

Although the competent draftsman almost always tries to achieve the greatest possible clarity, this is not the same as saying that he almost always tries to achieve the greatest possible precision. Optimum clarity for the draftsman is found in language that achieves a degree of precision commensurate with the client's objectives.[7] Over-precision and over-particularity not only needlessly circumscribe the actions of those who are affected by a legal instrument but make it harder to read, understand, and administer. The draftsman should not only avoid introducing unnecessary complexities of his own but weigh the appropriateness, under the circumstances, of taking up with his client the question of whether the client will best serve his objectives by pressing matters of apparently unnecessary detail. Over-precision especially afflicts old instruments that have been amended many times.

[6]Miller, Statutory Language and the Purposive Use of Ambiguity, 42 Va. L. Rev. 39 (1956).
[7]"[H]is words should be as flexible, as elastic, indeed as vague, as the future is uncertain and unpredictable. . . . A lawyer's words should be no more precise than his client's control of the future is both practicable and desirable." C. Curtis, It's Your Law 64 (1954).

§3.6. THE DISEASES OF OVER-GENERALITY AND UNDER-GENERALITY

A third concept, often confused with vagueness and sometimes even with ambiguity, is that of generality. A term is "general" when it is not limited to a unique referent and thus can denote more than one, that is, when it refers to a class. It would be hard to imagine a legal instrument, other than a purely dispositive one, that did not contain at least one general term.

The confusion of generality with ambiguity[1] is most likely to occur with respect to heterogeneous classes that include different referents that it is often useful to distinguish. For example, the general term "grandmother" is not ambiguous merely because it includes a paternal grandmother as well as a maternal one. The same is true for the general term "brother-in-law," which includes both a wife's or husband's brother and a sister's husband. The difference between heterogenerality and ambiguity is that the former permits simultaneous reference, whereas the latter permits only alternative reference. Which occurs usually depends on the context in which the term is used. In the sentence "A grandmother sometimes has heavy responsibilities," the word "grandmother" is general. In the sentence "My grandmother sometimes has heavy responsibilities," it may well be ambiguous, if both grandmothers are living.

Generality, like vagueness, is not necessarily a disease of language. Instead, it is an indispensable tool. The diseases, rather, are over-generality and under-generality. The classes referred to in a legal instrument should be neither broader nor narrower than appropriate to carrying out the client's objectives. Thus, unless context explains the intention, the draftsman should be careful not to say "crime" when he means to cover only felony, and conversely. This is the semantic counterpart of the draftsman's attempt to reduce the concepts inherent in the client's objectives to their lowest common denominator.

---

§3.6. [1]E.g., "If therefore a group of events is described in a statute, there must be at least two which will fit that description, and since events are unique, any description of a group is almost by definition ambiguous." Radin, Statutory Interpretation, 43 Harv. L. Rev. 863, 868 (1930).

Generality is more easily confused with vagueness than with ambiguity.[2] That most general terms are also vague in their marginal applications[3] makes it easy to overlook the fact that the leeway permitted by vagueness is not the same as the leeway permitted by generality. The word "many," for example, is both vague and general, and so is the word "automobile." The generality of the latter is exemplified by its capacity for simultaneously covering both Fords and Chevrolets without a tinge of uncertainty. Its vagueness is exemplified by the uncertainty whether it covers such three-wheeled vehicles as the post-war Messerschmidt, which bore a strong resemblance also to a motorcycle.

The most important difference between ambiguous or vague language and general language is that ambiguity and vagueness constitute uncertainties of meaning, whereas generality alone does not. As a means of granting leeway to those who will administer or officially interpret the instrument, it is preferable for the draftsman to rely on the generality of language rather than its vagueness, simply because, other factors remaining neutral, certainty is normally preferable to uncertainty. Vagueness, on the other hand, is a proper (though second-choice) vehicle for granting leeway when the client's uncertainty as to specific results is matched by the marginal uncertainty in the language and context of the instrument.

Although the draftsman cannot entirely eliminate vagueness, there is no inherent reason why he cannot find in the resources of current language a degree of generality substantially coextensive with the policies the instrument is intended to express.

---

[2]"Russell's definition of vagueness . . . as constituted by a one-many relation between symbolizing and symbolized systems is held to confuse vagueness with generality. . . .'. The finite area of the field of application of the word [chair] is a sign of its *generality*, while its vagueness is indicated by the finite area and lack of specification of its boundary." M. Black, Language and Philosophy 29, 31 (1949).

[3]E.g., the "prudent man" rule with respect to trust investments.

§3.7. THE DISEASE OF OBESITY

Obesity, another major disease of language in legal instruments, is a matter not of size but of excess. It consists of prolixity, circumlocution, avoidable redundancy,[1] and other unnecessary language. Obesity is a disease because it impedes rather than facilitates understanding. As James P. Johnson has said of wills, "Prolixity is much like obesity: in order to achieve a cure, each mouthful must be watched."[2] Prescriptions for dealing with particular forms of this disease appear in chapters 8, 9, and 11.

No word or phrase should be used in a legal instrument unless there is a good reason for including it. If none appears, it should be got rid of. Every word should pay its own way. An increase in clarity or readability is adequate payment.

§3.8. HOW FULL THE CURE?

It is sometimes said that every definitive legal instrument should be drafted so that no one reading it in bad faith could possibly misunderstand it. This made good sense so long as courts were generally unfriendly to draftsmen. However, as Professor Alfred F. Conard has pointed out,[1] the climate in which legal instruments are judicially examined has greatly changed. Today, it may be assumed that courts make an honest, generally unprejudiced attempt to extract the meaning of an instrument as it would be understood by a typical member of the audience to which it is addressed. The draftsman's main problem is to say what he means according to the standards of communication current in the relevant speech community.

A draftsman no longer must go to abnormal lengths to reduce the risk that his instrument will be misread. He may rely on the normal ways of reading language, even in the face of minority, competing usages. The law now accepts, for the most

---

§3.7. [1]Some redundancy is unavoidable, because it is built into the language. See C. Cherry, On Human Communication 115, 185 (1957).
[2]A Draftsman's Handbook for Wills and Trust Agreements 9 (1961).
§3.8. [1]New Ways to Write Laws, 56 Yale L.J. 458, 468 (1947).

part, the normal presupposition of communication that language has been used in its usual sense. This presupposition is generally valid, in and out of the law, because usage is what makes language.

If there is an evenly poised doubt whether the language will be read one way or another, the draftsman should be sure that he tips the scales toward the meaning that he intends to convey. As long as there is any significant possibility that his language will be misread by the typical reader, he should try to remove the uncertainty or reduce it to relative insignificance. In such matters there are few rules of thumb. There is no substitute for the judgment of an experienced draftsman sensitive to the nuances of text and context. He must have a feeling for how specific language hits the eye of a typical reader who has no access to the subjective intent except through the instrument and its shared environment. This is the essence of the editorial point of view.

It is sometimes said that a draftsman should leave nothing to implication.[2] This is nonsense. No communication can operate without leaving part of the total communication to implication. Implication is merely the meaning that context adds to express (dictionary) meaning. The draftsman may thus rely on any normal implication that attaches to the more significant features of the message that he has made express. Indeed, given the conditions that create them, the draftsman cannot escape the burdens of normal implication. The only reservation is that implications, like express language, vary in clarity and should be made as clear as reasonably possible without prolixity.[3] Implications can be ambiguous or vague. In general, they are subject to the same diseases, and respond to most of the same cures, as express language.

Although context is a powerful tool for controlling meaning, the draftsman should not rely on it to the point of becoming careless in the choice of words and specific syntax. Context

---

[2] E.g., "Legal composition . . . should also imply nothing which it does not express." Mackay, Introduction to an Essay on the Art of Legal Composition Commonly Called Drafting, 3 L.Q. Rev. 326, 334 (1887).

[3] I.e., by adjusting text and internal context.

should not be used to resolve needless uncertainty or to correct error. The elements of communication should support rather than contradict each other.

Although for the most part the draftsman can safely rely on the same likelihood of successful communication as the writer of a nonlegal document, areas remain where the courts read legal instruments with an unfriendly bias. An example is the seller's disclaimer of responsibility for quality in the sale of goods, especially to retail buyers. Courts tend to resolve doubts in favor of the buyer and even to restrict the sweep of normal implication of the instrument. The draftsman of such a provision must be much more explicit and precise than he would otherwise need to be. The same is true for insurance policies.[4] Another example is the criminal statute, which courts are said to interpret "strictly." Although this kind of lawmaking may be a justifiable exercise of the judicial power, it can hardly be rationalized in terms of legislative communication. The same is true for other instances of "strict construction." The draftsman should know when he is dealing with such an area so that he may take the necessary added precautions of explicitness.

The draftsman does not seek the unattainable goal of absolute clarity. He seeks the highest practicable degree of clarity that gets the message across to the typical member of his audience and to the skeptical reader in those situations in which courts want to be doubly sure that a probable result of some severity was actually intended.[5] If he can do this, he has suffi-

---

[4]C. Felsenfeld & A. Siegel, Writing Contracts in Plain English 54-55 (1981).

[5]This would seem to account for a recent tendency in statutory interpretation to refer to what Professors Henry M. Hart, Jr., and Albert M. Sacks were the first to call "policies of clear statement" (The Legal Process: Basic Problems in the Making and Application of Law 1240 (mimeo. 1958)). So far as courts adopt standards of statutory clarity, the prudent draftsman must, of course, take them into consideration. But whether any new or independent principle of statutory interpretation or drafting is involved is doubtful.

Professor William V. Luneberg says that clear-statement techniques function to free a court to deviate from the otherwise determined meaning of the statute. Luneberg, Justice Rehnquist, Statutory Interpretation, the Policies of Clear Statement and Federal Jurisdiction, 58 Ind. L.J. 211, 217 (1982). A more constitutionally congenial explanation is simply that strong constitutional con-

ciently overcome the diseases and other inadequacies of language.

§3.9. THE CANONS OF INTERPRETATION

It seems plain that the legal draftsman should know the canons of interpretation. We have seen, for example, the importance of recognizing the areas in which the courts tend to construe language strictly.[1] Even so, the draftsman rarely needs to consult the authorities on the interpretation of instruments. There are several reasons for this.

For the draftsman, many rules of interpretation are simply irrelevant. These are the rules by which courts resolve inconsistencies and contradictions or supply omissions that cannot be dealt with by applying the ordinary principles of meaning. They are irrelevant because the draftsman who tries to write a healthy instrument does not and should not pay attention to the principles that the court will apply if he fails. He simply does his best, leaving it to the courts to accomplish what he did not. The draftsman who adverts to what the courts will do in such cases is likely to relax his efforts, thus passing the drafting buck to the courts and forcing them to deal with an inferior instrument.

Although the rule *expressio unius est exclusio alterius* (negative implication) is useless for this purpose, the draftsman should sensitize himself to the kinds of situations that tend to generate negative implications. Compare the following situations, in which the mother says precisely the same thing:

Situation 1:

Son: "Mother, may I go swimming?"
Mother: "You may go swimming."

---

siderations or deeply entrenched notions of social policy, as part of external context, call for a more pointed formulation whenever the legislative intent is to impose limitations on those considerations or notions.

§**3.9.** [1]See §3.8 *supra.*

Situation 2:

Son: "Mother, may I go swimming and then to the movies?"
Mother: "You may go swimming."

In the first case, there is no negative implication against going to the movies. In the second, there presumably is. Accordingly, this so-called rule "is at best a description, after the fact, of what the court has discovered from context."[2]

Other principles of legal interpretation merely restate what the draftsman already knows about the general principles of meaning applicable to language. He needs no legal authority to tell him, as does the canon *noscitur a sociis* ("it is known by its companions"), that words are read in and restricted by context, nor is he ordinarily interested in what a particular court has said about the meaning of a particular phrase in a particular legal instrument.[3] Its irrelevance to the specific instrument he is writing lies in the fact that particular legal instruments taken in their respective environments tend to be unique.

On the other hand, he is interested in what particular words and phrases generally mean as a result of established usage. His interest in materials that can tell him these meanings includes court decisions, but it is not confined to them. For this purpose, judicial pronouncements have only such probative force as their inherent merits warrant. They have no legal status.[4] Although the meaning of a particular phrase in a particular document may be a matter of legal fiat in some cases, the general meanings of legal terms are not. The draftsman is interested in all reliable sources, judicial or otherwise. Although the codifiers of title 10 of the United States Code ("Armed Forces") were interested in the Court of Claims' definition of "grade" in *Wood v. United States,*[5] they did not feel bound by it. Their adoption of that

[2] R. Dickerson, The Interpretation and Application of Statutes 234 (1975).
[3] Dickerson, The Difficult Choice Between "And" and "Or," 46 A.B.A.J. 310 (1960).
[4] *Id.*
[5] "Grade is a step or degree in either office or rank." 15 Ct. Cl. 151, 160 (1879), *aff'd,* 107 U.S. 414 (1882).

definition resulted not from any legal authority the opinion had but from the conviction that the court's description of current usage was lexicographically accurate.

A few canons of interpretation describe specific current usage, and are, therefore, of direct interest to the draftsman. One of these is the canon *reddendo singula singulis* (refers each item in a series to its corresponding item in a matched series), which is a factual statement about a particular convention of language. It recognizes that in some cases the reader may properly infer that the author has intended a one-to-one correspondence of two juxtaposed series of ideas. Thus, it may be assumed that the phrase "my nephews, John, Harry, and Fred, who are 16, 19, and 26 years old," will be read "John is 16 years old; Harry is 19 years old; and Fred is 26 years old."

Although somewhat weaker, the doctrine of *ejusdem generis* ("of the same kinds") also expresses a general tendency. If there is a series of terms followed by a general catchall term, and the specific terms fall into a class narrower than the class defined by the catchall term, there is a rebuttable presumption that the catchall term is intended to refer only to things falling within the narrower class. For example, the phrase "pines, firs, spruce, or other kinds of vegetation" is intended to include vegetation of the same general kind as pines, firs, and spruce.

The trouble with the rule is that it does not tell us which of the various intermediate possibilities was intended. In this case, the narrower class could be trees, conifers, nondeciduous conifers (larches are deciduous), or the pine family of evergreens. This uncertainty is resolved, if at all, by total context.

The draftsman can reduce the uncertainty by interrogating the client to see which of these intermediate categories, if any, is most nearly congruent with his problem. If there is still doubt whether a significant category has been included, the draftsman can assure its inclusion either by naming the category or listing a species of it (e.g., "larches").[6]

---

[6]The "rule" is, of course, superfluous where it is already written into the provision in question, as in "fairs, shows, circuses, or similar functions in the park." Cf. Samuels, The Ejusdem Generis Rule in Statutory Interpretation, 1984 Stat. L. Rev. 180, 181.

Because few canons of interpretation describe actual usages of which he is not already aware, the draftsman has only a limited interest in them.[7]

---

[7]On the canons of interpretation generally, see Dickerson, *supra* note 2, at 4, 227-236.

IV

Steps in Drafting

§4.1. INTRODUCTION

We come now to the basic steps in the drafting process. The recommendations that follow are neither novel nor startling. Most of them have been thoroughly tested in practice and, where followed, they materially improve the end product. Unfortunately, they have not been as widely used as they should be.

These basic steps are best taken in two parts, divided by the distinction between the substantive and the verbal. Although these elements cannot be separated functionally, it is useful for understanding to distinguish the "think" part from the "write" part.

§4.2. SUBSTANTIVE STEP ONE: FINDING OUT WHAT THE CLIENT WANTS

On the substantive side, there are three basic steps. The first has already been referred to: Find out what the client wants to accomplish and what specific problems that involves.[1] Explore the detailed possibilities with him and help him think the problem through.[2] The emphasis here is on the analysis of the prob-

§4.2. [1]See §2.1 *supra.*
[2]"The draftsman must help the testator develop the latter's all-too-often vague and sketchy wishes and translate them into provisions which will be fully

lem and getting the relevant facts.[3] The draftsman may also want to explore (very tactfully!) his client's credibility, reliability, values,[4] and even sincerity and seriousness.[5]

At this stage, the draftsman pumps the client for information. He finds out specifically what the client wants and how much the client wants to leave to the draftsman's discretion. He points out any substantive inconsistencies that he thinks he sees in the idea, including in the case of legislation any constitutional problems that occur to him. He also mentions any administrative or other practical problems, and any drafting problems, that he thinks the client ought to know about. On matters of policy and substance, of course, he is ultimately subject to being overruled by the client.

The specific direction and content of the draftsman's questions should depend on the particular subject matter and the field of law involved. It is impossible here to do more than suggest the line of questioning the draftsman should take.

Professor Frank E. Cooper has described for us the kind of general considerations that are likely to interest the draftsman of a contract.

> The draftsman's first job is to learn of all the previous negotiations between the parties, so far as they are relevant to the proposed contract. Then — whether or not the parties think they have reached a meeting of the minds on all the terms of their agreement — the lawyer must consider what further matters should be made the subject of negotiation. He frequently discovers that although the parties assumed they were in complete

---

thought out and integrated." H. Schwarzberg & I. Stocker, Drawing Wills 3 (1956).

[3]This has been called the "Factual Sanction." K. Pantzer & R. Deer, The Drafting of Corporate Charters and By-Laws 11 (1968).

[4]These and other specific matters are listed by Mary Ellen Caldwell in Planned Research Protocol, from The Florida Approach, remarks made at International Seminar and Workshop on the Teaching of Legal Drafting, Indiana University School of Law, Bloomington, October 3-4, 1975, transcript, pp. 179-181 (MLD 115).

[5]Fred J. Carman, Bill Drafting Research, remarks made at legislative drafting workshop, National Conference of State Legislatures, Annapolis, November 10-11, 1977 (MLD 122). This is especially true of legislators, who sometimes merely want something to impress a constituent.

agreement, there remain a number of matters that require further negotiation. The lawyer must exercise his imagination to envisage all the possibilities that may be encountered. He must learn to forecast what may happen, and then consider both the legal and practical consequences that will ensue if the unexpected does occur.[6]

Cooper also includes a number of specific questions that commonly need asking:[7]

(c) If there are several promisors, should their obligations be joint, or several, or joint and several? . . .

(e) How about the time of performance? When is delay to be excused? How much delay will be permitted? Will delay excuse nonperformance by the other party?

(f) Should there be a limit on the duration of the contract? [Instead of providing for automatic termination] would it be better to provide that the party entitled to receive performance shall have an option to declare the contract terminated, in certain eventualities?

(g) Should provision be made for liquidated damages? . . .

(i) Will one party desire to examine the books and records of the other? . . .

(j) Should a performance bond be required?

Maurice B. Kirk recommends that the draftsman also try to determine the parties' common immediate objectives and, if possible, their respective ulterior purposes (which are likely to vary considerably).[8]

Where the number of contingencies is large, it is often desirable, as Cooper suggests,[9] to use a checklist. Not only will this remind him to ask the client all the relevant questions, but it may be useful in similar, future cases.

[6]Cooper, Writing in Law Practice 272 (1963). It is better, of course, when there have been no previous negotiations. The draftsman should be in on the negotiations from the beginning. See §2.1 *supra.*

[7]*Id.* at 273-274.

[8]Maurice B. Kirk, Legal Drafting: Some Reflections on Objectives, revision of remarks made at program on simplified legal drafting, American Bar Association, New York City, August 7, 1978 (MLD 113). See also Caldwell, *supra* note 5.

[9]Cooper, *supra* note 6, at 274.

A checklist may be borrowed from a book[10] (or friend) or accumulated out of the draftsman's own experience or that of his office. The easiest thing is to get someone else's list and, as necessary, perfect it through recurrent use. The other approach is to start from scratch and develop a mature checklist by gradual accretion. Much of the time the draftsman must develop his checklist *ad hoc.*

The importance of the draftsman's role in helping his client foresee all the significant contingencies has been emphasized by Dean Mason Ladd in connection with its effect on the sweep of the parol evidence rule.

> If all contracts were drawn by lawyers and they kept in mind the problems of the rule, the occasions to use the parol evidence rule would be negligible because writings would integrate in fact, every performance, obligation or promise contemplated by the parties. The careful lawyer should anticipate possible future troubles or difficulties which may arise under a contemplated transaction and find out what the desires of the parties are in respect to them before writing the agreement.[11]

In the drafting of wills, Charles M. Lyman suggests the kinds of specific background information that the draftsman needs to get.

> There are certain minima that a lawyer must know in order to be sure that the will is a proper one. He must know something of the client's family and relatives. He must have at least a rough idea of the nature and extent of his client's property, for it is obvious that a will that is adequate to dispose of an estate of ten thousand dollars would probably be quite insufficient for a wise disposition of a million dollars. If large amounts are involved, the lawyer ought to know whether the testator's wife also owns sub-

---

[10]A good example is M. Volz and A. Berger's checklist for partnership agreements in The Drafting of Partnership Agreements 5-11 (6th ed. 1976) (MLD 117). Fred J. Carman's remarks, *supra* note 5, provide a kind of general checklist of the things legislative draftsmen should be alert to. For a compilation of checklists, see B. Becker, B. Savin & D. Becker, Legal Checklists (1977).

[11]Cases and Materials on the Law of Evidence 720 (2d ed. 1955).

stantial property, because the tax consequences of large provisions for her might prove serious. (This is one of the cases where it is unwise to use the marital deduction.) Also for tax purposes, he ought to know about any jointly owned property, life insurance, and ante mortem transfers. Inquiry ought to be made as to the existence of any power of appointment under which the new will might operate. If one exists, questions arise as to whether the creating instrument requires that the exercise of the power must make specific reference to it and as to whether it would be tax-wiser to release or renounce it. It is well to know of any potential substantial increases in the testator's estate such as by inheritance or as the fruits of a recent royalty contract of which the real value has not yet been tested. Lack of knowledge of such a possibility may well result in the drafting of a will that would be perfect for a fifty-thousand dollar estate but grossly undesirable for one of a half-million dollars. Still other essential facts may appear relevant and important in the light of the lawyer's own experience.[12]

Each drafting project normally contains many elements peculiar to that project. This is true also of statutes.[13] Here is a highly edited version of some of the many questions that I asked a Congressman who wanted a bill emancipating Indians who could establish their general competency. Included are the answers that discussion with him and with the Bureau of Indian Affairs ultimately developed.

Q: Do you want to limit the bill to Indians of any particular age?
A: Yes. To those 21 or above.
Q: Who should determine the question of competency?
A: The local naturalization court.
Q: Should the court's jurisdiction depend on the applicant's domicile or on his residence?
A: His residence.

[12]C. Lyman, Practical Aspects of Drafting Wills 18 (1962).
[13]As between legislation and other definitive legal documents, ". . . the number of contingencies that a lawyer has to guard against in the case of a will or contract, while sometimes they are very numerous, are mere flyspecks compared with the contingencies that must be considered in the case of a statute. . . ." Middleton Beaman, Hearings on H.R. Con. Res. 18, Joint Committee on the Organization of Congress, 79th Cong., 1st Sess., 413, 419 (1945).

Q: Who should be notified of the hearing?

A: The head of the local governmental unit, the local welfare department, the Superintendent of the applicant's tribe, the head of its governing body, and any other persons the court considers appropriate.

Q: How much notice should be given?

A: 30 to 60 days.

Q: What factors should the court consider in determining competency?

A: The applicant's moral and mental qualifications and his ability to manage his own affairs.

Q: After a writ of competency is issued, what further steps, if any, need to be taken to assure full emancipation?

A: The Secretary of the Interior should be required to give the applicant all money and property that has been held in trust for him and to issue any necessary land patents.

Q: At what point should the applicant's tribal connection be severed?

A: When he and his tribe have fully settled all claims against each other.

Failure to build a solid base initially will probably result in a flimsy structure.

Whenever he is questioning his client about a complicated arrangement, the draftsman should be sure to tell the client how much effort is involved in putting together a professionally adequate instrument. Many inadequate legal instruments have resulted from drafts hurriedly prepared to meet deadlines fixed by clients who like to get things done but who have been inadequately briefed on what is entailed in turning out a satisfactory draft. It is true that some deadlines have to be met. It is also true that some deadlines are needlessly imposed on the preparation of instruments that are too complicated or critical to be properly handled within the time allotted. Some of these deadlines would be relaxed or dropped if it were explained to the client that either the time limit or the quality of the result must give way. The draftsman who is too easygoing about this winds up as a mediocre, short-order cook.

In many instances, the draftsman needs a factual background broader than can be supplied by the client. When this happens the draftsman must look elsewhere. Some draftsmen prefer independent research to asking the advice of a specialist. For technical matters not within the immediate reach of the draftsman, independent research normally takes too much time.[14] Even where the draftsman is not sure that his sources are reliable, he can save time by asking questions first and cross-checking the answers afterward. For legal rather than factual matters independent research is more desirable, because the primary sources are usually close at hand. But even here it is well to canvass the field for already completed studies and to telephone the available experts before formulating conclusions. Naturally, the draftsman cannot always pass the research buck if the drafting problem is new.[15]

[14]That research tends to preempt time badly needed for the conceptual, architectural, and compositional aspects of drafting is suggested by Professor Harry W. Jones's time study of a relatively modest drafting project conducted by a group that assumed the full research load and whose time sheet showed this breakdown (35 A.B.A.J. 941 (1949)):

Research time	58 hours
Conference time	18 hours
Writing time	4 hours

This is more typical: "We do not have time to take a lot of books or written material and pore over it. We have got to get the expert that knows it and dig it out of him in a hurry." Middleton Beaman, Hearings on H.R. Con. Res. 18, Joint Committee on the Organization of Congress, 79th Cong., 1st Sess. 413, 425 (1945).

[15]For a sample of a running debate on the propriety of passing the research buck, see colloquy on the draftsman as researcher, remarks made at International Seminar and Workshop on Teaching Legal Drafting, Indiana University School of Law, Bloomington, October 3-4, 1975, transcript p.402 (MLD 110-113). There is no basic disagreement on the kind of research needed for good draftsmanship (MLD 110). The disagreement, if any, lies only with respect to what kind of research is most appropriate for the typical draftsman to undertake personally.

Columbia University's Legislative Drafting Research Fund is an elite organization that selects its own clientele and accepts only projects that permit it to do the kind of careful and thorough research to which the typical draftsman cannot aspire. Somewhat similar organizations exist at Harvard, Yale, Notre Dame, Creighton, and Seton Hall, except that they are largely under student, rather than faculty, control.

The kind of drafting operation typified by Columbia University's group

When the draftsman is faced with revising an existing instrument prepared by another, perhaps the most important step is to research the instrument itself. This means intensively explicating it.

§4.3.   SUBSTANTIVE STEP TWO: EXPLORING THE LEGAL FRAMEWORK

The second important step is to explore the existing legal framework. A competent architect would not dream of remodeling a house without first taking a close look at it. Similarly, the draftsman of a legal instrument should closely examine the relevant existing instruments, if any, to see what to amend, what to repeal, and what to supplement. Failure to do this results in implied repeals, overlaps, and inconsistent terminology; in a word — confusion. If the instrument is a private one, he should also be familiar with the context of the law in which the instrument is to operate.[1]

For the most part, the form of private legal instruments is unregulated.[2] Most statutory forms, such as a short-form warranty deed, are optional rather than required. Where a form such as the uniform bill of lading is required, it is usually incidental to "achieving the public goals of a regulatory program."[3] However, form is the centerpiece in the simplification of "consumer" instruments, such as credit papers and product warranties, mandated in some states by "plain English" statutes.[4]

---

of draftsmen represents the exception, rather than the rule. Most legal draftsmen work under severe time constraints that even the most farsighted and diplomatic draftsmen cannot cure. Accordingly, they must pass the research buck, so far as necessary or prudent, to others or rely on other shortcuts to decently reliable knowledge.

§4.3. [1]The "Legal Sanction" according to K. Pantzer & R. Deer, The Drafting of Corporate Charters and By-Laws 13 (2d ed. 1968).

[2]For an excellent analysis of legal prescriptions relating to form, see Kirk, Legal Drafting: How Should a Document Begin? 3 Tex. Tech. L. Rev. 233, 247 *et seq.* (1972) (MLD 194-210).

[3]*Id.* at 247 (MLD 195).

[4]See §8.3 *infra.*

Wills, inter vivos trusts, leases (which are both conveyances and contracts), and many other private instruments are subject to substantive limitations that must be reflected in text but not necessarily in a prescribed form. The draftsman should become familiar with the local versions of such restrictions.

§4.4. SUBSTANTIVE STEP THREE: DEVELOPING A PLAN OF ORGANIZATION

The third "think" step is to select the right concepts and develop a concrete plan of organization and arrangement.[1] The instrument must substantively jell. This is the stage at which the legal architect develops what the real architect calls a "sketch," a blueprint without the details. This is the stage of general synthesis.

The job of selecting the most appropriate concepts[2] and then fitting them together is unquestionably the most elusive part of drafting. The specific pieces should cover the intended areas, and they should leave no gaps; they should not duplicate each other or overlap, and they should not contradict each other.

How does a person plan an office? He obtains the right space and equipment and then tries to achieve the greatest efficiency by arranging the elements to minimize the steps, effort, and expense required to operate it. Similarly, the draftsman, after confronting his conceptual problems, tries to achieve the greatest clarity and best organization by making an outline of the intended result. Unfortunately, he can never be sure of doing a perfect job. Although calculus provides us with a helpful parallel in the problems of maxima and minima, no one has yet perfected a calculus for drafting. Lacking this, the draftsman has to fall back on informed judgment. Even so, the time he spends

___

§4.4. [1]"[B]efore the draftsman commences his draft, the whole design of it should be conceived." E. Piesse, The Elements of Drafting 14 (5th ed. Aitken 1976). Pantzer and Deer call this the "Organizational Sanction." K. Pantzer & R. Deer, The Drafting of Corporate Charters and By-Laws 15 (2d ed. 1968).

[2]See §2.4 *supra*.

in developing and perfecting an outline is time well spent.

For some smaller drafting jobs an outline can be constructed mentally and remembered. For the more complicated and extensive projects a written outline is invaluable. Building one forces the draftsman to think the problem through, and it helps him determine whether he has exhausted his source material. Clearing up problems of basic arrangement at the outset saves valuable time, because readjustments in basic arrangement are more difficult later, and the risk of error becomes greater. Finally, an outline is the tool by which a big and complex problem can be divided into more manageable parts. With a good outline to work from, a draftsman can attack each discrete component separately, undistracted and unharassed, for the most part, by considerations affecting the other components. This is the most important single device for solving complicated problems.

An outline may be projected at various levels of particularity. The crudest kind simply divides the problem into general "titles" or subdivisions. A more detailed, more useful, and correspondingly more difficult outline sets forth specific chapter or part headings. The best outline is one that attempts to break the project down by major subdivision and by section. This is not always necessary or practicable, but, where it is, it is well worth the effort. It takes a high degree of discipline to resist the almost overwhelming temptation to omit this operation and "get on with the job."

Although most lawyers are familiar with the functions of an outline, in practice they underestimate its concrete utility and, especially, how hard it is to make. Nowhere is the typical lawyer more inept than at integrating the structural aspects of complicated legal problems into a well-organized instrument.

No outline, however carefuly developed, can be other than tentative, because it is almost never possible to anticipate all the relevant contingencies. The draftsman, therefore, must not fall in love with his own architectural accomplishments. He must keep his eyes open for whatever changes later developments make appropriate.

The problems of arrangement are so complex that chapter 5 is specially devoted to them.

§4.5. COMPOSITION: OBJECTIVES

After he has begun to get the substance of his message in hand, the draftsman gradually moves into the field of form and style. And thus he comes to the writing stage of drafting. The transition is not abrupt, and the two phases blend imperceptibly, because substance and form cannot be functionally divorced. The shift is mainly in emphasis, because the draftsman continues to be interested in substance up to the last minute. For one thing, he will want to take full advantage of the substantive improvements that a systematic attention to matters of form and style inevitably makes possible.

The proposed instrument should be written for the greatest possible accuracy. Accuracy, which (like clarity)[1] is not necessarily the same thing as precision, is the degree to which the proposed instrument expresses what the client intends it to express. A proposed ordinance, for instance, is "accurate" when it moves in the direction intended by the client and it is no more nor less general, and no more nor less vague, than is required by the considerations of substantive policy.[2]

Normally, this means that a draftsman need not try to provide a specific answer to every problem that might conceivably arise in connection with the instrument he is drafting. Not only is this impossible, but many situations are preferably or necessarily left to future administrative or judicial determination. Where underlying policy has been well crystallized, the great bulk of individually important problems and those that occur often enough to be significant can be foreseen and dealt with. In such cases, the draftsman's ultimate goals are (1) to eliminate semantic, syntactic, and contextual ambiguity, and (2) so far as vagueness is concerned, to leave for future interpretation only those borderline cases that are individually insignificant and unlikely to occur often enough to create a significant administrative burden that could be avoided by more specific drafting.

§4.5. [1]See §§3.3-3.8 *supra.*

[2]"The successful draftsman must steer a course between that of 'overemphasis on details' which defeats the author's purpose, and that overstatement which 'disguises matters.' " F. Cooper, Writing in Law Practice 19 (1963).

Where underlying policy has been developed intentionally only in general form, the development of more specific guidelines in particular situations may properly be left to the persons authorized to administer the policy. This is done by phrasing the relevant rules in correspondingly general and sometimes vague terms. Here, again, the client's wishes, after the draftsman has fully briefed him, ultimately control.

§4.6. COMPOSITION STEP ONE: PREPARING A FIRST DRAFT

Normally, there are five separate steps in establishing the final form of a legal instrument. First, the draftsman prepares an initial draft, paying general attention to the accepted rules of form, checking doubtful questions of substance, and handling new problems as they arise by asking questions or by doing individual research. At this early stage he is still interested in the broad essentials — the substance of his message and the problems of general arrangement. He does not worry over details and polish.

The draftsman will do well to keep each section on a separate sheet until the final draft, or one to be circulated for comment, is prepared. The draftsman can later revise individual sections as many times as necessary without having to retype materials belonging to other sections, and the sections can be freely rearranged without retyping. The draft should be double spaced or triple spaced.

§4.7. COMPOSITION STEP TWO: REVISING

Second, the draftsman revises his work as many times as necessary to produce the desired result. And here is a fact that should get him over a hurdle that pride puts in the path of most persons: It is no disgrace to revise a draft a dozen times. Somehow the idea has gone around that if a draftsman does not have a satisfactory draft by the third attempt, either he is beyond his depth or it is the best that could be done. Nonsense! A good draftsman may make as many as 15 to 20 revisions to iron out an extremely difficult provision. The important thing to remember is that, ideally, he should keep on revising until he feels that the draft is 99 percent right,[1] unless, of course, the economics of the situation make some compromise necessary.

The number of drafts required is a function of the difficulties of the immediate problem and the skill and experience of the draftsman. For myself, I have found that five or six drafts are enough for most provisions and that three or four are adequate for the mine-run of relatively simple drafting problems. Usually, it is desirable to revise a section or article extensively before starting the next one.

In revision, paper waste and unnecessary handling can be avoided by not preparing copies until they are needed for review by others. Some draftsmen have copies made simply to insure against losing the current draft. The same result is reached by saving the amended previous draft. This shows not only the earlier draft but, with its changes, the basis for the unamended current draft. Any attempt to keep more than one draft current should be avoided unless special circumstances make it advisable. When needed, photocopies are easily made, and they need no proofreading.

A clean draft should be run off as soon as the amended current draft becomes hard to read and work with. Only in emergencies should the draftsman release as his final effort anything less than a clean draft. Drafts that seem to read well when badly marked up usually still contain, when retyped, errors or

---

§4.7. [1]"[T]here is no such thing as good writing — there is only good rewriting." Rabkin, The Legal Draftsman: The Use of Forms in Tax Planning, 42 A.B.A.J. 137, 196 (1956). "Brandeis often rewrote an opinion a dozen times. Once, Justice Frankfurter tells us, there were fifty-three revisions." F. Cooper, Writing in Law Practice 33 (1963).

The point is especially important for legislation.

> You are all familiar with the story of the little boy who was asked what he would wish for if he had three wishes, and who said, first, all the candy he could eat; second, never to have to go to school; and third, after a long period of reflection, some more candy. Very similar should be the three wishes of the person called upon to express in effective form policies which have been determined upon; first, that he may exercise great care; second, that he may have plenty of time; and third, that he may be still more careful.

Beaman, Bill Drafting, 7 Law Lib. J. 64 (1948).

inconsistencies or awkwardnesses of expression, so that it is good policy to keep retyping and revising until a clean draft reads satisfactorily without further revision.

For identification, each draft should show in the upper right hand corner (1) the date and (2) if more than one draftsman is involved, the draftsman's initials. All drafts should be kept.

§4.8. COMPOSITION STEP THREE: MAKING ACROSS-THE-BOARD CHECKS

The third step in legal drafting is not always recognized as a separate operation, because for simple instruments it is usually taken as an incident of one of the other steps. But with more complicated instruments it is well worth special attention. This is the making of those specialized "across-the-board checks" that are necessary to tying the instrument together, to having internal consistency, and to realizing clarity. Here the draftsman gives the instrument a series of special "horizontal" treatments. He checks his definitions one by one, and then his cross references, and such other elements as recur and need to be treated uniformly. Each of these checks is a specialized testing of the instrument as a whole.

Across-the-board checks are necessary because through most of the earlier writing stage the draftsman has dealt with his material vertically. Having divided his subject matter into parts, divisions, or simply sections, he has tried to complete each unit from top to bottom before he tackled the next. This is essential in any long and complicated instrument. During the earlier phases, he kept in mind the relationships between the part before him and the other parts only so far as he could without dissipating his intellectual energies. No draftsman can work accurately and efficiently if he tries to solve all his problems at once. He may not be able to solve them at all; hence he must defer a number of matters that can be dealt with adequately only by a later series of across-the-board checks.

It should be plain that neither the vertical nor the horizontal approach is a substitute for the other and that the former is not necessarily complete before the latter begins. Although with the simplest instruments the two tend to run together, the draftsman will do well to keep each approach separately in mind. Once they have been ingrained, the draftsman will be able to apply them automatically as the needs of particular problems require.

Whereas under the vertical approach the draftsman tries to deal with all problems that affect each successive segment, under the horizontal, across-the-board approach he tries to deal with only one problem at a time for the instrument as a whole. For example, while he is checking the consistent use of definitions he is doing nothing else. Indeed, he will be wise to check his definitions one at a time.

One of the virtues of intensive, systematic, and specialized across-the-board checks is that even where they are applied to what appear to be only stylistic aspects of the instrument they often expose substantive discrepancies. This is most likely to happen when the draftsman is checking his definitions and terminology. Once he has made the draft speak with a single tongue, he often finds that the draft now states substantive results that he never before suspected. This may lead, in turn, to a reevaluation of the underlying thought and the discovery of important errors. In this way the systematic treatment of form is the means of substantive improvement. This is a big bonus to add to the improvements in organization and readability that formal and stylistic across-the-board checks seem mainly designed to achieve. Of course, across-the-board checks may be made of substantive aspects as well as of stylistic ones.

§4.9. COMPOSITION STEP FOUR: CHECKING WITH OTHERS

One very important step that is often overlooked, though it is sometimes impossible to take, is cross-checking with others.[1] Of

§4.9. [1]"[T]he best course is to have it considered and checked from end to end by someone else." E. Piesse, The Elements of Drafting 132 (5th Ed. Aitken 1976). "Important documents should be . . . gone over by at least one man in addition to the draftsman." Lewis, Legal Draftsmanship, 89 N.Y.L.J. 1914 (1933).

course, if the instrument is simple enough and covers sufficiently familiar territory, the draftsman may be safe in omitting
this step. At the same time, this is like saying that if a person lets
his fire insurance lapse his house may not burn down.

It is only in minor or routine jobs that the lawyer is safe in
performing solo. Collaboration is necessary in large, complicated jobs and it is desirable for many lesser ones. I have never
known a draftsman who could turn out a piece of work of substantial size that could not be materially improved by another.

The greatest barrier to seeking needed advice lies in the
draftsman himself. "Pride of authorship,"[2] in extreme form a
kind of emotional hemophilia, thrives in the neophyte and is
latent even in the sophisticate. Sooner or later he must learn that
his reputation as a draftsman depends on the quality of what he
is instrumental in producing, and his final accomplishments are
untarnished by the even considerable help he may have received
on the way. A draftsman who can carry a draft to only 80 percent
accuracy by himself but who can, by and through others, achieve
98 percent accuracy in the end product has a better batting
average than one who can achieve 90 percent accuracy by himself but who cannot work with others sufficiently to produce an
equally excellent result.

As a general rule, therefore, it is desirable to approach the
broad drafting problem on a team basis. In a well-run legislative
drafting group, for example, individual draftsmen are apt to
cross-check each other, especially on complicated instruments.
It is safe to say that a large part of drafting of nonroutine provisions involves complications too treacherous to be conquered
single-handed. It does not contradict this to say that every legal
instrument should be the ultimate responsibility of one person.[3]

For adequate testing there are several available methods.
The most usual is checking with individual fellow draftsmen or

[2]Pride of Authorship, 37 A.B.A.J. 209 (1951).

[3]It is significant that when the Constitutional Convention got to the final
writing stage, it assigned the job to a small committee, which then turned to
one of its members, Gouverneur Morris. 3 M. Farrand, The Records of the
Convention of 1787, at 499 (1937); C. Van Doren, The Great Rehearsal 160
(1948).

outside experts, or both. Indeed, it should be the practice in every law firm to have all but the simplest instruments read through by at least one lawyer other than the one preparing it. A second method, which is sometimes useful, especially for proposed legislation, is to submit the tentative results to a panel of critics, not much larger than a half dozen if the work is to move faster than a slow tortoise. A third device is to reproduce the instrument and circulate it for suggestion and comment to a carefully selected sampling of the kinds of persons who are going to have to live with it. The draftsman can use these devices separately or in combination, as circumstances make appropriate.

When a proposed legal instrument is circulated for suggestion and comment, this should not be done prematurely. If the original author does an inadequate job, those who review his work are correspondingly less able to deal with the errors that it is normal to expect in the work of a single individual. Instead, their attention is diverted by items that the original draftsman could, with reasonable effort, have eliminated in advance.

Those responsible for preparing a legal instrument should assume that they will have but one audience with a particular editorial panel or particular list of readers. Normally, it is both unnecessary and undesirable to submit different drafts of the same instrument to the same audience. Because the editorial point of view is sharpest the first time a critic sees an instrument, it is desirable not to squander this resource by permitting errors that could have been removed earlier.

The draftsman must not confuse the practice of getting help from others, which is very fruitful, with that of writing by conference, which wastes time and talent. Groups can mull over ideas, they can criticize, and they can give or withhold approval; but they cannot compose concisely, consistently, or clearly. The wise draftsman refuses to participate in such an endeavor.

In large organizations in which the functions of drafting and review are divided sequentially, an additional precaution is advisable. An important military doctrine of long standing is that of "completed staff work." Briefly, this means that an officer who is charged with carrying out a mission should submit nothing less than a completed job. This it is naturally impossible to do for every assignment, but the objective applies equally to any project that must pass through several or more hands before it is done. No one in the chain of responsibility can do his best job unless earlier handlers have done their best. Cumulative mediocrity cannot be abruptly wrenched into final excellence.

Organizational hierarchy can pose yet another problem. A tentatively complete draft often ascends to higher-ups, some of whom may disagree with aspects of the result. Since the superior normally associates his higher position with superior skill and knowledge, he is strongly tempted to improve the draft according to his own lights. This is sometimes necessary and it is often desirable. Let it also be said that it is very risky, unless the original draftsman either participates or is fully consulted. No matter how skilled the superior, he is usually less well informed on the background of the problem, and the considerations that affect the result, than the original draftsman. Failure to recognize this has trapped many an unwary supervisor or reviewer.

Drafts should be prepared in the lower echelons and, when finished, move to the higher, not the reverse. There are at least two reasons. First, many instruments call for a working knowledge of everyday detail that is usually denied the supervisor or general policy maker. Second, editorial inhibitions and a want of candor appear when the superior submits his workmanship to the critical scrutiny of the subordinate.

§4.10.　COMPOSITION STEP FIVE: APPLYING THE POLISH

The fifth and last step is to polish the result for the greatest clarity and simplicity. This brings us to a subject that has received much attention in recent years. There has been an increased interest in matters of form, particularly in those relating to the simplification of language. This is wholesome and praiseworthy. Much can yet be done to improve the ease with which many otherwise adequate legal instruments can be understood and used.

But this has led to the danger of becoming so style conscious that the more fundamental matters of substance and basic arrangement are neglected. Any approach to drafting that makes a sharp distinction between form and substance is likely to do more harm than good, because it diverts attention from the fact that clarity and simplicity are more than sentence deep. True clarity rests on the right statement of the right blend of the right concepts.[1] A draftsman who devotes himself entirely to obtaining structural coherence, with a contempt for style, is preferable to one who rushes to express his confusion "readably." Fortunately, substantive coherence and good style are entirely compatible, except where the pressure of time forces a compromise. But if anything must yield, let it be readability rather than logical coherence. In any event, no provision can be made simpler than the inherent, irreducible complexities of the underlying ideas allow.

With these reservations, it is safe to assert that form and style are important to a legal instrument because, even where they do nothing more, they have an important bearing on its success as a vehicle of communication.

Chapters 6 through 9 list many rules for writing that will help to make a legal instrument more understandable. Using them will not guarantee that the result makes sense (in some cases, however, deficiencies will become more obvious), but it will make much clearer and simpler whatever sense there is in the underlying idea. It is assumed at this point that the draftsman has thought through his ideas and has adequately organized them.

§4.11. USE OF FORM BOOKS

Before turning to the specific matters of form and style set forth in the following chapters, let us consider briefly the use of forms or form books, which is so often deplored.[1] The draftsman

§4.10. [1]The selection of the right words for a legal instrument has been called the "Orthological Sanction." K. Pantzer & R. Deer, The Drafting of Corporate Charters and By-Laws 16 (1968).

§4.11. [1]E.g., Beardsley, Beware of, Eschew and Avoid Pompous Prolixity and Platitudinous Epistles! 16 Cal. S.B.J. 65 (1941).

pressed for time naturally turns to any resource that will hasten his progress and perhaps even improve the result. But the problem is really broader: When are specific legal problems sufficiently similar that their treatment can be standardized in legal boilerplate? Besides form books, lawyers normally keep copies of their earlier efforts for possible use in dealing with later problems. Some of these develop into office forms. In the same way, legislative draftsmen look to existing statutes. Lawyers steeped in case precedent and heavily pressed for time readily see the value of instrumental precedent.[2]

But just as the values are generally the same, so also are the pitfalls. Just as blind adherence to judicial precedent is hazardous, so also is the blind use of forms, even when they have been developed by the lawyer for his own use or enacted in statutory form by a legislature.[3] Despite the similarities that make feasible the use of forms, new situations often present significantly different elements. And so the draftsman should carefully weigh the appropriateness of a form to the case at hand each time he is prompted to use it.[4] Indeed, the danger that the form will lull him into a false sense of accomplishment is so great that in other than the most routine situations he is wise to use it mainly as a cross check.[5] He must not forget that he has been engaged to exercise his professional judgment, not to serve as a mere retrieval system.

There is still another consideration. In their natural preoccupation with substantive results, some published form books

---

[2]"Should lawyers refrain from using legal boilerplate? They cannot operate efficiently without it. Indeed, they cannot operate even inefficiently without it." Dickerson, Some Jurisprudential Implications of Electronic Data Processing, 28 Law & Contemp. Prob. 53, 61 (1963). "Form books can also save you time in the selection of appropriate phrasing, though care should be exercised in lifting clauses bodily." L. Mandel, The Preparation of Commercial Agreements 9 (1955). "It is entirely impractical to draft conditional limitations, condemnation and similar clauses without the help of good forms. . . . If slavery is involved, let the draftsman be the master." M. Friedman, Preparation of Leases vii (1962).

[3]See, for instance, the standardized definitions in §13.7, *infra.*

[4]Thomas, Problems in Drafting Legal Instruments, 39 Ill. B.J. 51, 56, 57 (1950).

[5]Rabkin, The Legal Draftsman: The Use of Forms in Tax Planning, 42 A.B.A.J. 137, 196 (1956).

have treated matters of structure, form, and style so cautiously that they have tended to perpetuate the drafting ineptitudes of the past. In drawing heavily on adjudicated documents, they have included an unfortunate percentage of inadequately drafted provisions.[6]

§4.12.   TIME NEEDED TO COMPLETE

How long does it take to draft a legal instrument? Abraham Lincoln's answer is as good as any. When asked how long a man's legs should be, he answered, "Long enough to reach the ground." For the legal draftsman this means, "As long as it takes the particular draftsman to do the particular job." Unfortunately, the draftsman is often under time limitations that he cannot control, and he has to compromise accordingly. The real answer therefore is, "Longer than he has time for." There will even be times when he has to draft impromptu. At such times, when he has to get it right the first time or not at all, he crosses his fingers and hopes that his past experience and a little luck will keep him from going too far astray. As mentioned earlier, he can often reduce the time problem if he takes the trouble to educate his client on what is involved in producing a professionally adequate product.

§4.13.   SUMMARY OF STEPS IN LEGAL DRAFTING

It may be helpful at this point to summarize the steps normally involved in drafting. In preparing a legal instrument, the draftsman should:

> (1) find out what the client wants to accomplish and what concrete problems this involves;

[6]"An adjudicated form is a form that has attached to it a certificate that there is something terribly wrong with it. If there were not something terribly wrong with it, it would not have been adjudicated." Beardsley, Beware of, Eschew and Avoid Pompous Prolixity and Platitudinous Epistles! 16 Cal. S.B.J. 65, 66 (1941).

(2) explore the specific, detailed possibilities with the client, pointing out what the alternatives are, and by asking appropriate questions help him to think the problem through;

(3) explore the existing legal situation to find out what constitutional provisions and what statutes or other instruments, if any, already deal with the subject (Which need to be repealed? Which need to be amended? What administrative practices will be affected? What might be the collateral results?);

(4) develop a concrete and cohesive plan of organization and arrangement;

(5) prepare a draft of the instrument, paying attention to the principles outlined in the following chapters, and checking doubtful substantive and technical matters with the available experts or by such independent research as appears to be necessary to get a reliable result; and, as new problems come to light, get the answers from the client or the available experts, or by individual research;

(6) revise the draft as many times as may be necessary to produce a professionally satisfactory result;

(7) make appropriate across-the-board checks for consistency, coherence, and clarity;

(8) if the problem is very complicated or the result must be satisfactory to many persons, submit the tentatively complete draft to a panel of experts, circulate copies to a representative group for suggestions and comments, or hold hearings; and

(9) polish the language to make the draft as clear and easy to read as possible.

§4.14. THE IMPORTANCE OF TIMING: A STRATEGY FOR USING FORM TO IMPROVE SUBSTANCE

It is important not to view the described "steps" as an unvarying sequence of discrete operations, but rather as a flexible series of shifts in general emphasis. The reason is that the intimate connection between conceptualizing and verbalizing is a two-way, not one-way, street, one that carries an enormous potential for improving substance.

I first got some inkling of this when Professor Warren Seavey once confided in me, during a walk across campus, that he wrote his articles first and researched them later. At first I took this as academic wit, but now I believe that to disregard Seavey's insight is to waste time and impair quality. To avoid misunderstanding here, note that he did not say that he started writing with nothing in his head.

That Seavey had no patent on this approach was illustrated some years ago, when Joseph Heller was interviewed in the New York Times about his working habits in putting together the book, Something Happened. Again, what first appeared to be flippancy had real substance.

> My novels begin in a strange way. I don't begin with a theme, or even a character. I begin with a first sentence that is independent of any conscious preparation. Most often nothing comes of it: a sentence will come to mind that doesn't lead to a second sentence. . . . As I sat there worrying and wondering what to do, one of those first lines came to mind. . . . Immediately, the lines presented a whole explosion of possibilities and choices. . . . Ideas come to me in the course of a sort of controlled daydream, a directed reverie. It may have something to do with the disciplines of writing advertising copy . . . , where the limitations involved provide a considerable spur to the imagination. There's an essay of T. S. Eliot's in which he praises the disciplines of writing, claiming that if one is forced to write within a certain framework the imagination is taxed to its utmost and will produce its richest ideas.[1]

Briefly, then, Heller, like Seavey, doesn't hold off writing until he has his substance fully in hand. Starting with at least something to say, he exploits the resources of composition to inspire and condition his own thinking. Legal drafting, involving probably the most disciplined writing outside mathematics,

§4.14. [1]New York Times, sec. 7, October 6, 1974, p.1.

offers this potential in its fullest measure. Heller's idiosyncracy is that he starts writing with very little mental warm-up.

Confirmation exists also in a letter of E. B. White:

> I always write a thing first and think about it afterward, which is not a bad procedure, because the easiest way to have consecutive thoughts is to start putting them down.[2]

The central idea here is that in the course of writing, the author, after what may seem like trying to strike a damp match, soon finds that he is party to a two-way conversation with what he has put on paper.[3] The manuscript is talking back to him. In current computer jargon, it is producing "feedback." I call it "talk-back." For the legal writer this talk-back is mostly in the form of questions. And here we should remind ourselves that in the development of workable ideas the primary thing is not to rush for right answers, but not make sure that we are asking the right questions.[4] This is what disciplined writing helps to do.

The main devices for exploiting substantive talk-back have already been described briefly in section 2.3, above: semantic and formal consistency, the architecture of hierarchical arrangement, and general adherence to normal usage, as explained and refined elsewhere in this book and, indeed, as supplemented by anything that improves clarity.

Writing also helps research. Research is inefficient unless we know what we are looking for, and trying to express and systematize a fuzzy question helps us sharpen it.[5]

[2] Letters of E. B. White (D. Guth ed., Harper & Row, 1976), p.225. S. I. Hayakawa, writing in the Chicago Tribune, sec. 1. August 12, 1977, p.14, asked, "Why is it that I don't feel I have understood a difficult theory until I can write it in a way that everyone can understand?" See also H. Martin & R. Ohmann, The Logic and Rhetoric of Composition 1-5 (rev. ed. 1963); and MLD, ch. 6(A).

[3] "[W]riting is an aspect of dialogue, rather than merely monologue . . . an act of communication, and not of broadcasting." Van Nostrand, 77 Brown Alumni Monthly 12, 17 (1976).

[4] "The worst, the most corrupting, lies are problems poorly stated." Georges Bernanos, French theologian quoted by Senator Daniel F. Moynihan at Baruch College, Chicago Tribune, sec. 1, June 24, 1977, p.11.

[5] "[P]eople acquire knowledge about any subject simply by writing about it. They do so by being forced to perceive relationships among the data that pertain to the subject." Van Nostrand, *supra* n.3, at 15. "[T]raining in writing

I once had eight summer weeks to do a legal management project for the Federal Aviation Agency. My research in this instance was confined largely to finding the experts and asking questions. Did I wait until the end of the seventh week to start writing my report? I began writing it at the end of the *first* week. Although the first draft was scrawny and feeble, my attempts to organize it brought to the surface inconsistencies, gaps, and other defects.

Writing that first draft at an early stage helped sharpen my sense of the relevant in time to get full mileage out of it in my later interviewing. The writer who tries to do all his research before he starts to write often finds out later that he has re-searched many irrelevant or insignificant things, thus wasting precious time, while he failed to research things that came to light too late to handle adequately. It is good to find the basic defects, and the earlier the better. Besides, if he over-researches before starting to write, he risks snuffing out potentially valuable insights of his own before they have had a chance to germinate in the delicate air of intellectual innocence. He also risks creat-ing a formidable psychological hazard by inundating himself with detailed materials, distracting in their wide irrelevance, to the point of sapping his will to write.

The best part of the "write early" approach is that it works. The important fact is that this method provides, for future test-ing, the sharpest possible hypotheses. This means that the sup-portive research will be highly relevant, highly focused, and highly efficient. The result is quicker and more useful results.

The lesson for legal writing is clear. Unless his problem is simple, the writer does not try to do all his research first. In-stead, he should begin to write, or at least to systematically organize his material, as soon as he has a fairly good idea of what his problem is and a generous inkling of the answer. Indeed, he should repeat the process whenever his later research accumu-lates enough material that it starts to become indigestible or hard to cope with. These phases correspond to the scientist's

---

. . . is a way of discovering things we didn't know were there in our minds. . . . How will we know what we think until we see what we have written?" Lerner, On the Art of Reading and Writing, Indianapolis Star, Feb. 14, 1977.

periodic switches from hypothesis to verification to modified hypothesis.

While writing, the draftsman should use every chance to encourage talk-back. For instance, suppose he is typing energetically, trying to develop a coherent line of thought. He discovers a bad gap in his information. Should he turn off his machine and run to the law library or a telephone? Not unless he has reached a basic fork in the road. Instead, he should fill the gap with statements that blend logically with his current information or argumentation. This gives him important, specific hypotheses that he can test later. Most important, it heads off what could be a serious interruption.

If he takes the other approach, insights that are perched precariously on the tip of his mind may be gone by the time he comes back to his machine. The same applies to minor imperfections of spelling, grammar, or form. While the draft is talking to him, he should not fuss with details, but get the gist of its message on paper. Besides allowing the talk-back to continue, careful interpolation or extrapolation will produce not only relatively specific hypotheses (which will focus later research) but ones that have the best chance of being verified.

If the legal writer follows this general approach, much of the talk-back will relate to matters of substantive policy that, properly dealt with, will make the final product a better instrument of the client's will. Recognition of this contribution is likely to earn the writer an opportunity to participate earlier in the development of substantive policy.

The one real danger in the write-early approach is that the writer may get so carried away with the beauties of his tentative results that he forgets to follow up with the research needed to verify them.[6] (Every good thing carries some risk.)

The general strategy just described seems fully applicable to legal drafting.

---

[6]"The only people who can safely start writing with very partial information are those who don't get emotionally committed to their own early formulations . . . . I normally try to make a few talks or write a magazine piece when about halfway through a job to establish a reference point — but there are lots of people for whom it's a gamble." Letter from Martin Mayer, May 19, 1979.

§4.15. "DON'T SHOOT THE PIANO PLAYER"

One of the less attractive features of legislative drafting is that even when the draftsman has taken all the steps prescribed by this chapter the net accomplishment may not be commensurate with the quality of his efforts. It is not always safe, therefore, to judge the draftsman by the final product. For one thing he may not have full control of the draft even before it is introduced. This is true of English draftsmen as well as American.

> There are often good reasons, political or tactical, sometimes more easily appreciated by the politician than by the lawyer, but in many cases very sound and cogent, against the adoption of counsels of perfection urged, and properly urged, by the draftsman from the legal point of view. . . . Whether the minister who had to decide between the risk of losing his bill and the responsibility for leaving the law obscure adopted the right course is a nice question of political ethics.[1]

Even if he is initially successful in convincing his client and executing a thoroughly professional draft, it will still have to run the gauntlet of many minds. As Sir Frederick Pollock has pointed out,

> Many an Act of Parliament, originally prepared with the greatest care and skill, and introduced under the most favourable circumstances, does not become law till it has been made a thing of shreds and patches hardly recognisable by its author, and to any one with an eye for the clothing of ideas in comely words no less ludicrous an object than the ragged pilgrims described by Bunyan: "They go not uprightly, but all awry with their feet; one shoe goes inward, another outward, and their hosen out behind; there a rag and there a rent, to the disparagement of their Lord."[2]

§4.15. [1]C. Ilbert, The Mechanics of Law Making 18, 22 (1914).

[2]Sir Frederick Pollock, quoted in Ilbert, *supra* note 1, at 14. ". . . [S]ome of the criticisms passed on the form of our statute law, especially those which animadvert upon desultory and fragmentary legislation, indicate an imperfect appreciation of the difficulties with which modern legislators have to contend, and a misconception of the task which popular legislatures have to perform. . . . It is a marvel that our English Acts are as decent in form as they are, considering the conditions under which they are produced." *Id.* at 186, 195.

It is important to know these things because otherwise the critical analysis of results is likely to be misconstrued as a personal attack or a charge of professional incompetence. This impairs the flow of constructive criticism. Besides, it is unfair to judge people by events that are beyond their control. Professor Harry W. Jones gives us this poignant instance:

> A few days ago, I heard a group of lawyers and businessmen denouncing the "wretched drafting" embodied in a statute of great current significance. I happened to know in this instance that the act under fire was written by one of the ablest legislative draftsmen in the country. Every problem mentioned here existed in relation to that statute — the inexactness of words, the unpredictable range of future fact-situations, and the rough-and-tumble of the practical legislative process. There are times in legislative work when one finds it an irresistible temptation to reply, in the terms of the old maxim: "Don't shoot the pianist. He's doing the best he can."[3]

What is so harrowing for a legislative draftsman plagues also the draftsman of regulations, ordinances, and even private legal instruments, but normally not so severely. Anyone who serves a client rarely has a free hand. Where the client is a group of people with individual clout, it becomes increasingly hard to reconcile fairness and coherence with diplomacy. The professional sacrifice that commonly results is rarely recognized and even more rarely honored.

---

[3] 36 A.B.A.J. 321, 322 (1950). "It may be well to warn the draftsman that in his case virtue will, for the most part, be its own reward, and that after all the pains that have been bestowed on the preparation of a Bill, every Lycurgus and Solon sitting on the back benches will denounce it as a crude and undigested measure, a monument of ignorance and stupidity. Moreover, when the Bill has become law, it will have to run the gauntlet of the judicial bench, whose ermined dignitaries delight in pointing out the shortcomings of the legislature in approving such an imperfect performance." H. Thring, Practical Legislation 8 (1912). For a more recent cry of anguish, see §8.26 note 3 *infra*.

V

The Architecture of Legal Instruments

§5.1. INTRODUCTION

The desirability of an adequate framework is clear. The problem is to make one. The draftsman cannot develop a satisfactory plan for a legal instrument unless he understands the general principles of arrangement. This is the most fundamental, and possibly the hardest, part of making his ideas jell. It is certainly the most elusive and the hardest to describe.

For this purpose, a satisfactory outline is something more than numbered paragraphs and subordinate tabulations. It is a logical pyramid in which the location of specific items in the hierarchy of substantive ideas shows their interrelationships and relative importance. Unless the draftsman has some real grasp of this fact, he has little chance of marshaling his ideas so as to get the client's message expeditiously across.

The draftsman should distinguish the outline form as an aid to analysis from the outline form as a means of expressing final text. The former must, in the interest of analysis, be severely hierarchical; the latter, in the interest of clarity,[1] predominantly linear. Thus, an instrument whose apt concepts and logical sequence reflect a sophisticated, detailed working outline may finally appear merely as a series of numerically coordinate sec-

___

§5.1. [1]How the hierarchical form may impair readability may be seen in appendix B. See also §6.3 *infra,* par. 1.

tions.[2] Even in the final text of longer and more complicated instruments, the hierarchical form must be used with restraint.

§5.2.   OBJECTIVES

The chief aim in arranging an instrument is to make the final product as clear and useful as possible. The draftsman should carefully select the subjects to be covered and arrange them so that they can be found, understood, and referred to with the least possible effort.

There is, of course, no all purpose arrangement that is the most suitable for all sets of ideas; nor is there even a single ideal arrangement for a specific set of ideas. Every sensible arrangement reflects a point of view.[1] What may be the best arrangement from one point of view may not be the best from another. The draftsman should make sure that he is reflecting the point of view that best advances the purposes of his client.

When the client issues instruments addressed to audiences favored by the consumer movement, the client will probably want to pay special attention to the usability of those instruments to their respective audiences. Every legal communication should, of course, be audience oriented, but consumer instruments present a special challenge because of the imbalance of information and understanding that inheres in the relationship between supplier and individual consumer. On the substantive side, this has produced such concepts as "unconscionability" and "contracts of adhesion."[2] On the understandability side, it has produced a heightened sensitivity to the consumer's greater vulnerability to damaging ignorance. According to Carl Felsenfeld and Alan Siegel, this "means concentrating on giving the reader a sense of the situations that underlie the concept being described," as by "interpolating short examples."[3]

---

[2]One way of expressing a specific hierarchical relationship in such a case can be seen in the first example in §8.23 *infra.*

§5.2. [1]See H. Martin & R. Ohmann, The Logic and Rhetoric of Exposition 152 (rev. ed. 1963).

[2]See §2.1.

[3]C. Felsenfeld & A. Siegel, Writing Contracts in Plain English 83 (1981).

What general arrangement is appropriate in a particular case depends on the needs of the persons who will be making the fullest use of the text. The draftsman should arrange provisions relating primarily to administration from the viewpoint of the persons who will administer them. He should arrange provisions relating primarily to the conduct, rights, privileges, or duties of persons not administering them from the viewpoint of the persons so affected. He should arrange all provisions with due regard for the persons who may later be called on to amend them. Reasonable convenience of amendment is desirable for statutes, regulations, ordinances, corporate charters, by-laws, and contracts (especially labor agreements). This is not merely out of solicitude for the future draftsman, but as insurance against mistakes and the resulting loss to those whom the legal instrument is to serve in the future as distinguished from those whom it will immediately affect. Finally, the draftsman should consider not only who and how many will use a provision but how often they will use it. Although this advice has special relevance to legislation, it has some bearing also on private legal instruments. In wills and trusts, for example, the dispositive provisions, which interest all parties concerned, should precede the administrative provisions, which interest mainly the trustee.

One important objective is to arrange the specific elements so as to illumine the meaning of the instrument, including its internal relationships. Thus, the draftsman should, so far as practicable, arrange the materials to reflect their underlying rationale. This will help persons using the instrument to interpret it correctly. But, if a choice is required, it is more important to indicate what than why.

§5.3. GENERAL PRINCIPLES OF ARRANGEMENT

The arrangement of a legal instrument should always be functional in the sense that it should serve the objectives set forth in the preceding section. In each case the central problem is to develop the most effective hierarchy of relevant ideas and at each level in the hierarchy to choose the most useful principle of order.

Always in the background is the broad aim of simplicity and economy. In general, the better the arrangement the less page turning required. The draftsman should avoid any arrangement, for instance, that requires substantially more cross references between parts or sections than is required by an alternative arrangement offering equal or better findability, clarity, and usability.

In developing a specific arrangement, the draftsman is confronted with three kinds of problems:

(1)   problems of division;
(2)   problems of classification; and
(3)   problems of sequence.

Respecting these three kinds of problems, which are closely interrelated, every good arrangement should meet the minimum standards prescribed for the following skeleton outline. Suppose, for example, that subject "X" has been arranged as follows:

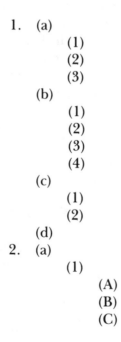

1.   (a)
          (1)
          (2)
          (3)
     (b)
          (1)
          (2)
          (3)
          (4)
     (c)
          (1)
          (2)
     (d)
2.   (a)
          (1)
               (A)
               (B)
               (C)

                    (2)
            (b)
                    (1)
                    (2)
        3. (a)
            (b)
            (c)
                    (1)
                    (2)
                    (3)
            (d)
            (e)

If the arrangement is satisfactory for the client's purposes, it will show the following characteristics.

1. The most fundamental principle of division is that for the 1, 2, 3 sequence. The next most fundamental principles are those for the several (a), (b), (c), etc., subsidiary sequences. The next most fundamental principles are those for the several (1), (2), (3), etc., subsidiary sequences. And so forth, in descending order of significance. The measure of significance here is the point of view the instrument is intended to reflect.

2. For each such sequence the elements are developed by a single principle of division.

3. The principle of division for the (a), (b), (c), (d) subsidiary sequence under topic 1 is not necessarily the same as that for the (a), (b) subsidiary sequence under topic 2, and so forth. Thus, it may represent the order of procedural steps in one case and the order of importance in another.

4. Each element in a sequence is a functional unit of classification.

5. The elements of each segment are placed in some kind of logical sequence, so that they form, in mathematical terms, "ordered sets." Thus, one subsidiary sequence may be arranged in descending order of importance, while another may follow the simple chronology of events.

6. Each sequence can hypothetically be of any length, but for practical purposes will be finite.

These six characteristics may be summarized mathematically by stating that a satisfactorily arranged legal instrument is an ordered set of ordered sets in which there are subsets to the order n and in which each subset expresses a principle less significant than that expressed by its parent set or subset. This is perhaps the most concise description of the characteristics of good legal architecture. Unfortunately, in this naked form such a summary is not very helpful. On the other hand, careful attention to the six named characteristics may make the principles of good arrangement less mysterious.

That there are few ideas harder to convey than the basic idea of hierarchy may tell us why the books on exposition are almost devoid of help in matters other than paragraphing and designation. Fortunately, a few published examples of good arrangement and bad arrangement are available.[1] Supplementary insights into hierarchy may be found below in sections 6.3, on tabulation, and 12.3, on logic trees and flowcharts.

Problems of division, classification, and sequence are discussed in more specific terms in the next three sections.

§5.4.   PROBLEMS OF DIVISION

Problems of division are those involved in determining the respective bases on which the main and subordinate divisions are to be made. Here the draftsman should choose the most fundamental basis of arrangement for his primary breakdown and, for subsidiary breakdowns, the next most fundamental bases of arrangement in descending order of importance.

Here is a very simple example. In a recent agreement[1] among the next of kin, legatees, and creditors of a decedent whose complicated estate consisted of personal effects too small in value to warrant the expense of administration, the main breakdown was as follows:

---

§5.3.   [1]See, e.g., J. Harris & R. Blake, Technical Writing for Social Scientists 86-87 (1976) (MLD 144-145); R. Pirsig, Zen and the Art of Motorcycle Maintenance 92-94 (1974) (MLD 135-136). And see note on the differentiation and classification of widgets, MLD 139-143.

§5.4.   [1]Set forth in full in §14.8, *infra*.

1. Why ("Purpose")
2. Who ("Parties")
3. What ("Terms of Agreement")
4. When ("Effective Date")

Section 3 first listed the steps required or permitted to be taken and then named the persons responsible for taking them. The specified steps are named in chronological order, as follows:

(a) Will to be filed but not probated.
(b) Storage company to exercise storage lien by public auction.
(c) Any next of kin or legatee to be permitted to bid.
(d) Remainder of proceeds of sale to be paid to other creditors in the order named.
(e) If the proceeds are insufficient, non-stored property of decedent to be applied to unsatisfied claims, subject to options in two named next of kin to buy named items at named prices.
(f) Remaining property, if any, to be distributed according to the will.

In many cases it is helpful to base the primary division on the kinds of persons affected, administrative organizations involved, or fields in which they operate, and to deal with such matters as chronology separately for each major subdivision as subsidiary bases of arrangement.

The problem of division with respect to each set of elements is, to use a homely metaphor, like that of selecting the most appropriate implement for cutting a pie. The cutting implement may, for example, be chronology, age, importance, size, weight, or rank. Whichever is selected for the job, it must be used until the entire pie has been cut.

This has been well stated by James MacKaye:

Concerning division Jevons may be quoted as follows:
"*Logical division* is the name of the process by which we distinguish the species of which a genus is composed. Thus we

85

are said to divide the genus 'book' when we consider it as made up of the groups folio, quarto, octavo, duodecimo books, etc., and the size of the books is in this case the ground, basis or principle of division, commonly called the *Fundamentum divisionis.* . . . Three rules may be laid down to which a sound and useful division must conform:

(1) The constituent species must exclude each other.

(2) The constituent species must be equal when added together to the genus.

(3) The division must be founded upon one principle or basis."

The wag who divided the genus human being into women, men and French violated all three of the above rules. The three species into which the genus is divided (1) do not exclude each other, (2) omit the portion of the genus consisting of children, and (3) found the division on two principles, (a) sex and (b) nationality, instead of one. A division into male and female, or into French, Russian, Japanese, and all other nationalities, would have obeyed all three rules.[2]

It is common to assume either that division and the other problems of arrangement are a matter of discovering the ideal arrangement or that it is a matter of indifference. Neither assumption is proper. Good arrangement involves neither finding what inheres in nature nor flipping a coin. It involves deploying specific ideas to fit an assumed point of view. This requires professional judgment of a high order.

The point, which is not peculiar to the law, has been fully stated by the logicians. Morris R. Cohen and Ernest Nagel have pointed out that

> [t]he various traits selected as a basis of classification differ widely in their fruitfulness as principles of organizing our knowledge. Thus the old classification of living things into animals that live on land, birds that live in the air, and fish that live in water gives us very little basis for systematizing all that we know and can find out about these creatures. The habits and the structure of the

---

[2]The Logic of Language 31 (1939). See also L. Stebbing, A Modern Introduction to Logic 433-435 (7th ed. 1950).

porpoise or the whale have many more significant features in common with the hippopotamus or the horse than with the mackerel or the pickerel.[3]

L. Susan Stebbing tells us that the key to selecting the most logical basis of division is the purpose for which the classification is undertaken.[4] The Minister of Transport, when confronted with the problem of street traffic in London, would be interested in such bases of division as the ability of a vehicle to change its route, the relative flexibility of route as between buses and taxis, speed capability, bulk, and weight. On the other hand, the Chancellor of the Exchequer, who is interested in imposing taxes, would be interested, instead, in such bases of division as kind of ownership (public or private), cost, and horsepower. "Vehicles are susceptible of any order that the practical man or the logician may impose upon them. . . . This process of splitting a class into its constituent sub-classes is known as *logical division.*"[5]

§5.5. PROBLEMS OF CLASSIFICATION

Once the draftsman has selected the proper implement for cutting the legal pie (to continue our simple metaphor), his next problem is to determine at what places in the pie to insert it. Thus, once a basis for division has been tentatively selected at any level, its application to the materials at hand leads inevitably to the problem of classification, the problem of determining the appropriate subjects, groupings, or other elements that are to be placed in logical sequence.

The problem of what is a unified "subject" or topic for the purposes at hand is one of the most elusive in the field of arrangement. In general, the modern view is that the draftsman's problem is not the metaphysical one of discovering absolute,

[3]An Introduction to Logic and Scientific Method 223 (1934).
[4]J. MacKaye, The Logic of Language 434 (1939).
[5]L. Stebbing, A Modern Introduction to Logic 433-435 (7th ed. 1950). For related conceptual problems, see §2.4 *supra*.

preexisting "subjects," but that of determining what groupings are the most useful in dealing with the particular situation.[1] Here, again, professional judgment of a high order is required.

The concepts and groupings used in the text of a legal instrument should correspond to those necessarily involved in the substantive problems faced by the persons to whom the instrument is primarily addressed. The "logical pull" of a proposed heading or grouping depends on how fully it meets this test.

One important rule of classification is that the draftsman must not dismember a functionally indivisible subject merely because it falls partly within one parent heading and partly within another. If the draftsman were sorting dogs by color and placing them in separate pens, he would hardly cut off the brown ears of white dogs and throw the ears into the pen for brown dogs! He would either include in the white pen all dogs that were predominantly white or create a special pen for dogs of mixed color.

An example of the latter approach occurred in the preparation of title 10 ("Armed Forces") of the United States Code. Separation and retirement were for the most part separate problems that could be dealt with in separate chapters. But, where the cause was physical disability, the fact that the selfsame administrative proceeding might result in either separation or retirement meant that a division would be administratively impractical and confusing to the reader. The logical pull of "physical disability" being thus stronger than the logical pull of either "separation" or "retirement," a chapter called "Retirement or Separation for Physical Disability," following the other

---

§5.5.   [1]Despite §2.5, this book takes no hard position on the validity or utility of the often made distinction between "natural" classes and "artificial" classes discussed in M. Cohen and E. Nagel, An Introduction to Logic and Scientific Method 223 (1934); J. Locke, An Essay Concerning Human Understanding, bk. 3, ch. 5, §9 (1854); 1 J. S. Mill, A System of Logic 137 (4th ed. 1856); Williams, Language and the Law (pt. 2), 61 L.Q. Rev. 179, 189 (1945). The draftsman is only concerned with selecting, creating, or tailoring the concepts best suited to the needs of his client. That some classes may or may not be "natural" in no wise limits his range of choice. If a "natural" class is unsuited to his purpose, he is free to select or create an appropriate "artificial" one.

chapters on separation and preceding the other chapters on retirement, seemed the most appropriate.[2]

In a situation such as this, the draftsman might be tempted to place the materials on physical disability under both main headings. However, he should not state the same rule or requirement at more than one place. Not only is it unnecessarily wasteful of paper and space, but it creates confusion as to which provision controls and it creates a hazard for the draftsman in case the provision needs later to be amended. A true repetition is one in which the same rule is addressed at more than one place to the identical circumstances. On the other hand, the same rule may be addressed at more than one place to comparable (as distinct from identical) circumstances, without offending the principle just stated.

Although the draftsman can sometimes lessen the difficulty by narrowing or otherwise changing the scope of the respective headings, in many cases conflicting pulls between overlapping or otherwise competing headings cannot be removed. In these cases, he should treat the subject under the heading that is judged to have the strongest logical pull and, if feasible, develop cross references to that heading for the other sections under whose headings the materials also literally fall.

§5.6. PROBLEMS OF SEQUENCE

Once a particular legal pie has been cut, the third step with respect to that particular division is to arrange the resulting pieces or elements in the most appropriate logical sequence. In mathematical terms, this makes the set of elements an "ordered set." There will be as many such sequences as there are bases for division used in the instrument. Except for the sequence of elements in the principal division used in the instrument, each sequence will represent the division of an element that appears in a higher sequence.

In the spatial dimension, the draftsman will find the follow-

[2] 10 U.S.C. ch. 61.

ing rules of thumb helpful, particularly for the main divisions of the instrument:

(1) General provisions normally come before special provisions.

(2) More important provisions normally come before less important provisions.

(3) More frequently used provisions normally come before less frequently used provisions (i.e., the usual should come before the unusual).

(4) Permanent provisions normally come before temporary provisions.

(5) Technical "housekeeping" provisions, such as effective date provisions, normally come at the end.

In practice, these principles sometimes produce conflicting results. In such a case the draftsman must decide for himself which is the more important under the circumstances.

Provisions relating respectively to the components in a series of classes of people may be ordered, as judgment directs, according to such criteria as degree of consanguinity, rank, age, length of service, wealth, or amount of income or property. Provisions relating respectively to the components in a series of physical entities may be ordered, as judgment directs, according to such criteria as location, size, weight, density, or color, or alphabetically according to name.

In the temporal dimension, the normal ordering of provisions follows the chronology of successive actions or events. This, of course, is one of the most frequently used principles of logical sequence.

When replacing old, heavily used instruments, the draftsman may properly depart from historical groupings if alternative groupings offer substantially greater accessibility, clarity, and usability. However, unless an alternative grouping offers more of these functional advantages, it is better to keep the traditional arrangement, because it requires less readjustment by the reader.

Unfortunately, there is no simple principle by which the

draftsman can determine, in a particular case, which complex of these elements and sub-elements will produce the optimum general result. Because there is as yet no practical mathematics for dealing with these things, aided perhaps by a computer, there is no substitute for sound personal judgment grounded on a thorough grasp of the facts and long practice in ordering the elements of particular problems.

Even so, the following primary sequence may be useful for many legal instruments:

(1)   Title, if any.
(2)   Statement of purpose or policy, if any.
(3)   Definitions.
(4)   Statement of to whom or to what the instrument applies.
(5)   Most significant general rules and special provisions.
(6)   Subordinate provisions, and exceptions large and important enough to be stated as separate sections.
(7)   Sanctions, if any.
(8)   Temporary provisions.
(9)   Specific repeals and related amendments, if any.
(10) Severability clause, if any.
(11) Expiration date, if any.
(12) Effective date, if it is different from the date of issuance and if the instrument is not a will.

This order is, of course, only a safe starting point. It may be changed to fit the needs of particular instruments.

§5.7.   RECURRING SITUATIONS

Some of the most baffling problems of arrangement involve recurring situations. If a term recurs throughout the instrument, title, part, or other subdivision, it can be handled once and for all in a single provision, located usually at or near the beginning of the segment involved, where custom suggests that it is most likely to be looked for. However, problems that recur in part but not throughout pose a special dilemma: If they are solved at each place where they arise, the solutions appear where they are most readily found and considered, but at the expense of repetition. This means a longer instrument and the chance of unintended differences. If they are given a single, unified solution, it is hard to place the provision where it may serve as a usable answer to the problem in all the places where it arises. This makes the provision harder to find and creates the risk that some of its important applications may be overlooked.

Although the draftsman can sometimes lessen the difficulty by internal cross references (e.g., "Subject to section 4, the seller may . . ."), these cost heavily in readability and clarity and should be kept to a minimum. Although editorial cross references (being no part of the text) are not subject to this objection, the draftsman cannot always control the editorial treatment, if any, that the instrument will receive after it takes effect. Often there is no entirely satisfactory solution and the result represents what judgment considers the best compromise.

An excellent example of how a very complicated problem of this kind was handled appeared in the consolidation of the military laws of the United States (title 10, "Armed Forces," United States Code). Some of the source laws applied only to a single service (Army, Navy, or Air Force). Others applied to two but not the third (Army and Air Force, Army and Navy, Navy and Air Force). Still others applied to all three. Following the principle that each service ought to have a title containing all the law that applied to it would have produced three titles, but at the expense of stating all bi-service law twice and all tri-service law three times. On the other hand, following the principle of economy that all similar provisions should be consolidated in a single statement would have produced seven titles (General Military Law, Army, Navy, Air Force, Army-Navy, Army-Air Force, and Navy-Air Force). After much soul-searching, it was decided to compromise by stating all tri-service law in one title and repeating the bi-service law. This produced four titles; General Military Law, Army, Navy, and Air Force. It meant that the benefits of consolidating tri-service law could be retained at the expense of requiring a person interested in Air Force law, for example, to look in two titles instead of one. One of these benefits was to facilitate the drafting and enactment of an ever-increasing number of unified military laws.

Recurring problems that cut across a number of different legal instruments pose an even more extreme dilemma. The desire for contiguity suggests that the rule be stated at each place. The price of this benefit is, again, a multiplicity of provisions, much greater difficulty in amending the rule in all its applications when a change is later necessary, and the corresponding danger in nonuniformity in treatment. The burden of this price depends on the length and complexity of the rule, its importance, and the amount of repetition involved. Conversely, economy, ease of amendment, and uniformity entail the risk of incompleteness, lack of findability, and consequent misunderstanding.

Here the draftsman must choose between (1) repeating the provision, (2) placing it where it has its most important application and making it generally applicable, either positively or by incorporation by reference, (3) framing it as an independent instrument, or (4) a combination of these approaches.

The problem here discussed is not confined to statutes or even to public documents. It inheres, for example, in insurance policies.

The problem became a major one during World War II, particularly in the agencies responsible for maintaining and guiding America's enormous economic complex. A pioneer in dealing with this problem was the Office of Price Administration. What the problem was and how it was dealt with is best described in these excerpts from the Statement of Considerations issued with Food Products Regulation No. 1:[1]

> The establishment of maximum prices for a large number of processed dry groceries involves a certain inevitable multiplicity of pricing methods because of the necessity of adapting these methods to the varying peculiarities of the commodities dealt

§5.7.   [1]9 Fed. Reg. 6711 (1944), discussed in Dickerson, FPR No. 1, An Experiment in Standardized and Prefabricated Law, 13 U. Chi. L. Rev. 90 (1945). For excerpts, see appendix C.

with. This multiplicity is not enlarged by stating separate pricing methods in separate documents nor is it lessened by stating them in a single document. The hard fact is that these diversities inhere in price control and no amount of "simplification" can reduce them beyond a certain minimum.

In spite of inescapable differences of treatment, however, there are many pricing problems, situations, and concepts which tend to recur as common, in greater or less degree, to large classes of products. Thus, problems of discounts and allowances, brokerage, storage, compliance, amendments, uniform delivered prices, definitions, and other matters, are found to repeat themselves in the face of substantial differences in product and differences in basic price treatment.

These facts have forced OPA into a troublesome dilemma in the writing and administration of its maximum price regulations. On the one hand, it has been tempted to write a separate price regulation for each group of food commodities requiring individual treatment. On the other hand, it has been under pressure to emphasize the recurring problems and lump otherwise divergent pricing methods into common regulations. That neither alternative is universally satisfactory has been fully demonstrated by experience. The difficulties of this position have not been lightened by frequent insistence that OPA go in both directions at once!

The piecemeal approach of early price control which expediency required has given OPA the fullest opportunity to try the former alternative. . . . In each case, it was found necessary to deal with a large number of recurring problems.

The difficulties which this approach produced stem not from the fact that different documents have been issued for each group of commodities, but from the fact that it was necessary to restate in each case a number of provisions intended to cover pricing and enforcement problems common to all. This led to some lack of uniformity in these provisions and in their interpretation, with consequent confusion to the public and loss of time to the staff.

Attempts have been made to minimize these disadvantages by consolidating commodities into larger, more comprehensive regulations. . . .

In the administration of such attempts to simplify and consolidate, OPA learned certain fundamental principles of organization. One of these is the fact that mere physical consolidation does not necessarily mean greater workability and simplicity of understanding. For one thing, differences in pricing methods cannot always be successfully reconciled within the compass of a single instrument without causing confusion both within and outside of OPA. . . . Moreover, there is no virtue in collecting in a single document pricing methods respectively addressed to diverse groups of sellers which have nothing in common. . . . In short, one document is not always simpler than two documents. . . .

Food Products Regulation No. 1 is an attempt to resolve the fundamental dilemma, existing in some fields, between the desirability of consolidation and the desirability of treating different pricing problems differently.

The conflict is resolved, it is believed, by segregating, standardizing and unifying the recurring provisions and by stating them in a single autonomous pricing document. The non-recurring provisions, on the other hand, are stated separately from the recurring provisions and in turn are stated separately from each other according to their natural groupings. In this way, common provisions can be dealt with as a unit, while separate individual pricing methods are handled on an individual basis, with a minimum of confusion.

Food Products Regulation No. 1 is set up as an autonomous document separate from its supplements, which set forth the various basic pricing methods. It attempts to gather into a single document the provisions most commonly used in regulations fixing maximum prices for the sales of processed dry groceries. Having gathered together these provisions, the regulation operates in a manner exactly opposite to the way in which a supplementary order works. Instead of inserting itself in a number of specified regulations listed in the order itself (which usually requires a separate order for each provision) the regulation is able to operate comprehensively as a single document by having effect on particular commodities only to the extent that particular supplements specifically adopt its various sections. Thus, the normal order of . . . reference is almost exactly reversed.

This latter feature of the regulation is believed to be essential to its most efficient use. The ultimate aim has been to consolidate the largest possible number of recurring provisions with respect to the largest possible number of commodities. If no provision were included in Food Products Regulation No. 1

which did not apply to all supplements, then an attempt to consolidate a substantial number of provisions would mean that only a relatively small number of commodities could be included within the particular plan. Conversely, if an attempt were made to include a wide group of commodities, the number of 100 percent recurring provisions would be reduced to a point where much of the value of the consolidated regulation would be lost.

OPA constructed frequency charts showing the extent to which the various types of provisions now used tend to recur. By including in the basic regulation a number of provisions which these charts demonstrate to have large although not universal applicability, the usefulness of the plan has been greatly enlarged. This means, of course, that in some supplements not all of the sections of Food Products Regulation No. 1 will be adopted. However, this minor disadvantage creates no difficulty which is not already in many regulations of the "appendix" type, where experience has shown the frequent necessity of including a clause to the general effect that "if any special provision is contrary to or inconsistent with any general provision, the special provision shall be controlling." . . . On the contrary, Food Products Regulation No. 1 frankly recognizes the normal impossibility of writing any comprehensive over-all document of 100 percent applicability. Troublesome questions of the applicability of the general provisions of the main regulation to specific situations arising in connection with particular commodities are largely avoided because of the fact that each supplement forthrightly states which general provisions are applicable, and (by necessary implication) which are not.

To summarize, the essential plan of Food Products Regulation No. 1 and its family of supplements is built upon three basic principles:

(1) The basic regulation, as distinct from its supplements, is an autonomous document, printed and administered separately from its supplements.

(2) Each supplement, in addition to being separate from the basic regulation, is an autonomous document, printed and administered separately from other supplements to the basic regulation.

(3) The basic regulation applies to a given group of commodities only to the extent that the applicable supplement expressly adopts its provisions.

Similar boilerplate regulations were issued for other products in the general grocery products field and for spirituous liquors. All appear to have been successful.

The most significant aspect of this device is that in the boilerplate provisions it takes the passive approach, rather than the traditional active approach exemplified by most construction acts and other provisions that purport to lay down across-the-board definitions or principles applicable even to future legal instruments. For example, section 3 of title 1, United States Code, purports to lay down the meaning of the word "vessel," even for future enacted statutes. Similarly, section 8301(a) of title 5, United States Code, provides for rounding out the date of retirement to the first day of the following month, presumably even for retirement systems enacted after its enactment.

The difficulty with the active approach is two-fold. First, it purports to place semantic or other limitations on future authors of legal instruments who have the same legal capacity to prepare and issue effective instruments. It is, therefore, of doubtful effect on later instruments that have been issued without apparent regard to the earlier pronouncement. Moreover, experience has shown that it is impossible for the author of such a provision to anticipate the appropriateness of including the provision in every instrument that has entered or may enter the field. This is witnessed, for example, in the preface to most definition sections, which provide, in effect, that "the following meanings are intended except where they are not."

The value of the passive approach, on the other hand, is that its legal effect with respect to other instruments (1) is selective and (2) is made explicit in each case by the other instrument. Under the active approach, the generating force is the instrument containing the boilerplate. Under the passive approach, the generating force in each case is the other, often later, instrument.

That the appropriateness of the passive approach was not limited to OPA in World War II is shown by its adoption for writing insurance on automobiles. At least one insurance company issues a combination automobile policy consisting of nine designated coverages and a long list of standardized conditions and exclusions. As printed, the basic policy applies to no named insured and to no specified automobile. Nor is there any place on the policy where these items can be entered. Instead, these are entered on a short strip of paper called an "extension certificate." This contains all the information that is peculiar to that policy: policy number; effective date; expiration date; name and address of insured; year, make, and number of automobile; the specific coverages and their respective premiums; and the countersignature of the issuing officer. As with Food Products Regulation No. 1, the generating legal force is the supplement or extension certificate rather than the longer document containing the legal boilerplate. For example, if the extension certificate carries the notations "A7," "B1," and "I," it means that the specific coverages so designated in the basic policy are incorporated by reference and made a part of the extension certificate. In this example, it means that the insured has $100,000-$300,000 of bodily injury liability coverage, $25,000 of property damage liability coverage, and towing and labor costs coverage on the terms specified in the basic policy.

The advantages of the passive approach are, again, that if the insured has several automobiles, he has as many extension certificates as he has cars but only one statement of the standardized provisions. Although for each car the insured must consult two documents, the total bulk is greatly reduced. If the company decides to broaden any coverage, it need only distribute a new edition of the basic policy without the labor of reissuing each separate contract, each of which is necessarily a custom-tailored instrument. Variations of this approach have been adopted also for deeds of trust.[2]

Alternative methods of handling legal boilerplate, made feasible by the development of computers, are considered in chapter 12.

---

[2]Bird, Incorporation by Reference — Key to Shorter Security Instruments and to Lower Recording Costs, 10 Prac. Law. 39 (March 1964).

§5.8. OVER-COMPLEXITY

In his zeal for logical, coherent, and economical arrangement, the draftsman must take care, particularly in the case of a long, complicated instrument likely to need amending, lest he make the result so tightly complicated that he alone is capable of repairing it without danger of stripping its gears. A looser, less economical framework may be necessary to having a plan sufficiently flexible that later draftsmen of reasonable skill can adjust it to changing circumstances without undue risk of wrecking the whole machine. A system of arrangement is suspect whenever changing one part means changing many other parts. The seriousness of the risk is somewhat less for one-shot documents such as wills and other documents, which if amended at all are likely to remain within the control of the original draftsman.

§5.9. ARRANGEMENT OF PARTS

The principles that apply to shaping the general outlines of the legal instrument apply also, so far as relevant, to the internal organization of the logically separate parts, whether they are titles, parts, sections, paragraphs, or sentences. In the broadest sense, anything that relates to the ordering of words is a matter of arrangement. However, although they shade imperceptibly into the more general aspects of arrangement, the problems of putting together paragraphs, sentences, clauses, and phrases raise special questions that it is better to treat separately. These are reserved for the chapters that follow.

VI

Substantive Clarity: Avoiding Ambiguity

§6.1. SYNTACTIC AMBIGUITY: UNCERTAINTY OF MODIFICATION OR REFERENCE

Probably the biggest source of uncertainty of meaning in legal instruments, as in other writings, is the unclear use of modifiers or reference, technically known as "syntactic ambiguity."[1] According to William Strunk, Jr., and E. B. White, "The position of the words in a sentence is the principal means of showing their relationship. . . . The writer must, therefore, bring together the words and groups of words that are related in thought and keep apart those that are not so related."[2] There is no serious excuse for any writer to construct a sentence like this: "John looked at the boy eating the sundae with envious eyes," even though context makes it unambiguous.

Perhaps the simplest form of syntactic ambiguity and one of the commonest is the squinting modifier, already mentioned in section 3.4. Ambiguities of this kind are sometimes the result of avoiding the split infinitive. However offensive it may be to many persons, the split infinitive makes clear beyond all doubt what the adverb modifies. The same is true of other split verb forms. There can be no doubt, for example, as to the meaning of "shall promptly require." The draftsman, therefore, should

§6.1. [1] See §3.4 supra.
[2] The Elements of Style 28 (3d ed. 1979).

not hesitate to split an infinitive or other verb form if to do otherwise would create the significant possibility of ambiguity.[3]

Unfortunately, it is often impossible to imbed a modifier in the term that it modifies. Although the safest approach is to place the two elements next to each other, even this is not always possible. For example, it is impossible (without repetition) when a modifier relates to multiple terms (e.g., "charitable institutions or organizations") or when there are multiple modifiers of the same term (e.g., "medical, hospital, or burial expenses"). Problems of multiple modification or reference are discussed in the next section.

Another common form of ambiguity is uncertainty of pronominal reference. Much of this can be avoided by putting the pronoun as close as possible to the word or phrase to which it refers, making certain that the two agree in number. However, the force of uncongenial context is often so strong that closeness is not enough. When context leaves a significant uncertainty, the pronoun should be replaced by the name of the person or thing to which it refers, or the context should be appropriately changed. Similarly, a simple reference to "the Corporation" is adequate in an instrument, or severable part of an instrument, in which only one corporation is involved. However, if several corporations are involved, it is safer to refer to the particular corporation by name unless the context makes clear which one is meant.

One of the most troublesome problems of ambiguity is that of determining the scope of a modifier and the scope of the thing modified. When the two are juxtaposed, it is often hard to tell whether a particular word is part of the modifier or part of the thing modified. To take a simple example, the title "Green Bay Tree" may be read, grammatically, as meaning either "Tree in Green Bay," or "Bay tree that is green." Does "Bay" have the prior affinity with "Green" or with "Tree"?[4]

---

[3]"[Y]our first duty is to be exact and clear and brief, and if that requires you to split an infinitive, or to do anything else that the books frown on, do so, and leave any one who pleases to bruise himself against your work." E. Piesse & J. Smith, The Elements of Drafting 5 (2d ed. 1958).

[4]Montrose, Mock Turtle: A Problem in Adjectival Ambiguity, 59D M.U.L.L. 28 (1959).

It is unfortunate that English has so few symbols for showing that specific phrases form a unit. The hyphen has only limited utility for this purpose (e.g., "run-of-the-orchard fruit"). Mathematics has solved the problem largely through the use of parentheses and contiguity. To avoid the ambiguity in the expression "x plus y times z," a mathematician would write either "$(x + y) z$" or "$x + yz$," depending on the substantive result intended. Although, in general, writing convention permits only a sparing use of parentheses, they are sometimes usable for this purpose. For example, in the phrase "active duty (other than for training) performed before July 1, 1984," it is clear that the phrase "before July 1, 1984," refers to "active duty (other than for training)" and not to "training."

A pair of commas is sometimes useful for setting off a group of words as a verbal unit. Unfortunately, commas are a weak device for this purpose, because, unlike parentheses, they are nondirectional. When used in the vicinity of other commas, it is often uncertain how they are to be paired.

A terminal "because" clause is often ambiguous in that it is not clear whether the clause applies to the entire statement or merely to the phrase immediately preceding. For example, in the sentence, "The union may not rescind the contract because of hardship," it may not be clear whether the draftsman intends to say, "The union may not rescind the contract, because to do so would cause hardship," or "The union may not rescind the contract, using hardship as the justification." The ambiguity lies in the doubt whether the word "not" negates the broad power to "rescind the contract" or the narrower power to "rescind the contract because of hardship." If he intends the former, the draftsman should at least insert a comma after the word "contract." Even better would be to place the "because" clause at the beginning. If he intends the latter, he might say, "The union may not rescind the contract on the ground of hardship."

A similar problem often arises when two prepositional phrases are juxtaposed.[5] For example, the provision "Every

---

[5]E. Driedger, The Composition of Legislation — Legislative Forms and Precedents 25 (2d ed. rev. 1976). Driedger handles problems involving participles and gerunds at 16-17, 21-22 (MLD 241-243).

member of a chapter in Indiana" may create doubt whether the words "in Indiana" refer to the word "chapter" or to the phrase "member of a chapter." If the former is intended, doubt can be dispelled by saying, "Every member of a chapter organized in Indiana." If the latter, it can be dispelled by saying, "Every member of a chapter who is in Indiana." In each case the problem is solved by adjusting the context so that the modifier is incapable, semantically or syntactically, of modifying anything other than the intended term.

From these examples, we see that syntactic ambiguity, as a disease of context, is ordinarily cured by adjusting context. Unfortunately, modern English, unlike German or Latin, has few inflections, or special endings, to show the relation between words.

Some of the devices for dealing with syntactic ambiguity are discussed in the following sections.

§6.2.　SEMANTIC AND SYNTACTIC AMBIGUITY: UNCERTAINTIES IN THE USE OF "AND" AND "OR"; PROBLEMS OF MULTIPLE MODIFICATION OR REFERENCE

Problems of multiple modification or reference are perhaps best approached through the peculiar uncertainties involved in the use of "and" and "or." The difference between "and" and "or" is usually explained by saying that "and" stands for the conjunctive, connective, or additive and "or" for the disjunctive or alternative. The former connotes "togetherness" and the latter tells you to "take your pick." So much is clear. Beyond this point, difficulties arise.

One problem is that each of these two words is semantically ambiguous. It is not always clear whether the writer intends the *inclusive* "or" (A or B, or both) or the *exclusive* "or" (A or B, but not both). This long-recognized uncertainty has given rise to the abortive attempt to make "and/or" a respectable English equivalent to the Latin "vel" (the inclusive "or").[1]

---

§6.2.　[1]The development of the "and/or" combination represents an attempt to compensate for the failure of the English language to separate the

What has not been so well recognized is that there is a corresponding, though less frequent, uncertainty in the use of "and." Thus, it is not always clear whether the writer intends the *several* "and" (A and B, jointly or severally) or the *joint* "and" (A and B, jointly but not severally). This uncertainty will surprise some, because "and" is normally used in the former sense. Even so, the authors of documents sometimes intend things to be done jointly or not at all. This idea inheres in the purchase of a pair of shoes (try to buy one shoe separately!) without, however, posing any grammatical problem. On the other hand, a reference to "husbands and wives" may create a grammatical uncertainty as to whether the right, privilege, or duty extends to husbands without wives, and vice versa, or whether it may be enjoyed or discharged only jointly.[2] When such a doubt exists, it is desirable to recognize and deal with it.

---

inclusive "or" (the Latin "vel") from the exclusive "or" (the Latin "aut"). Modern mathematics accomplishes this distinction through the symbols "$\sim$ ($\sim$P$\sim$ Q)" (shortened for convenience to "P v Q") and "$\sim$ ($\sim$ P $\sim$ Q) $\sim$ (PQ)." J. Rosser, Logic for Mathematicians 13, 14 (2d ed. 1978). (And see works on logic cited *infra* note 3.) Some logicians would add a third meaning of "or," that of equivalence. Thus, the sentence, "The canine, or dog, is a useful animal," can be viewed as asserting the equivalence of the things respectively designated by the words "dog" and "canine." From this it might seem that in such a context "or" means "which is equivalent to." On the other hand, it seems unnecessary to postulate a third meaning here, because the use of "or" in the quoted statement can be justified without it. Thus, the statement can be viewed grammatically, not as an assertion of the equivalence of the things to which the words "dog" and "canine" refer, but as an assertion that the identical thing may be referred to by either of two alternative names. The former is a statement about things; the latter, a statement about words. It is questionable, therefore, whether such a use of the disjunctive "or" in the metalanguage involves any more than a shift in context. Fortunately, the principle that synonymous expressions are taboo in legal drafting makes the question for present purposes moot. For a fuller discussion of "and/or," see R. Dick, Legal Drafting 104-108 (2d ed. 1985).

[2]E. Driedger, The Composition of Legislation, Legislative Forms and Precedents 20 (2d rev. ed. 1976). Some logicians have expressly recognized variations in the use of the word "and." For example, A. Frye and A. Levi, Rational Belief 180-181 (1941), contrast the enumerative "and" (mere conjunction) with the wholistic "and" (conjunction involving logical relation). The same distinction seems to underlie the differentiation of conjunctive compounds and implicative compounds in H. Veatch, Intentional Logic 336-339 (1952). See also *infra* note 4. This distinction is not necessarily the same as that drawn in the text because, for one thing, the simple package deal is not

Observation of legal usage suggests that in most cases "or" is used in the inclusive rather than the exclusive sense,[3] while "and" is used in the several rather than the joint sense. If true, this is significant for legal draftsmen and other writers, because it means that in the absence of special circumstances they can rely on simple "or's" and "and's" to carry these respective meanings. This, incidentally, greatly reduces the number of occasions for using the undesirable expression "and/or" or one of its more respectable equivalents, such as "A or B, or both," or "either or both of the following."

Special circumstances in which it is unsafe to rely on general

---

the only kind of logical relation that can exist between conjoined entities. Moreover, it seems questionable that the draftsman of a legal document would have legitimate occasion to use mere conjunction, that is, to use "and" to connect wholly unrelated statements. If this is true, the distinction drawn in the text is for the most part between two kinds of implicative compounds, to use Veatch's terminology, and does not ordinarily involve conjunctive compounds at all. For legal instruments, therefore, the distinction drawn in the text would appear to be more significant than that drawn, for quite different purposes, by Frye and Levi or Veatch.

[3]Webster, New International Dictionary 1585 (3d ed. 1972), defines "or" only in its exclusive sense. To the same effect is 1 B. Bosanquet, Logic, ch. 8, §1 (1888). The following agree that usage supports the exclusive "or": F. Bradley, Principles of Logic, ch. 4 (2d ed. 1922), and A. Ushenko, The Theory of Logic 45 (1936). In H. Joseph, An Introduction to Logic 187 (2d ed. 1916), this is considered the "safer" interpretation. On the other hand, L. Stebbing, A Modern Introduction to Logic 70-71 (7th ed. 1950), says:

> It is not usual to interpret the "or" in an alternative proposition as expressing the *exclusion of one alternative.* That is, "or" is consistent with "perhaps both." . . . The *onus probandi* lies on those who assert that the *logical* interpretation of "or" should be exclusive. It cannot be maintained that the common use is exclusive. . . . It is not to be denied that it is sometimes clear that two alternatives exclude each other. But the exclusion is due to the nature of the alternatives, not to the form of the proposition.

To the same effect is J. Keynes, Formal Logic 278n (4th ed. 1906). The following agree that usage supports the inclusive "or": E. Burtt, Right Thinking, note at 134 (3d ed. 1946); A. Frye & A. Levi, Rational Belief 178 (1941); W. Gibson, The Problem of Logic 135 (1908); C. Mace, Principles of Logic 61 (1933); and W. Quine, Methods of Logic 4 (1950). Whatever general overall usage may be, it is believed that general legal usage conforms to Stebbing's statement. In A. Tarski, Introduction to Logic 21-23 (2d ed. 1946), it is suggested that "or" be used to denote the inclusive "or" and "either . . . or" to denote the exclusive "or."

usage exist, on the other hand, whenever the courts have shown an unfriendly or biased attitude in interpreting language. Thus, in drafting a criminal statute, with respect to which the courts are inclined to make law restrictively under the euphemism of "strict construction," it is safer not to rely on the chance that "or" will be given its normal inclusive reading but to say expressly "shall be fined not more than $5000 or imprisoned not more than three years, *or both.*"

Another and more perplexing difficulty in the use of "and" and "or" is that it is often unclear, because of conflict between grammar and immediate context, whether the draftsman has attempted an enumeration of persons or institutions, on the one hand, or of their characteristics or traits, on the other. Take the phrase "every husband and father." If it is intended as an enumeration of two classes of persons, that fact can be less equivocally expressed by saying, "every husband and every father" or, taking another approach, by saying, "every person who is either a husband or a father." If, on the other hand, it is intended as an enumeration of characteristics or traits necessary to identify each member to be covered, that alternative can be less equivocally expressed by saying, "every person who is both a husband and a father."[4]

---

[4]See E. Driedger, The Composition of Legislation — Legislative Forms and Precedents 20-21 (2d ed. rev. 1976). This uncertainty must be distinguished from that involved in choosing between the joint "and" and the several "and." The ambiguity in the phrase "every husband and father," unlike that in the phrase "husbands and wives," lies not so much in the meaning of "and" as in the immediate context in which it appears. Thus, the central question is not, "What does 'and' mean?" but, "What is 'and' being used to enumerate?" This becomes clear when the phrase is used in a mandatory sentence, e.g., "Every husband and father shall report annually." In such a case, "and" is necessarily joint whichever kind of enumeration is involved. It is easy to confuse the two issues because in some permissive sentences "and" would be several if the enumeration were of people, but joint if it were of characteristics.

J. Keynes, Formal Logic 469 (4th ed. 1906), says that *"and* and *or* occurring in a predicate are understood as expressing a conjunctive or an alternative *term;* but occurring in a subject they are understood as expressing a conjunctive or an alternative *proposition.* " The latter is true of the sentence, "John and George are boys," i.e., "John is a boy and George is a boy." It is not true of the sentence, "John and George are friends." R. McCall, Basic Logic 70-71

As the foregoing examples show, the former alternative meaning can be expressed, without changing substance, either by an enumeration of persons, using "and," or by an enumeration of their identifying characteristics or traits, using "or." This does not say that "and" means "or." It says that whether we use "and" or "or" in such a case depends upon whether we identify the affected persons by enumerating the several classes into which they may fall or, defining them as a single class, by enumerating their qualifying characteristics. A corollary of this is that shifting from "and" to "or" without shifting from a listing of persons to a listing of characteristics or traits changes the grammatical meaning. For example, compare these two provisions:

Provision A:

The security roll shall include:
(1)   each person who is 70 years old or older;
(2)   each person who is permanently, physically disabled; *and*
(3)   each person who has been declared mentally incompetent.

Provision B:

The security roll shall include each person who:
(1)   is 70 years old or older;
(2)   is permanently, physically disabled; *or*
(3)   has been declared mentally incompetent.

Although both provisions say exactly the same thing, "and" is necessary to provision A because it enumerates three separate

---

(1948). Nor does it appear to be true of enumerations of adjectives and other modifiers. Thus, the normal interpretation of the sentence, "Red and white banners are beautiful," is not "Red banners are beautiful and white banners are beautiful," but "Banners that are both red and white are beautiful."

classes of persons each of which must be included, whereas "or" is necessary to provision B because it names a single class of persons by enumerating its three alternative qualifications for membership.

To illustrate some typical problems of multiple modification or reference involving "and" or "or," let us now consider four basic variations of phrase that are commonly used. The discussion of these variations is not intended to imply that either "and" or "or," or the phrase in which it is used, can be interpreted in specific instances apart from the context in which it appears. Clearly, it cannot. Even so, we are not prevented from making appropriate generalizations about the usual meanings of such phrases, which imply useful generalizations about the context of the legal writing in which they tend to appear. Even when read out of specific context, particular words and phrases retain much of the flavor of their usual associations.

One of the normal functions of context is to provide the basis for limiting otherwise overly broad general terms. There is, for instance, no risk in referring to "the Company" in a paragraph or section in which the organization is otherwise identified. Context limits also in other ways. Thus, the following discussion recognizes that the choice of grammatical alternatives is determined by whether the enumeration appears in a mandatory or permissive sentence. It further recognizes that these alternatives are also conditioned by whether the connective in question links characteristics that are potentially cumulative or mutually exclusive.

More specifically, the examples dealing with the modifiers "charitable" and "educational" must be appraised in the light of the fact that these terms are potentially cumulative: the same institutions can be both charitable and educational. On the other hand, those phrases dealing with the modifiers "hospital" and "burial" must be considered in the light of the fact that these terms are not potentially cumulative, but mutually exclusive. An expense can be a hospital expense or a burial expense, but it cannot be both.

Phrase (1): "Charitable and educational institutions"

Does this mean:
(a)   "institutions that are both charitable and educational";
      or
(b)   "charitable institutions and educational institutions"?

If we tabulate phrase (1), remembering that strings of adjectives are normally used cumulatively, rather than distributively,[5] we get this:

"Institutions that are:
"(1)   charitable; and
"(2)   educational."

Although sense (b) is sometimes intended by this phrase, sense (a), as expressed in the tabulation, is the normal grammatical reading, that is, the way it is usually read in practice. This is true whether the sentence is mandatory or permissive. Phrase (1) is therefore a proper way of expressing the idea of "institutions that are both charitable and educational." If sense (b) is intended, it is better to express the phrase as sense (b) is expressed above (see also phrase (3), below), or in some other way different from phrase (1).

Compare phrase (1) with the phrase "hospital and burial expenses," in which the modifiers are mutually exclusive. Because the same expense cannot be both "hospital" and "burial," only sense (b) is possible, and the phrase can mean only "hospital expenses and burial expenses." Although the phrase "hospital and burial expenses" is shorter and has the sanction of usage, it would seem grammatically preferable to say "hospital expenses and burial expenses," reserving the shorter form for use with potentially cumulative modifiers where sense (a) is both possible and intended.

[5]See *supra* note 4, par. 2.

Phrase (2): "Charitable or educational institutions"

Does this mean:
  (a) "institutions that are either charitable or educational, but not both";
  (b) "institutions that are either charitable or educational, or both";
  (c) "charitable institutions or educational institutions, but not both"; or
  (d) "charitable institutions or educational institutions, or both"?

If we tabulate phrase (2) similarly to phrase (1) and infer the normal inclusive "or," we get this:

"Institutions that are:
"(1)   charitable;
"(2)   educational; or
"(3)   both."

Sense (b) is the normal grammatical reading. This is true whether the sentence is mandatory or permissive. Phrase (2) is therefore a proper way of expressing the idea of "institutions that are either charitable or educational, or both." If sense (a), (c), or (d) is intended, it is better to express it differently from phrase (2).

On examination, it appears that sense (d), which is apparently different, is in most cases substantively the same as sense (b), because it is normally inferred that if we may or must have institutions that are either charitable or educational or both we may also have both charitable institutions and educational institutions. Conversely, it is normally inferred that if we may or must have both charitable institutions and educational institutions we may also have institutions that are both charitable and educational.

Compare phrase (2) with the phrase "hospital or burial expenses," in which the modifiers are mutually exclusive. Here, sense (b) is impossible. Sense (c) is also eliminated if we infer the normal inclusive "or." Instead, sense (a) is the normal grammatical reading. Examination similarly shows that sense (d) is substantively the same as sense (a) in most cases, because if we may or must pay expenses that are either hospital or burial it is normally inferred that we may pay both kinds.

> *Phrase (3):* "Charitable institutions and educational institutions"

Does this mean:
  (a) "both charitable institutions and educational institutions," which may include institutions that are both charitable and educational; or
  (b) "charitable institutions or educational institutions, or both," which may include institutions that are both charitable and educational?

If the sentence is mandatory, we must have both kinds of institutions (i.e., a "package deal" is intended). "And" is joint rather than several, and sense (a) is the normal grammatical reading.

If the sentence is permissive, it is normally inferred that we may have one kind without the other (i.e., no "package deal" is intended). Here, "and" is several rather than joint, and sense (b) is the normal grammatical reading.

Compare phrase (3) with the phrase "hospital expenses and burial expenses," in which the modifiers are mutually exclusive. The alternatives are the same, except that the possibility of including an expense that is both "hospital" and "burial" is excluded from both sense (a) and sense (b).

> *Phrase (4):* "Charitable institutions or educational institutions"

Does this mean:
  (a) "charitable institutions or educational institutions, but not both," which may not include institutions that are both charitable and educational; or

(b) "charitable institutions or educational institutions, or both," which may include institutions that are both charitable and educational?

If we infer the normal inclusive "or," sense (b) is the normal grammatical reading. This is true whether the sentence is mandatory or permissive.

Compare phrase (4) with the phrase, "hospital expenses or burial expenses," in which the modifiers are mutually exclusive. The alternatives are the same, except that the possibility of including an expense that is both "hospital" and "burial" is excluded from sense (b).

It is interesting to note that for the cumulative modifiers "charitable" and "educational" senses (b) and (d) of phrase (2), sense (b) of phrase (3), and sense (b) of phrase (4), the normal grammatical ways of reading these respective phrases, are substantively the same when the sentence is permissive. Thus, if we intend that the person covered by the instrument is to be free to have either, neither, or both, we may use any of these three sentences to express the idea:

(A) "He may contribute to charitable or educational institutions."

(B) "He may contribute to charitable institutions and educational institutions." Here, "and" is several, not joint.

(C) "He may contribute to charitable institutions or educational institutions." Here, "or" is inclusive, not exclusive.

Sentences (B) and (C) differ only in that the former uses "and," whereas the latter uses "or." Because both sentences mean the same thing, it follows that "and" and "or" produce the same result in such a context. Stating the matter broadly, we can say that in a permissive sentence the inclusive "or" is interchangeable with the several "and." Again, this does not say that "and" means "or." It says that in such a context the two words are reciprocally related: The implied meaning of one is the same as the express meaning of the other.

Of the three ways of extending permission, sentence (B) is to be preferred. Sentence (A) is open to the objection that its applicability to both charitable institutions and educational institutions is based on inference (a strong one, however). Sentence (C) is open to the objection that in the wider context of the instrument as a whole it is more likely that "or" will be read as exclusive than that "and" will be read as joint.

With respect to the alternative modifiers "hospital" and "burial," the same analysis applies, except that, because they cannot be cumulative, there is the fourth alternative of using phrase (1):

(D) "He may pay the hospital and burial expenses."

As pointed out in connection with phrase (1), sentence (D) is not as desirable grammatically as sentence (B).

The reader is warned that many of the foregoing generalizations are based only on personal observation. So far as they have not (to my knowledge) been confirmed by exhaustive scientific investigation they remain subject to honest skepticism. Even so, they may retain some value as potential conventions that, if adopted, would ultimately crystallize the usages that I believe them now to reflect. While I do not rest my analysis on this kind of bootstrap pulling, it is comforting to recognize its supporting effect.

The reader is also warned that, even if sound, the foregoing generalizations on usage are valuable not because they eliminate all possibility of ambiguity or other uncertainty (they are incapable of discharging this responsibility), but because they establish sufficiently probable meanings. Fortified in particular cases by general and specific context, these meanings are strong enough to reduce any uncertainty remaining, after a careful reading of the whole statement in its proper setting, to the point where an attempt to eliminate it altogether would cost more in prolixity and unreadability than would be gained by attaining the unattainable ideal of absolute certainty.[6]

---

[6]For further discussion of "and" and "or," see D. Hirsch, Drafting Federal Law 31-32 (1980); Kirk, Legal Drafting: The Ambiguity of "And" and "Or," 2 Tex. Tech. L. Rev. 235 (1971).

§6.3. TABULATION: A DEVICE FOR DEALING WITH AMBIGUITY IN MULTIPLE MODIFICATION OR REFERENCE

As the last section may suggest, tabulation is one of the drafts-man's most useful devices.[1] It is particularly useful in avoiding ambiguity in multiple modification or reference. It is, in substance, an intensive and detailed form of outlining. It is useful both as a tool for analyzing and testing the internal structure of paragraphs and sentences and as a form of clear presentation in the final text. Although it may be used without limitation for the former purpose, it must be used sparingly for the latter. As noted in section 5.1 above, overuse of this hierarchical form impairs readability (and complicates amendment).

The conventional rules for tabulation are these:

(1) All items in the tabulated enumeration must belong to the same class. (The enumeration must have a common theme or thread.)

(2) Each item in the tabulated enumeration must be responsive, in substance and in form, to the introductory language of the enumeration (the material immediately before the colon).

(3) If the sentence of which a tabulated enumeration is a part continues beyond the end of the enumeration, the part of the sentence that follows it must be appropriate to each item.

(4) All of each item in the enumeration must be indented.

(5) Material immediately preceding or following the enumeration must not be indented, unless it marks the beginning of a paragraph.

(6) If the tabulated material takes the form of a sentence in which the enumeration is an integral part, each item should begin with a small letter and end with a semicolon, except that (1) the penultimate item should end with a semicolon followed by an "and" or an "or" and

§6.3. [1]See E. Driedger, The Composition of Legislation — Legislative Forms and Precedents ch. VII (2d ed. rev. 1976).

       (2) if the last item ends the sentence, it should end with a period.

(7)   If the tabulated material takes the form of a simple list following a sentence that is otherwise complete, each item should begin with a capital letter and end with a period. No "and" or "or" follows the penultimate item.

The following provision exemplifies the *sentence* form of tabulation:

    Any person punishable under this chapter who:

       (1)   commits an offense punishable under this chapter, or aids, abets, counsels, commands, or procures its commission; or

       (2)   causes an act to be done that if directly performed by him would be punishable under this chapter;

   is a principal.

The following provision exemplifies the *list* form of tabulation:

    The Trustee may buy any of the following:

       (1)   United States Government bonds.
       (2)   State bonds.
       (3)   Municipal bonds.
       (4)   Preferred stock.
       (5)   Common stock listed on the New York Stock Exchange.

The features of tabulation that make it useful for avoiding syntactic ambiguity are (1) the form of indentation and (2) the convention that the introductory and subsequent language must be appropriate to each item in the enumeration. For example, introductory language that applies to the first item necessarily applies to each of the other items. Thus, if the draftsman wishes to show that particular language applies to some, but not all, of the items, he includes it as part of each item to which it is intended to apply and omits it elsewhere. That it is part of a particular item is supported by its indentation.

In the following tabulation, for example, it is clear that the exception for deed restrictions applies to interior lots and through lots as well as to corner lots:

"front lot line":
> (1) for an interior or through lot, means the line marking the boundary between the lot and the abutting street; and
> (2) for a corner lot, means the line marking the boundary between the lot and the shorter of the two abutting segments;

except as deed restrictions specify otherwise.

If the draftsman wants to make the exception apply only to corner lots, he should draft clause (2) as follows:

> (2) for a corner lot, means the line marking the boundary between the lot and the shorter of the two abutting segments, except as deed restrictions specify otherwise.

The following tabulation is defective, because clause (5) is not responsive to the introductory language:

The report shall include information regarding the following:

> (1) The historical importance of the memorial.
> (2) The nature of the site.
> (3) The cost of establishing the memorial.
> (4) The cost of maintaining the memorial.
> (5) Recommendations.

The defect may be cured either by removing clause (5) from the enumeration and setting it up as an independent requirement or by striking the words "information regarding" from the introductory language and putting them at the beginning of each of the first four clauses.

Normally, it is unnecessary or undesirable to tabulate an enumeration in the final text, unless it contains more than two items or unless the two items are cumbersome or complicated. Also, it is undesirable to carry subtabulation beyond the third level of division.

Here is an example of how tabulation can help to clarify the meaning of a very complicated provision, without exceeding this limit:

§1201.   *Regulars and members on active duty for more than 30 days: retirement*

If the Secretary concerned determines that a member of a regular component of the armed forces entitled to basic pay, or any other member of the armed forces entitled to basic pay who has been called or ordered to active duty (other than for training) for a period of more than 30 days, is unfit to perform the duties of his office, grade, rank, or rating because of physical disability incurred while entitled to basic pay, the Secretary may retire the member, with retired pay computed under section 1401 of this title, if the Secretary also determines that —

    (1)   based upon accepted medical principles, the disability is permanent;

    (2)   the disability is not the result of the member's intentional misconduct or wilful neglect, and was not incurred during a period of unauthorized absence; and

    (3)   either —

        (A)   the member has at least 20 years of service computed under section 1208 of this title; or

        (B)   the disability is at least 30 percent under the standard schedule of rating disabilities in use by the Veterans' Administration at the time of the determination; and either —

            (i)   the member has at least eight years of service computed under section 1208 of this title;

            (ii)   the disability is the proximate result of performing active duty; or

> (iii)   the disability was incurred in line of duty in time of war or national emergency.[2]

Because future amendments can greatly increase the incentive to proliferate sectional subdivisions and their designations, it is important to keep each section, in its original form, from being unduly long. That this is feasible even with very complicated statutes is shown by the Uniform Commercial Code, which, except for its general definition section, "has few sections longer than a page and none longer than two pages."[3] This offers hope that future Internal Revenue Codes can avoid such enormities as a section 3121 that is more than 11 pages long and that a Railroad Retirement Act can avoid a 6-page section 5. In the Internal Revenue Regulations, Peacock once discovered a 30-page section with an 18-page subsection![4] For most sections, however, even one page is too long. "For what better argument for such a course than that afforded by the mere citation of Section 30.742-2(b)(3)(ii)(B) Example (1)(i) . . ."[5]

The beauty of the tabular form of presentation is not only that it removes syntactic ambiguity but that it clarifies the structure of a complicated paragraph by exposing to view the "and's" and "or's" that tell the reader which provisions are alternative and which are cumulative.

Even when it is unnecessary or undesirable to use tabulation as a means of presentation in the final text, it is a highly useful device for testing the structure of sentences and paragraphs. It is particularly useful in exposing instances of what has been called "bastard enumeration".

Take, for example, the familiar phrase, "the several States, Territories, and the District of Columbia." Although it commits the sin of bastard enumeration, the fact is not obvious until the phrase is put in tabular form:

[2]10 U.S.C. §1201 (1958) (slightly edited, otherwise as originally enacted, 70A Stat. 91).
[3]J. Peacock, Notes on Legislative Drafting 10 (1961).
[4]*Id.* at 17.
[5]*Id.*

. . . the several:
    (1)   States;
    (2)   Territories; and
    (3)   the District of Columbia.

Clause (3) is unresponsive to the introductory language, either in form or in substance.

One appropriate retabulation of this provision would be this:

    (1)   the several States;
    (2)   the several Territories; and
    (3)   the District of Columbia.

After such a tabulation has been verified as meeting the tests listed above, it may be translated back into simple linear form: "the several States, the several Territories, and the District of Columbia" and so used in the final text.

Another, and probably preferable, approach in this instance would be to use a principal enumeration of two, the first of whose elements contained a subordinate enumeration of two:

    (1)   the several:
          (A)   States; and
          (B)   Territories; and
    (2)   the District of Columbia.

Although this alternative is more complicated in its tabular form, it is probably more economical and more easily read in its linear form: "the several States and Territories and the District of Columbia."

When using the tabular form, the draftsman may be tempted to draw into the introductory language any initial wording that would otherwise need to be repeated in each item in the enumeration. However, this may be done only with proper regard to the language that follows the enumeration. For example, the following provision makes no sense grammatically:

. . . shall be transferred on the date when he becomes a member of:
   (1)   the American Geophysical Society or one of its affiliates; or
   (2)   a recognized foreign organization of equivalent standing;
whichever is earlier.

In some instances this provision may also be confusing, because the word "whichever" necessarily refers to clauses (1) and (2) as the only available alternative elements, whereas the rest of the concluding phrase can refer only to dates or events rather than to organizations. There is no alternative to restoring "date" language to both clauses, as follows:

. . . shall be transferred:
   (1)   on the date when he becomes a member of the American Geophysical Society or one of its affiliates; or
   (2)   on the date when he becomes a member of a recognized foreign organization of equivalent standing;
whichever is earlier.

At this point the reader is invited to sharpen his tabulation sense by doing a complete tabulation of the following provision. This means putting every enumeration in tabular form, making only the minimal changes in text necessary to support that form. Because there are subordinate tabulations, the result will necessarily be hierarchical in form. The exercise is worth doing, because if done properly it will greatly sharpen the draftsman's nose for cases of bastard enumeration, which abound in legal instruments. It will also improve his architectural sense. Because the exercise is not easy, the reader may want to compare his final effort with my own, which appears in appendix B. Here is the provision:

[A]ny key, any identification card, identification tag, or similar identification device, and any other small article which the Postmaster General by regulation may designate, which bears, contains, or has attached securely thereto —

(1) a complete, definite, and legible post office address, including (if such exists) the street address or box or route number, and

(2) a notice directing that such key, card, tag, device, or small article be returned to such address, and guaranteeing the payment, on delivery, of the postage due thereon, may be transmitted through the mails to such address at a rate of postage of 5 cents for each two ounces or fraction thereof.[6]

Through the use of symbolic logic, this approach has been expanded and refined by Layman E. Allen and others to the point where it is capable of portraying the many permutations and combinations of multiple syntactic ambiguities that may be juxtaposed in the same sentence or paragraph.[7] This highly formalized system, which Allen calls "language normalization," is useful in analyzing the syntactic structure of extremely complicated provisions, such as many in the Internal Revenue Code.[8] On the other hand, because it tends to impair readability, it has only limited utility for purposes of inclusion in the final text.

The system's utility for analysis has been exaggerated by the fact that it treats each potential syntactic ambiguity as an actual ambiguity, even when the larger context clearly resolves it.[9] In the overwhelming majority of cases, the number of juxtaposed actual ambiguities in the draft of an instrument is relatively small. For such drafts, the more formal system seems

[6]Act of Aug. 4, 1955, chap. 560, §1, 69 Stat. 497, 39 U.S.C. §302a.

[7]Allen, Symbolic Logic: A Razor-Edged Tool for Drafting and Interpreting Legal Documents, 66 Yale L.J. 833 (1957); Allen, Interpretation of California Pimping Statute, 60S M.U.L.L. 114 (1960); Ely, The Limits of Logic, 63S M.U.L.L. 117 (1963); Stern, Syntactic Ambiguity in Clayton Act, Section 5(a), 60D M.U.L.L. 129 (1960).

[8]Allen, Beyond Document Retrieval Toward Information Retrieval, 47 Minn. L. Rev. 713, 747-756 (1963). (At that time, Allen called his system "systematic pulverization.")

[9]The difference between a potential ambiguity and an actual one is pointed out in the materials cited in Montrose, Syntactic (Formerly Amphibolous) Ambiguity, 62J M.U.L.L. 65, 70 n.R1 (1962).

unnecessarily elaborate.[10] Allen's system is discussed further in chapter 12.

Neither the system of tabulation described above nor Allen's "language normalization," just referred to, pinpoints ambiguities in the sense of specifically pointing them out. By laying bare the essential structure of the paragraph or sentence, both systems are valuable in making its shortcomings more readily observable.[11] Ultimately, therefore, the detection of a specific ambiguity remains a matter of recognition by the draftsman. Even with these systems, he needs a nose sensitive to ambiguity.

When a sentence contains two coordinate enumerations that it is desirable to tabulate in the final text, some draftsmen designate the elements of the second enumeration as if they were a continuation of the first. This avoids having two clause "(1)'s," and so forth, in the same designated unit, which would create the possibility of ambiguous citation. However, the problems of citation seem less significant than the danger in using forms that suggest that two enumerations, with possibly different bases of division, form parts of the same enumeration.

Fortunately, there are preferable alternatives. One is to divide the provision so that each enumeration falls in a separate subsection, paragraph, or other designated unit. If this is not feasible, it may be possible to put the clearer and simpler of the two in undesignated linear form or, if both tabulations must be retained, to use a different system of designation (e.g., "(A)," "(B)," etc.) for the second. In many years of drafting, however,

[10]See Allen, Symbolic Logic and Law: A Reply, 15 J. Legal Ed. 47 (1962), and two succeeding comments; Summers, A Note on Symbolic Logic and the Law, 13 J. Legal Ed. 486 (1961).

[11]"Circuit and isomer diagrams may make explicit the ambiguity involved, but they do not assist in the resolution of the ambiguity. . . . Allen considers that the arrow diagram is a procedure 'for the systematic detection of such syntactic ambiguity' . . . It is submitted, however, that the construction of a diagram is possible only after the ambiguity has been detected. It is of course true, as Allen has pointed out, that the attempt to construct a diagram helps in the discovery of an ambiguity." Montrose, Syntactic (Formerly Amphibolous) Ambiguity, 62J M.U.L.L. 65, 69, 70 n.R3 (1962).

I have never met a situation where the latter device became necessary.

§6.4. SEMANTIC AMBIGUITY: PASSIVE PAST PARTICIPLES

As Elmer A. Driedger has shown,[1] the passive past participle is sometimes ambiguous, a fact important to instruments that refer to past events. The phrase "a person who was married on January 1, 1984," can be read as meaning either a person who entered into a contract of marriage on January 1, 1984, or a person who had the status of a married person on that date. The ambiguity lies in the doubt whether the verb is "was" (a form of the verb "to be") or "was married" (a form of the verb "marry"). Unless context clearly resolves the uncertainty, the draftsman should recast the phrase.

§6.5. SEMANTIC AMBIGUITY: NUMBER

So far as substantive meaning permits, it is desirable to use the singular rather than the plural. This will avoid the question whether the predicate applies separately to each member of the subject class or jointly to the subject class taken as a whole.

Don't say	*Say*
The architect shall issue certificates for the stages listed in section 403.	The architect shall issue a certificate for each stage listed in section 403.

unless you mean
The architect shall issue certificates for each stage listed in section 403.

§6.4. [1]E. Driedger, The Composition of Legislation — Legislative Forms and Precedents 23 (2d ed. rev. 1976).

or

The architect shall issue certificates, each of which shall
be for all the stages listed in
section 403.

If it is necessary to use the plural, the draftsman can change
to the singular, whenever desirable, by using the following device.

Example:

Employees who have earned 15 or more point credits are
eligible for positions under section 9. *Such an* employee . . .

When number is a matter of indifference, the simplest form
that makes this clear is neither the singular nor the plural, but
the generic.

Example:

Proof of hardship may be by affidavit [i.e., by one or more
affidavits].

§6.6.   SEMANTIC AMBIGUITY: REDUNDANT NUMBERING

Edward Vanneman, Jr., has justifiably ridiculed the still common
practice of using both written and arabic numbers.[1] Why should
we take this precaution in some instances ("ten (10) days") and
not in others ("329 Mass. 453" or "chapter X")? The risk of
striking a wrong word processor key would justify abandoning
arabic (and roman) numbers altogether. Repetition is a poor
substitute for careful proofreading.

If clarification of the arabic form is the reason, wouldn't it

---

§6.6.   [1]Blame it All on O.P.E.C.? 65 A.B.A.J. 1266 (1979) (MLD 177).

make better sense to say "6 (six)"? If kiting of numbers is a problem, the written form alone should be enough.

The redundant form sometimes leads to ambiguity ("two (3)"). The conventional judicial resolution in such a case is to go with the written form. But what would the court do with a sequence like this: "one (1), two (2), two (3), four (4)"?

§6.7.   SEMANTIC AMBIGUITY: MOOD

· The words "shall" and "shall not" normally imply that to accomplish the purpose of the provision someone must act or refrain from acting. Draftsmen often use these words merely to declare a legal result, rather than to prescribe a rule of conduct. In this usage the word "shall" is not only unnecessary but involves a circumlocution in thought ("false imperative") because the purpose of the provision is achieved in the very act of declaring the legal result. Worse, use of the false imperative (e.g., "Each person shall be required to . . .") may create doubt in particular instances whether the result is self-executing, as it is in a declaratory provision, or is effective only when required action is taken.

In declaratory (i.e., self-executing) provisions, therefore, the draftsman should use the indicative, not the imperative, mood.

Don't say	*Say*
The term "person" shall mean	The term "person" means
The equipment shall remain the property of the lessor.	The equipment remains the property of the lessor.
No person shall be entitled	No person is entitled

The indicative mood is also appropriate for conditions. The draftsman should avoid the subjunctive.

Don't say	*Say*
If it be determined that	If it is determined that

§6.8. SEMANTIC AMBIGUITY: PROBLEMS OF TIME[1] AND AGE

When used to fix the beginning or end of a period, the word "time" is liable to be read as referring to the exact time during the day or night when the event occurs. If the draftsman intends that the period is to be measured in whole days only, he should say "day" instead of "time."

Don't say	*Say*
120 days after the time when	120 days after the day on which

When specifying a period, the draftsman should make clear what the first and last days are.

Don't say	*Say*
from July 1, 1984, to . . .	after June 30, 1984, and . . .
between July 1, 1984, and . . .	after June 30, 1984 and . . .
to ["until," "by"] June 30, 1985	before July 1, 1985

Because a legal provision of continuing effect, in contrast to the purely dispositive provisions of a will or conveyance, is considered to be continuously speaking, the draftsman should not use words such as "now," "present," "already," "heretofore," or "hereafter" to relate events to the time when the instrument takes effect. He should relate them expressly to that event ("when this . . . takes effect," "before this . . . takes effect," and so forth).

If the draftsman means a calendar year or a continuous period of a year and the context creates no special ambiguity, he should say "year." If he means a continuous period but in the context reference to "two years' service" might be interpreted as permitting the addition of different periods totaling two years, he should say "service for a two-year period."

§6.8. [1]See generally E. Piesse, The Elements of Drafting, Ch. 11 (5th ed. Aitken 1976).

If something must be done by the end of a specified period that is to begin in the future, the draftsman should be sure to show whether the act may be done before the period begins or whether it must be done within that period.

If the former, say	*If the latter, say*
before the expiration of six months after the end of the period during which he was unemployed	within the six-month period immediately following the period during which he was unemployed

Ambiguities similar to those described above for periods of time exist also for ages.

Don't say	*Say*
between the ages of 17 and 45	17 years old or older and under 46

Although the phrase "less than 46 years old" is clear (it means anyone who has not reached his 46th birthday), the phrase "more than 17 years old" is ambiguous because it is not clear whether a person becomes "more than 17" on the day after his 17th birthday or on his 18th birthday.

Don't say	*Say*
who is more than 17 years old	who has passed his 17th birth-day
	unless you mean who is 18 years old or older

§6.9.   SEMANTIC AMBIGUITY: PROVISOS

Provisos have been used for so many purposes (to state conditions or exceptions, or simply to add material) that they tend to be ambiguous. At best they constitute archaic legalisms. Accordingly, provisos should be avoided. To introduce a condition, the draftsman should say "if." To introduce an exception or limitation, he should say "except that," "but," or "however," or simply start a new sentence. To add other material, he should start a new sentence or paragraph.[1]

§6.10. CONTEXTUAL AMBIGUITY: CONDITIONS AND REQUIREMENTS

To state as a command what is intended only as a condition precedent often creates ambiguity. The draftsman should make clear what he really means.

Don't say	*Say*
The security officer shall be a citizen of the United States.	To be eligible for security officer, a person must be a citizen of the United States.

In some contexts, the "Don't say" version can be read as merely requiring a security officer to become a citizen.

§6.11. CONTEXTUAL AMBIGUITY: GILDING THE LILY

Adjectives such as "real," "true," "complete," and "actual" and adverbs such as "duly," and "properly" should be avoided except when needed for special contrast. Because these ideas are normally implied, expressing them in some, but not all, instances creates doubt that they are implied elsewhere.

Don't say	*Say*
He shall write his actual age in the appropriate blank.	He shall write his age in the appropriate blank.

[1]§6.9. [1]For more detailed analyses, see R. Dick, Legal Drafting §92-100 (2d ed. 1985); E. Driedger, The Composition of Legislation — Legislative Forms and Precedents ch. 9 (2d ed. rev. 1976).

§6.12. CONTEXTUAL AMBIGUITY: INCORPORATION BY REFERENCE

References that conceptually incorporate other (usually external) provisions instead of restating them in the incorporating instrument constitute "incorporation by reference."[1] Incorporation by reference saves space and sometimes valuable time for the draftsman (if not for users). Where parallel results are desirable, it guarantees them. Exact uniformity is sometimes important, especially when the problem continually recurs. To restate long or complicated provisions risks creating unintended differences.

The advantages of uniformity, however, carry risks. The big one is that the incorporated language may not adequately fit the immediate situation.[2] The risk is increased by the fact that the time pressures that often lead the draftsman to incorporate existing materials may prevent him from making sure that what look like parallel situations are in fact so. That incorporated language is less likely to be checked by the draftsman or his client increases the chances of mistake or deception.[3] Most of the trouble arises when the draftsman incorporates by reference materials that lie outside the instrument he is preparing.

If the material considered for incorporation does not adequately fit the case at hand, the draftsman should reject it or

---

§6.12.   [1]On incorporation by reference generally, see E. Driedger, The Composition of Legislation — Legislative Forms and Precedents, ch. 13 (2d ed. 1976); C. Ilbert, Legislative Methods and Forms 259-266 (1901), C. Ilbert The Mechanics of Law Making 130-132 (1914); J. Sutherland, Statutes and Statutory Construction §21.13 (4th ed. 1985); H. Thring, Practical Legislation 52-58 (1902); Brabner-Smith, Incorporation by Reference and Delegation of Power — Validity of "Referential" Legislation, 5 Geo. Wash. L. Rev. 198 (1937); Cullen, The Mechanics of Statutory Revision, 24 Ore. L. Rev. 1, 21 (1914); Dosland, Statutory Drafting, 9 Tenn. L. Rev. 158, 164 (1931); Fertig, Hints on Bill Drafting, 35 Pa. B.A.Q. 151, 153 (1938); Poldervaardt, Legislative Reference — A Statutory Jungle, 38 Iowa L. Rev. 705 (1953); Read, Is Referential Legislation Worth While?, 25 Minn. L. Rev. 261 (1941); Statutory Cross References — The "Loose Cannon" of Statutory Construction in Florida, 9 Fla. St. U.L. Rev. 1 (1981).

[2]A. Russell, Legislative Drafting and Forms 59 (4th ed. 1938).

[3]Poldervaardt, *supra* note 1 at 707; Read, *supra* note 1 at 261-277.

revise it appropriately for inclusion in the new instrument, even though doing so takes substantial space and time. Actually, the time legitimately saved by incorporation is less than first appears, because it takes time to screen even compatible incorporated material.[4] Sometimes the draftsman can adopt language by reference subject to minor, clear-cut exceptions. This is dangerous and he shouldn't try it unless the advantages are overwhelming.

When a statute incorporates by reference material from another source, the draftsman should make clear whether the borrowed material is taken only in its current form or includes later changes as well. Otherwise, he leaves the question to the uncertainties of interpretation. Courts tend to hold that in the absence of words to the contrary the incorporation of specifically named provisions picks up only current text, whereas the incorporation of a general area includes future changes. But the line between the specific and the general is hard to draw and there is always the chance that the court will find some unintended sign of contrary intent. It is safer to nail the point down, for example, by referring to "the provisions of . . . in effect when this Act [or "instrument"] takes effect" or "the provisions of . . . in effect when this Act [or "instrument"] is being applied."[5]

One reason for being specific is that, if the incorporated language was not enacted by the legislature that the draftsman is serving, the inclusion of future changes may jeopardize the constitutionality of the incorporating provision. The borrowed material may be in a law enacted in another jurisdiction or it may be material that has not been enacted by any legislative body. If only current text is adopted, no problem arises in most cases.[6] But if the incorporation, properly construed, includes future

---

[4]"The method rarely, if ever, saves the draftsman any trouble, for the work of framing modifications of the enactments applied requires extreme care, and is often a matter of great difficulty." C. Ilbert, The Mechanics of Law Making 132 (1914). See also Read, *supra* note 1 at 296-297.

[5]Brabner-Smith, *supra* note 1 at 198, 203; Poldervaardt, *supra* note 1 at 724-729; Read, *supra* note 1 at 270-276.

[6]Even here some courts take a dim view of the incorporation by reference of the laws of another jurisdiction. See, e.g., *Wilentz v. Sears, Roebuck & Co.*, 12 N.J. Misc. 531, 172 Atl. 903 (Ch. 1934); Poldervaardt, *supra* note 1 at 719.

changes, the incorporating provision may be found to make an unconstitutional delegation of the legislative power to the persons authorized to change the incorporated material.[7]

Even if future changes in an adopted provision from the same legislature are not being included, the draftsman should consider spelling out the intended result instead of incorporating it by reference. Otherwise, the reference may be functionally orphaned by later changes in the incorporated law, making it necessary to exhume dead law to find out what the live law refers to.

The most fruitful field of legislative incorporation, therefore, is the incorporation of laws enacted by the same legislature, including future changes in those laws. But even here the draftsman must move carefully.

In any event, he should make clear that he is adopting the substance of the other law and not amending it to extend its coverage. This is important in states whose constitutions require that amended provisions be restated in full in the amending law. Especially in those states, the draftsman should *not* say:

> For the purposes of this section, the Act of March 19, 1923, ch. 243 (5 U.S.C. 593), applies also to any person who has made a declaration to become a citizen.

Such a provision can easily be read as amending the earlier law. Instead, he should say:

> For the purposes of this section, a person who has made a declaration to become a citizen has the same rights and duties as the Act of March 19, 1923, ch. 243 (5 U.S.C. 593) prescribes for a citizen.

In New Jersey and New York, statutory incorporation by reference is expressly forbidden by the state constitution.[8] In

---

[7]Brabner-Smith, *supra* note 1 at 204-222; Poldervaardt, *supra* note 1 at 714; Read, *supra* note 1 at 232-294.

[8]New Jersey, Art. IV, §VII (5): New York, Art. III, §16. However, these provisions have been construed as allowing the incorporation of statutory systems of procedure. *Hutches v. Borough of Hohokus,* 82 N.J.L. 140, 81 Atl. 658

Louisiana, the constitutional prohibition hits only the incorporation by reference of "any system or code of laws."[9] In Arkansas, New Mexico, and possibly Pennsylvania, constitutional provisions requiring that laws "extending" other laws must set forth the extended provision in full have been construed as outlawing incorporation by reference as a means of making "substantive," as distinct from "procedural," changes in the law.[10] Although the cases so holding that involve true incorporation by reference are of doubtful validity, draftsmen in those states must accept them as correct.[11] Doubt has also arisen in several other states as to whether similar results would not be reached even though their constitutional provisions affect only laws that amend, revise, or revive.[12]

Incorporation by reference is, of course, the essence of the "passive boilerplate" approach represented by Food Products Regulation No. 1[13] and some automobile insurance policies.[14] This is ordinarily preferable to the "active boilerplate" system represented by 1 U.S.C. §§1-11 (definitions), 5 U.S.C. 8301(a) (effective dates of federal retirements), or the Model Statutory Construction Act,[15] which impose themselves on other laws, except as context indicates otherwise, without specifically identifying them.

(1911); *People ex rel. Everson v. Lorillard,* 135 N.Y. 285, 31 N.E. 1011 (1892). See also Poldervaardt, *supra* note 1 at 714; Read, *supra* note 1 at 280.

[9]Art. III, §15(B).

[10]*Farris v. Wright,* 158 Ark. 519, 521, 250 S.W. 889, 890 (1923); *Yeo v. Tweedy,* 34 N.M. 611, 628, 286 Pac. 970, 977 (1929); *Commonwealth v. Wayne Sewerage Co.,* 287 Pa. 42, 47, 134 Atl. 390, 391 (1926). The *Wayne* case did not deal with a clean-cut incorporation by reference. See also Poldervaardt, *supra* note 1 at 711-714; Read, *supra* note 1 at 279.

[11]"A court may get rid of its mistaken precedents by overruling them or by distinguishing them out of existence, but the official draftsman must accept judicial decisions, however inimical to sound drafting, as the supreme canons of legislation." E. Freund, Legislative Drafting 7 (1916).

[12]E.g., *Carroll v. Hartford Fire Ins. Co.,* 28 Idaho 466, 479, 154 Pac. 985, 988 (1916); *Holmes v. State,* 146 Miss. 351, 359, Ill. So. 860, 862 (1927). See also Poldervaardt, *supra* note 1 at 709-711.

[13]See §5.7 *supra* and appendix C.

[14]See §5.7 *supra.*

[15]Formerly the Uniform Statutory Construction Act, 14 Uniform Laws Annotated 513 *et seq.* (1980).

The active approach affects future law only so far as the boilerplate is sufficiently taken for granted by author and audience that its existence and relevance can be said to be part of the conditioning fund of tacit assumptions that comprise the later law's external context. In this way, even new law can yield to preexisting limitations.[16] But this is exceptional and the approach is not safe for general use.

§6.13.   CONTEXTUAL AMBIGUITY: KIND OF INSTRUMENT INVOLVED

As Maurice B. Kirk has pointed out, it is important that a legal instrument disclose what kind of instrument it is intended to be.[1] In most instances, the necessary information appears on the face of the instrument or emerges from a casual reading. How the instrument describes itself is not as important as including the kind of provisions that are mandated by applicable law. Thus an instrument that is intended to operate as a lease should have "operative words of grant" to distinguish it from a mere contract to make a lease.[2] For the most part, substance controls rather than form. "In the absence of an explicit (usually statutory) requirement otherwise, a beginning is sufficient if it identifies the parties and the attempted legal action."[3]

§6.14.   AVOIDING AMBIGUITY: THE MOST EFFECTIVE TOOLS

Consistency, good arrangement, and adherence to established usage have already been strongly advocated as aids to perfecting

---

[16]See e.g., 5 U.S.C. 8301(a) (effective dates of federal retirements).

§6.13.   [1]Kirk, Legal Drafting: How Should a Document Begin?, 3 Tex. Tech. L. Rev. 233.

[2]*Id.* at 248, 254, 257.

[3]*Id.* at 263.

the substance of the legal message.[1] It should now be emphasized that the same three tools are the most effective for avoiding ambiguity. Here again, consistency, which sharpens the
tools of language, is the ranking principle. Nothing will contribute so much to general clarity as following it, and nothing will
contribute so much to obscurity as neglecting it.

§6.14.　[1]See §2.3 *supra.*

VII

Substantive Clarity: Definitions[1]

§7.1. THE ROLE OF DEFINITIONS

In a legal instrument a definition should be used only to explain the meaning that a term is intended to carry. Although this advice might seem to be obviously sound, many draftsmen disregard it.

The first thing to remember about definitions in legal instruments is that they should be used only when necessary and should be only as full as necessary.[2] It is hard, and often risky, to try to formulate definitions that describe the ways in which the draftsman actually uses the defined terms elsewhere in the same instrument. (It is apparently easier to use words properly than to define them accurately.) Draftsmen are prone to define a word in one sense and then, without realizing it, use it in a very

---

§7.1. [1]On definitions generally, see H. Martin & R. Ohmann, The Logic and Rhetoric of Exposition 7-47 (rev. ed. 1963); R. Robinson, Definition (1954). On legal definitions generally, see E. Driedger, The Composition of Legislation — Legislative Forms and Precedents, ch. 5 (2d ed. rev. 1976); E. Piesse, The Elements of Drafting, ch. 6 (5th ed. Aitken 1976).

[2]"A definition does not necessarily have to set forth everything which is included and everything which is excluded by the use of a particular word. Frequently it may be desirable to exclude certain things without stating what is included by the use of a word. Or the draftsman may wish to state only some of the things which are included within a certain word." R. Cook, Legal Drafting 37 (1951).

different sense.[3] The main use of definitions in legal instruments is, of course, to achieve clarity and consistency without burdensome repetition. Just as every word in any legal instrument ought to pay its own way, every definition ought to be limited to filling a real need. Fortunately, definitions "are seldom used in simple private documents."[4]

§7.2.　KINDS OF DEFINITIONS

Some authorities divide definitions into "real" and "nominal." Because the former relate to the refinement and crystallization of concepts rather than to the meanings of words, many persons do not consider them to be definitions at all.[1] This discussion concerns for the most part the latter, which do relate to the meanings of words.

Nominal definitions are called "lexical" insofar as they assert a meaning corresponding to actual usage in the given speech community.[2] They are called "stipulative" insofar as they declare a meaning different from actual usage in that speech community.[3] Lexical definitions attempt to record usage. Stipulative definitions attempt to create it. Because they describe actual use patterns, the former have truth value. The latter do not.[4]

Definitions may be usefully classified also in terms of their methods. Whether lexical or stipulative, the following kinds of definitions are useful in legal instruments. The first, definition by synonym, although infrequent, is occasionally useful. A term is defined by equating it to a more familiar term whose meaning

---

[3]"No more disastrous mistake can occur than to formulate a definition that gives to a word a meaning other than that intended." Thomas, Problems in Drafting Legal Instruments, 39 Ill. B.J. 51, 55 (1950). "There is no more reason why a person who uses a word correctly should be able to tell what it means than there is why a planet which is moving should know Kepler's laws." B. Russell, My Philosophical Development 147 (1959).

[4]R. Cook, Legal Drafting 37 (1951).

§7.2.　[1]R. Robinson, Definition 7-11 (1954).

[2]*Id.*, ch. 3.

[3]*Id.*, ch. 4.

[4]*Id.* at 35-39 and 62-66.

is presumably sufficiently clear to the audience to whom the instrument is addressed.[5] For example: "The term 'fracture' means break." A second kind of definition is definition by analysis. The draftsman defines the subject in terms of (1) a parent class, (2) a subclass, and (3) the features that distinguish the subclass from others of the same parent class.[6] For example: "The term 'cosmetic' means an article intended to be applied to the human body to cleanse or beautify it or change its appearance." Such a definition must apply to all the individual members included in the subject and to nothing else. A third (and very similar) kind of definition is definition by synthesis. The draftsman defines the subject by its relation to something of which it is a part.[7] For example: "The term 'carburetor' means a part of a motor vehicle." Whereas the analytical definition speaks in terms of parent class, subclass, and distinguishing characteristics, the synthetic definition speaks in terms only of parent class and subclass. It is correspondingly less informative. Both kinds are connotative in that they define in terms of significant characteristics. All three methods presume that the described meaning is exhaustive in the sense that it purports to give the full sweep of the term (none of the three is necessarily detailed). Because equivalence is assumed, the word "is" may be substituted for the normal connective "means."

A fourth kind of definition useful to lawyers is denotative definition, that is, definition by listing all or some of the things to which the term refers.[8] Here, particular characteristics are ignored. Such a definition may be exhaustive (e.g., "The term 'narcotic drug' means opium, coca leaves, cocaine, isopecaine, opiate, or a salt, derivative, or preparation of any of those products") or partial (e.g., "The term 'narcotic drug' includes coca leaves"). Other kinds of definitions, which are of interest mainly to logicians and the philosophers of language, need no consideration here.

[5] *Id.* at 94.
[6] *Id.* at 96. This is a definition in the classical, Aristotelian sense. Here the corresponding technical terms are "genus," "species," and "differentia."
[7] *Id.* at 98.
[8] *Id.* at 108.

What kind of definition should the draftsman choose in a particular case? Should he choose the method of synonym, analysis, synthesis, or denotation? If denotation, should he make the definition exhaustive or partial? The problem in each case is the purely practical one of selecting a method that is no more complicated or elaborate than necessary to deal with the relevant doubt or uncertainty in the minds of his audience. If he is creating a new technical term for a complicated idea, he will probably choose a comparatively detailed analytic definition. If the problem is merely to put to rest several specific doubts in the margin of uncertainty surrounding a modestly vague but generally adequate term, he will probably choose a partially denotative definition (e.g., "The term 'income' includes [or does not include] capital gain"). In each case he tells his audience all that he thinks it needs to know, but no more. Definition for its own sake has no place in legal instruments.

§7.3.   "FREEDOM OF STIPULATION"

For many years philosophers such as John Stuart Mill[1] have beat the drums for what they call "freedom of stipulation." James MacKaye has stated this freedom succinctly as follows: "Any person is free to stipulate any meaning he pleases for a word and his meaning shall always be accepted."[2] Although MacKaye was not a lawyer, he could not have stated more accurately a principle that has been dear to the heart of the traditional legal draftsman.

    The appeal of this position has come from both a desire to have language grow fruitfully and a rebellion against the now generally repudiated notion that words have inherently proper meanings, that is, that there is some natural affinity between a word and the thing to which it refers. The possible outcome of this outmoded view is found in the statement of the person who said to an astronomer: "I feel *such* an admiration for you

§7.3. [1]A System of Logic 18 (8th ed. 1900).
[2]The Logic of Language 61 (1939).

astronomers because of your many wonderful discoveries about the universe. But the most wonderful of all it seems to me is your discovery of the names of the planets. How for instance did you ever manage to find out that the red planet named Mars really *is* Mars?"[3]

With the thorough repudiation of this point of view, it has been easy to go the whole hog in exercising the freedom of stipulation. As early as Plato's Cratylus, we find Hermogenes saying: "I . . . cannot convince myself that there is any principle of correctness in names other than convention and agreement; any name which you give, in my opinion, is the right one, and if you change that and give another, the new name is as correct as the old."[4]

This point of view found perhaps its ultimate expression in the famous exchange between Humpty Dumpty and Alice in chapter 6 of Lewis Carroll's Through the Looking-Glass.[5] What may surprise some, however, is that the world of legal drafts-manship has produced the lawyer's counterpart of Humpty Dumpty in a group of bills that stated that for their purposes the term "September 16, 1940," meant "June 27, 1950"![6] This feat of legal draftsmanship is not likely to be equaled, let alone excelled, in this century. Less spectacular but more insidious is the instrument that says that for its purposes the term "sup-plies" includes buildings. In a short, isolated legal instrument this may do little harm. But confusion is certain in a long, com-

---

[3]*Id.* at 95.

[4]3 Dialogues of Plato 42 (Jowett trans. 4th ed. 1953).

[5]L. Carroll, Alice in Wonderland 163 (Gray ed. 1971):

> "When I use a word," Humpty Dumpty said, in rather a scornful tone, "it means just what I choose it to mean — neither more nor less."
>
> "The question is," said Alice, "whether you *can* make words mean so many different things."
>
> "The question is," said Humpty Dumpty, "which is to be master — that's all."

[6]E.g., H.R. 353, 474, 1624, 1882, 2335, 4171, 6391, 6757, 82d Cong., and several other bills culminating in the enactment of the Veterans' Readjustment Assistance Act of 1952. "Seldom has this gone farther than the English statute which, it is said, provided: 'Whenever the word "cows" occurs in this Act it shall be construed to include horses, mules, asses, sheep and goats.' " F. Cooper, Writing in Law Practice 7 (1963).

plicated one in which well-accepted and clearly delineated terms are twisted to extend or restrict its coverage. The problem is even more acute when an instrument must be read in relation to other instruments using different terminology. Here we have the modern Tower of Babel.

Hermogenes, Humpty Dumpty, and a long line of generally respectable legal draftsmen went wrong in falsely assuming that, because language is for the most part conventional, its users have carte blanche to attach whatever meanings they like. What they failed to grasp is the nature of convention and its relation to effective communication. Bernard Berenson has perhaps best expressed for us the relationship between convention and communication. The fact that he was talking about modern art makes his comments no less apt.

> *Representation is a compromise with chaos* . . . The compromise prolonged becomes a convention. . . .
> The alphabet is a convention. So is all arithmetical notation. So is mathematics . . .
> . . . And the joy of creative art comes when one is lured to hope that he has found the cypher, the symbol, the generic shape or scrawl, the hieroglyph, the convention, in short, that will do it. . . .
> So long then as we want to have . . . contact with others of our own species, we can have it only through conventions. If we shed any instinctively or throw them over deliberately, either they are replaced before too long or we fall back into private universes, self-immured *incommunicado*. . . .
> Literature, Anglo-American literature certainly, is now overshadowed by the glossolaly of Gertrude Stein and still more by the polyglot etymological puns and soap-bubbles of James Joyce. . . .
> It is worse in the visual arts. Words drip with sub-meanings. Take a word out of the colour-vat in our own minds where it soaks; do what you can to wring it clean, to dry it, to harden it, to crystallize it, as the French have done with their language for three whole centuries until the other day: yet some trace of meaning, besides what is intended, sticks. . . .
> A tradition, a convention, needs constant manipulation to

vivify it, to enlarge it, to keep it fresh and supple, and capable of generating problems and producing their solution. To keep a convention alive and growing fruitfully requires creative genius, and when that fails it either becomes mannered and academic or runs "amok."[7]

Why the link between language and convention has a psychological basis is suggested by Colin Cherry's comment that the fact that communication works at all "depends principally upon the vast store of habits which we each one of us possess."[8] The key word here is "habit," and anyone familiar with Pavlov's dogs[9] knows that the basis of language convention is something akin to the conditioned reflex. This is not to say that meaning is necessarily "behavioral." It says merely that communication is based on shared psychological habits and that these habits are not easily or quickly unlearned. Richard Robinson summed it up neatly when he said that "it is not possible to cancel the ingrained emotion of a word merely by an announcement."[10]

The lawyer who defines "wheat" as including rye is laying a trap not only for his readers but also for himself. Even a legislature is powerless to repeal the psychological law on which this is based. Like ghosts returning to a haunted house, established connotations return to haunt the user who attempts to banish them. The draftsman who has resorted to this slovenly device has often forgotten his special definition and reverted unconsciously to the established sense, thereby introducing either an unintended result or an intended result disguised as something else.

[7]Seeing and Knowing 7, 9-13 (1953).

[8]On Human Communication 12 (2d ed. 1966). "[A] child acquires the habit of using the word 'dog' on appropriate occasions exactly as he acquires any other habit." B. Russell, My Philosophical Development 146 (1959). "[T]he fixed meaning represents, not a state of consciousness fixed by a name, but a recognition of a habitual way of belief: a habit of understanding." J. Dewey, Essays in Experimental Logic 187 (1916).

[9]Cherry, *supra,* note 8 at 61. See also C. Ogden & I. Richards, The Meaning of Meaning 56 (10th ed. 1956).

[10]R. Robinson, Definition 77 (1954). See also H. Martin & R. Ohmann, The Logic and Rhetoric of Exposition 26-29 (rev. ed. 1966); Hall, Reason and Reality in Jurisprudence, 7 Buffalo L. Rev. 351, 386 (1958).

The temptation to use a Humpty Dumpty definition is, of course, strong. If a long and complicated instrument makes many references to wheat, and it becomes desirable to extend the instrument to include rye, it is far simpler to make a single insertion in the definition section ("The term 'wheat' includes rye") than it is to insert the words "and rye" after each appearance of the word "wheat." At the same time it would be hard to find a better example of the penny-wise-pound-foolish approach. For these reasons it is important for the legal draftsman not to define a word in a sense significantly different from the way it is normally understood by the persons to whom it is primarily addressed. This is a fundamental principle of communication, and it is one of the shames of the legal profession that draftsmen so flagrantly violate it. Indeed, the principle is one of the most important in the whole field of legal drafting.

This injunction, of course, does not rule out the use of nicknames, e.g., "the Great American Corporation (called 'the Corporation' in this lease)," or appropriate fictions. When a fiction is appropriate, the draftsman should continue to use his words in their normal senses and label the fiction plainly by using "as if" language.

Don't say	*Say*
The terms "child" and "issue" include an adopted child.	A child adopted by any person shall be treated as if he were a child of the blood.

But even before turning to fictions such as this, the draftsman should exhaust the possibilities of amending each relevant provision to make it say expressly what it is intended to mean. More of his time is required, but in the long run it often saves the time of many more readers and avoids unnecessary confusion.

§7.4. USES OF STIPULATIVE DEFINITION AND LEXICAL DEFINITION

Though Humpty Dumptyism is out, freedom of stipulation and stipulative definition have legitimate uses, which can best be understood by examining the true purpose of definitions in legal instruments. Because a legal instrument is not intended to supplant the dictionary, one that hews as closely as possible to accepted usage need not define the great bulk of the terms that it uses. Instead, it need define only those terms for which accepted usage in the given speech community is inadequate to carry the intended message. A lexical definition is thus necessary only where a partially established usage is still gaining currency, competing usages pose the threat of ambiguity, or a critical element of established usage is not sufficiently plain.

Stipulative definitions, on the other hand, are necessary on two general kinds of occasions. One is when the instrument deals with a new concept for which usage has not yet established a name. Here the draftsman may even have to create a term. If he does, he is well advised to choose one that puts no greater strain on the reader than the burden of facing the unfamiliar. He should avoid a term whose established connotations are sufficiently similar to and at variance with the intended meaning to create the strong likelihood of confusion.

A second, and more often necessary, use of stipulative definitions is to resolve uncertainties in the cloudy areas surrounding vague terms. A full and more precise definition may be substituted for the looser meaning of accepted usage, in which case it is partly lexical and partly stipulative ("In this ordinance, 'mobile home' means a vehicle or other portable structure more than 30 feet long that is designed to be moved on the highway and designed or used as a dwelling"). Or a partial definition may be used to resolve a specific marginal uncertainty, in which case it is wholly stipulative (e.g., "In this Act, 'automobile' includes an amphibious passenger motor vehicle"). In neither case is the reader called on to make a significant adjustment in his normal response habits.

Much of the need for stipulative definition grows out of what some philosophers of language have called "real definition," that is, the improvement and perfection of underlying concepts, rather than out of the need to explain how a term is being used. As Robinson has said,

> To "analyse" a concept sometimes means to improve it, that is, to substitute for it a very similar concept which is superior.

145

. . . Concepts are improved, other things being equal, when they are altered so as to fit into a system, or into a better or larger system. Thus the famous definition of implication in *Principia Mathematica*, "*p* implies *q* if and only if either *p* is false or *q* is true," while inconvenient in many respects, had the great advantage of building the notion of implication into a large and detailed system of ideas.[1]

The perfection of legal concepts is, of course, one of the principal functions of the legal draftsman. As mentioned earlier, it took OPA more than a year of trial and error to perfect the concept of "processor" for the purposes of price control.[2]

Once a concept is perfected, the draftsman is faced with the problem of naming it. Whether to retain the old name and add a stipulative redefinition of it or substitute a new name is the practical problem of Humpty Dumptyism, discussed above. If the center of gravity of the concept has not been substantially shifted, the former approach seems indicated. Robinson has commented aptly: "Every improvement of a concept carries along with it a stipulative redefinition of the word expressing the concept."[3] On the other hand, if the new concept could not be called by the old name without forcing the reader to make a substantial semantic readjustment, the wiser course is to find a different name. Whether such a name requires a stipulative definition of its own depends on what that name suggests to the mind of the ordinary reader in the particular speech community.

Again we see the legal draftsman operating on two planes.[4] On the conceptual plane, he is the selector or sculptor of concepts appropriate to carrying out his client's purposes. On the verbal plane, he is the selector or sculptor of words. The two planes are as closely interrelated as two adjoining layers of plywood.[5]

This, then, is the proper scope of stipulative definition.

§7.4.   [1]R. Robinson, Definition 180, 184 (1954).
[2]See §2.4 *supra.*
[3]R. Robinson, Definition 187 (1954).
[4]See §1.2 *supra.*
[5]See §2.2 *supra.*

Indeed, if the foregoing analysis is correct, the competent draftsman has occasion to define only sparingly and, when he does, most of his definitions are appropriately stipulative in whole or in part. Not often does he need a purely lexical definition.

§7.5. FORMAL ASPECTS OF DEFINITIONS

A legal definition should show whether it is intended to be exhaustive or partial. In the former case, the draftsman should use the word "means"; in the latter, the word "includes." Although he should never use the ambiguous expression "means and includes," he may follow an exhaustive definition in which he uses the word "means" with a supplementary partial one in which he uses the word "includes."

Example:

In this agreement, "mobile home park" means an area of land on which two or more mobile homes are regularly accommodated with or without charge. It includes any building or other structure, fixture, or equipment that is used or intended to be used in providing that accommodation.

The word "means" is normally followed by a comparable equivalent to what precedes it.[6] Thus in the definition, " 'Settle' with respect to a claim means consider, ascertain, adjust, and dispose of, whether by full or partial allowance or by disallowance," what follows the verb "means" exactly equals what precedes it. If the defined word is a verb, the explanatory equivalent should carry the comparable verb form. If it is a noun, the explanatory equivalent should carry the comparable noun form.

Sometimes it is not feasible to use a comparable equivalent. In this situation, the words "refers to" may often be used.

[6]H. Martin & R. Ohmann, The Logic and Rhetoric of Exposition 19-20 (rev. ed. 1963).

Example:

In this lease, "settle" and "settlement" refer to the consideration, ascertainment, adjustment, determination, and disposition of a claim, whether by full or partial allowance or by disallowance.

Another contingency is illustrated by the following example:

In this indenture:
  (1) "Shall" is used in an imperative sense.
  (2) "May" is used in a permissive sense.

Definitions should be placed where they are the most easily found. A term that is used only in one section should be defined in that section. A term that is used only in one title should be defined at the beginning of the title. A term that is used throughout an instrument should be defined at or near the beginning of the instrument.[7]

§7.6.   KINDS OF DEFINITIONS TO AVOID

In general, the draftsman should avoid every definition that he does not need. In particular, he should avoid definitions of the kinds described below.

§7.6.1.   Definitions that recite the obvious

Years ago, the following section appeared in the regulations of the Atomic Energy Commission:

---

[7]Cf. C. Felsenfeld & A. Siegel, Writing Contracts in Plain English 98 (1981). For readability the authors prefer definitions "in context," but for terms that recur often throughout an instrument this would involve burdensome repetition.

041 *Form.* A form is a piece of paper containing blank spaces, boxes, or lines for the entry of dates, names, descriptive details or other items.

What significant problems of state this definition helped to solve would be hard to imagine. Further comment on the obvious and useless seems unnecessary.

§7.6.2. Humpty Dumpty definitions

For reasons already stated with some vigor,[8] Humpty Dumpty definitions should be assiduously avoided. Although a militant opposition to such atrocities often attracts charges of "fanatic" and "pedantic quibbler," the battle is worth the winning for clarity of communication and for clarity of thought.

§7.6.3. Degenerate definitions

A degenerate definition, according to Robinson, is one that "leaves us bereft of any means of indicating an important distinction that could be indicated by the word in its previous sense."[9] Ben Ray Redman further describes this as "impoverishing the language by using certain words in such a way as to rob them of their special meanings and make them do forced labor as mere synonyms of other words."[10]

Many lawyers have been guilty of implying a degenerate definition of the word "ambiguity" by using it indiscriminately to cover both ambiguity and vagueness.[11] Although "equivocation" is available for taking its place, the word is only infrequently used in this legal context. As a result, it is difficult to discuss the concept of ambiguity (in its classical sense) with the

[8]See §§2.3.3 and 7.3 *supra.*
[9]R. Robinson, Definition 82 (1954).
[10]The Saturday Review, March 2, 1957, p.22.
[11]See §3.5 *supra.*

typical lawyer. He is not used to making the important distinction between ambiguity and vagueness.

During the recodification of the military laws of the United States, top-level officials in the Pentagon made things unnecessarily difficult for the codifiers and complicated the art of communication by insisting that the term "Department," which is the traditional governmental name for the headquarters concept, be defined as covering the entire military establishment, which includes all field installations.[12] The purpose of this insistence was to emphasize the plenary powers of the Secretary of Defense over all elements of the military establishment, a result that could have been easily achieved without resorting to a degenerate definition. This left the headquarters concept bereft of its normal label and required the codifiers to improvise a substitute, somewhat cumbersome, term, "executive part of the Department."[13]

It should take no extended argument to establish the undesirability of definitions that tend to obscure significant distinctions between underlying concepts.

§7.6.4. One-shot definitions

Draftsmen sometimes define a word in a legal instrument and then use it only once. Although this is not likely to confuse, it introduces a circumlocution that wastes the draftsman's time as well as the reader's.[14] Here is an example, slightly condensed:

> Each judge shall be paid all necessary traveling expenses and all reasonable maintenance expenses while attending court or transacting official business at a place other than his official station.

---

[12]10 U.S.C. §101(5) (1958).

[13]*Id.* §101(6).

[14]"Humpty Dumpty stipulates a new meaning and uses it once only. He is like the man who, wishing to say that the sky is overcast, says instead: 'By "soda" I shall mean that the sky is overcast. Soda.' He uses eleven words to say what four would say better, and these four are included in his eleven." R. Robinson, Definition 80 (1954).

The official station of such judges for this purpose shall be the District of Columbia.

What would be lost by restating this provision as follows?

Each judge shall be paid all necessary traveling expenses and all reasonable maintenance expenses while attending court, or transacting official business, outside the District of Columbia.

§7.6.5. Stuffed definitions

Draftsmen often abuse definitions by stuffing them with substantive rules that it would be more appropriate to state elsewhere. An example appeared in the Civil Air Regulations of the Federal Aviation Agency:

A periodic inspection is an inspection of an aircraft required each 12 calendar months and is a complete airworthiness inspection of such aircraft and its various components and systems in accordance with procedures prescribed by the Administrator.[15]

Such a provision should be divided into a definition ("The term 'periodic inspection' means an inspection made at least once during each 12-month period") and a substantive requirement ("Each periodic inspection shall completely cover the airworthiness of the aircraft and its components and shall be made in accordance with procedures prescribed by the Administrator").

A stuffed definition is sometimes developed in connection with formulas and computations. It takes the form of a definition of a complicated technical term, specially created and usually without previous connotations. The temptation here is to make a complicated problem seem simpler than it is. The effect is heightened by putting the new definition with other definitions at the beginning of the instrument. This, unfortunately, not only

[15]14 C.F.R. §43.70 (rev. Jan. 1, 1962).

does not solve the basic problem but creates two additional difficulties, one of arrangement and the other of clarity. With an essential part of the substantive rule placed elsewhere, it is correspondingly harder to fit together the two parts of an integrated idea. Furthermore, it may make the basic rule, taken by itself, unclear or deceptively simple. Even if the definition is placed where the term is used, it is at best circuitous, because the same result is reached more directly by stating the result intended or by simply referring to the related provision (e.g., "as computed under section 16").

A good working test of whether a substantive rule and its accompanying definitions are adequately stated is whether the reader can get a generally accurate and complete impression of the substantive rule without referring to the pertinent definitions. If he cannot, the chances are that the draftsman has either used words in unnatural senses or put too much of the substantive rule in the definition.

Stuffed definitions not only impair clarity and good arrangement but may produce unintended results. For example, a recently proposed zoning ordinance included the following definition:

> "Parking space" means a space, no smaller than 9 feet by 20 feet, for the off-street parking of one motor vehicle.

This definition looked innocent enough until the reader examined some of the basic provisions. For example, one provision of the proposed ordinance forbade the location of parking spaces in front yards in some residential or business districts. Under this definition, an owner might have safely located a 9-by-19-foot parking space in his front yard, because not being within the definition of "parking space," it would have fallen outside the prohibition. On redraft, the definition ("The term 'parking space' means a space for the off-street parking of one motor vehicle") was stated separately from the substantive requirement ("No parking space may be less than 9 feet by 20 feet"). Stuffed definitions, therefore, are not only inartistic but dangerous.

VIII

General Factors Affecting Clarity and Readability; Simplification

§8.1. GENERAL PROBLEM OF CLARITY AND READABILITY; SIMPLIFICATION

During the early stages of writing the skillful draftsman still concentrates on substance and arrangement. There are substantive errors to be corrected. Some of the specific pieces do not fit. During this period he pays only as much attention to the principles of form and style as is consistent with concentrating on the more basic elements of his draft.

Unfortunately, the draftsman does not always have a free hand. For example, when preparing an amendment to an existing instrument, he must adapt his approach to the necessity of meshing the new with the old. In varying degrees this may circumscribe his choice of arrangement, terms, and style. But, even within these limitations, there is usually room for the play of sound drafting principles. Paramount among them are complete consistency of expression, logical arrangement, and close adherence to accepted usage.[1]

Almost equally important to clarity and simplicity is the economy of expression involved in achieving the greatest degree of generality consistent with the substance of the ideas to be expressed. This is substantially the same as the notion that the good draftsman always looks for the lowest common denom-

§8.1. [1] See §§2.3 and 6.14 *supra.*

inator.[2] Thus, a reference to a broad class is easier to understand than a listing of its constituent subclasses.

In the treatment of specific language, simplification is often a matter of segmenting language on the basis of recurrent partial similarities, an operation similar to factoring in mathematics. Simple examples are the use of a defined legislative nickname to avoid burdensome repetition ("In this policy, the term 'Company' means the Equitable Life Assurance Society of America") and the practice of including in the introductory language of a tabulation, so far as substance permits, all the information that applies to each item listed in the tabulation.[3]

The fact is that, beyond their substantive impact, clarity of ideas and clarity of organization make the intended message much more accessible. Thus, James P. Johnson's insight into the value of searching for the lowest common denominator, previously mentioned as a useful conceptualization device,[4] can here be seen as having the beneficial side effect of simplifying the end product, not only substantively but verbally.

Indeed, simplification can sometimes be achieved *only* by reconceptualization and architectural reform. An extraordinary example appeared in the New York County Lawyers Association House and Library Rules, which, without relying on big words, legalisms, or other kinds of gobbledygook, achieved this magnificent enigma:

> The Office of the Association shall be open on weekdays, other than Saturdays and holidays, from 9 A.M. to 5 P.M. The building of the Association and its library and reading rooms shall be open from 9 A.M. to 10 P.M. on weekdays, other than on Saturdays; and on Saturdays the library shall be open from 9 A.M. to 6 P.M.; excepting that on weekdays in July and August it shall close at 6 P.M. with the exception of Wednesday when it shall be open until 10 P.M. and be closed on Saturdays; and it shall be closed entirely on all Sundays and holidays, excepting Columbus Day, Lincoln's Birthday, Veteran's Day and Election Day, other

[2]See §2.4 *supra.*
[3]See §§7.3 and 6.3 *supra,* respectively.
[4]See §2.4 *supra.*

than presidential elections, when it shall be open from 9 A.M. to 6 P.M., and on Christmas Eve and New Year's Eve it shall close at 4 P.M.

Here there are only two significant ways to improve clarity and readability: Improve the conceptualization and improve the architecture.[5]

After exploiting these more basic approaches, the draftsman tries to give his conclusions the clearest and most readable form, leaving the fewest possible language barriers between himself and his audience. In the final stage of writing the draftsman thus shifts his emphasis mainly to style and form, keeping always in mind that, properly followed, these principles will inevitably reveal more fundamental inadequacies. The shift is never abrupt, and there is never a time when he is not trying to improve basic concepts and the underlying structure. The main benefit will be greater general clarity. This will come, not from the isolated application of a single principle, but as the cumulative reward for persistence in complying with all the principles in the many, and individually insignificant, places where they apply.

[5]Most of the difficulties involve the library. To make them more manageable, it is useful to deal with the other facilities separately. The library rules can then be handled as a separate package. This approach is functionally sound, because the typical reader is likely to be interested in only one of the four facilities at a time. It also makes it easier for draftsman and reader alike to cope with the complexities of the library schedule.

In conceptualizing the latter, the draftsman may want to break the year into two main segments, September–June and July–August, and cluster the several rules for the former by similarity of schedule, stating the results in descending order of incidence of use. But he will probably find it more helpful simply to take, as his main basis of division, the difference between the general and the specific, stating the most general library schedule first and then the more specific ones, clustered on the basis of shared schedules for special periods or days taken in descending order of incidence, thus placing the 9-to-4 schedule for December 24 and 31 at the end. Putting the results in tabular form helps. (The reader may find this an enlightening exercise!)

In one of my drafting classes, two students conspired to take the final step in simplification by turning in as their joint effort a large card on which "OPEN" appeared on one side and "CLOSED" on the other. This earned hearty applause.

§8.1.   General Factors Affecting Readability: Simplification

Besides these broad guides there are many specific aids to clarity. Some of the more important ones are considered in this chapter; others are considered in chapter 9. But before we plunge into detail, we may benefit from a historical perspective.

§8.2.   A BIT OF HISTORY[1]

Although it is hard to say when the complaints against "legal" language began, outrage is hardly new. Legal prolixity came under fire as early as 1566.[2] Thomas Jefferson took up the cudgel in 1778.[3] Jeremy Bentham fumed about legislative long-windedness early in the nineteenth century.[4] Fred Rodell, writing in 1939, said, "Almost all legal sentences . . . have a way of reading as though they had been translated from the German by someone with a rather meager knowledge of English."[5] Two years later an Arizona official observed that statutes were being spoken of as "disgraceful, unworkmanlike, defective, unintelligible, abounding in errors, ill-penned, inadequate, loosely-worded, depraved in style, [full of] peculiar absurdities, mischievous, baneful in influence, . . . confusing, obscure, . . . overbulky, redundant, entangled, unsteady, disorderly, complex, to say nothing of being 'uncognoscible.' "[6]

The modern push for clear and readable legal instruments began in the early 1940s, following Maury Maverick's coinage of "gobbledygook" and the Office of Price Administration's first

§8.2.   [1]In §§8.2 through 8.9, I have drawn heavily from my paper, Should Plain English Be Legislated?, in Plain English in a Complex Society (The Poynter Society, Indiana Univ. 1980), at 18.

[2]*Milward v. Welden,* 21 Eng. Rep. 138 (Ch. 1566). See also Chancery Ordinance 55, 15 The Works of Francis Bacon 362 (Spedding, Ellis, and Heath eds. 1864); Edward Coke, 2 Coke Rep. xii–xiii (new ed. 1826).

[3]2 The papers of Thomas Jefferson 230 (Boyd ed. 1950). See also MLD 256.

[4]3 The Works of Jeremy Bentham 239-253 (Bowring ed. 1838-1843); 7 *id.* 280-283.

[5]F. Rodell, Woe Unto You, Lawyers! 185 (1939).

[6]Indictment of the Form of Laws, Arizona Newsletter No. 15 (January 1941), 7, 9.

attempts to impose price controls at the beginning of World War II. Finding that America's small businessmen could not understand its regulations without the intervention of lawyers, OPA engaged Professor David F. Cavers of the Harvard Law School and Rudolf Flesch to help the agency communicate more effectively with the people whose prices it regulated.

From OPA's experience came a body of expertise useful in simplifying regulations and statutes.[7] This was improved during the Pentagon's ten-year post-World War II recodification of the nation's military laws[8] and later during the Federal Aviation Agency's recodification, in the early 1960s, of the vast accumulation of regulations relating to aviation. Indeed, this expertise, since refined and extended to private legal instruments, remains useful even today.

Despite these developments, the public visibility of the movement to simplify faded with the end of the war pressures that supported price control. The resulting public passivity went undisturbed, even by the Korean and Vietnamese wars, until the explosion of the consumer movement, which in the late 1960s and early 1970s turned its attention to instruments that the typical consumers of goods and services are being persuaded to accept: insurance policies, product warranties, and credit documents. At the same time, many small, relatively unsophisticated businessmen were being subjected to a barrage of detailed regulations from agencies such as the Occupational Safety and Health Administration and the Environmental Protection Agency. As a result, public pressure to simplify legal instruments became even greater than it was during World War II.

For many years, private legal instruments have increasingly been prepared by large, sophisticated, and economically powerful organizations for use in transactions with unsophisticated

---

[7]See, e.g., Cavers, The Simplification of Government Regulations, 8 Fed. B.J. 339 (1949); Conard, New Ways to Write Laws, 56 Yale L.J. 458 (1947); Dickerson, FPR No. 1: An Experiment in Standardized and Prefabricated Law, 13 U. of Chi. L. Rev. 90 (1945).

[8]See A Manual for Drafting Federal Legislation, 11 Fed. B.J. 238 (1951) (authorship suppressed), later expanded into R. Dickerson, Legislative Drafting (1954).

and economically weak individuals, the kinds of individuals that the consumer movement is designed to protect. The substantive aspects of this were touched on earlier in our consideration of "unconscionability."[9] These people need to be protected against instruments that are unnecessarily complicated or hard to read.

The state of the drafting art has long made it possible to write simpler legal instruments but, until the recent resurgence of the consumer movement and the flood of government regulations affecting small businessmen, the legal ground was uncongenial to widespread germination.

§8.3.   MANDATING PLAIN ENGLISH: FIRST EFFORTS

The most dramatic development in the drive to simplify the language of private legal instruments came with the emergence of the "plain English" movement. The first visible glimmerings came in 1972 or 1973, when Pennsylvania's Insurance Commissioner, Walter Dennenberg, induced Blue Cross/Blue Shield to simplify its customer agreements; in 1974, when Nationwide Mutual Insurance Co. and Sentry Life Insurance Co. introduced simplified automobile insurance policies; and in 1975, when Citibank and First National Bank of Boston introduced simplified consumer loan agreements.[1] The first week in February 1977 saw the introduction of the Sullivan bill in New York, which became law the following year,[2] and President Carter's television "fireside chat" (complete with rocking chair and cardigan sweater), which culminated in an executive order that we will examine later.[3]

The first efforts to legislate "plain language" show widely differing approaches. New York's Sullivan law, brainchild of a

[9]See §2.1 *supra.*
§8.3.   [1]Hathaway, An Overview of the Plain English Movement for Lawyers, 62 Mich. B.J. 945, 946 (1983).
[2]N.Y. Gen. Oblig. Law §5-702 (1977, 1979).
[3]See §8.11 *infra.*

Citicorp lawyer, Duncan A. MacDonald, protects "consumer" instruments, which are defined as residential leases or contracts for money, property, or services for "personal, family, or household purposes" involving $50,000 or less.[4] The mandated standard is "plain language," defined as language "written in a clear and coherent manner using words with common and everyday meanings," and "[a]ppropriately divided and captioned." In case of noncompliance, the consumer is entitled to actual damages and a civil penalty of $50, but not attorneys' fees or court costs. Defenses include good faith and full performance. The Attorney General may bring an action for an injunction or restitution. Other states have followed suit.

Because it applies only to insurance policies. Massachusetts's plain language law[5] follows a different legislative tradition. There is no money limit and the standards require (1) scoring at least 50 on the Flesch (or equivalent) readability test, applied according to detailed statutory instructions, and (2) meeting typeface standards, avoiding undue prominence of particular provisions, supplying a table of contents or subject index, maintaining appropriate margins and ink-to-paper contrast, and providing an organization and summary "conducive to understandability." Compliance is required only to obtain clearance from the insurance commissioner.

Connecticut's law[6] requires "plain language" for the same general kinds of consumer contracts as New York's, but only those involving up to $25,000. Again, the standard is "plain language," except that it is tied to two alternative sets of supple-

---

[4]For some of the background here, see MLD 256-259. When I asked MacDonald to verify the authorship of the Sullivan law, he replied, by letter of May 10, 1985, "I wrote it all myself, warts and all. . . . Morever, if you really want to trace the origins of the recent plain language movement, you need only look to yourself. It started in your classroom at I.U. back in 1966. Certainly your effect on me got the ball rolling at Citicorp." The sponsor of the bill was Assemblyman Peter M. Sullivan.

[5]Mass. Ann. Laws §175:2B (1977, 1979). This law has been a model for other states that have "plain English" laws peculiar to insurance. For a recent list, see Hathaway, An Overview of the Plain English Movement for Lawyers, 62 Mich. B.J. 945, 947 (1983).

[6]Conn. Gen. Stat. §42-151 through 158 (1979).

mentary standards. The first has nine criteria such as sentence length, typography, verb forms, and captions. The second has eleven criteria such as words-per-sentence, syllables-per-word, length of paragraphs, and space between paragraphs. There are elaborate instructions for counting words and determining what is a "sentence" or "syllable." Offended consumers may recover a civil penalty of $100 plus attorneys' fees. Defenses include good faith, preparation of the contract by the consumer, attendance by plaintiff's attorney at its signing, full performance, and the expiration of six years.

Maine's plain language consumer loan law[7] covers "loans made to a consumer by a supervised lender for personal, family or household purposes, if the debt is payable in instalments or a finance charge is made," unless the amount involved exceeds $100,000. Each such consumer loan contract must be in "plain language," defined (as in New York's Sullivan law) as "written in a clear and coherent manner using words with common and everyday meanings" and "[a]ppropriately divided and captioned by its various sections." Noncompliance is subject to legal action by the superintendent of the Bureau of Consumer Protection. On the other hand, a supervised lender may gain immunity from suit by securing the Bureau's certificate of compliance.

West Virginia's plain language law,[8] which applies to consumer agreements for the rental of residential space or the sale of goods or services, follows the Sullivan law formulation of appropriate language and supplements it with type size and ink-to-paper contrast requirements. These standards are enforceable by a consumer action to reform the agreement. Language otherwise authorized by law is exempt.

Hawaii's law[9] follows the general Sullivan law pattern but with a monetary limit that is reduced and made inapplicable to residential leases and an extended list of exemptions.

Minnesota's "Plain Language Contract Act"[10] adopts the Sullivan law prescription for the language usable in consumer

[7]Me. Rev. Stat. Ann. §§1121 through 1126 (1979).
[8]W. Va. Code §46A-6-109 (1981). See also 36-29-1 *et seq.*
[9]Haw. Rev. Stat. tit. 26 §487A-1 (1981).
[10]Minn. Stat. Ann. §325G 29 through 36 (1981, 1983).

contracts involving sales of service or personal property, pledges of personal property, and residential leases for not more than three years. It provides for the judicial reformation (or limiting) of provisions that confuse the consumer enough to risk "financial detriment." It authorizes judicial orders where needed to avoid unjust enrichment. Civil penalties apply, except where the defendant made "a good faith and reasonable effort" to comply. Actual damages are recoverable, but only if the violation substantially confused the consumer regarding his position under the contract. Certification of the contract form by the attorney general absolves the seller, creditor, or lessor.

The New Jersey law[11] requires that six kinds of consumer contracts be written "in a simple, clear, understandable and easily readable way." This is a third kind of formulation. Language acceptable under any other law is excepted. Also excepted are provisions supplied by the consumer. Technical terms are not necessarily fatal. As a partial guide to compliance, the law lists six kinds of defects (such as double negatives, bad cross referencing, and over-long sentences) that make for hard-to-read instruments. The statute favors a table of contents for contracts of more than 3000 words and the setting of exceptions in at least 10-point type. This law also provides for protective certification by the attorney general (commissioner of insurance in the case of insurance policies). There are numerical limitations on punitive damages and attorneys' fees in class action. Full performance and good faith are defenses in civil actions. The statute also provides for injunctive relief.

The federal government has set a few, very general standards of clarity and readability.[12] Under the Consumer Product Warranty Act,[13] for example, the Federal Trade Commission has, by regulation,[14] required that written consumer product warranties "clearly and conspicuously disclose" specified items

[11]N.J. Stat. Ann. §56:12-1 through 12-18 (1980, 1982).
[12]See Saferstein & Richie, Plain Language in Consumer Contracts — An Overview of Federal Regulations, in Drafting Documents in Plain Language 1981 at 61 (Practising Law Institute, Commercial Law and Practice Course Handbook Series No. 254, 1981); Hathaway, *supra* note 5 at 947.
[13]15 U.S.C. §§2301 *et seq.*
[14]16 C.F.R. 701.3.

of information "in simple and readily understood language."
The Truth in Lending Act[15] and its supplementary Regulation
Z[16] require that the disclosures required by that Act be made
"clearly and conspicuously." Neither of these examples has
much to offer in the present context. A more useful guideline
appears in the Employee Retirement Income Security Program:
"The summary plan shall be written in a manner calculated to
be understood by the average plan participant."[17]

§8.4.   STATING THE PROBLEM

What is the best way to solve the problem of formal clarity and
readability? First, we have to understand it. This involves,
among other things, knowing how lawyers got into this mess.
The traditional explanation has been that every discipline needs
its own technical terms, some of which may be meaningless to
outsiders. Also, the law often deals with matters that are inherently complicated owing to an irreducible minimum of substantive considerations that no amount of simplification can
remove.[1] Both statements are true. It is also true that many legal
terms have perfectly adequate "plain English" equivalents and
some matters need not be as complicated as they at first seem.
Here, a good case for simplification can be made.

[15]15 U.S.C. §1667a ("in a clear and conspicuous manner"). §1604(b)
requires the Federal Reserve Board to "publish model disclosure forms and
clauses for common transactions to facilitate compliance with the disclosure
requirements . . . and to aid the borrower or lessee in understanding the
transaction by utilizing readily understandable language to simplify the technical language of the disclosure."

[16]12 C.F.R. §226.5(a) ("clearly and conspicuously").

[17]29 U.S.C. §1022(a)(1).

§8.4.   [1]See, e.g., military retirement statute, in text for §6.3, note 6, *supra.*
"The demand for simple legal documents cannot be satisfied if the ideas which
have to be expressed are complex." E. Piesse, The Elements of Drafting 17
(5th ed. Aitken 1958). "We are also told that simple language should be used,
so that the layman can understand the bill; but it is unfortunately true that
many of our modern statutes, dealing as they do with intricate and complex
social phenomena and attempting to fit these phenomena into existing law,
itself intricate and complex, require for their understanding a knowledge
which the ordinary layman cannot have." Beaman, Bill Drafting, 7 L. Lib. J.
64 (1914).

Unfortunately, drafting tradition retains the heavy flavor of now-extinct conditions that prevailed for a long period beginning in 1487, when drafting by the judiciary ended. According to William Craies, "English superseded Latin and Norman French, and Parliament appears to have handed over the drafting of statutes to conveyancers."[2] Craies attributes the wordiness of statutes and deeds of conveyance, which has prevailed long enough to contaminate legal drafting as a whole, to the invention of printing and to the precaution of using strings of synonyms.[3]

The practice of using strings of synonyms may well have started with the use of couplets. Couplets such as "devise and bequeath" and "fit and proper" have been said to date from the time when the use of a word from the native tongue along with one from Norman French, Old Norse, Celtic, or Latin made the meaning easier to understand.[4] Couplets of Old English words such as "have and hold" have been tentatively explained by the "uncertainty as to which of several English words accurately rendered a Latin or Norman French law term."[5] This uncertainty, incidentally, was undoubtedly inflated by the practice of paying for the preparation of legal documents according to length.[6]

> Sometimes for clarity, sometimes for emphasis, and sometimes in keeping with the bilingual fashion of the day . . . , they joined synonyms. And what they did not join their successors did.[7]

But, so long as courts remained unfriendly to legislative changes in the common law or adoption of extreme penalties, a draftsman had good reason to sprinkle his text with synonyms to guide judges who responded only to special incantations. Fortunately, this need has, for the most part, disappeared.

[2]W. Craies, Statute Law 22 (7th ed. Edgar 1971).
[3]*Id.*
[4]C. Jones, Statute Law Making in the United States 123 (1912).
[5]Craies, *supra* note 2 at 22 n.11.
[6]D. Mellinkoff, The Language of the Law 190 (1963).
[7]*Id.* at 121.

Another factor, according to David Mellinkoff, was the capability of the typical draftsman. Long after modern English became the language of the law, the bulk of routine private instruments were drafted not by the best-educated lawyers but by persons, such as court clerks and scriveners, who were hardly distinguishable from laymen.[8] Even recognizing that most legal instruments are still drafted by inadequately trained lawyers (and many laymen), none of these factors is a compelling reason for perpetuating the drafting idiosyncrasies of the past.

Legislative gobbledygook apparently reached its peak in the eighteenth century,[9] a peak so high that even the massive statutory reforms that Bentham generated early in the nineteenth century[10] have not succeeded in leveling it.

As a consequence, lawyers have long been enmeshed in an accumulation of outworn forms that they have been reluctant to revise if the forms have been adjudicated in court, and unable to revise if they do not understand them, which is often the case. A thorough purging of offending forms would be a happy event.

But do we need a law?

§8.5.   THE CASE FOR A STATUTE

The idea of legislating the specifics of good writing is, for professional draftsmen, highly repugnant and not merely because most of the people who have been writing these laws have failed to get an adequate handle on the principles of clear communication. It is desirable not to tie the hands of draftsmen who need elbow room.

A normal first reaction to the Sullivan law was that, while a minor political miracle, it was naive, inadequately framed,

[8]*Id.* at 195.

[9]"A redundancy of language that would now be thought almost beyond endurance became common, and it has taken generations to prune it." Piesse, *supra* note 1 at 6.

[10]C. Ilbert, The Mechanics of Law Making 96 (1914); Mellinkoff, *supra* note 6 at 261-266.

and unenforceable.[1] Many members of the bar still think so. But they may be missing the main point. Despite its weaknesses, it dramatically symbolizes the current public distaste for ineptly crafted laws, regulations, and consumer instruments, and the failure of the legal profession to keep abreast of modern planning needs. Although the bar is beginning to wake up (along with some law schools), the pace has until recently been glacial.

The main value of the plain English laws appears to be symbolic. Although New York's Sullivan law is probably in any serious sense unenforceable because of its "good faith"[2] defense (most bad draftsmen operate in good faith), the results that it seems to have helped to produce in that state are impressive.[3] Decently readable insurance policies and consumer warranties are now common.

To accelerate this trend, the organized bar (and indirectly the law schools) needs a similar legislative jolt in other states, which can be delivered without seriously compromising the principles of good draftsmanship. Because a highly developed (but too often overlooked) expertise for simplifying legal instruments already exists, it is time that it be put to more effective use.

And so, a modest case can be made for a law to help the legal profession overcome its present, partly justifiable inertia.[4] Without it, the organized bar is unlikely to initiate effective action to improve the clarity and readability of legal instruments.

---

§8.5.   [1]See e.g., Friedman, The "Plain English" Law, Amended but Not Improved, N.Y.L.J., June 22, 1978, pp.1, 3 (MLD 256-259).

[2]This is so even though this exception probably does not extend to suits for actual damages, which are of course hard to prove.

[3]In view of the dearth of litigation, it is impossible to accurately trace the causal nexus here.

[4]"It would be better that legal writers mend their ways on their own; they can. But without the goad of some legislation, they won't. They need some encouragement, and not only on 'consumer' agreements. The 'plain language' movement may speed the disposal of much of the trash in the language of the law." D. Mellinkoff, Legal Writing: Sense and Nonsense 218 (1981).

§8.6.   SOME RESERVATIONS

One problem is that the "plain English" ideal, if not carefully focused, can be seriously off the mark. "Plain English" is in many legal contexts anything but plain. Besides, the concept suggests that there is an ideal way to say things that will fit all legal audiences.

Because legal audiences differ widely, the draftsman should be permitted to adjust his focus accordingly. On the other hand, no great harm is involved if such a law focuses solely on professionals who deal with unsophisticated consumers, where mandating a higher level of understandability makes sense. It makes less sense if the effort is spread over a wider base within which audiences differ materially.

A plain language bill recently proposed in the District of Columbia included governmental regulations, which are addressed for the most part to varying audiences. In addressing such heterogeneity, it is hard, if not impossible, to provide other than a broad statement of ultimate objectives and general standards common to all legal drafting, which are voluminous enough to warrant remaining in textbooks. For symbolic purposes, it is questionable whether it is worth the effort. A better approach is to require agencies with rule-making power to operate with professionally trained draftsmen. Legal education, too, needs beefing up.[1]

Judge Harold Leventhal's observation that simplifying private instruments would make it harder to charge what they are worth[2] is relevant but not persuasive. His explanation too readily becomes an excuse for the status quo, which is deplorable. The answer is that in most cases the matter can be handled by educating the client, preferably in advance, about what is involved.[3] This will head off most of the unpleasant surprises.

Another commentator has been concerned (orally) lest the

§8.6.   [1]See appendix F.
[2]R. Dickerson (ed.), Professionalizing Legislative Drafting — The Federal Experience 27 (1973).
[3]Kirk, Legal Drafting: How Should a Document Begin?, 3 Tex. Tech. L. Rev. 233, 247 n.133 (1972).

simplification movement "sacrifice the language of the law," pointing out that words have many different meanings and that they carry many nuances and connotations. Fortunately, simplification need not founder on those truths. Homonyms create little trouble, because they involve multiple meanings that in normal context sort themselves out automatically.

Nor is ambiguity our most serious problem. First of all, most ambiguities are syntactic rather than semantic. The former can be resolved by sharpening the focus of modification; the latter either by supplying needed context or by including a definition showing which competing alternative is being used.

Problems of vagueness are harder to handle. But vagueness is not always bad; indeed, it is a virtue when, within the sweep of semantic leeway, the client wants to delegate line-drawing authority to the courts or an administrator. The problem is not to avoid vagueness, but to avoid too much or too little.[4]

§8.7. TERMS OF ART

Another basis for skepticism has been the generally acknowledged necessity of honoring legal "terms of art." This is a problem for a legal term only if there is no usable replacement.

What is a legal "term of art"? Mellinkoff says that it is a "technical word with a specific meaning."[1] A technical meaning, of course, is likely to be unfamiliar to the general public. But the determining factor, he says, is "specificity," which he equates with "precision."

But if unique aptness is not the determining factor, where is the problem? If Mellinkoff is right, the concept of "term of art" is here irrelevant. Semantic precision is not the ultimate, or even main, goal in drafting and its presence does not guarantee suitability. The appropriate measure of aptness is, rather, the draftsman's substantive mission, for which generality and even

---

[4]See §3.5 *supra.*
§8.7. [1]D. Mellinkoff, The Language of the Law 16 (1963); Legal Writing — Sense and Nonsense 7 (1981).

vagueness are often preferable. The Sherman Act is the classic example.

Mellinkoff's definition of "term of art" may look like a paraphrase of the definition in Webster's Third International Dictionary ("a word or phrase having a specific signification in a particular . . . department of knowledge"), but it is not. Because "specific" is closer to "special" than to "precision" and "signification" refers, not to the concept, but to the relation between it and its technical name, the gist of "term of art" would seem to be its uniqueness for practical use.

Ironically, Mellinkoff supports this view of semantic precision by many of his own examples. "Laches," "comparative negligence," "merchantable," "tort," and "stare decisis," which he lists as legitimate "terms of art," are all highly general and highly vague.[2] Precision is not the problem. The problem is irreplaceability: To what extent is the draftsman stuck with technical legal terms that are unfamiliar to the general public? Mellinkoff associates terms of art with irreplaceability in his questionable contention that the greater its precision ("sharpness") the greater the chance that a term "has no synonym in ordinary English."[3] Many of his nonspecific terms of art likewise have no equivalent in plain English. The importance of irreplaceability is hard to avoid.

What we are really concerned with in legal drafting is otherwise apt, but generally unfamiliar, language for which no familiar language is a suitable substitute. This may mean suitable in law or suitable in fact. As an example of the former, the law might permit only one way of expressing an idea. A classic example is *D'Arundel's Case*,[4] which held that if a person wanted to convey land in fee simple, he had to say "to A and his heirs." No substitute, no matter how clearly synonymous, would do.

A modern counterpart is section 3-104(1)(d) of the Uniform Commercial Code, which provides that to be negotiable,

[2]D. Mellinkoff, The Language of the Law 17 (1963); Legal Writing — Sense and Nonsense 203, 228 (1981).
[3]D. Mellinkoff, Legal Writing — Sense and Nonsense 108 (1981).
[4]Bracton's Notebook, case no. 1054 (1225).

a note must "be payable to order[5] or to bearer." This means that it must say "order" or "bearer." Although modern law contains little of this kind of mandated legal suitability, the draftsman must remain alert to the danger.

What about factual suitability? Here, we are talking about a term that refers to a body of law and for which there is no usable substitute with equivalent legal connotations. Examples are "surrender" (of a lease), "merchantable," "unconscionable," and "venue." Until a suitable synonym appears, there is no practicable alternative to using the accepted term or perhaps creating equivalence by express definition. Example: "In this policy, the term 'legal cause' means proximate cause." Here, it is safe to use "legal cause" throughout the rest of the instrument without losing the benefit of the established legal connotations of "proximate cause." Unfortunately, in this instance, the substituted term would not be very helpful. In many cases, the only other acceptable alternative is a supplementary explanation[6] or referral to a lawyer.

In any event, the outer limits of "term of art" need not concern us. Indeed, it is unnecessary even to refer to the concept. The important thing is that the instances in which the draftsman has no legal or practicable choice as to how something may be effectively stated are few enough to leave him considerable opportunity to simplify or otherwise improve the language of legal documents. As for the unavoidable terms, he always has the option of adding explanatory material if he believes that it would be helpful and not unduly cumbersome. Experience with the Securities Act of 1933 and the recent Truth in Lending Act shows that the danger of "information overload" is a real one.[7]

In any event, technical terms are not the main source of trouble. As Janice Redish has pointed out, "The complexity of

[5]See C. Felsenfeld & A. Siegel, Writing Contracts in Plain English 40-43 (1981).

[6]Mellinkoff, *supra* note 3 at 83.

[7]C. Felsenfeld & A. Siegel, Writing Contracts in Plain English 40-43 (1981).

the sentence structure is a much greater barrier to understanding . . . than the technical vocabulary."[8]

§8.8.   SUBSTANTIVE CONCESSIONS TO CLARITY AND READABILITY

On the preeminence of substance over clarity and readability, Professor Frank P. Grad has spoken as follows:

> Many problems that need legislative resolution are complex and difficult. To pretend that they are susceptible of "plain" statement is as misleading as to assert that such problems are susceptible to simple, easy solution. We need complex language to state complex problems of law or fact. A "plain," simple statement of issues does not itself simplify them — on the contrary, such a simple statement may actually mislead. I do not defend complicated, obfuscatory legal language. I simply assert that here, too, form follows function. The language of drafts of legislation should address itself to the problem to be resolved. If complex problems require complex language for their resolution, so be it.[1]

Grad makes a solid point here, but he is not necessarily trying to refute the case for workable, understandable language in documents pitched largely at audiences unfamiliar with legal or other relevant technical language, even though beyond such documents the notion of some kind of universal language of clarity and readability is highly unrealistic. In any event, as Elmer A. Driedger has pointed out, the substantively unsophisticated reader who is confronted with a substantively and un-

[8]Redish, Drafting Simplified Legal Documents: Basic Principles and Their Application, in Drafting Documents in Plain Language 121, 126 (Practising Law Institute, Commercial Law and Practice Course Handbook Series No. 203, 1979).

§8.8.   [1]Grad, Legislative Drafting as Legal Problem Solving — Form Follows Function, in Drafting Documents in Plain English 481, 489 (Practising Law Institute, Commercial Law and Practice Course Handbook Series No. 203, 1979) (MLD 277).

avoidably sophisticated legal document will probably rely on a simpler, collateral explanation.[2]

Once substance jells, clarity and readability must normally yield to it. On the other hand, Felsenfeld and Siegel make a good case for an exception for consumer documents: It may be desirable to sacrifice substantive points that are not likely to cause significant trouble, if omitting them will substantially improve clarity and readability and thus relations with the consuming public. They suggest this rule of thumb: "For commercial agreements, if a problem can be foreseen, draft for it. For consumer agreements, unless a problem seems likely, consider dropping it."[3] There can be a useful trade-off here, but the client calls the shots.

With this reservation, simplification is spurious whenever it reaches its goal by significantly compromising substance. The aborted proposed Uniform Age of Majority Act is a good example of how a simplistic solution to a complicated problem almost inevitably produces an undesirably complicated result.[4]

Felsenfeld and Siegel's exception must not be confused with the recurrent recommendations that American legislators curb their passion for detail and emulate the European countries that have enacted extensive codes of laws composed for the most part of general legal rules. Naturally, such codes tend to be more readable and thus less troublesome to "plain English" enthusiasts. Their main proponents, however, have been moved by other considerations, such as the desirability of greater flexibility to deal with the chronic problem of legislative obsolescence.[5] There is much to be said for these recommendations.

There are also reasons for doubt. First of all, most of the detail that the general-principle approach avoids must still be

[2]Driedger, Public Administration and Legislation, 1 Canadian Pub. Admin. 14, 19 (1958) (MLD 278).

[3]C. Felsenfeld & A. Siegel, Writing Contracts in Plain English 57 (1981).

[4]For the first tentative draft and commenting letter, see MLD 272-277.

[5]See, e.g., Note, Intent, Clear Statements, and the Common Law: Statutory Interpretation in the Supreme Court, 95 Harv. L. Rev. 822 (1982). See also W. Dale, Legislative Drafting — A New Approach 335 (1977).

dealt with, either by the delegated legislation of a rule-making administrative agency, in which the problem of complexity is simply shifted from statute form to regulation form (for which the problems of drafting remain the same), or by leaving supplementation to the courts, as in the Sherman Act.

How the former alternative could be more conducive to the generation of "plain English" would be hard to explain, because every statutory fiasco has been more than matched by regulatory ones. Nor is delegation to the courts an adequate alternative. Not only are courts already overburdened, but they are not noted for their ability, restricted as they are to sporadic action, to integrate a vast amount of governmental detail.

Overriding even these considerations are the political tensions among the three branches of government that currently make such speculations purely academic, especially for the legislative draftsman. While testifying before the Renton Committee in London some years ago, I was asked what I thought about the general-principle approach. I replied that for statutes the problem was mainly political rather than one of draftsmanship and thus one over which the draftsman had little control.

Like any respectable pedagogue, I would prefer to formulate general doctrine than become entangled in a web of legislative detail. But we have to be realistic. Is it not fatuous in today's world to expect that a legislature that trusts neither the executive branch nor the judicial branch will confine itself to general principles? Many of the statutes that begin life in general form eventually sprout exceptions and qualifications. This pessimistic assessment extends also to regulations.[6]

---

[6]"The automatic gravitational tendency of a regulatory system is not toward simplicity, but toward greater complexity. [One reason is that] [t]hose aspects of the system which do not work well always invite further elaboration to correct the deficiencies. As these in turn show deficiencies, they can also be further elaborated until a multi-layered cheesecloth is created with exceptions, exception[s] to the exceptions, and so on." Givens, The New York "Plain Language" Law, in Drafting Documents in Plain Language 1981, 9, 31 (Practising Law Institute, Commercial Law and Practice Course Handbook Series No. 254, 1981).

§8.9.   READABILITY FORMULAS

Some "plain English" statutes (usually those relating to insurance policies) measure readability by readability formulas, especially that developed by Rudolf Flesch. Ironically, these statutes have provoked attacks on readability formulas generally.[1] Here, we should distinguish between the use of these formulas as general measures of readability, for which they have a fairly good track record, and their use as guides to the specifics of simplification, for which they are almost useless.[2] The difference can be documented by Flesch's own works. Although for reading purposes Flesch relies only on word length and sentence length, for writing purposes he relies also on such factors as use of the active voice, use of the first or second person, and preferment of verb forms over synonymous noun forms.

In a "plain English" statute, no readability formula should be adopted unless it is adequate also as a guide to redrafting, which it probably cannot be.[3] Otherwise, the conscientious redrafter may be lured into a false sense of accomplishment by emphasizing the factors relied on by the readability test to the neglect of the many other factors needed for clarity and readability.

Clarity and readability differ significantly. In their study of jury instructions,[4] Robert and Veda Charrow concentrated on clarity; Flesch has concentrated on mere readability. A document can meet the Flesch (or Gunning) test 100 percent without

§8.9.   [1]See, e.g., C. Felsenfeld & A. Siegel, Writing Contracts in Plain English 224-227 (1981).

[2]Redish & Selzer, The Place of Readability Formulas in Technical Communication, 32 Technical Communication 46, 50 (4th quart. 1985); Charrow, What is "Plain English," Anyway?, Publication C1 (Document Design Center, American Institutes for Research, 1979), p.4 (MLD 279). As for what the future may hold, see Holland, Psycholinguistic Alternatives to Readability Formulas (American Institutes for Research, Wash. D.C. 1981).

[3]Redish, Readability, in Drafting Documents in Plain English 157, 165 (Practising Law Institute, Commercial Law and Practice Course Handbook Series No. 203, 1979).

[4]Charrow & Charrow, Making Legal Language Understandable: A Psycholinguistic Study of Jury Instructions, 1979 Colum. L. Rev. 1306.

rising above gibberish.[5] What is needed here is a general performance standard of decently readable substantive clarity (as adopted by New York's Sullivan law and the laws of some other states), without mandating a readability formula or a myriad of grammatical detail (as in Connecticut's plain language law and a number of state insurance laws).

Fortunately, clarity and readability are more complementary than competitive. Up to a point we can have both. A preoccupation with clarity alone implies that optimum readability is automatic. A response to that implication appears below in section 14.5(b).

Flesch's preoccupation with readability even to the point of derogating from clarity (and, in some instances, substance) is revealed in his recent attack on a piece of "shredded law," which he unsuccessfully undertook to redraft.[6] Although he might have produced a more adequate result had he done the kind of checking that for the professional draftsman should be routine, his kit lacked many necessary tools.[7]

During a recent conference on "plain English," one critic of simplification believed that he had exposed a fatuity by citing instances in which "simplification" had produced longer rather than shorter results. But for a person who seeks clarity rather than adherence to a mechanical formula, this is no occasion for embarrassment. The point is especially relevant to the short sentences favored by the readability formulas. Psycholinguists have recently shown that, because the structure of an unavoida-

[5]"The Flesch test cannot differentiate between sentences and non-sentences; between sense and nonsense; between the comprehensible and the incomprehensible." Charrow, Let the Rewriter Beware 6 (mimeo, available from the author at American Institutes for Research, Wash. D.C., 1978).

[6]R. Flesch, How to Write Plain English 102-105 (1979).

[7]To achieve greater technical "readability," Flesch sacrificed substantive accuracy. He also impaired clarity by introducing ambiguities, elegant variation, lack of structural parallelism, confusing syntax, and a more complicated hierarchy of contingencies. To complete the irony, he adopted the very device he castigated — tabulation — and then, by failing to indent the tabulated material, created a syntactic ambiguity. For details, see MLD 285-288.

But defects in Flesch's redraft in no way lessen the original's possible vulnerability. What, if anything, could be done to improve its readability without impairing accuracy or clarity?

bly complicated idea is normally hierarchical, it is better grasped if framed in sentences long enough to accommodate appropriate clauses and subclauses than if chopped up into short sentences whose interrelationships are accordingly obscured. "[W]hen we remove relative clauses, we remove the logical connectors that give meaning and coherence to a sentence."[8]

Redish has summarized it well:

> The potential harm in writing directly to the formula is that you may not be changing the aspects of the passages that are really causing the difficulty. Moreover, the results may end up sounding like a first grade primer, like what has been called the "Dick and Jane" style of writing. This can be insulting, uninteresting and in fact less understandable than more normal writing.[9]

Some wit has called it "baby talk."

§8.10. SPECIFICATIONS FOR A "PLAIN ENGLISH" STATUTE

It would be useful to have a uniform or model language simplification act addressed to "consumer" transactions (appropriately limited and defined), where it is desirable to require language that is clear to a modest level of readership. It should be general, rather than detailed, and it should rely mainly on general performance standards of clarity and readability,[1] bolstered, perhaps, by suggested, otherwise neglected specifics to be taken into account, without requiring semantic precision or forbidding technical language that is generally familiar to the audience or for which no satisfactory "plain English" substitute exists.

[8]Charrow, *supra* note 2.
[9]Redish, §8.7, *supra* note 8 at 127.
§8.10. [1]To help courts apply such a subjective test, Felsenfeld and Siegel suggest relevant considerations. Writing Contracts in Plain English 220 (1981). For other surveys of what is appropriate in a plain language law, see Black, A Model Plain Language Act, 33 Stanford L. Rev. 255 (1981); Karlin, Readability Statutes — A Survey and a Proposed Model, 28 Univ. Kan. L. Rev. 531 (1981).

§8.10. General Factors Affecting Readability: Simplification

The suggested specifics should be limited to matters of format (such as typeface, ink-to-paper contrast, paragraphing, and cross-referencing) that are usually ignored or played down in the standard texts on legal writing or legal drafting. Attempts to list the full range of professionally useful devices that improve clarity or readability would be cumbersome, controversial, and inevitably incomplete. And to avoid any undesirable negative implication that might arise from the inclusion of some devices and omission of others, the act should do no more than recite that the draftsman should keep in mind the full range of relevant professionally accepted drafting devices that improve clarity and readability.

It seems undesirable, in such a law, to try to control the drafting of legal instruments generally, many of which can smoothly accommodate language that would subvert a consumer "plain English" law.

Because many of the enterprises concerned do business in more than one state, a uniform act, if feasible, would be appropriate. The main argument for a model act is that a "plain English" law should be dovetailed with existing laws dealing with particular kinds of instruments such as insurance policies. This accounts for the main differences between Hawaii's law and New York's. Nonuniformity is guaranteed by any provision that sanitizes all provisions that are required or permitted by existing law, which undoubtedly differ considerably among the states. The problem can be alleviated by amending the related laws.[2]

First of all, language that is merely permitted by other law should not be allowed to preempt an important consumer safeguard. Merely permissive provisions can be repealed or, if needed for other purposes, overridden or supplemented, by the more stringent requirements of the "plain English" law.

Preexisting legal rules that mandate specific language should likewise be examined. If the mandate relates to a mere phrase or provision, the legislature may want to preserve it. But this would not necessarily require exempting the rest of the

---

[2]Except, of course, that a state legislature could not tamper with a federal requirement.

instrument from simplification. The uniform act could simply exempt the mandated provision or require that mandated provisions likely to cause significant trouble for the consumer be supplemented by appropriate definitions, examples, or explanations.

New Jersey's recognition of the validity of "technical terms and terms of art"[3] might be more effective if it provided that under the standards of its act any unfamiliar technical term for which there is no suitable replacement, definition, or explanation may be disregarded for the purposes of the act.[4]

When an entire form is involved, the chances are great that it is afflicted with many of deficiencies that the language simplification acts are intended to discourage. If mandated by statute, the form should be carefully scrutinized and appropriately amended. If mandated by regulation, it should not be exempted from coverage.

In general, requiring specific language in a statute or regulation makes it harder to maintain standards of good draftsmanship. Felsenfeld and Siegel cite this instance:

> A look at one form used for the instalment sale of an automobile revealed ten different statutes or regulations. One effect of those particular requirements was to turn what might have been a clear and expository contract into a thicket of legal boiler plate.[5]

Even as modest an example as the Federal Trade Commission's requirement that a consumer product warranty state that "This warranty gives you specific legal rights, and you may also have other rights which vary from state to state"[6] creates a dilemma for the draftsman who finds it more appropriate to draft in the third person or to follow the Fowler convention of using "that" instead of "which" when introducing a restrictive clause.[7] It is preferable that the statute or regulation state the

---

[3]N.J. Stat. Ann. §56:12-2.
[4]See §8.7 *supra.*
[5]C. Felsenfeld & A. Siegel, Writing Contracts in Plain English 50 (1981).
[6]16 C.F.R. 701(3)(a).
[7]H. Fowler, Dictionary of Modern English Usage 625-628 (2d ed. rev. Gowers 1965).

substance of the requirement and let the draftsman select the language that best fits the particular instrument. The Federal Trade Commission's door-to-door sales rule provides the needed leeway by requiring the statement concerned be "in substantially the following form: . . . "[8]

It seems appropriate that a "plain English" law fix monetary limits on the transactions covered and on penalties and attorneys' fees. The former help define the kind of consumers that need protection. The latter help avoid penalties so disproportionate that juries would be tempted not to apply them.

New Jersey's exemption of provisions supplied by the consumer makes good sense. A lessor, warrantor, or contractor should not be responsible for the self-inflicted disappointments of a complainant.

As for enforcement, a suit for reformation to reduce the risk of financial loss helps forestall later and more burdensome litigation. Injunctive relief is also helpful. Whether a disposition or contractual arrangement should be voided for bad draftsmanship should be left to general principles of common law regarding unconscionability, bad faith, lack of necessary intent, and so forth. A statement to this effect would head off negative implications that might otherwise arise out of the express remedies.

Full performance is a suitable defense to a suit for damages, because it eliminates the element of injury. It should also be a defense to a suit for reformation, because the need has disappeared. Under conventional doctrine, it would also head off punitive damages.[9] Whether it should make undesirable a separate statutory action for a penalty is debatable.

In view of the chronic ineptitude of lawyers in matters of drafting, the mere presence of plaintiff's attorney at the time of signing should not disqualify a plaintiff from taking action, as it does in New York. Nor should "good faith" be a defense in any

---

[8] 16 C.F.R. 429(a), 17 F.R. 22934.

[9] J. Ghardi & J. Mircher, Punitive Damages Law and Practice §5.37(1980). However, nominal damages are usually enough to support an award.

instance, because the predominant cause of bad drafting is ineptitude rather than bad faith. Lawyers need to be more fully motivated to improve their performance in this area.[10]

§8.11. MANDATING "PLAIN ENGLISH" IN STATUTES, REGULATIONS, AND PRIVATE INSTRUMENTS OTHER THAN "CONSUMER" INSTRUMENTS

In his television "fireside chat" of February 2, 1977, President Carter announced that his administration would cut down on government regulations and make sure that those that are written are in "plain English."[1] On March 23, 1978, he issued Executive Order No. 12044,[2] which adopted as its basic policy this requirement: "Regulations shall be as simple and clear as possible." The head of each agency was required to make sure that "the regulation is written in plain English and is understandable to those who must comply with it."

For government regulations, which are usually highly technical and addressed to a multitude of audiences of differing sophistication, this general statement needed improving.

As for "simple" and "clear," their parallel form suggested (1) that simplicity and clarity are coordinate values (which they are not) and (2) that "as possible" qualifies clarity in the same way that it qualifies simplicity. Also, it is not clear in either case what standard of "possibility" was intended. The government should shoot for as much clarity as it can get that is consistent with substance and as the government believes it should insist on. It should then shoot for as much readability as it can get without significantly compromising substance or clarity. The

---

[10]For alternative approaches to legislatively mandated readability, see Black, A Model Plain Language Act, 33 Stan. L. Rev. 255 (1981); Karlin, Readability Statutes — A Survey and a Proposed Model, 28 U. Kan. L. Rev. 531 (1980).

§8.11. [1]N.Y. Times, February 3, 1977, p.22 (MLD 262).

[2]43 F.R. 12661 (MLD 263).

reference to "possibility" in the executive order did not adequately reflect this hierarchy of drafting values. The executive order was revoked on February 17, 1981.[3]

A "plain English" or "plain language" standard has no place here. Too often everyday public-at-large English is not plain enough for the substance covered. Neither term is apt where technically sophisticated problems are involved and the instrument is addressed to a correspondingly sophisticated audience.

A general requirement of understandability for the kinds of persons who must comply, on the other hand, is squarely on target. Its central notion of clarity is properly beamed in each case at the kind of audience involved, which in some cases may be the public at large. In extreme cases such as federal income tax law, draftsmen would seem justified in addressing their words to members of the tax bar, upon whom taxpayers are accustomed to rely, and in relying, therefore, on the established sources of supplementary guidance that continue to be available.

The same strictures apply to "plain English" statutes that apply to regulations. As for those that apply also to private instruments addressed to individuals other than those whom the consumer movement is designed to protect, either the requirement should be confined to a simple requirement of understandability to the kind of persons who must respectively comply or such instruments should be exempted from coverage.

Any statutory attempt to control the language of future statutes is unenforceable in any practical sense. It is probably also unconstitutional, because a legislature cannot tie its own hands. It can, of course, control by resolution the activities of its own draftsmen. The best approach is simply to engage or train qualified legislative counsel.

[3]E.O. 12291, 47 F.R. 13198.

§8.12. OTHER FACTORS AFFECTING READABILITY

Except for instruments aimed at consumers or the general public, the notion of "plain English" or "plain language" should be abandoned in favor of a concept of readability, appropriate to the audiences addressed, that is deferential to the superior values of substance and clarity and is realizable only through the application of a large miscellany of well-tested rules. Many of these are covered by the readability conventions set forth in the rest of this chapter and in chapter 9.

Despite the skeptics and the necessary reservations, we know that without violating any significant substantive objective we can do for legal instruments generally a considerable amount of useful simplification. We know it, because it has been done, not only in the academic ivory tower, but in the sterner environment of the so-called real world.

Taken individually, few of the following rules have great significance. Certainly, a single application of one of them will have only slight effect. Rather, they are valuable for their cumulative effect; and their cumulative effect can be considerable. This is what Cavers meant by "the importance of the inconsequential."[1] Overall clarity and readability are the aggregate results of a myriad of small operations.

Strategically, this fact is important to the successful defense of a specific change that, taken by itself, can only be viewed as trivial. It is more persuasive in such a case to rely on the cumulative effect of the broad range of principles underlying clarity and readability.

§8.13. BREVITY

Tight compression of language does not insure clarity and simplicity. The draftsman should condense his language only so far

§8.12.   [1]The Simplification of Government Regulations, 8 Fed. B.J. 339, 345 (1949).

as it helps rather than hinders understanding. Sometimes the longer statement is the simpler.[1]

Don't say	*Say*
Trailer Interchange contractors allocated less-than-carload freight shipment refunds	Refunds that Trailer Interchange contractors allocate for less-than-carload freight shipments.

§8.14.   SENTENCES

The draftsman should avoid long sentences when shorter ones will say the same thing as well.[1] Ordinarily, he should state the circumstances in which the rule is to apply before he states the rule itself.[2] However, he should not start a sentence with an exception if he can conveniently avoid it.

Examples:

Whenever the distributor finds that a conflict exists, he shall convene a bargaining committee of five representatives from the territory concerned . . .

If, after hearing both parties to any such challenge, or acting on his own initiative with respect to a prospective voter, the official in charge of the polling place reasonably believes the prospective voter is unqualified to vote, he shall allow the prospective voter to cast a ballot marked "challenged."

On the other hand, if the circumstances in which the rule is to apply involve numerous contingencies or conditions, the

§8.13.   [1]"Terseness should not be carried to the point that it interferes with readability." J. Johnson, A Draftsman's Handbook for Wills and Trust Agreements 8 (1961). See also R. Flesch, The Art of Plain Talk 120 (1946); E. Piesse, The Elements of Drafting 2-3 (5th ed. Aitken 1976).

§8.14.   [1]Flesch, *supra,* ch. 4; C. Ilbert, The Mechanics of Law Making 117 (1914); Piesse, §8.13, note 1, *supra* at 31-32.

[2]G. Coode, On Legislative Expression 22, 31, 34 (2d ed. 1843), reprinted in E. Driedger, The Composition of Legislation — Legislative Forms and Precedents, 317, 334, 342, 344 (2d ed. rev. 1976).

draftsman may find it desirable to state the rule first. (In this case it may be appropriate to put an exception at the beginning.)

Example:

> Except as provided by section 9, the tenant may by written notice terminate[3] this lease at any time, but only if the notice is received at least 60 days before the day on which the termination is to take effect, the notice states that the tenant does not intend to acquire membership in the Association during the calendar year in which the termination is to take effect, and the Board of Trustees approves the termination in writing.

When there are a number of unwieldy contingencies, it is desirable to make each a separate clause. As seen in section 6.3, statement in tabular form is often clearer and makes it easier to determine which ideas are central and which are subordinate.

Example:

The Company may by written notice terminate this lease at any time:

(1) effective immediately, if the tenant becomes ineligible to live in Company housing;

(2) effective no sooner than 10 days, if the tenant fails to pay a monthly installment of rent by the 10th day after it becomes due;

(3) effective no sooner than 5 days, if the tenant violates section 2 or 3(a); and

(4) effective no sooner than 60 days, if the premises will be needed for Company construction within a reasonable time after the termination is to take effect.

---

[3]Although shorter, "cancel" is frowned on as tending to suggest retroactivity. I would gladly opt for "end," except that "ending" seems awkward as a replacement for "termination" and I am reluctant to commit "elegant variation."

§8.15. DIRECTNESS

When an idea can be accurately expressed either positively or negatively, it should be expressed positively.

Don't say	*Say*
This section does not apply to bondholders who have not been paid in full.	This section applies only to bondholders who have been paid in full.
Indigents other than those with no children may . . .	Indigents with children may . . .

The negative form (No person may . . . unless . . .) "is appropriate, however, when the provision is intended to be 'mandatory'" (i.e., compliance is a condition precedent to the validity of the transaction).[1] Conversely, it should not be used in provisions that are intended to be only "directory" (i.e., compliance is not such a condition).

§8.16. EXCEPTIONS

Exceptions should be used only when necessary. They can be avoided whenever the draftsman can find a named category co-extensive with that involved in carrying out the client's objective. In the phrase "all persons except those who are 60 years old or older," the exception is unnecessary because the client intends to deal with a category that is narrower than "all persons" and can be directly described, i.e., "persons who are less than 60 years old."

An exception is proper, of course, when to avoid it would require a long and cumbersome enumeration or an elaborate description of what is covered. Thus, it is far preferable to say "all States, except Texas, New Mexico, and Arizona" than to enumerate the other 47.

§8.15. [1]J. Sutherland, Statutes and Statutory Construction §57.09 (4th ed. 1985). On mandatory and directory provisions generally, see C. Jones, Statute Law Making in the United States, ch. 8 (1912).

§8.17.   TENSE

For the most part, the draftsman should stay with the present tense. A provision of continuing effect, unlike the purely dispositive provisions of a will or conveyance, speaks as of the time it is being read, not merely as of the time it took effect.[1]

When it is necessary to express a time relationship, the draftsman should recite facts concurrent with the operation of the instrument as present facts, and facts precedent to its operation as past facts.[2]

Examples:

> If, having been convicted of a felony, an alien is found physically incapable of being deported within the time otherwise prescribed by section 402, he may . . .

> Any person who is or has been a member of the Communist Party is disqualified from further participation, if he . . .

If it is necessary that a provision include past as well as future events, the draftsman should use the present tense but insert before the appropriate verb the phrase "before or after this ['title,' 'part,' 'section,' etc.] takes effect."

Although the future tense is rarely appropriate (apart from what inheres in the imperative "shall"), it is sometimes necessary to use it.

Example:

> If the contractor finds that service under section 3.02 of this contract will contribute to a violation of the law by the Company, it may . . .

---

§8.17.   [1]"Although a general formal statement to this effect may not be found in the reports [with respect to non-statutory instruments] there can be no doubt that this is the case." E. Piesse, The Elements of Drafting 83 (5th ed. Aitken 1976).

[2]This sentence is a paraphrase of G. Coode, On Legislative Expression 66 (2d ed. 1843), reprinted in E. Driedger, The Composition of Legislation — Legislative Forms and Precedents, 317, 375 (2d ed. rev. 1976).

§8.18. VOICE

In general, the active voice is more readable, but not necessarily clearer, than the passive. (The passive voice is acceptable when the actor is unidentified or when it is clear who he is but it would be cumbersome to name him expressly.)

Don't say	*Say*
Dealers for each territory shall be appointed by the distributor from persons for firms who are financially responsible.	The distributor shall appoint the dealers for each territory from persons or firms who are financially responsible.

In sections conferring powers or privileges or imposing duties, using the active voice will help to avoid vagueness by forcing the draftsman to name, as the subject of the sentence, the person in whom the power or privilege is vested or upon whom the duty is imposed.[1]

§8.19. PERSON

Because it is standard practice to draft in the third person in statutes, ordinances, and most regulations, its use in such instruments may usually be taken for granted. It is also appropriate in many private instruments.

Beginning with World War II, when for greater readability the Office of Price Administration used the second person (in a singular context) to address the retailers and wholesalers of grocery products, the second person has often been used in regulations and other instruments that are addressed to audiences consisting for the most part of individual members of the public, including those operating small businesses. Most typical are "consumer" instruments such as insurance policies and

---

§8.18. [1]This sentence is a paraphrase of Uniformity of Legislation in Canada — An Outline, and Rules of Drafting 33 (1949), also published as Rules of Drafting, 26 Can. B. Rev. 1231, 1239 (1948). See also E. Piesse, The Elements of Drafting 66 (5th ed. Aitken 1976).

product warranties.[1] The advantage of the second person is, as Flesch has shown,[2] greater readability.

The first person is appropriate in a proclamation, an executive order, or a private dispositive instrument such as a will. As for the first person plural, I remember but one use in a legislative instrument, where "we" appeared in an inept legislative preamble. It is more appropriate in introducing a constitution ("We, the People, adopt . . .").

Although Felsenfeld and Siegel approve of personal pronouns in private instruments, they warn that:

> Pronouns affect tone. For example, if the consumer is called *you,* beware of a peremptory tone. Otherwise, the consumer's obligations may sound like burdens instead of responsibilities that have been assumed voluntarily.[3]

A good point.

§8.20. LIVE WORDS

Whenever possible, the draftsman should arrange his sentences so as to make the fullest use of finite verbs instead of their corresponding participles, infinitives, gerunds, and other noun or adjective forms denoting action.[1]

Don't say	*Say*
give consideration to	consider
give recognition to	recognize
have knowledge of	know
have need of	need

§8.19. [1]See also §§2.1 and 8.2 *supra.*
[2]The Art of Plain Talk, ch. 6 and *passim* (1946).
[3]C. Felsenfeld & A. Siegel, Writing Contracts in Plain English 116 (1981).
§8.20. [1]R. Flesch, The Art of Plain Talk, ch. 8 (1946). Compare J. Bentham, Nomography 267, in 3 Bentham's Works 231 (Bowring ed. 1843), where the exact opposite is urged: "Where a substantive is employed, the idea is stationed as it were upon a rock: — where no substantive is employed, but only a verb, the idea is as it were a twig or a leaf floating on a stream, and hurried down out of view along with it." By today's standards floating twigs are easier to read than ideas on rocks.

in the determination of	in determining
is applicable	applies
is dependent on	depends on
is in attendance at	attends
make an appointment of	appoint
make application	apply
make payment	pay
make provision for	provide for

§8.21.   PUNCTUATION

Many conventions of punctuation have crystallized sufficiently to be reasonably helpful aids in buttressing intended legal meanings. Although low in relative persuasiveness, punctuation marks are today often relied upon by the courts, together with other evidence, in interpreting legal instruments.

Accordingly, punctuation is a tool that the draftsman can ill afford to neglect.[1] He should master it and use it as a finishing device, together with other typographical aids, in carrying meaning. But he should not rely solely on it to do what an arrangement of words can do. It is here that punctuation marks are the most abused.

Draftsmen who carefully adhere to accepted conventions in punctuating textual material that has already been made as clear as possible do much to make punctuation a more useful and reliable drafting tool. Scrupulous consistency in punctuating a legal instrument reassures the reader that marks have not been haphazardly inserted.

Most of the current uncertainty involves the comma, the most useful and yet the most dangerous of the marks of punctuation. But, whatever the general uncertainties, there are at least three useful conventions of punctuation the draftsman can safely adopt:

(1)   He should use commas to set off clauses that describe a subject that is otherwise identified (e.g., "The Comp-

§8.21.   [1]This is true even of statutes.

troller, who shall be appointed as provided in section 403, may . . .").

(2)   In a series of more than two items, he should put a comma after the next to last item (e.g., "wheat, corn, and rye"). Omitting it may create a syntactic ambiguity.

(3)   Where two conjoined adjectives are intended to modify the same noun independently of each other (so that the first adjective modifies the noun unlimited by the second adjective) the intention can be shown by separating the adjectives by a comma, the equivalent of "and" (e.g., "other, more lucrative branches of the legal profession"). Here, the modifiers are correlative, not hierarchical.

Parentheses, though generally frowned upon, are sometimes more reliable than commas in setting off a phrase when there is possible uncertainty as to how the ideas that follow the phrase are linked to those that precede it.

Examples:

If it is necessary to order individuals to active duty, other than for training, without their consent . . .

is not as clear as

If it is necessary to order individuals to active duty (other than for training) without their consent . . .

§8.22.   CAPITALIZATION

The draftsman should use capitalization sparingly. He should use initial capital letters only where required by good usage, as for proper nouns. The following terms should be capitalized at least in federal legislation (state legislative styles may differ):

Federal, Government (when referring to the Government of
the United States)
State (when referring to a State of the United States)

The following terms should not be capitalized:

title, part, chapter, article, section, etc.

The Government Printing Office Style Manual (ch. 4) is a helpful
guide.

§8.23.   HEADINGS

A neglected device for making legal instruments more readable
is the topic heading. Because topic headings are helpful and
involve little extra work and risk (in case of later amendment),
it is desirable to use them on the major breakdowns, including
sections, of all legal instruments of substantial length that are
intended to have continued effect. However, in normal circumstances, the draftsman should not attach a heading to anything
smaller than a section. The crowding of headings is self-defeating.

Headings should be as short as consistent with helping the
reader quickly find what he wants. They need not exhaust the
ideas expressed in the text. However, if a section title cannot be
made both succinct and illuminating, it may indicate that the
section covers too much territory and should be divided into
several sections. Phrases, rather than sentences, should be used
as headings. No part of an opening sentence of text should be
treated as a heading. The draftsman should include in the heading only ideas that are equally plain in the text, or the court may
not give them weight.

When sections fall into logical groupings, the draftsman
may want to reflect this fact by giving each section in a group
a compound heading stating first the common idea and then the
subject of the particular section, with the parts separated by a
colon.

Example:

Sec. 201. General safety standards
Sec. 202. Speed of motor vehicles: Passenger cars
Sec. 203. Speed of motor vehicles: Trucks and buses
Sec. 204. Speed of motor vehicles: Motorcycles
Sec. 205. Enforcement.

Sometimes it is desirable to put several coordinate subjects in the same section rather than in separate sections. For this purpose a compound heading, with the parts separated by semicolons (not colons), is appropriate.

Example:

Sec. 703. Appointment of commissioner; tenure; removal for cause

§8.24.   NUMBERING OF SECTIONS

So long as it is appropriately simple, internally consistent, and compatible with any general scheme of which it may be a part, the numbering of sections is not a significant problem for most legal instruments. However, if an instrument such as a union contract or a securities registration statement is very long, the draftsman may find helpful some of what follows.

With legislative instruments such as statutes and regulations numbering can be a sticky problem. Sections can be numbered by simple arabic numbers that run serially throughout the instrument (with or without gaps to accommodate later sections)[1] or that (like all state constitutions except Kentucky's) start over in each succeeding title (or part), in which case each title has its own "section 1."

That the former approach is to be preferred for "free-

---

§8.24.   [1]J. Peacock, Notes on Legislative Drafting, ch. 11 (1961).

standing"[2] legislation is suggested by Donald Hirsch's description of the prevailing federal practice:

> If a bill has titles, all sections under title I should be in the 100 series, those under title II should be in the 200 series, and so forth. If a title is divided into subtitles or other parts (designated "I," "II," or "A," "B," and so forth), each part should begin at the beginning of a 10 series, e.g., part A begins at 100, part B at 120, part C at 140. This leaves room to add sections to a part, after the bill becomes law, without complicated renumbering of the entire title. It also makes it convenient to add new sections to successive drafts of the bill.[3]

Another important advantage of such a numbering system is that it allows every section within the system to be identified by a unique number without identifying any subcategory of which it may be a part. This is important, because it permits simpler references and makes it easier to find a particular section (what intermediate categories it falls under become irrelevant). These values were best realized in the numbering system used in title 10 of the United States Code.[4]

The central assumption here is that for legislative instruments the basic unit is the section.

Statutes that are part of comprehensive state-enacted codes often use compound numbers in which the first number designates the relevant title, (e.g., "24") the second designates either the chapter and section (e.g., "101," meaning "section 1 of chapter 1"), or just the chapter (e.g., "10"), in which case the third designates the section. Indiana uses a four-fold breakdown of title, article, chapter, and section (e.g., "§14-6-22-4").

[2]A statute that establishes a continuing program as distinct from an amendatory one (see §11.2(5) *infra*).

[3]D. Hirsch, Drafting Federal Law 9 (1980). Ontario Senior Legislative Counsel, Arthur H. Stone, (letter of August 20, 1985) writes that a "system of numbering should provide a unique identification of each unit that may be cited . . . [and] be capable of expansion for the insertion of amendments. . . . The method of expansion is more important when periodic revision and reprinting of the statutes is not available."

[4]As originally enacted, 70A Stat. iii *et seq.* (1956).

Compound numbers with three or four number-units can produce highly formidable references, especially where long sections and inherent complexity have combined to produce intra-section breakdowns to the third or fourth degree, with a potential of producing designations such as "section 17-6-34-19(c)(1)(A)(iii)."[5] It is far preferable to drop from section numbers the numerical units that designate title and part, and to develop more and shorter sections, preferably short enough not to require a high degree of internal proliferation.

Some states, such as New Mexico, separate the numerical units by dashes, and some by colons. New Jersey uses a colon and then a dash, which constitutes "elegant variation" because the shift does not signify anything that is not signified by using the same kind of separator throughout (i.e., a step-down to the next lower level in the hierarchy).

Indiana's code numbering system, as originally adopted, used a period to introduce both the next contiguous provision (the usual spatial sequence) and the next replacement version of the same provision (the temporal sequence),[6] an ambiguous approach that guarantees ultimate confusion for the ordinary run of lawyer. It compounded this by using both dashes and periods as separators without indicating the resulting hierarchical relationships.[7] (In such a system, a dash introduces a step down in the hierarchy; a period does not.) Although Hoosier lawyers may be more than ordinarily perceptive, the Indiana system has little to commend it and the effort to reflect temporal sequences has since been abandoned.

[5]In Indiana, the reference could even have looked like this: 17-6.1-34-19.1(c)(1)(A)(iii). See *infra* note 7.

[6]The theoretical argument for this is apparently that it provides the aesthetic values of redesignation while alleviating any problem of semantic readjustment. See text accompanying §11.3 note 4. But is this not over-subtle and counterproductive?

[7]For example, in the current designation "20-6.1-4-9.1" the first ".1" is intended to show that article 6.1 is a replacement for the original article 6, whereas the second ".1" is intended to show that a new section has been inserted immediately after section 9. It is interesting to speculate on what the draftsman would have done had there been simultaneous moves to replace a section and insert a new one immediately after it.

Indiana's system, whether or not the worst of all possible legislative numbering systems, could easily have been improved by following the example of such states as Arizona, which uses a single split, indicated by a dash, between the number showing the relevant title and the number showing the relevant section within that title (e.g., "section 6-539"), the latter of which run serially similarly to the federal system described above by Hirsch.

But even Arizona's system carries unnecessary baggage. Its apparent advantage is that it avoids the more awkward external reference "section 539 of title 6." But this advantage is partly illusory, because it appears that most sectional references in statutes are internal to the relevant title and not to sections in other titles. If so, the price of Arizona's dubious advantage is the unnecessary references to title in the larger bulk of internal references.

Nor is Arizona's approach needed to handle multiple external references, which can often be batched (e.g., "sections 539, 661, and 802 of title 6"). Even where there is no batching, references to title often need not be repeated for additional sectional references that lie within a common context.

What about the vast numbers of references that lie in such unenacted materials as cases, articles, and textbooks, all of which are inherently external? For them, the considerations mentioned in the preceding paragraph would seem to apply.

At least partial verification of these conclusions would seem to lie in the experience with title 10 of the United States Code (Armed Forces), which was part of one of the longest and most complicated pieces of legislation ever enacted and whose numbering system was evolved only after seven weeks of concentrated work. No internal sectional reference uses a number of more than four digits (e.g., "section 8002") and no further complication is needed except where it is necessary to pinpoint an internal fragment (e.g., "section 8002(a)(1)").

If this approach is taken, no section designation need contain a separator of any kind, including spaces, which appear with good reason in Social Security and credit card numbers and whose use for segmentation invites the attention of psychologists and psycholinguists.

The trouble with the systems just described is that they tend to break down in areas where amendments are prolific. Deletions leave gaps that if unexplained tend to create perplexities about sequence.[8] Concentrations of additions tend not only to fill the spaces, if any, left to accommodate new provisions (whose distribution can be only crudely anticipated) but to clutter the sequence with alphabetical insertions when gaps in the arabic sequence do not exist (e.g., "section 476a, 476b", etc.).[9]

In jurisdictions that follow a policy of periodic statutory reconsolidation or revision, awkwardnesses of sequence are washed out on those occasions at the expense of considerable redesignation (see section 11.4 below), problems of which are exacerbated if a considerable time does not elapse between revisions.

Oregon and Wisconsin have adopted continuous (yearly) looseleaf revision, which not only postpones general revision indefinitely but, in confining itself to continual, sporadic action, makes the wholesale overhaul of section numbering a rare event. This greatly increases the incentive to redesignate (with its attendant headaches).

As insurance against redesignation, these states used compound numbers (e.g., "14.101") in which the first number represents the chapter of the compiled whole, the second represents the section number, and the period represents a decimal point. As James Craig Peacock has pointed out, a decimal system facilitates "the insertion in logical sequence between any two sections of an almost infinite numbers of new sections. Thus, new sections between sections 43.8 and 43.9 can be numbered

---

[8]See §11.3 *infra.*

[9]Where letters are used for this purpose, they are not encased in parentheses, as is the case with letter designations of parts of sections. See §8.25 *infra.* Canadian federal statutes avoid possible confusion here by using arabic numbers (set off by periods, e.g., "15.1") instead of letters. But periods can be confused with decimal points.

43.81 and 43.82."[10] and new sections between 43.81 and 43.82 can be numbered 43.811, 43.812 and so forth. Here, moving to a lower decimal place to squeeze in a new section does not assign it to a lower order in the conceptual hierarchy, which is the case with mere separators. It also guarantees permanence of designation, and thus avoids the dire consequences of redesignation.

Peacock contends that such an approach is not unduly troublesome so long as the period remains a true decimal point and not a mere separator, as it is in the Code of Federal Regulations.[11] There a "reader looking for Section 73.348 who opens to either 73.3 or 73.34 is entitled to assume that 73.348 is just a page or two further on. But . . . 73.3 is in the Code's pattern followed by 73.4, 73.5, and so on, and 73.348 is 150 pages further on."[12] The latter approach is more appropriate in private instruments in which a profusion of new sections is unlikely. In such a case, the period serves as a mere separator (as it does in this book).

My prejudice is that in statutes use of a period either as a decimal or as a mere separator tends to create an ambiguity, and that there are simpler ways to handle the insertion problem than to introduce a decimal system, which tends to confuse readers.[13]

[10]Peacock, *supra* note 1 at 11. James W. Ryan, in Decimal System of Numbering, 1968 Proceedings, Conference of Commissioners on Uniformity of Law in Canada 27, 76 (at 56-59 of the report) says:

> The decimal systems now used for regulatory or statutory provisions show considerable variation, but nearly all seem to show some debt to the Dewey decimal system as developed for library cataloguing purposes.
> The Dewey system classified subjects by three digit numbers, such as 300, 500, etc., and permitted subdivision within the general class by using the two extra spaces held by the zeros, as well as permitting digits to the right of a decimal point, e.g. 310.10, 501.1, etc.

[11]Peacock, *supra* note 1 at 19. Although the numbering of sections in this book does just that, textbooks are not ordinarily inhibited by the semantic connotations of specific number designations. See §11.4 *infra*.

[12]*Id.*

[13]The problem is further complicated by the fact that in any jurisdiction in which all or part of the existing code of laws is developed editorially rather than enacted, the code numbering is likely to differ from that used in the enacted version.

Evaluating the trade-off here is not easy, which suggests that the problem deserves further study. A description of the decimal system designed by James W. Ryan, which has been adopted in several instances for federal regulations in Canada and, more recently, by provinces for use in loose-leaf consolidations, is worth examining.[14]

My own inexperience with decimal systems disqualifies me from commenting further.

§8.25. DESIGNATION OF PARTS OF SECTIONS

For identification it is usually desirable to designate each paragraph of text by a letter or number.[1] Simple enumerations, whether or not in tabular form, may or may not be designated. For designating paragraph groupings within a section, these conventions are useful: For divisions of a section (called "subsections"), use "(a)," "(b)," "(c)," etc. For divisions of a subsection (called "paragraphs"), use "(1)," "(2)," "(3)," etc. For divisions of a paragraph (called "subparagraphs"), use "(A)," "(B)," "(C)," etc. Further subdivisions should be avoided whenever possible. When an additional designated breakdown is necessary, use "(i)," "(ii)," "(iii)," etc.

When designating a tabulation in a section that has no subsections, use "(1)," "(2)," "(3)," etc., to designate the clauses.

Example:

Sec. 232. *Failure to comply with posting requirements*
If a distributor fails to comply with the posting requirements prescribed in section 203:

---

[14]Ryan, *supra* note 10. Examples of Canadian decimal systems include the regulations under the Food and Drug Act and the Queen's Regulations for Canada relating to the armed forces.
§8.25. [1]Thomas, Problems in Drafting Legal Instruments, 39 Ill. B.J. 51, 55 (1950).

(1)   the shipment shall be seized under section 301(a);
(2)   he shall be fined not more than $1,000; and
(3)   his license shall be withdrawn.

§8.26.   REFERENCES

It is often desirable in a legal instrument to refer to another provision of the same instrument, to a provision of another instrument, or even to extralegal materials such as commercial life tables or industrial standards of construction. Although the practice is useful and sometimes necessary, it should be approached warily. There are pitfalls.[1]

Textual cross references to other parts of the same instrument help pull it together. Unfortunately, unless used sparingly and carefully, they can be as much a hindrance as an aid. Taken in isolation, an internal cross reference is easy to justify. Taken in the aggregate, they can make material hard to read[2] and, in some cases, unintelligible. The Internal Revenue Code has been a frequent offender. Here is perhaps the most notorious example:

(a)   General Rule — For purposes of this title, the term "private foundation" means a domestic or foreign organization described in section 501(c)(3) other than —
   (1) . . .
   (2) . . .
   (3) . . .
   (4) . . .
   For purposes of paragraph (3), an organization described in paragraph (2) shall be deemed to include an organization described in section 501(c)(4), (5), or (6) which would be

§8.26.   [1]For example, James B. Minor points out that reference to a definition (e.g., " 'apple' as defined in section 1") may create a problem of negative implication, unless the reference is repeated every time the term is used in the instrument involved. If a definition is properly introduced ("In this contract, the term 'apple' means . . ."), reference to the definition is redundant.

[2]J. Johnson, A Draftsman's Handbook for Wills and Trust Agreements 12 (1961).

described in paragraph (2) if it were an organization described in section 501(c)(3).[3]

The usual purpose of an internal cross reference is to call attention to another provision that qualifies, makes an exception to, or otherwise affects the provision containing the reference. In such a case, it may be purely informational, rather than determinative, and thus optional. On the other hand, if the reference is needed to establish the applicability of a provision that it is preferable not to repeat, it is a substantive necessity. The incidence of cross references normally depends on the bulk and internal complexity of the subject matter being expressed, which may justify some of the apparent excesses of the Internal Revenue Code.[4]

References that are purely informational should be enacted

[3]Internal Revenue Code of 1954, §509(a). Edward O. Craft, former Legislative Counsel to the United States House of Representatives, comments as follows:

> I suspect that every draftsman that participated in the drafting of the last sentence of section 509(a) (private foundation defined) would deny it. I can assure you that the problem is much more fundamental than the cross references. If you have a Code at hand, it is relatively simple to flip a few pages to read the appropriate reference. Taking account of the number of 501(c)(3) organizations that are (or could possibly want to know whether they are) covered by the offending sentence, should the cross references be avoided in light of the material required for replacement? Note that section 509(a) applies to an organization described in section 501(c)(3). Note also the words in the last sentence: "If it were" [!] such an organization.
>
> I think that the number of individuals who have read this provision to apply the tax law is very small indeed. Unfortunately, there are many other provisions in the Code of like ilk.
>
> It has been popular almost from the beginning of the federal income tax to cite tax provisions as examples of bad drafting, obfuscation, and materials in urgent need of redrafting. At one time, I had a rather voluminous file of published examples. The early ones were from Middleton Beaman going back at least to 1922. Both the draftsmen and the policymakers (legislative and Treasury) received their lumps. Over the same years high praise was bestowed on the quality of the drafting of other legislation, sometimes by those who had been most severe in their criticism of the internal revenue laws. It was interesting to observe the reaction when it was disclosed that the same individuals had, as legislative draftsmen, drafted both sets of provisions.

See also §4.15 *supra.*

[4]An interesting analysis of the kinds of situations that generate references appears in V. Bhatia, An Applied Discourse Analysis of English Legislative Writing, ch. 5 (Language Studies Unit, U. of Aston, Birmingham, U.K. 1983).

as part of the statute only where the instrument concerned is long or complicated enough that the typical reader is likely to remain uninformed of a limiting provision because the instrument is one that it is customary to consult as the need arises and not read in full. If supplied only editorially, they be freely used.

A short, simple instrument normally needs few cross references. In any event, the need for internal cross references can be reduced by achieving the simplest feasible arrangement. Even when cross references are unavoidable, the threat to readability can be lessened by keeping the references as simple as possible. This can be done by taking three precautions, each of which helps reduce the number of numerical signposts needed in the reference. The first is to draft more, but shorter, sections (as suggested in section 8.24, above). This will simplify their internal structure and internal designations.

The second is to adopt a system of numbering sections (as also suggested in section 8.24) that assigns each section of the instrument a unique numerical designation that makes it unnecessary to refer to any of the broader organizational categories within which the section may fall.

The third is to avoid unnecessary pinpointing of specific parts of sections where mere reference to the relevant section or subsection takes the reader to a point where he can easily find his way to the relevant provision.

A cross reference should refer specifically to the related provision by its technical designation (e.g., "section 4") rather than by its relative location (e.g., "the preceding section," "the last section," etc.) or merely by its subject matter. A reference to relative location may be upset by the insertion of new provisions. A reference merely to subject matter risks a muddy result.

Even if the specific provision referred to is technically identified, it is often desirable to show parenthetically what it is about (e.g., "This computation is subject to section 38, which explains how to compute interest"; "under section 39 (penalties)"; "the provisions on adoption (sections 37-49)"; "chapter 42 of the Execution of Wills Act"). Otherwise, references provide a rich soil for bafflement, misjudging aptness, and even deception.

When pinpointing, the draftsman should use the most compact technical identification.

Don't say	Say
Paragraph (4) of subsection (c) of section 25	Section 25(c)(4)

Because multiple references, whether in tandem or sequence,[5] risk confusion, they should be used sparingly. On the other hand, trying to avoid references altogether may be undesirably restrictive.

In an internal cross reference, it is unnecessary to refer to any category (e.g., "this Act," "this contract," "this title," "this article," "this part," "this chapter," "this section," etc.) that contains both the reference and the item referred to.

Conversely, if the material referred is in another subsection or section, that category should be reflected in the reference. This is true also of references to material in other subtitles, articles, parts, chapters, etc., of an instrument, but only if it uses independent section numbering for each article or title, as most state constitutions do (e.g., "article VI, section 1"). If, instead, the instrument uses unique section designations, an internal reference to material in another section need not identify any category larger than the section, even when referring to sections in other articles or parts. Thus, "section 4712," which appears in section 2575 of chapter 153, part IV, subtitle A of title 10 of the United States Code, is an appropriate reference even though section 4712 is in chapter 445, part IV, subtitle B of that title.

What about materials outside the instrument?

Ordinarily, an instrument that amends another instrument cannot adequately identify what is being changed without referring to it.[6] Here express reference is not only permissible but

---

[5]J. Peacock, Notes on Legislative Drafting 24-27 (1961).

[6]One apparent exception is the Uniform Determination of Death Act, which defines "death" for all legal purposes as the irreversible cessation either

necessary. The same is true of the incorporation by reference of external boilerplate materials discussed in section 6.12 above.

§8.27.   TABLES

Although tables are relative newcomers to legal instruments, there is no reason why they should not be used whenever they are otherwise appropriate. Indeed, technical data can often be more clearly portrayed in tables than in conventional language.[1] The same care, of course, should be taken in preparing tables as in preparing the other parts of the instrument. Like those parts, tables are vulnerable to ambiguity.

§8.28.   COMPUTATIONS

Although it is common to prescribe computations in terms of mathematical formulas, it is often easier and clearer to use the "cookbook" approach, that is, to list in chronological order the steps leading to the intended result.

---

of the circulatory and respiratory functions or of all brain functions. This clearly displaces the common law definition of death and, so far as any statute was previously served by that definition, it has arguably been amended. It is also arguable that it has not, because nothing already in the statute needs changing. All that could be usefully changed would be the addition of the new definition (or a reference to it), which in the aggregate of such statutes could be more cumbersome than useful.

On the other hand, any differing *statutory* definition of death would, by hypothesis, be amended and its parent statute should expressly reflect that fact. With the widespread computerization of statutory materials, this should be feasible in most cases. It is now probably feasible also for provisions such as §8301(a) of title 5 of the United States Code, which postpones all federal retirement dates otherwise falling after the first of the month to the first of the following month.

§8.27.   [1]A related approach, says Johnson, "is to attach to contracts exhibits containing compilations of facts. Among other things this device permits drafting to go forward while the facts are being compiled." Letter from James P. Johnson to E. Blythe Stason, Jan. 27, 1964, on file at the American Bar Foundation.

Example:

The seller shall compute the price of any item that is packed in a new container type or size as follows:

(1)   He shall first determine the most similar container type for which he has established a price for that product. From that container type he shall select the nearest size that is 50 percent or less larger than the new size, or if he has no such size, the nearest size that is 50 percent or less smaller. This is the base container.

(2)   The seller shall take as his base price his price for the product when packed in the base container. If this price is a price delivered to any point other than the shipping point, he shall convert it to a price f.o.b. shipping point and deduct the transportation charges that are reflected in it.

(3)   From the price f.o.b. shipping point, the seller shall subtract the direct cost of the container.

(4)   If the new container differs in size from the base container, the seller shall adjust the figure obtained by this deduction by dividing it by the number of units in the base container and multiplying the result by the number of the same units in the new container.

(5)   The seller shall add to the figure so adjusted the direct cost of the container in the new type and size. The resulting figure is the seller's price f.o.b. shipping point for the product in the new container.

(6)   If the seller's base price for the product in the base container is a delivered price, he shall compute transportation charges as follows: He shall take the transportation charges that he deducted from his base price and adjust them in proportion to the difference in shipping weight. If the product in the new container will move under a different freight tariff classification, the seller shall figure his transportation charges (by the same means of transportation and to the same destination) on the basis of the new shipping weight. He shall then add these transportation charges to his f.o.b. shipping

point price for the product in the new container. The resulting figure is his delivered price for the product in the new container.

§8.29.   FORMAT AND LAYOUT

A matter stressed by Felsenfeld and Siegel[1] and the Document Design Center of the American Institutes for Research is the importance of format and layout.[2] See, for example, the sample pages from the Massachusetts insurance policy reproduced in section 14.9, below. How well that instrument has worked in practice I do not know, but its two-dimensional approach would seem to be functional as well as attractive. Format includes typeface and size, margins, blank spaces, line length, space between lines, and other typographical features. Paper color and ink-to-paper contrast also affect readability. These efforts are bearing fruit.

Except where it is prescribed by law, the draftsman has wide control over the format of private legal instruments. He has much less control over the format of statutes and regulations.

§8.30.   EXTERNAL READER AIDS

If the draftsman retains control of the form and presentation of the instrument after it is drafted and issued, he can supply additional reader aids to accompany the instrument even though they are no formal part of it. The advantage of such external aids is that they can be supplied, changed, or deleted without the necessity of amending or reissuing the instrument. Thus examples, diagrams, footnotes, marginal headings, and cross references can be added by the draftsman (or even by others) to enhance the clarity and usability of the instrument. This is commonly done in compilations of statutes.

§8.29.   [1]C. Felsenfeld & A. Siegel, Writing Contracts in Plain English, ch. 8 (1981).

[2]D. Felker (and others), Guidelines for Document Designers (American Institutes for Research, Wash., D.C., 1981).

§8.31. TOO MUCH OF A GOOD THING

Unfortunately, too much help to the reader can boomerang. The following excerpts from an analysis of a critical manual prepared by a federal agency outline the problem and suggest a solution. Where the shoe fits, the analysis seems appropriate to other legal instruments.

> Briefly, the Manual suffers from an overdose of reader aids. The result is as self-defeating as the overuse of neon signs on a commercial street. Taken in the aggregate, there is too great a use of boldface type, capitals, italics, and other devices for catching the eye. An equally distracting factor is the interruption of the continuity of the text with notes, examples, diagrams, and editorial cross references.
>
> This kind of one-dimensional presentation is hard to read and to understand. Moreover, it impairs the reader's access to the materials, because it requires him, when trying to find the provisions on a particular subject, to check through not only the text but the accompanying notes, examples, diagrams, and editorial cross references.
>
> Beyond their normal uses for initial capitalization and abbreviations . . . , capitals are used in the Manual . . . to emphasize important phrases. Unfortunately, this not only impairs readability but implies that there are only two levels in the hierarchy of importance. Also, it implicitly downgrades mandatory provisions that have not been so capitalized. Instead, it would seem preferable to put all such materials in ordinary roman type and let the [user] underscore in pencil what he considers the most significant. . . .
>
> It is believed that the usability of the Manual could be significantly improved by changing to a two-dimensional presentation in which the basic text of the procedures is confined to the left-hand column and all supplementary reader aids such as notes, diagrams, examples, and editorial cross references are placed in the right-hand column opposite the particular provisions of text to which they respectively relate. . . .
>
> Such a format would have several advantages. It would:
>
> (1) Improve the accessibility of specific topics by making it easier to find the relevant provisions of basic text.

(2) Make the text more unified and thus easier to understand.

(3) Make possible the fuller use of editorial cross references to related materials in the same or other manuals, and of other supplementary reader aids, without interrupting the normal flow of basic text.

Although it would require about a third more paper, this would be a small price to pay for improved accessibility, usefulness, and general efficiency in a critical area of operations where even lives are at stake. . . .

To avoid the self-defeating consequences of overuse, boldface type also should be used sparingly. It is proper for section numbers and catchlines and for defined terms in the section on definitions. . . . Otherwise, it should not be used.

IX

Miscellaneous Suggestions on Specific Wording

§9.1 OBJECTIONABLE WORDS

The draftsman should avoid the following terms altogether (they are pure gobbledygook):

above (as an adjective)
above-mentioned
afore-granted
aforementioned
aforesaid
before-mentioned
henceforth
herein
hereinafter
hereinbefore
hereunto
premises (in the sense of matters already referred to)
said (as a substitute for "the," "that," or "those")

same (as a substitute for "it," "he," "him," etc.)
thenceforth
thereunto
therewith
to wit
under-mentioned
unto
whatsoever
whensoever
wheresoever
whereof
whosoever
within-named
witnesseth

§9.2. CIRCUMLOCUTIONS AND REDUNDANCIES

The draftsman should avoid combinations of words or expressions having the same meaning.[1]

§9.1. [1]See §§3.7 and 8.4 *supra*.

alter or change
assumes and agrees
authorize and empower
bind and obligate
by and with
cease and come to an end
chargeable or accountable
convey, transfer, and set over
covenant and agree
deemed and considered
due and owing
each and all
each and every
final and conclusive
finish and complete
for and during the period
for and in behalf of
full and complete
full force and effect
furnish and supply
kept and performed
kind and character
kind and nature
known and described as
made and entered into

mentioned or referred to
null and of no effect
null and void
order and direct
over and above
perform and discharge
perform or observe
power and authority
relieve and discharge
remise, release, and forever quitclaim[2]
shall and will
shall have and may exercise (the power)
sole and exclusive
stand and be in full force
suffer or permit
supersede and displace
then and in that event
true and correct
type and kind
under and subject to
understood and agreed
when and as
within and under the terms of

The draftsman should avoid pairs of words or expressions one of which includes the other (he should use the broader or narrower term as the substance requires):

all and every
any and all
authorize and direct
authorize and require
by and between
by and under
desire and require

from and after
have and obtain
may have access to and examine
means and includes
request and demand
shall have and may exercise (the power)

[2]However, in some states this language is prescribed by statute.

The draftsman should avoid circuitous or otherwise unnecessary expressions such as:

is guilty of . . . (if a punishment is separately prescribed for the crime)
it is herein provided that
mutually agree
now these presents witness that
none whatever
now, therefore,
shall be considered (or "deemed") to be, may be treated as, have the effect of (unless a fiction is intended)
shall be construed to mean

§9.3. PREFERRED EXPRESSIONS

The draftsman should pay careful attention to the recommended language in the following list. However, the preferences expressed are not meant as absolute prescriptions. Individual tastes differ, usages vary, and terms of art often must be honored. The point is that following the "Say" column will in general produce a result that is easier to read than following the "Don't say" column. Some of the items are suggested only as conventions for attaining uniformity. For these, the individual draftsman may have an alternative that will serve as well or better.

Don't say	Say
accorded	given
adequate number of	enough
admit of	allow
afforded	given
all of the	all the
approximately	about
assist, assistance	help
attains the age of	becomes . . . years old
at the time	when
attempt (as a verb)	try

Don't say	*Say*
by means of	by
calculate	compute
category	kind, class, group
cause it to be done	have it done
cease	stop
commence	begin, start
complete [as a verb]	finish
conceal	hide
consequence	result
contiguous to	next to
corporation organized and existing under the laws of New Jersey[1]	New Jersey corporation
deem	consider
does not operate to	does not
donate	give
during such time as	while
during the course of	during
effectuate	carry out
endeavor (as a verb)	try
enter into a contract with	contract with
evince	show
excessive number of	too many
expedite	hasten, speed up
expend	spend
expiration	end
feasible	possible
for the duration of	during
for the purpose of holding (or other gerund)	to hold (or comparable infinitive)
for the reason that	because
forthwith	immediately
frequently	often
hereafter	after this . . . takes effect

---

§9.3. [1]Johnson suggests that in a warranty the phrase "corporation legally organized and existing in good standing under the laws of New Jersey" does add something. Letter from James P. Johnson to E. Blythe Stason, Jan. 27, 1964, on file at the American Bar Foundation.

Don't say	*Say*
heretofore	before this . . . takes effect
in case	if
in cases in which	when, where (say "whenever" or "wherever" only when you need to emphasize the exhaustive or recurring applicability of the rule)
indicate (in the sense of "show")	show
inform	tell
in lieu of	instead of, in place of
in order to	to
inquire	ask
in sections 2023 to 2039, inclusive	in sections 2023-2039
institute	begin, start
interrogate	question
in the event that	if
in the interest of	for
is able to	can
is authorized	may
is binding upon	binds
is empowered	may
is entitled (in the sense of "has the name")	is called
is unable to	cannot
it is directed	shall
it is the duty	shall
it shall be lawful	may
law passed	law enacted
loan (as a verb)	lend
locality	place
locate (in the sense of "find")	find
majority of	most
manner	way
maximum	most, largest, greatest
minimum	least, smallest
modify	change
necessitate	require

Don't say	*Say*
negotiate (in the sense of "enter into" a contract)	make
no later than June 30, 1984	before July 1, 1984
obtain	get
occasion (as a verb)	cause
of a technical nature	technical
on and after July 1, 1984	after June 30, 1984
on his own application	at his request
on or before June 30, 1984	before July 1, 1984
on the part of	by
or, in the alternative	or
paragraph (5) of subsection (a) of section 2097	section 2097(a)(5)
Party of the First Part	[the party's name]
per annum, per day, per foot	a year, a day, a foot
per centum	percent
period of time	period, time
portion (other than in the sense of "measured share")	part
possess	have
preserve	keep
prior	earlier
prior to	before
proceed	go, go ahead
procure	obtain, get
prosecute its business	carry on its business
provision of law	law
purchase (as a verb)	buy
pursuant to	under
remainder	rest
render (in the sense of "cause to be")	make
render (in the sense of "give")	give
require (in the sense of "need")	need
retain	keep
specified (in the sense of "expressly mentioned" or "listed")	named

Don't say	*Say*
state (in the sense of "utter")	tell, give
State of Kansas	Kansas
subsequent, subsequently	later
subsequent to	after
suffer (in the sense of "permit")	permit
sufficient number of	enough
summon	send for, call
terminate[2]	end
the Congress	Congress
the manner in which	how
to the effect that	that
transmit	send
under the provisions of	under
until such time as	until
utilize, employ (in the sense of "use")	use
within or without the United States	inside or outside the United States
with reference to	for
with the object of changing (or other gerund)	to change (or comparable infinitive)

The draftsman should not change a term of art merely because it contains words on the "Don't say" list.

§9.4. "SHALL," "MAY," AND "MUST"

The problems of "shall", "may", and "must" are best seen against the broad spectrum of creating or negating rights, legal authority, duties, or conditions precedent. For these basic legal contingencies the following conventions seem to be lexicographically sound:

[2]But see §8.14 note 3 *supra*.

(1) To create a right, say "is entitled to."
(2) To create discretionary authority, say "may."
(3) To create a duty, say "shall."
(4) To create a mere condition precedent, say "must" (e.g., "To be eligible to occupy the office of mayor, a person must . . .")
(5) To negate a right, say "is not entitled to."
(6) To negate discretionary authority, say "may not."
(7) To negate a duty or a mere condition precedent, say "is not required to."
(8) To create a duty not to act (i.e., a prohibition), say "shall not."

Respecting item (1):

The draftsman should avoid the common error of using "shall" to confer a right when the recipient is the subject of an active sentence. A right should not be stated as a duty to enjoy the right.

Don't say	*Say*
He shall receive compensation of $72,000 a year.	He is entitled to compensation of $72,000 a year.

or

His compensation is $72,000 a year.

Respecting item (2):

If a power conferred on a public authority is liable to be construed by the courts as a duty, the word "may" should be followed by words such as "in his discretion" unless "may" has been expressly defined as being only permissive.

Respecting items (5) and (6):

Although every right to act carries with it the discretionary authority to take the relevant action (but not conversely), merely

214

negating the right ("is not entitled to") does not normally negate the authority. What about the converse? Does negating the authority negate the right? Normally, it does.

In most cases, negating the relevant authority is equivalent to a direct prohibition. On the other hand, in some cases (mainly cases in which the enactment in question is not the exclusive source of authority to act) denial of the authority to act under the enacting instrument does not necessarily negate the authority to act that otherwise flows from other instruments of political power (normally, another and earlier statute). Weakening this possibility is the fact that in most legal contexts it is common to read "No person may" as expressing, however inartistically, an intention to negate all relevant authority to act in the defined circumstances, whatever the source. Where that is the case, negation produces the same result as direct prohibition.

A broader objection to "No person may" (and "No person shall") is that "No person" is the negative counterpart of "Any person," where "any" is normally a form of verbal overkill that provides unneeded emphasis in the routine situation where "A person" alone would be adequate.[1]

Respecting item (7):

Although every duty carries with it the authority to perform the relevant act (but not conversely), negating the duty ("is not required to") does not ordinarily negate the discretionary authority to perform the act.

Read literally, "No person shall" means "No person has a duty to," and is thus equivalent to "A person is not required to," thus negating the duty or condition precedent.[2] However, in most legal contexts, "No person shall . . . ," however inartistic, is likely to be read as a direct prohibition against performing the relevant act. On the other hand, "No person may" negates also the permission and is probably the stronger prohibition.

§9.4.   [1]See §9.5 *infra.*
[2]Cf. E. Driedger, 1 A Manual of Instructions for Legislative and Legal Writing 5, Department of Justice, Canada (1982).

What about the converse? Would negating the authority negate the duty? In most legal contexts, the answer would seem to be yes.

Respecting item (8):

Literally, "A person may not" negates only the authority to act, but in most contexts it is intended to bar action and is thus synonymous with "A person shall not," thus creating a duty to refrain from doing the specified act. Accordingly, this form is an acceptable substitute for "A person shall not." In case of doubt, it is probably safer to use the latter form.

Passive voice:

Sometimes it is not feasible or desirable to identify the person charged with a duty, the recipient of a right or discretionary authority, or the person from whom a right or discretionary authority is withheld or withdrawn. In such a case, the same conventions are respectively appropriate, with the reservation that the person, property, or condition immediately affected by the legal action replaces the unnamed person as the subject of the sentence. The following appear to be appropriate examples:

(1)   "The by-stander shall be treated as if he were the consumer." (Creates a duty in the unnamed person.)

(2)   "The applicant may not be required to pay a fee." (Negates authority in the unnamed person.)

(3)   "A mobile home shall not be moved on a public highway, unless. . . ." (Creates a duty not to act in the unnamed person).[3]

---

[3]Kirk, Legal Drafting: Some Elements of Technique, Tex. Tech. L. Rev. 297, 301-303 (1973).

§9.5. "ANY," "EACH," "EVERY," ETC.

The draftsman should use adjectives such as "each," "every," "any," "all," "no," and "some" (technically known as "pronominal indefinite adjectives") only when necessary. If the subject of the sentence is plural, it is almost never necessary to use such an adjective (e.g., "Qualified state officers shall" rather than "All qualified state officers shall").

If the subject of the sentence is singular, the draftsman should use the pronominal indefinite only when the article "a" or "the" is inadequate, as when the use of "a" would allow the unintended interpretation that the obligation is to be discharged (or the privilege exhausted) by applying it to a single member of the class instead of to all of them. "Any" and "no" should be reserved for instances where the context would otherwise raise a significant doubt as to whether the draftsman intended to cover everyone in the described class.

If it is necessary to use a pronominal indefinite, he should follow these conventions:

(1) If a right, privilege, or power is conferred, use "any" (e.g., "Any qualified state officer may").

(2) If an obligation to act is imposed, use "each" (e.g., "Each qualified state officer shall").

(3) If a right, privilege, or power is abridged, or an obligation to abstain from acting is imposed, use "no" (e.g., "No qualified state officer may").

§9.6. "SUCH"

Although the word "such" is commonly used by lawyers as a demonstrative adjective (i.e., as a word pointing at a particular person, object, or entity already referred to), this use is undesirable because (1) it is contrary to general writing usage, (2) it is a stilted way of saying something better expressed by "that," "the," "those," "it," "them," etc., and (3) it is easily confused with the more appropriate uses of the word (e.g., as a synonym, when followed by "a" or "as," for "that kind of").[1]

Don't say	*Say*
. . . to pay to such child the income and such amounts of the principal as my trustee considers appropriate for the welfare of such child.	. . . to pay to that child the income and such amounts of the principal as my trustee considers appropriate for the child's welfare.

§9.7. "RESPECTIVELY" AND "AS THE CASE MAY BE"

If the draftsman wants to apply A to X, B to Y, and C to Z, but it is awkward to state it that way, he should say, "A, B, and C apply to X, Y, and Z, respectively." The three relationships are concurrent, not alternative. The verb in such a sentence is plural. If he wants to apply A if X occurs, B if Y occurs, and C if Z occurs, and it is awkward to state it that way, he should say "If X, Y, or Z occurs, A, B, or C applies, as the case may be." The three relationships are alternative, not concurrent. The verb in such a sentence is singular.

§9.8. PLACEMENT OF THE NEGATIVE

The draftsman should use care in placing the negative. For example, the sentence "The trustees may not appoint more than ten directors" is not necessarily equivalent to the sentence "The trustees may appoint not more than ten directors." The former expresses a prohibition against their appointing more than ten directors, and in context may or may not imply authority to appoint directors not exceeding ten; whereas the latter ex-

§9.6.   [1]H. Fowler, A Dictionary of Modern English Usage 602, para. 4, 5 (2d ed. Gowers 1965).

presses authority to appoint directors not exceeding ten, and in context may or may not imply a prohibition against appointing more than ten. Thus, the two sentences are equivalent only in a context in which each implication arises.

§9.9. AVOIDING THE "UNDISTRIBUTED MIDDLE"

When creating a mutually exhaustive dichotomy, the draftsman should take care not to leave an "undistributed middle." For example, if the draftsman describes one class as "an employee who is at least 65 years old *or* has at least 35 years of service," he should describe the remaining class as "an employee who is under 65 years old *and* has less than 35 years of service," or, preferably in this instance, "any other employee." For the same reason, he must not refer to two exhaustive classes as "persons born before January 1, 1984," and "persons born after January 1, 1984." To do so omits persons born on that date.

X

Verbal Sexism

§10.1. THE PROBLEM

One of the aims of feminists has been to remove from statutes (and other forms of law) provisions that discriminate against women. An old offender was the Mississippi statute that limited jurors to "male citizens."[1]

Discontent with similarly offensive federal laws prompted President Carter to issue his memorandum of August 26, 1977,[2] requesting federal agencies "to cooperate in eliminating sex discrimination from the laws and policies of the United States." This launched a movement that, aided by computerized research, has reached not only substantive discrimination but "verbal sexism."[3]

§10.1. [1]Miss. Code 1942 Ann. §1762, repealed by Gen. Law 1968, ch. 335, §1.

[2]MLD 186. The impetus was probably the U.S. Commission on Civil Rights' report, Sex Bias in the U.S. Code (1977).

[3]"Substantive discrimination" unfairly denies to women a right, privilege, power, or immunity that is granted to men. (An example appears in the second sentence of this chapter.) "Verbal sexism" consists of uses of the masculine gender (e.g., "chairman" and "he") to refer also to women. This chapter is concerned only with the latter. It also bypasses the problem of interpreting statutes and other instruments that fail to make clear whether their use of the masculine gender includes women. It is assumed, of course, that such ambiguities should be resolved, preferably by clearer drafting. Substantive discrimination and the problem of ambiguity are discussed in Comment, Sexism in the

In the federal government, an attack on "sexist" terms was formally mounted in the Federal Register's Legal Drafting Style Manual,[4] which admonished government draftsmen not to use gender-specific job titles such as "chairman" or "chairwoman" or to use gender-specific pronouns (which occur only in the third person singular) to refer to people generally, unless they were paired, as in "he or she." Corresponding state efforts began with a directive by Washington's Governor Dixy Lee Ray and spread to other states.[5]

Substantive sexism may be totally exclusionary or something less discriminatory. It may be intentional, accidental, or incidental. Verbal sexism includes language that is conducive to treating women unfairly. It may be expressly or impliedly condemnatory or scornful, but at worst this would be rare in any legal instrument to which this book is directed. Or it may consist only of including women in terms that have connotations of maleness. Male connotations may be active, moribund, dead, merely apparent, or subliminal. Sexism may result from distrust of women, condescension, or mere laziness.

What sex-related evils would conscientious feminists like to stamp out? Certainly, unfair exclusion or discrimination. Certainly, condemnatory, scornful, derogatory, condescending, or otherwise demeaning language. But what about words that include women but do not generate sexism beyond apparently carrying connotations of maleness?

In cases not involving substantive discrimination, two general questions arise: How sexist are the verbal targets of this movement? What effect would a thorough verbal "desexification" have on definitive legal instruments?

People who are both sympathetic to the women's movement and sensitive to factors affecting clarity and readability may find it hard to reconcile some of the things now being done

---

Statutes: Identifying and Solving the Problem of Ambiguous Gender Bias in Legal Writing, 32 Buffalo L. Rev. 559 (1983).

[4]§§19.1-19.3 (MLD 187).

[5]The Civil Rights Division of the U.S. Department of Justice has issued a booklet listing the actions taken by the several states.

in the name of removing verbal sex bias from legal instruments.[6] The problem is to determine not only what is currently and significantly sexist but the extent to which removal is, under the circumstances, the wisest alternative or even feasible.

Fortunately, there are some measures (to be discussed later) that may help alleviate verbal sexism without producing undesirable side effects. Fortunately, too, appropriate concessions to legal clarity and readability can at the same time reduce significant risks from the simplistic, the sometimes counterproductive, and ultimately the unworkable. We need a sense of proportion here and perhaps even a sense of humor.[7]

§10.2. CONSIDERATIONS OF BALANCE

Although the widespread aversion to verbal sexism needs no defending here, such sexism is hard to identify and ferret out without disturbing the law's sensitive communication process. This chapter is more than normally conservative in this respect, because, while general, it is addressed to the formulation of definitive legal instruments, the authors of which are more restricted than are the authors of any other kind of writing.[1]

Caution is advisable, because (1) there is no point in trying to categorically rid legal instruments of "sexisms" that, because of death or false etymology, appear to be such only to the biased or uninformed, (2) it is not always possible to find an appropri-

---

[6]The moral validity of the feminist cause does not qualify even its most dedicated adherents to change the extraordinarily complex system of communication that comprises the English language, if they have not complied with the fundamental principles of semantics.

[7]See, e.g., McFadden, In Defense of Gender, The New York Times Magazine, August 2, 1981, reprinted in M. Hogan, ed., Words and the Writer: A Language Reader 200-202 (1984).

§10.2.   [1]D. Hirsch, Drafting Federal Law 31 (1980).

Do not forget . . . that as a draftsman your overriding objective is to express an idea as clearly and simply as you can, not to pursue a social ideology, no matter how lofty.

. . . [I]nnovation in devising new meanings for words is a flaw, not an asset in a draftsman. . . . Certainty of meaning largely depends upon the draftsman's unbendingly conservative use of language. *Id.*

ate replacement that does not contribute to an exorbitant cumu-lative price in clarity or readability,[2] and (3) it is impossible to follow through thoroughly without disfiguring the language and trivializing the feminist cause. Finally, established sex stereo-types can be dislodged only gradually and then, not by fiat, but by general usage.

§10.3. THE SEXIST "MAN"

The word (or root) "man" has incited probably the worst en-mity. Like many other words, it has at least two meanings, going back in this instance to Old English.[1] Where multiple meanings are widely disparate and normally sorted out in usage, their verbal counterparts are called "homonyms,"[2] for which (despite surface appearances) the different meanings define functionally different words.

One meaning of "man" is sex-oriented in that it differenti-ates a male person from a female person. The other principal meaning denotes human beings as a comprehensive class; in appropriate contexts, it embraces both sexes and is therefore sex-neutral. But can these meanings, which are not widely dispa-rate, be safely put aside as supporting a harmless pair of homo-nyms?

Consider this: Friedrich Waismann has pointed out that "man" is similar to other words in having several meanings, one of which clearly differentiates itself from something else while another meaning includes it.[3] "Day" in one sense differs from

[2]Readability is not necessarily clarity. See §§8.9 and 8.11 *supra* and the discussion, in MLD 284-288, of Flesch's attempt to simplify 10 U.S. Code §1201.

§10.3. [1]C. Miller & K. Swift, Words and Women: New Language in New Times 27-28 (1976); Clubb, And God Created Person, letter to Modern Lan-guage Association Newsletter, March 1974, MLD 190.

[2]E.g., "If he *can,* the buyer shall return the empty *can.*" See §3.4 *supra.*

[3]Analytic-Synthetic V, 11 Analysis (No. 1, October 1957), p.3; reprinted as The Resources of Language, M. Black, ed., The Importance of Languages 107-109 (1962) (MLD 190). O'Connor, in Toward an Inclusive Theology, The Christian Century, November 30, 1983, 1114, 1117, calls this an example of "synecdoche," but if it is, note that referring to a ship as a "sail" in no wise demeans the hull, mast, or anchor.

"night," but in another sense includes it ("He was gone for three days"). "Old" in one sense differs from "young," but in another sense includes it ("How old is your youngster?"). "Far" in one sense differs from "near," but in another sense includes it ("How far is it to the nearest mailbox?"). So also for "man."

As with simple homonyms, the important thing is that in their respective contexts the connotations of the narrower meaning do not contaminate the broader meaning,[4] unless (as sometimes happens) context in the particular situation is too frail to tell us which meaning is operating.[5] This suggests that tinkering with internal context may, in many cases, be the most appropriate option. If a gender definition[6] is used, it should be included in the particular instrument and not merely in some omnibus "interpretation act."

This analysis does not absolve compound words such as "fireman," "policeman," and "middleman," each of which over the years has carried an express male reference sustained by the fact that their respective activities were, until recently, performed almost exclusively by men. On the other hand, persons familiar with the dead metaphor[7] should not find it hard to envision the possibility of dead or dying sexism.[8] Recognition of

---

[4]That "man" is a homonym does not mean that connotations of "man" in its narrow, male sense carry over to "man" in its broad, mankind sense any more than "day"'s connotations of daylight, when contrasted with night, carry over to "day" in its time-measuring sense.

[5]See Comment *supra* §10.1 note 3.

[6]On the basis of what I currently know about gender and sex, I would write something like this:

> Unless the context shows otherwise, use of the masculine gender includes female persons [and all organizations] and use of the feminine gender includes male persons [and all organizations].

The bracketed words are to be included where appropriate. Cf. Driedger, *infra* §10.5 note 3 at 670-672.

[7]W. Alston, Philosophy of Language 99, 101-102 (1964). To communicate metaphorically is to use words that refer only to something analogous to what we are referring to, but in a context that steers the reader to the intended meaning. ("He is a bag of wind.") A dead metaphor is one in which the original express allusion has disappeared and the expression now refers directly to its analogue. ("He took a fork in the road.") Thus, a metaphor dies when the audience gets the intended meaning without adverting to the original meaning. So, too, for dying sexism.

[8]W. Strunk & E. White, The Elements of Style 60 (3d ed. 1979).

the suggestive value of etymology does not imply that the original meaning of a word necessarily controls its current meaning.[9]

Let us first consider sexism that has long since died. Is there not dead sexism in such Greek or Latin-based words as "enthusiasm," "puerile," and "virtue?"[10] Although the law fraternity that recently expunged "brotherhood" from its ritual was not sensitive enough to recognize the sexist "fraternal," inconsistency may be the lesser evil in this area. Potentially, we have a bottomless pit, unless the original sexism has died or been cured in the process of assimilation and modified use.

Except where there is a substitute congenial[11] to definitive legal instruments (for example, "firefighter" for "fireman"), the best approach is to adhere to "man" where it clearly refers to human beings without regard to sex or where, as part of a compound word ("craftsmanship"), it refers to a class that originally included only men but is now generally understood in the relevant context or speech community as including women.[12]

§10.4.   SEXIST SUFFIXES

"Man" is not the only offending word or root. What about the once-male or in some cases still-male, suffixes "-er," "-or," and "-ar"?[1] The fact that the enemies of "draftsman" and "workman" are willing to respectively substitute "drafter" and "worker" suggests that they are not necessarily offended by dead sexism (assuming, of course, that they recognize it). This

[9]MLD 52-53. See also *supra* note 8. This principle was recognized by the U.S. Commission on Civil Rights in its report, *supra* §10.1 note 2 at 106:

> Although ["fellowship"] is masculine in origin, it need not be replaced since fellowships have not been awarded solely to men in recent years, and the term now has a sex-neutral connotation.

[10]"Enthusiasm," literally "God inspired," has as one of its roots the Greek-based prefix "the-" or "theo-," referring to God or a god, a male concept. "Puer," of course, is Latin for "boy"; "vir," Latin for "adult male."

[11]That is, familiar, grammatical, and not awkward. The important thing is to minimize significant semantic readjustment.

[12]Weihofen, Legal Writing Style 19 (2d ed. 1980).

§10.4. [1]See D. Mellinkoff, Legal Writing: Sense and Nonsense 47 (1982).

is reaffirmed by a general willingness to accept, as decently neutral, terms such as "lawyer," "doctor," and "scholar."[2] This is fortunate, because many of the words so accepted have no satisfactory female counterparts and no acceptable across-the-board neutral alternatives.[3]

Stickier are words such as "administrator," "aviator," and "prosecutor," which have female, but less-used, counterparts (for example, "prosecutrix") and no general neutral alternatives. David Mellinkoff notes that "[t]hose female versions . . . are headed for extinction. The once male forms may eventually become as sex neutral as the once equally male 'juror.' "[4] The growing acceptance of these terms to cover both sexes is significant, because the vestigial use of their female counterparts remains to remind us even of dying sexism. May we not conclude that, where the residual sex connotations are minimal, it may not be worth the cumulative effort of doing away with them?

What about words such as "waiter" and "waitress," whose respective sex connotations have been undiluted by applications to the opposite sex and for which there is no neutral term in current use? The connotations of sex are hardly dead or dying here. And what about male forms for which there is a female, but no congenial neutral, counterpart that is generally viewed in the kind of context involved as including women. "Actor" meets the test, but "waiter," as yet, does not.

"Waitperson" is an interesting invention, but it will not fly (what about "server," which appears on many meal checks?). Together with "freshperson"[5] "watchperson," and "personhole," it will stay on the ground, where "chairperson" still belongs.

There is no easy across-the-board fix here. Each term (in each of its respective contexts) should be examined separately. It is also important to keep in mind that the drafting of definitive

---

[2]Has any theatrical group objected to "Screen Actors Guild"?

[3]"Attorney" is not satisfactorily synonymous with "lawyer" and, in any event, it is no less etymologically sexist, being derived from the past participle masculine of "atourner." Oxford English Dictionary.

[4]Mellinkoff, *supra* note 1 at 48.

[5]This word surfaced briefly at Southern Illinois University.

legal instruments is already so sensitive that draftsmen do not need to be burdened further by the unnecessary.

§10.5.   SEXIST PRONOUNS

It is harder to deal with the third person singular pronouns "he" and "she" (and their variants), which, in or out of context, can hardly be classed as other than "masculine" and "feminine." Can homonymity or dead sexism vindicate these?

    Elmer A. Driedger has found partial vindication in the concept of "gender."[1]

> English is an uninflected language, and gender declensions have disappeared except in the personal pronouns singular. . . .
>   The situation is quite different in inflected languages, such as German and French. In those languages, gender is not equated to sex; masculine is not necessarily male, feminine is not necessarily female, and an inanimate thing could be masculine or feminine instead of neuter. "Gender" says Eric Partridge "refers to words; as a synonym for sex it is jocular and archaic."[2] . . .
>   The problem in modern English is that it is difficult to dissociate gender from sex in personal pronouns. In referring to words that denote persons in general, when sex is inconspicuous or unimportant, . . . why *he*? Why not *she* or, as in the French, sometimes *he* and sometimes *she*? The answer is probably that English simply follows its ancestor languages [which are primarily Teutonic. — ED] . . .
>   The situation seems to be that although gender forms and declensions have disappeared, gender still remains, hidden but nevertheless active in a few situations. The result is that words like *man, one, everyone, each, every person* are just like their ancestors, masculine gender. The pronoun representing these words must also be masculine, and all we have available is *he, his* and *him.*

    §10.5.   [1]On the widespread confusion regarding sex and gender, see Mellinkoff, *supra* §10.4 note 1 at 47. Despite their close correlation, the real offender is sex, not gender.

    [2]The significance of this is in no wise compromised by the recent popular use of "gender" as a euphemism for sex.

When used in this way, these pronouns indicate the gender of the words they represent, and have nothing to do with sex.[3]

A more persuasive fact is that our primary interest is not in what is generally true of the language but in what is true in areas where context makes clear that sex is irrelevant. Here, the overriding fact is that in these contexts long-established usage (sometimes reinforced by a gender definition) has made clear that "he" includes both sexes.[4] The sexism, if any, consists of residual overtones of maleness significant mainly to persons hypersensitized by a preoccupation with feminist concerns.

What approaches to singular pronouns in legal instruments are available? At least seven have been proposed:

(1) Adopt the "he or she" approach.
(2) Avoid third person singular pronouns and in each case repeat the noun.
(3) Substitute "they," "their," and "them," respectively, for "he," "his," and "him."
(4) Use plural nouns (for which the applicable pronouns are sex-neutral).
(5) Convert the instrument from the third person to the second.
(6) Shift to the passive voice.[5]
(7) Continue to use "he," "his," and "him" until the

[3]Driedger, Are Statutes Written for Men Only?, 22 McGill L.J. 666, 667, 669-670 (1976) (quoted with permission). For another excellent discussion of gender and sex, see R. Waddell, Grammar and Style 48-50, 61-62 (1951). See also G. Block, Effective Legal Writing 14 (1981); Mellinkoff, *supra* §10.4 note 1 at 47-48. Theoretically, Canadian draftsmen could face a special problem. Driedger (in conversation) has pointed out that, if they accepted without limitation the strictures against gender-specific words, it would be impossible to apply them to the mandated French versions, because every French noun or pronoun is either masculine or feminine. If French-speaking Canadians do not consider this a problem, no one else is likely to. For the Australian view, see Avoidance of "Sexist" Language in Legislation, 11 Commonwealth L. Bull. 590 (1985).

[4]Strunk & White, *supra* §10.3 note 8. There seems to be general agreement on this.

[5]Simply Stated (No. 28, August 1982) 2 (monthly newsletter of Document Design Center, American Institutes for Research, Wash., D.C.).

normal processes of usage have created congenial substitutes.

The first approach[6] is clumsy, sometimes to the point of being intolerable.[7] Theodore Bernstein dismisses "his or her" simply as "stilted."[8] Even worse, Driedger reminds us that in many statutes "person" includes organizations,[9] in which case the multiple third person singular pronouns would have to be "he, she, or it," "his, hers, or its," and "him, her, or it."

Note also that, whereas "he" alone is in many legal contexts *not* sexist, "he or she" *is* sexist in giving priority to the masculine. Strunk and White anticipated this problem by alternately

[6]Approved by A Style Guide for CBO: About Writing and Word Usage 21 (rev. ed. Cong. Budget Off. 1985); L. Squires & M. Rombauer, Legal Writing 232 (1982); R. Wydick, Plain English for Lawyers 61 (1979), if used sparingly. So also by the Legislation Committee of Cabinet in Australia, but without the reservation, 58 Aust. L.J. 685, 686 (1984).

[7]Strunk & White, *supra* §10.3 note 8 at 61. Implicit support comes from an interesting source, The Anatomy of Power, a recent book by John Kenneth Galbraith, who, according to columnist James K. Kilpatrick, is "acutely aware of the sensitivity of many females to the male nuances of the English language." Indianapolis Star, November 27, 1983, p. 6F. Kilpatrick notes that Galbraith dutifully used "he or she" until he reached page 42, where his feminist views finally yielded to his deep respect for good style in exposition. There he wrote:

> The individual who has access to the instruments of power has a natural attraction for those who wish to share his influence, live in his shadow. It would not be seemly to tell him that his access . . .

In the following legal excerpt, the change of heart, after two tries, was even quicker:

> For example, an individual's performance may be used without *his or her* consent. People will normally pay to watch *that entertainer,* but where the performance is misappropriated, *he* is unable to reap the benefits of *his* talent and capitalize upon the public demand for *his* performance. [Emphasis added.]

Ausness, The Right of Publicity: A "Haystack in a Hurricane," 55 Temp. L.Q. 977 (1982).

Unfortunately, the need in any definitive legal instrument for a consistent style rules out switching back and forth as complexity waxes and wanes. Fortunately, large clusters of "he"'s are not so likely to appear in definitive legal documents.

[8]T. Bernstein, The Careful Writer 351 (1973).
[9]Driedger, *supra* note 3 at 667.

reversing the order.[10] This not only compromises readability but produces "elegant variation," thus violating the basic principle of clear legal drafting that shifts in form are justified only by corresponding shifts in substance.[11]

One possible compromise would be to continue to use the generic "he" (bolstered as needed by a gender definition)[12] in statutes, regulations, and ordinances, where it has had long professional acceptance and no congenial replacement is available, and to use the more awkward "he or she" (1) in instruments intended for lay audiences that are likely to view the otherwise generic "he" as sexist or that are the more intimately involved as individuals, or (2) where, as Bernstein says, "the issue of sex is present and pointed."[13] Conversely, in the relatively few situations in which the class dealt with, such as nurses, continues to be overwhelmingly female, use of "she" alone is appropriate. But this needs to be bolstered by a gender definition, because it is still unusual enough to raise the interpretive question of whether use of the feminine gender announces an intent to exclude males.[14]

The second approach,[15] which involves repeating the nouns, adds a degree of awkwardness that legal utterances hardly need and it thus helps frustrate current efforts to alleviate a writing malaise that remains a continuing embarrassment to the legal profession.

The third approach, which commonly bastardizes "their" in conversation, is assiduously avoided by almost all serious writ-

[10]*Supra* §10.3 note 8; also suggested by the Federal Register style manual, *supra* §10.4 note 2. Mellinkoff, §10.3 *supra* note 1, says of alternating use, "This is the equal time doctrine. Sexist madness."

[11]See §§2.3.1, 6.14, 8.1 *supra;* MLD 168-171.

[12]See §10.3 note 6 *supra.*

[13]Bernstein, note 8 *supra.* E.g., "In the case of spouses, each must make his or her own choice separately."

[14]See Comment, *supra* §10.1 note 3.

[15]Adopted by the National Conference of Commissioners of Uniform State Laws and the State of Indiana. So also by the Legislation Committee of Cabinet in Australia, 58 Aust. L.J. 685 (1984). I have yet to find an authority on language who accepts it as having more than the most marginal use. Even so, it may be the least objectionable alternative to the status quo.

ers of exposition.[16] Were this to become an accepted convention for writers, it would provide a simple and clear solution. Unfortunately, definitive legal instruments do not provide an appropriate opportunity for this kind of semantic innovation.[17]

The fourth approach,[18] which resorts to plural nouns, works in many cases, but in many others it creates a syntactic ambiguity indigenous to the plural: Does the predicate apply separately to each member of the subject class or jointly to the subject class taken as a whole?[19]

The fifth approach,[20] which involves resort to the second person, is universally considered out of place in statutes and ordinances and appropriate only in some regulations. It is more appropriate in private, personalized legal instruments. The main objection is that adoption of the second person would normally extend to the whole document and that the choice between adopting and not adopting usually depends on other, more significant considerations such as the level of formality appropriate in the circumstances to the users of the instrument. Also, the second person would probably look silly in a statute or regulation whose addressees included corporations and other organizations.

---

[16]Recognized, but not approved, by Block, *supra* note 3 at 14; disapproved by 95 percent of the 103-member Usage Panel of the American Heritage Dictionary of the English Language (1969), p.xxiv; classified as "informal" by its Second College edition (1982), p.1260 ("many words that are perfectly acceptable in conversation with friends or colleagues would be unsuitable in . . . formal prose" p. 48); classified as "colloquial" by Webster's New Word Dictionary of the American Language (2d coll. ed. 1982), p.1474; unclassified by Webster's Ninth New Collegiate Dictionary, p. 1232, while apparently fitting its "nonstand[ard]" usage label ("disapproved by many, but [having] some currency"), p. 18.

[17]See §10.2 note 1 *supra*. Mellinkoff says, "If you can't find a way out of *he, his,* or *him* other than illiteracy or bad grammar, you had better stick with what you've got. . . ." §10.4 note 1 *supra* at 50. Most legitimate semantic innovation in legal drafting consists of definitional line-drawing in the fringe areas surrounding undesirably vague terms.

[18]Approved by Weihofen, *supra* §10.4 note 8, at 20; Wydick, *supra* note 6 at 61. *Cf.* Hirsch, *supra* §10.2 note 1 at 30-31.

[19]§6.5 *supra;* Hirsch, *supra* §10.2 note 1 at 30-31.

[20]Approved by Squires & Rombauer, *supra* note 6 at 232; Weinhofen, *supra* §10.4 note 8 at 20; Wydick, *supra* §10.5 note 6 at 61.

The sixth approach of switching to the passive voice, while not impairing clarity,[21] concededly impairs readability.[22]

The seventh approach[23] is to stay for the most part with the least objectionable current alternative, the accepted, semantic legal conventions, where context stands as an effective bastion against at least significant verbal sexism and where the addition of females is steadily eroding it.

For personalized private legal instruments, such as wills and leases (which can be tailored to the individual situations of the participants), the problem is easily handled. On printed forms, "he/she" can be sex-personalized by striking the inapplicable pronoun. For computerized boilerplate, alternative male and female versions can be stored in the electronic memory.[24]

In other cases, hypersensitive draftsmen (or draftsmen with hypersensitive clients) can at least partly assuage semantic guilt by adhering to otherwise sound drafting principles that incidentally remove even the false appearance of sexism. These include:

(1) avoiding unneeded pronominal references;[25]
(2) using the second person throughout the instrument in instances where use of the second person is otherwise preferable; and
(3) using "he or she" where substance occasionally requires a sex distinction.[26]

These principles can be applied for the most part without adverting to the problem of apparent sexism. On the other hand, using the plural noun, generally considered to be unnecessarily risky unless substance requires it, is acceptable only

[21]Charrow, What is "Plain English," Anyway?, Publication C1, Document Design Center, American Institutes for Research 2, 9 (Wash. D.C. 1979), MLD 278-282.

[22]§8.18 *supra.*

[23]Approved by Strunk & White, *supra* §10.3 note 8 at 60-61.

[24]See §8.1 *supra.* Good boilerplate is hard to draft and easy to over-rely on. The number of checkpoints can be reduced modestly by a judicious elimination of unneeded pronouns.

[25]Wydick, *supra* note 6 at 61.

[26]E.g., see note 13 *supra* and accompanying text.

if the draftsman is consistently on guard against syntactic ambiguity. It is much easier (and safer) to opt, wherever possible, for the singular.[27]

§10.6. SEX-NEUTRAL TERMS

In statutes, regulations, ordinances, and other instruments addressed to large groups of people, the generality of the terms used should reflect the generality of the classifications being referred to. If there is a congenial generic form that is sex-neutral, that form can safely be preferred to forms with any significant chance of being read with a sex orientation. Thus, the British can use "Sovereign" or "Crown" in preference to "King," "Queen," or "King or Queen." Nor is there any awkwardness in referring to airline stewards and stewardesses as "flight attendants." "Firefighter" creates few ripples. With "actor" and "actress," on the other hand, there is no comparatively neutral third term (except where the context permits an unstrained transfer to "performer" or "player"). Fortunately, "actor" is becoming sex-neutral. The residual sexism is at worst minimal, a small price to pay to help the consumers of legislative or regulatory instruments read and understand what they read.

   Where an acceptable replacement is found for a word designating a class of people, it does not follow that a similar substitution is appropriate in a compound word of which the discarded word is a part. Thus, the substitution of "worker" for "workman" or "drafter" for "draftsman" would not necessarily call for a corresponding change in "workmanship" or "draftsmanship". Not only would such a substitution be highly awkward but "workmanship" and "draftsmanship" refer to activities, not persons.[1]

---

[27]See *supra* note 19 and accompanying text.
   §10.6. [1]Those who feel impelled to substitute "humankind" for "mankind" (which does not involve even dead sexism) have a double problem. First, whatever might be theoretically offensive about "mankind" persists in "humankind." Second, those who are willing to look at etymology to vindicate "manual" and "management" as derived from "manus" (Latin for hand), or

§10.7. LINGERING DOUBTS: DEALING WITH LEGAL STEREOTYPES

If there are lingering doubts here, they challenge the psycholinguists to determine whether, despite the otherwise impressive force of context, a significant subliminal residue of sexism remains.[1] Even if it does, the question remains as to the extent to which the benefit of removing it justifies the cumulative price.

In the meantime, even the most ardent equalitarians should realize that over-zealousness, egged on by false etymology or the mistaken view that etymology irrevocably shapes the present (and thus the future), fosters a spurious perfectionism that helps exacerbate the very semantic problem they are trying to solve.[2]

"mantle" as derived from its Latin name "mantellum," should be willing to look at etymology to vindicate "mankind" as derived from the German word for the whole human race (see also §10.7 note 3 infra). In any event, the curative power of "hu" remains unexplained.

§10.7.   [1]The studies cited in Miller & Swift, supra §10.3 note 1 at 21-25 may not be wholly persuasive. For one thing, lawyers do not draft for infants. Also, for any mixed class that is predominantly male, it seems plausible to assume a natural tendency to visualize in terms of the most typical members ("stereotypes"), even if the name of the class is theoretically neutral and "he or she" is used. If such visualization is "sexist," its roots are inherently psychological rather than verbal and therefore hard, if not impossible, to change, unless the physical constitution of the class is changed. But it is no more sexist to visualize the typical plumber as male than it is "racist" to visualize the typical symphony conductor as white. The studies relied on by Miller and Swift are suspect because the pictorialization required in the tests tended to sharpen normal visualization (which is derived from mere words) by encouraging sex specificity. Cf. Collins, Language, History, and the Legal Process: A Profile of "The Reasonable Man," 8 Rutgers Camden L. J. 311, 322 (1977). Maybe we should take another look here.

[2]Friendly, Language and the Woperson's Movement, Washington Post, May 2, 1978, MLD 188.

> [A]mong the worthy and long-overdue goals of the women's-rights movement is a world in which the activity of women in all pursuits of life on an equal basis with that of men is so normal and accepted that it would be ridiculous to remark on it. Yet the insistence of the strident fringe of the movement on *spokeswoman* and *chairperson* is in fact a remark on it, and perpetuates rather than extinguishes an invidious discrimination.

Much of the problem would go away, if the verbal feminists concentrated on substantive sex discrimination and allowed erstwhile sexist terms not otherwise smoothly avoidable to automatically adjust and ultimately self-destruct.

Although etymology is an unreliable guide to current meaning, it may be needed to dispel the verbal fallacies of persons who have misused or been confused by it.[3] To this, the conscientious equalitarian may reasonably reply that even sexism that is based on false assumptions is nonetheless undesirable and worth eliminating. How should a conscientious draftsman respond?

The answer lies in the legal audiences respectively involved. What speech communities do draftsmen address? They owe primary consideration to the relevant speech communities that it is the business of current standard dictionaries and similar reference services to reflect. What the extreme equalitarians may not realize is that, in often finding sexism where sexism does not exist, is dying, or exists only subliminally, their heightened sensitivity has led them to believe that they are members of a recognizable speech community in which they constitute the predominant element, whereas they remain in most instances a hard-to-measure minority element in each of a number of traditional speech communities defined by other considerations.[4]

Identifying the speech communities relevant to any intended message is important, because in each case it determines the nature of the reader stereotype ("the typical reader")[5] at which the message is mainly aimed and the methods best cal-

---

[3]Johnson, Words Between the Sexes, 9 Student Law. (No. 1) 64 (September 1980). Johnson uses etymology to justify "man" in "manage", but she repudiates it as a justification for "man" in "mankind" (see *supra* §10.6 note 1), on the ground that in the latter case English misuse has tainted the once-neutral meaning. But if the typical reader, who is unversed in etymology, cannot (even with the help of context) distinguish the "man" in "mankind" from the "man" in "fireman," how does he easily distinguish the "man" in "manage" or the "man" in "mantle" (see *supra* §10.6 note 4)? The answer is that in *both* cases he distinguishes on the basis of connotations flowing from their established uses in context. Johnson merely describes what has happened in still-limited feminist speech subcommunities, discussed later.

[4]The main exceptions, of course, are communications (such as this chapter) that are addressed, at least partly, to extreme feminists. As for feminists generally, it has yet to be shown that the extreme feminist is the appropriate stereotype.

[5]Being psychologically inevitable, stereotypes are not necessarily bad. (Every concept used in serious exposition invites a stereotype.) The problem is to avoid the untypical and the irrelevantly specific.

culated to score a hit. It is not fruitful to impair the communication process appropriate to typical members of the audience being addressed. Legal instruments of general applicability can only be drafted with the guidance of stereotypes, many of which have in the past been unequivocally male. Indeed, keeping in mind the typical member of the legal audience (which is increasingly female) is the essence of sound drafting.

Are the meanings of words restricted to the *visual* stereotypes that the underlying concepts tend to generate? By no means. That an author may visualize stereotypes does not mean that he intends to deal only with them or that the language he uses is limited to them.[6] This is true even where at the time of composition the stereotype exhausts the class.

This does not mean that sex-related words are a good thing. It means that, as writers, we need a perspective that recognizes that the English language is laced with language defects, many of which are far more serious than those relating to third-person singular pronouns or the fact that "man" has twin uses as a separate word and even more uses as a root.

§10.8. THE ULTIMATE CURE (DO NEW NAMES WORK?)

Here is the critical point: The current nature of a referent is ultimately more determinative of connotations than the name attached to it. Thus, prolonged changes in usage easily override the vagaries of verbal history. As women enter areas previously reserved for men, the habitual associations of words with our respective perceptions of reality (which generate word meanings) generate compensating changes in connotations as they erode earlier ones. Although subject to cultural lag, the process is automatic. That is why the male connotations of "fraternity" have been gradually disappearing with the admission of women

[6]R. Dickerson, The Interpretation and Application of Statutes, 23, 80 (1975); C. Nutting & R. Dickerson, Cases & Materials on Legislation 503-504 (5th ed. 1978). "[O]ne may mean a good many things one does not consciously intend." Jacobson, Satanic Semiotics, Jobian Jurisprudence, 19 Semeia 63, 64 (1981).

into law fraternities, which may explain why there is no significant demand for a formally balanced term such as "fratority."[1] (Even "guys" is now being used to include women.) Language has a built-in capacity to adjust its connotations to reflect new denotations and new kinds of denotations.

"Freshman," despite its etymologically male ending, clearly includes women, and almost no one seems to be uncomfortable with the verbal result,[2] because with coeducation the original connotations of maleness have long since died. The same would seem to be true of "chairman."

"Conductor" (orchestral) is another matter. Not only does it have a masculine ending, but the masculine visual stereotype is strong, because the overwhelming proportion of orchestral conductors continues to be male. But does the word exclude or demean women?

Substitute a new, neutral term for "freshman" and it will carry no male connotation, that of its predecessor having previously expired. Substitute the same word for "conductor" and it will quickly acquire the male connotations of its predecessor. Why? Because the visual stereotype in the latter case is undoubtedly male and will remain so at least until there is a stronger representation of women who conduct musical performances. Changing names would make a relevant difference in neither case.

This does not say that names are unimportant. Words with offensive connotations are worth trying to avoid. "Bitch," when applied to a woman, is offensive, not merely because it refers to a dog, but because as a dead metaphor it has become, through usage, an epithet with strong connotations of scorn. But no demeaning or exclusionary connotations attach to "draftsmanship" or "chairman," except in fringe speech subcommunities.

---

§10.8.   [1]The musical organization Sigma Alpha Iota describes itself as a "music fraternity for women." The recommendation of the U.S. Commission on Civil Rights to replace "fraternity and sorority chapters" with "social societies" misfires because the replacement, undefined, is too loose to be adequately synonymous and is thus uncertain and novel enough to impair clarity and readability. Report, *supra* §10.1 note 2 at 169.

[2]But see §10.4 note 5 *supra.* See also §10.3 note 9 *supra.*

The present problem thus arises largely from the current prevalence of male visual stereotypes, which result, in turn, not from names so much as the overwhelming presence of males in the categories concerned. (The converse is true in the case of "nurse," where the visual stereotype continues to be overwhelmingly female). Changing names on any large scale would be semantically very hard, would come at a cumulatively high price in clarity or readability, and would accomplish little. On the other hand, paying greater attention to the substantive inequities that still plague women will facilitate their greater representation in various activities and to the same extent facilitate the natural demise of verbal sexism, because changes in the referents of traditional terms are a more effective force in controlling meaning than any wholesale infusion of new terms.

The conscientious legal draftsman should try on a case-by-case basis to estimate the relative sensitivity to verbal sexism of the stereotypes being addressed and be guided accordingly, remembering always to weigh in the balance the cumulative cost to the author in time and effort, and to the audience in clarity and readability, of adopting any semantic innovation.

XI

Amendments; Redesignation

§11.1. IN GENERAL

Although little has been written on the amendment of legal instruments (other than statutes), amendments are important enough to warrant attention.

For statutes, amendments are especially important, because most enacted text amends existing legislation. For private instruments, amendments appear to be a problem mostly for wills, insurance policies, and the constitutions and bylaws of private institutions, instruments either of long life or subject to oft changing conditions. Without more documentation, we may surmise that for other private instruments amendments are only occasionally a problem. Anyway, the experience reflected here is probably useful whenever amendments to legal instruments are involved.

§11.2. AMENDING STATUTES, REGULATIONS, AND ORDINANCES

There are at least five ways to amend a statute.[1] Although addressed specifically to statutes, the following comments apply,

§11.2. [1]See E. Driedger, The Composition of Legislation — Legislative Forms and Precedents 171-172 (2nd ed., revised 1976); G. Thornton, Legis-

for the most part, also to "rule-making" regulations and to ordinances. The main difference is that state constitutional limitations requiring full textual restatement or forbidding incorporation by reference normally do not apply to regulations or ordinances.

§11.2.1. Amendment by inconsistent enactment

The simplest way to amend a statute is to enact the new rule of law and let it override by inconsistent action the statute that it changes or displaces. Until a long-standing constitutional idiosyncracy was corrected, this was a common approach in Indiana. The method is rarely justified,[2] because it confuses readers as to the state of the law and complicates editorial compilation. Nor is its undesirability lessened by including a general repealer. ("All laws inconsistent with this Act are repealed.") Although adding the words "Notwithstanding any other law" may help reduce the risk that a court will resolve doubts against the new law in favor of the old, the main vice of the method is that it does not come to grips with the policy decisions necessary to mesh the new with the old.

§11.2.2. Amendment by general reference

The eleventh amendment to the United States Constitution changed the substantive thrust of the Constitution without spell-

---

lative Drafting, ch. 15 (2nd ed. 1979); Note, The Form of Amendatory Statutes, 43 Harv. L. Rev. 482 (1930); Note, Drafting Amendatory Statutes, 43 Harv. L. Rev. 1143 (1930); and the local state legislature's drafting manual, if any.

[2] A possibly justifiable exception is 5 U.S.C. §8301(a), providing that retirements from government service take effect "on the first day of the month following the month in which retirement would otherwise be effective," which is intended to blanket all federal retired pay entitlement statutes, including even future ones, that do not specifically provide otherwise. But this is a dangerous precedent that, if multiplied, is better handled by shifting to the passive boilerplate approach outlined in §5.7 *supra.*

ing out its specific verbal impact or even indicating that it would constitute an appended numbered article.[3] Although widely used in England, this approach is undesirable, because (unlike the eleventh amendment) it often fails to make clear the degree to which the new rule displaces the old. It also complicates editorial compilation.[4] It is even less desirable than incorporation by reference,[5] because it tells the readers of the act only minimally about what it refers to. Outside of federal or state constitutions and substantive provisions found in "interpretation" acts,[6] it is rarely used in the United States. England's Parliamentary counsel are now turning more to textual amendment.

§11.2.3. Textual amendment

In most cases, the best way to amend is to show specifically how the old text is being changed. There are two kinds of textual amendments. One names the deletions and insertions necessary to change the affected provision ("section 5 is amended by striking out the words '* * *' and substituting the words '* * *' "). The other states in full the affected provision in its changed form ("section 5 is amended to read as follows: * * *"). Both methods facilitate compilation by requiring greater discipline in determining what changes are to be made.

[3]"The Judicial power of the United States shall not be construed to extend to any suit in law or equity, commenced or prosecuted against one of the United States by Citizens of another State, or by Citizens or Subjects of any Foreign State."
A more typical example is found in England's Civil Amenities Act 1967:

4.(1) The power conferred by subsection (1) of section 4 of the Historic Buildings and Ancient Monuments Act 1953 to make grants for the purposes mentioned in that subsection shall include power to make loans for those purposes. . . .

[4]See the partial compilation of the United States Constitution in Constitutions of the United States National and State 1-23 (2d ed. 1984).
[5]On incorporation by reference, see §8.26 supra.
[6]See R. Dickerson, The Interpretation and Application of Statutes 267-268 (1975).

The former is more helpful in that it pinpoints the specific changes, but less helpful in that it is often mysterious until the changes are physically carried into the affected provision. (This is why, as "blind," it has been constitutionally outlawed in most states). It also takes less space. The latter is more helpful in that the affected provision is immediately accessible in its changed form, but less helpful in that a word-for-word comparison with the old version is needed to identify the specific changes (a different kind of "blindness").

Both approaches are available to the federal draftsman. In general, the strike-out-and-insert approach is better if the changes are few and especially if they affect a long, indivisible provision. Full restatement is better if the changes are extensive.

In normal circumstances, selection of the more useful approach for the situation at hand should be made from the point of view of the users of the bill. It is undesirable to compromise the ultimate usability of the new law for reasons of temporary expediency to meet the needs of legislators during the course of enactment (not all of whom may agree).

Problems of clarity for legislators can be handled by providing accompanying editorial aids. For example, where the strike-out-and-insert approach has been adopted, a collateral explanation showing the text of the new provision should be enough.[7] Where prompt compilation can be expected, greater concessions to the immediate needs of the legislators can be made in the amendatory act itself.[8]

---

[7]In the United States House of Representatives, the *Ramseyer* rule (House Rule XIII (3)) requires that when a bill that amends or repeals is reported out of committee it must be accompanied by a document showing "by stricken-through type and italics, parallel columns, or other appropriate typograph devices the omissions and insertions" that would be made by the bill as introduced.

In the United States Senate, the *Cordon* rule (Senate Standing Rule XXIX (4)) imposes a similar requirement, except that it applies to the bill in the form recommended by the committee.

Canada's Parliament has a rule comparable to the *Cordon* rule. Such reader aids are deleted once the bill is enacted. In Indiana, similar statutory reader aids are even carried into the session laws. They do not appear, of course, in the Indiana Code.

[8]Donald Hirsch warns that "restating a major or sensitive operative provision . . . in a [federal] bill to make substantively minor amendments" some-

Donald Hirsch adds this suggestion:

> Good drafting practice calls for grouping amendments by subject [instead of following the sequence of the law being amended]. . . .
> . . . A subcommittee may . . . wish to discuss or vote on the various sections during a formal reading of the bill. . . . [It] would have difficulty following a single concept that is spread among widely scattered amendments.
> Modular construction simplifies the draftsman's task if the subcommittee chooses to accept some but not all of the amendments. . . .
> . . . [E]arly amendments should not anticipate later ones; if they do, they will not be readily intelligible.[9]

The draftsman of state legislation has fewer options in most jurisdictions. The constitutions of these jurisdictions forbid amendments of a law "by reference to its title only" (as it is usually expressed) and require that amended provisions be set forth fully in their changed form. The state draftsman will naturally check the applicable constitution (see appendix D).

Constitutional provisions such as these make it necessary to distinguish between acts that amend other acts and acts that incorporate by reference materials from other acts. An act providing that the rules of law in the Act of July 20, 1982, applicable by its terms only to railroads, "apply to trucking concerns" creates doubt as to whether the new law amends the Act of July 20, 1982, by extending its coverage (placing truckers under the amended earlier act), or adopts by reference the old rule for railroads as a part of the new law (placing truckers under the later act). The former method is widely proscribed; the latter, in most states, is not. Even when a constitutional provision is not involved, it is desirable to make clear which approach is being used, because it will be necessary to know which act to invoke in a future case involving truckers or to amend if a change respecting truckers becomes necessary.

---

times gives "the appearance to a legislator or his staff of intending more than it" does. Letter to the author dated July 22, 1985.

[9]D. Hirsch, Drafting Federal Law 23, 24 (1980).

§11.2.4.   Amendment by repeal and enactment

Amendment by repeal and enactment is a form of textual amendment in which the affected section or subsection is repealed and its desired substitute is enacted and inserted in its place. Its special usefulness is confined to cases where a substantial segment of material is being entirely replaced. A suggested test is whether the "new material is essentially unrelated to the material it is to replace."[10] But whether this succeeds in telling the reader whether he is looking at a revised version of the current section depends on its becoming a generally accepted convention.

§11.2.5.   Amendment by redefinition

Amendment by redefinition extends or restricts the reach of an existing act by redefining one or more of its terms. This device is especially tempting for any word that is used repeatedly in the act, because it makes across-the-board substantive changes without making multiple verbal changes. Technically, such an amendment is textual, but if, as is often the case, the redefined term extends to matters not normally comprehended by it (" 'Dog' includes cat") or, conversely, excludes matters normally within it (" 'Active duty' means active duty other than for training"), the evil of Humpty-Dumptyism[11] arises with its strong risk of confusing not only the reader but the draftsman himself. If Humpty-Dumptyism is involved, this kind of textual amendment should be avoided.

---

[10]*Id.* at 26.

[11]See §7.3 *supra.* Whatever kind of express amendment is used, James Craig Peacock tells us, it "should ideally be as complete and self-contained as is possible. . . . Except for the date of enactment, there should seldom be occasions to look beyond the four corners of an amendment in order to find its full meaning and effect." This is directed at the common legislative practice of "splitting" amendments, that is, locating the main provision in one part of a code or major or permanent statute and provisions relating to its applicability in another part, sometimes many provisions apart. Notes on Legislative Drafting, ch. IV (1961).

§11.2.6. A word of caution: Meaning of "act"

For legislative amendments, it is important to keep in mind the two senses in which the word "act" is used. (The same is true of the term "Public Law.")

First, it is used to denote a specific legislative action whereby Congress or a state legislature creates new law or changes or repeals existing law. Here, "act" refers to a particular historical event. In this sense, the Miller amendment to the Food Drug Cosmetic Act of 1938, was, as the Act of June 24, 1948, ch. 613,[12] as fully an "act" as the Food Drug Cosmetic Act itself.

The term "act" is also used in another sense. In the title, "Food Drug Cosmetic Act of 1938," the word "Act" means more than what Congress did on June 25, 1938. It is a continuing legislative frame of reference into which new parts may be inserted, and from which existing parts may be removed. It can be compiled and, when compiled, shows each subject in its proper place.

Briefly, an act is, in the former sense, a fleeting event; in the latter, a continuing concept. Every enactment is an act in the former sense, but only some enactments are acts in the latter sense. Enactments that are acts in both senses have a continuing status. Enactments that are acts only in the former sense are considered executed as soon as they go into effect.

The distinction is important. Suppose the Act of July 23, 1980, established a new general program for unemployment compensation and section 402 of that act has already been amended by section 5 of the Act of April 6, 1983. The draftsman now wants to make a further change in the amended provision. Should he amend section 402 of the Act of July 23, 1980, or section 5 of the Act of April 6, 1983? Although the substantive result would be the same (subject to problems and pitfalls), the cleaner and generally accepted way is to amend the original act "as amended." Similarly, repealing the Act of July 23, 1980, automatically repeals all express amendments of that act.

[12]62 Stat. 582.

It is unfortunate that adequate terminology for distinguishing basic from amendatory action, such as exists for administrative regulations, is lacking for legislation. "Amendment No. 16 to Regulation No. 4" is not likely to be confused with the parent regulation.

Confusion between the two kinds of enactments affects even amendments to the United States Constitution. The draftsmen of those following the first ten have wavered between treating them (1) as actions (conceptually, but not physically) replacing particular provisions already in the Constitution (the twelfth and seventeenth amendments), (2) as new articles additional to or inconsistent with existing provisions (the thirteenth through the sixteenth amendments and the eighteenth through the twenty-sixth amendments), and (3) as a wholly independent, unintegrated action (the eleventh amendment). In several (the eighteenth, twentieth, twenty-first, and twenty-second amendments), permanent provisions are scrambled with immediately executed housekeeping provisions. If this practice continues, it will become increasingly hard (as in Massachusetts) to compile the Constitution and within it to separate the live provisions from the dead ones that later provisions have superseded but not physically expunged.

The problem here, while conceptual, has important practical implications. The draftsman who keeps his lines straight benefits users generally by making it possible for editorial compilers to publish a clear, integrated, and well-ordered statute simply by following the express directions of the amendments. The draftsman who does not produces uncompilable scraps and patches and uncertainty, inconvenience, or confusion.

For statutes, some of the difficulty may be removed by flagging basic legislation with appropriate "short titles" (e.g., "The Fair Employment Practices Act"). Any law that is to be the charter for a continuing program should be given an appropriate short title, not only to make it easier to cite, but to earmark it as such a law. Any later act whose main rather than incidental purpose is to amend should not ordinarily be given a short title; but if it is, the short title should show its amendatory character.[13] The material covered by the title should not include the basic charter for another program.

Often a bill setting up a continuing program must specifically amend other laws to make the new law dovetail with the old. Here the draftsman can separate the permanent from the temporary by making the short title apply only to the parts of the bill that establish the new program, and not to the amendments, the repeal section, the savings and severability clauses, and the effective date section. In this way the amendatory or one-shot provisions will not clutter up a later compilation of the basic provisions.

§11.3. AMENDING PRIVATE INSTRUMENTS

Because ideally a will should be a single, integrated instrument to help assure that the testamentary scheme hangs together

[13]Unfortunately, the short title "Futures Trading Act of 1982," P.L. 94-444 (96 Stat. 2294), does not reveal that the Act's sole purpose is to amend the Commodity Exchange Act and the Futures Trading Act of 1978. The Garn-St. Germain Depository Institutions Act, P.L. 97-320 (96 Stat. 1469), by its title, gives no hint that the Act is 100 percent amendatory. Four of its eight titles carry their own short titles, none of which repair the omission. Each is a temptation to amend the wrong law.

Although essentially amendatory, the recent Orphan Drug Act, P.L. 97-414 (96 Stat. 2049), does not expressly disclose that fact. (The long title does, but such a title is not readily available when the Act is consulted in its Code form.) When the formal amendments to other acts are executed, only sections 5, 6(b)-(f), and 7 remain to constitute permanent residents. Of these, section 7(a) ("In carrying out section 301 of the Public Health Service Act, the Secretary . . . shall"), being in effect an amendment of section 301, should have been handled as such. Also, being directed to thyroid cancer and not a "rare disease or condition," it is unresponsive to a title focused, in substance, on rare diseases. What section 6(b)-(f) might have appropriately amended is not clear beyond the fact that these subsections focus, not on "orphan" drugs, but on "home health services." All that is left to legitimate the Orphan Drug Act as a free-standing repository of permanent law is section 5, which authorizes grants to support clinical testing. The thinking here seems unbecomingly fuzzy.

Canada's Gerard Bertrand asks, "Would it not be easier to provide that amending acts should not, under any circumstances, have a short title?"

conceptually and physically, the preferred method of amending a will is to restate and reexecute it.[1]

A codicil, on the other hand, amends the will conceptually but not physically. As a competing, independent instrument, a codicil increases the chances of loss, risks the introduction of interpretative problems, and may even complicate probate where a beneficiary is being eliminated.[2]

Accordingly, James P. Johnson recommends that a codicil be used only if:

(1)   lack of time precludes redoing the whole will, in which case a new will should be executed as soon as feasible;

(2)   the codicil deals with a temporary situation (such as vacillation over specific current pecuniary bequests) that is likely to clear up before death; or

(3)   the testator wants minor changes at a time when his capacity is in doubt.[3]

As for multiple codicils, "[i]t is only in very rare instances that a second codicil can be justified."[4] This does not include a codicil that merely replaces an earlier one.

Because most insurance policies have relatively short lives, amendments are usually handled by supplementary instruments ("endorsements") that spell out the specific changes. These are physically compiled with succeeding issuances and renewals, but not, of course, with policies currently in force. For the company draftsman, the choice is inevitably textual amendment either by striking and adding or by full restatement, depending on the considerations already stated for legislative amendments. Where the amendments affect insurance boilerplate that is intended to apply also to successive renewals, an accumulation of endorsements likely to confuse the insured could pose problems

---

§11.3.   [1]J. Johnson, a Draftsman's Handbook for Wills and Trust Agreements 239-240 (1961) (MLD 340-341).

[2]*Id.*

[3]*Id.*

[4]*Id.* at 240 (MLD at 341).

of consumer relations and, indeed, legality under state "plain English" insurance laws.[5]

As for amending other private instruments, I can only suggest creatively applying the general principles already set forth in this chapter or self help through further investigation of the legal literature.

§11.4. REDESIGNATION

Although material can often be added, changed, or removed without disturbing existing number or letter designations, amendments often affect the existing system of designating parts, sections, subsections, paragraphs, clauses, and simple enumerations.

When designated material is being added or deleted, the conscientious draftsman is tempted to preserve a smooth sequence of letters or numbers as a "necessary technical change." For legislative instruments, unfortunately, yielding to this normal impulse can wreak a havoc of confusion far out of proportion to any aesthetic value that it preserves.

Judge Shirley Abrahamson's classic analysis of the redesignation trap,[1] which she prepared while serving Columbia University's Legislative Drafting Research Fund, gives as an example the following 1954 amendments to the Social Security Act of 1935.[2]

> Section 210(a) of such Social Security Act is amended by striking out paragraph (3) and redesignating paragraphs (4), (5), (6), (7), (8), (9), (10), (11), (12), (13), and (14), and any references thereto

[5]See §8.3 *supra.*

§11.4. [1]Abrahamson, Redesignation: Lawyer's Nightmare (mimeo 1958) (MLD 341). See also J. Peacock, Notes on Legislative Drafting, ch. 5 (1961).

[2]Abrahamson, at MLD 342. For a recent example, see section 427 of the Garn-St. Germain Depositary Institutions Act of 1982, P.L. 97-320 (96 Stat. 1524).

contained in such Act, as paragraphs (3), (4), (5), (6), (7), (8), (9), (10), (11), (12), and (13) respectively.

Section 210(a) of the Social Security Act is further amended by striking out paragraph (15) and redesignating paragraphs (16) and (17), and any references thereto contained in such Act, as paragraphs (14) and (15), respectively. . . .

Section 214(a) of the Social Security Act is amended by redesignating paragraph (3) as paragraph (4) and inserting after paragraph (2) the following new paragraph:

"(3) In the case of . . ."

The total substantive accomplishment in the three provisions, it will be seen, is to strike out two old paragraphs and to insert a new one. But, on top of that, the draftsman has piled fourteen pieces of redesignation. As a matter of fact, the number of redesignations in this statute alone is lifted to 38 by other provisions.[3]

There are other problems. For provisions that are constantly referred to, letter and number designations become semantically cemented to the substantive legislative concepts that they respectively denote.[4] For these, unrestrained redesignation can challenge the worst excesses of Humpty-Dumptyism.[5]

Another problem created by redesignation, if the affected statute is referred to by other laws, is illustrated by still another provision of the Social Security amendments:

References in the Internal Revenue Code of 1939, the Internal Revenue Code of 1954, the Railroad Retirement Act of 1937, as amended, or any other law of the United States to any section or subdivision of a section of the Social Security Act redesignated by this Act shall be deemed to refer to such section or subdivision of a section as so redesignated.[6]

[3]By Peacock's count, the 1954 act ran up "more than 70 additional such redesignations." Notes on Legislative Drafting 37 (1961).

[4]Abrahamson, at MLD 343.

[5]See §§2.3.3 and 7.3 *supra.*

[6]Abrahamson, at MLD 342. The Act of October 14, 1982, P.L. 97-314 (96 Stat. 1463), redesignating a building in Greenville, South Carolina, as the "Clement F. Haynesworth, Jr. Federal Building", adds this fatuity:

This last effort was a poor substitute "for careful research and an understanding of the effect of the new law on existing legislation,"[7] which make possible appropriate amendments to that other legislation and thus disclose more fully the true price being exacted by redesignation.

This problem prompted the National Conference of Commissioners on Uniform State Laws to direct its draftsmen to "avoid reference to other sections or divisions" in all Conference acts.[8] The computerization of statutes and other legal instruments has reduced the burden of research here, but not enough. For one thing, it does not touch the problem of references in collateral aids such as texts or search services not included in the data base or not favored with prompt updating.[9] "What could better demonstrate the possibilities or error that attend the vast job of adjusting cross-references after redesignation?"[10]

Sometimes there is a readily available substitute for redesignation. For example, when striking out a designated item, the draftsman can delete the item but retain the designation, which can then be followed by "[repealed]" in the amendment itself or added later by a compiling editor.[11] When a new item is to

---

Sec. 2 Any reference in any law, regulation, document, record, map or other paper of the United States, to the building referred to in the first section of this Act hereby is deemed to be to the "Clement Haynesworth, Jr., Federal Building."

Translated, this must mean that official references to that building (which, therefore, already refer to the Haynesworth building) shall be read as if they referred to it *as* the "Haynesworth" building. In actual human behavior, how is this accomplished psychologically? How can something written in French be read as if it were written in German? Conceptually, the provision is nonsense. It accomplishes nothing.

[7]Abrahamson, at MDL 343, n.8.

[8]1980 Yearbook of the National Conference of Commissioners on Uniform State Laws 431 (Rule 13).

[9]Peacock, *supra* note 1 at 42, says:

Indeed by the very nature of redesignation its potential for spreading indefinite confusion and uncertainty can never be measured. . . . [W]ho can say in what opinion or ruling or regulation, or even in what instructions on what form, a redesignated provision may have been referred to.?

[10]Abrahamson, at MLD 346; Peacock, *supra* note 1 at 43.

[11]Abrahamson, at MLD 347.

be inserted in a designated sequence instead of merely added at the end, it can be designated by the number of the immediately preceding item followed by "a" and so forth.[12]

For alphabetized material, the problem can be avoided altogether by not designating the items originally listed. (This works particularly well with definitions.) This approach is becoming standard for federal regulations.

Is redesignation *ever* appropriate? For statutes, regulations, and ordinances, the answer is "rarely."[13] One of the few exceptions is a drastic overhaul such as the recodification of the whole or a major segment. Except for this, James Craig Peacock would outlaw it completely for legislative instruments.[14] Donald Hirsch, while cautioning that "the larger the subdivision and the older the statute the more you should try to avoid redesignation," says that "there is probably little risk in redesignating a paragraph or subparagraph of a recently enacted law with which the draftsman has had experience."[15] For statutes and regulations, such an exception should be narrowly construed.

On the other hand, redesignation has been standard practice with the American Bar Association's Constitution and Bylaws Committee and, if there have been resulting difficulties, they have not been readily apparent, presumably because routine use of the instruments has been light. This may be true also of private constitutions and bylaws generally. There are undoubtedly other relatively simple legal instruments that are only occasionally changed, that are not used (or have not yet been used) often enough for specific designations to take semantic root, and to which other sources will not create (or have not yet created) a significant reference problem. Here, aesthetic considerations may be persuasive.

Even so, Judge Abrahamson's general stricture seems appropriate: "[S]urely it is reasonable to demand as a minimum that a draftsman, before indulging in redesignation, take careful stock of the advantages he hopes to get and the difficulties and

[12]*Id.*
[13]Abrahamson, at MLD 347-348.
[14]Peacock, *supra* note 1 at 44.
[15]D. Hirsch, Drafting Federal Law 28 (1980).

damage he is likely to bring about."[16] As King Lear has reminded us, "Striving to better, oft we mar what's well."[17]

These principles also apply, though with less force, during any protracted drafting exercise involving the creation or codification of a large, complicated body of law. For example, the initial numbering system developed for the projected codification of the laws then editorially compiled in titles 10, 32, and 34 of the United States Code was changed as little as possible until the very last phase of the project, nine years later.[18]

[16]Abrahamson, at MLD 348.
[17]Act 1, Scene 4.
[18]This approach proved helpful even in the preparation of this book.

XII

Computers and Other Scientific Aids[1]

§12.1 ELECTRONIC AIDS

For some time, voices have been heard claiming that lawyers are drafting legal instruments by computer. But, unless photocopying and cutting up an existing will can be considered "legal drafting," there is little to support such a claim. The simple fact is that drafting by computer is impossible in any but a peripheral or incidental sense.[1] On the other hand, there are steps during the overall drafting process at which a computer or comparable device may be significantly helpful.

The trouble with considering drafting problems mainly in terms of equipment is that the underlying problems are broader than the range of devices, electronic or mechanical, that are available to help solve them. For this reason, it is more fruitful to concentrate on systems than on equipment. Many useful sys-

---

[1]This chapter draws for the most part on Dickerson, Electronic Aids to the Drafting of Legal Instruments, 1 Rut. J. Computers & L. 75 (1970); Sprowl, Automating the Legal Reasoning Process: A Computer That Uses Regulations and Statutes to Draft Legal Documents, 1979 A.B.F. Res. J. 1; Sprowl & Staudt, Computerizing Client Services in the Law School Teaching Clinic: An Experiment in Law Office Automation, 1981 A.B.F. Res. J. 699; Wason, The Drafting of Rules, 118 New L.J. 548 (1968) (MLD 311); and Allen & Engholm, Normalized Legal Drafting and the Query Method, 29 J. Leg. Educ. 380-400 (1978) (MLD 316). See also Saxon, Computer-aided Drafting of Legal Documents, 1982 A.B.F. Res. J. 685.

§12.1 [1]Dickerson, *supra* note 1 at 75.

tems require little or no equipment. Examples of generally comparable nonmechanized systems or devices appear in sections 5.7, 6.3, and 12.3 and in appendices B and C.

If drafting can be said to include supporting research, electronic storage and retrieval systems such as Lexis, Westlaw, and Dialog are highly useful (especially as they extend their data bases) for locating relevant statutes and case law, and, increasingly, secondary legal materials such as articles and treatises. Because the equipment involved is that used for general legal purposes and continues to undergo frequent technical refinements, there is little about computerized research for drafting purposes that could profitably be discussed here.

Computers are useful also for making calculations that it would be impossible or onerous to do by other means.[2] Ordinarily, calculations of this magnitude are not involved in the preparation of legal instruments. However, it is often desirable, especially in the field of estate planning,[3] to estimate the probable tax consequences of the available alternatives. Fortunately, computerized programs are available for figuring for specific hypothetical situations the estate and inheritance taxes that it is reasonable to anticipate. So far as that information affects the testator's judgment, it can be a valuable aid. Commercial enterprises are active in this field.

As for the handling of language, electronic devices dedicated specifically to text entry, revision, and printing, commonly called "word processors,"[4] have long been useful to anyone creating and editing legal text. General purpose computers[5] have the additional capacity to organize, assemble, and retrieve standardized legal provisions, usually called "boilerplate," that are needed to deal with frequently recurring situations. As a

---

[2]*Id.* at 79.

[3]*Id.*

[4]Word processors have been classed as "dedicated" computers, because they are programmed for only one general function. Sprowl & Staudt, *supra* note 1 at 703. For an "ideal" word processing system, see Walshe, What to Consider When Selecting Text-editing Equipment, 67 A.B.A.J. 45 (1981).

[5]A general purpose computer is one controllable by a number of different programs. Sprowl & Staudt, *supra* note 1 at 703.

kind of sophisticated cut-and-paste operation, use of such devices saves time, helps achieve uniformity, reduces the chances of typographical error, and, when set up as a mechanized checklist, guards against unintended omissions.

Although reliance on legal forms and other kinds of boilerplate needs no explaining here,[6] it is useful to know how computers can be used to handle it. But before boilerplate can be handled, it must be created.[7] General purpose computers are useless during initial composition (as distinct from revision), except as they can perform the modest editorial functions of a word processor. Not only must this step be taken first, but it is critical that boilerplate reflect the principles of good drafting. Failure to do this will compromise all that follows. Accordingly, an effective delivery system should, in James A. Sprowl's phrase, be built from the "top down":[8] First build solid boilerplate and then the computer support for it.

The history of computerized lawyering is strewn with instances in which the technical allurements of equipment absorbed the attention of users to the point that they overlooked important aspects of legal drafting. No computer can compensate for basic inadequacies in the drafting process. Taking adequacy for granted thus sets a trap for the unwary. Boilerplate deserves special attention to accuracy and detail because it is marked for multiple use.

The simplest systems for handling legal boilerplate merely store and deliver a miscellany of loosely indexed prefabricated provisions. (One such system, now almost obsolete,[9] uses magnetized cards; another uses an automatic typewriter.)[10] Because

[6]See §4.11 *supra;* Dickerson, *supra* note 1 at 76.
[7]See Sprowl, *supra* note 1 at 52.
[8]*Id.* at 58.
[9]*Id.* at 74.
[10]E.g., see Moses, In the Beginning was the Word, Legal Economics 15 (summer 1975).

There are a number of variations: Cantwell, Bonapart, and others, "Automated" Drafting Techniques, 3 Real Property, Probate & Trust J. 475 (1968); DeMeo, Check-In Forms for Instant Drafting, 16 Prac. Law. 57 (November 1970), DeMeo, How to Develop Manuals of Forms and Procedures, 17 Prac. Law. 33 (December 1972); Lipson, File Your Forms as a Computer Would

digital computers readily respond to algorithmic programming (any systematic set of instructions),[11] stored boilerplate can usefully include bracketed information gaps representing matters that vary according to the nature of the client or the peculiarities of specific situations. Spaces can thus be reserved for names, addresses, ages, sex, financial worth, dimensions, and other common variables. This capability, combined with a matching computerized checklist of matters about which each client should be interrogated, not only facilitates the client interview but makes it possible to feed the answers into the computer to fill the bracketed spaces.[12]

This match-up is achieved by taking a hard-copy version of the boilerplate provisions to be stored and inserting in each blank space a bracketed description of what needs to be inserted at that point (e.g., "the lessor [name of the lessor]"). When these have been completed, the respective bracketed materials can be matched in the checklist by corresponding questions ("Q: What is the name of the lessor?" followed by "A:" and a space for the client's answer).

Each set of answers constitutes a profile of the client's current needs respecting the matter to which the boilerplate is addressed. The completed questionnaire-checklist not only guides the interrogator in the current instance but may be useful in future matters involving that client.[13]

In brief, the two main features of such a system are the (1) boilerplate as developed by a person expert not only in the legal area concerned but in legal drafting, and (2) the program for adapting it to the needs of specific clients. The former constitutes both "an outline of all possible document structures" and

---

— Without a Computer, 60 Mich. B.J. 451 (1981); Pasquesi, A First Step in the "Automated" Drafting of Wills — The Preprinted Page, 60 Ill. B.J. 958 (1972), Pasquesi, A First Step in the "Automated" Drafting of Wills — A Second Application of the "Preprinted Page" System, 61 Ill. B.J. 40 (1972); Tilton & Tilton, Basic Considerations in Designing Forms, 26 Prac. Law. 55 (July 1980); Wright, Establishing a Workable Forms System, 23 L.O.E.M. 29 (1982).

[11]Id. at 63; Sprowl & Staudt, *supra* note 1 at 705.

[12]Sprowl, *supra* note 1 at 18-19, 22, 36; Sprowl & Staudt, *supra* note 1 at 706-707.

[13]Sprowl, *supra* note 1 at 73, 74.

a computerized checklist.[14] The latter combines with the boiler-plate the information supplied by the draftsman that is needed to adapt it to specific needs. Besides information supplied by the client, designated gaps can also relate to legal categorization by the lawyer, factual information available from accepted sources, the results of mathematical calculations made by the computer, and relevant materials already stored in the computer for later incorporation by reference. (Bracketed instructions self-destruct when the material called for is inserted.)[15]

To computerize the assembly of separate boilerplate provisions into an integrated legal instrument, it is necessary to put the materials in a standardized form keyed to standardized computer commands via a list of operators that trigger the appropriate computer responses.[16] For example, the American Bar Foundation's highly sophisticated system ("ABF") first translates the boilerplate into Layman E. Allen's "normalized" form, an intensively paragraphed format designed to head off omissions and ambiguities of modification and useful also in tying in with a computer.[17] The same language is used to formulate the operating instructions to the computer.

[14]Saxon, *supra* note 1 at 706.
[15]Sprowl, *supra* note 1 at 65.
[16]*Id.* at 24, 38-40.
[17]*Id.* at 10-11, 35 note 52. For a sample of "normalized" drafting, see Allen & Engholm, Normalized Legal Drafting and the Query Method, 29 J. Legal Educ. 380 (1978). Cf. "tabulation," §6.3, *supra*.

The ABF system drew much from a computer-assisted drafting system that Thomas Chatterton and Richard McCoy developed for the Cook County Assistance Foundation of Chicago under a grant from the Legal Services Division of the Office of Economic Opportunity. Although phased out, years later, when Legal Services terminated its support, the project provided valuable experience. In a letter to the author dated January 11, 1985, Chatterton wrote:

> The Legal Services operation lent itself very well to computerization. They had a high volume of relatively routine cases and were chronically short-handed as far as attorneys were concerned.
>
> The operating system essentially consisted of a central computer located in downtown Chicago with terminals in storefronts throughout Cook County. Clients would come to storefronts and be interviewed by the computer. Appropriate documents would be computer-generated at the central office for use by the attorneys.
>
> The system operated much as you described such systems in your chapter.

On the other hand, it is doubtful that language so fragment-edly taxonomic in form should be carried into the final boiler-plate as presented to its users. Rudolf Flesch has savagely attacked this form (along with tabulation) as being "shredded law" and consequently hard to read.[18] But Allen's tests show that lawyers understand substance faster when legal text is couched in "normalized" form than when it is left in its original legislative form, which undoubtedly results from the fact that normalization (like tabulation) forces the reviser to deal with syntactic ambiguities that he might otherwise overlook.[19] The ABF system delivers the final product in familiar legal language.

The same general approach has been taken in several less elaborate systems. Legal Management Systems, for example, uses an inexpensive microprocessor that, unlike the ABF sys-tem, handles both the word processing function and the selec-tion and assembly functions that only a general computer can handle. One disadvantage is that its modest size limits it to using document programs that are hard to read and audit even by computer professionals. User acceptance, in any event, has been good for both systems.[20]

The questions were essentially formatted to elicit answers as follows: yes, no, don't know, or don't understand, or with fill-in-the-blanks type questions.

Based on the answers given, documents would be constructed by the com-puter by stringing together appropriate boiler plate.

The interviews and documents were flow charted. Many of the cases involved simple divorces. Depending upon the answers given, the computer could deter-mine whether jurisdiction was present, whether grounds were present, etc. and could construct appropriate complaints, affidavits, orders, etc. If a don't-know answer was given, a print-out could be generated and given to the client to obtain the necessary information. If a don't-understand answer was given, a short tutorial could be given so that the client could respond to the question.

[18]R. Flesch, How to Write Plain English (1979), at 102-105, discussed in MLD, at 285-288.

[19]But not necessarily easier to read and understand than what a sparing use of tabulation in a modern, simplified, and more conventional legislative form can provide. See, e.g., §6.3, *supra.* To take a similar example, the useful-ness of logic trees in "critical path analysis" does not necessarily validate them as "common . . . species of communication." Jamieson, Swinging from Logic Trees (Part II), 124 New L.J. 1120, 1121 (1974).

[20]Saxon, *supra* note 1 at 700-702. For a detailed description of the Legal Management System's approach, see Boyd & Saxon, The A-9: A Program for Drafting Security Agreements under Article 9 of the Uniform Commercial Code, 1981 A.B.F. Research Journal 639.

In the more complicated legal areas, the client's answer to a question may introduce a network of legal consequences each of which calls for a special piece of boilerplate. In such a case, the bracketed material can include automatic computer commands to that effect keyed by the entry of special symbols representing the insertions.[21]

In the case of a will, for example, a computer can be programmed so that, if informed that the testator is a male, it will use "husband" or a male pronoun, when referring to him, and "wife" or a female pronoun, when referring to his wife. A mere word processor cannot handle such operations.

Indeed, the permutations of legal possibilities can become hard to handle without a computer or other organized system whenever there are multiple questions involving multiple networks of legal consequences. In such a case, the person preparing the bracketed hard-copy form may find it helpful to prepare a logic tree or flowchart tracing the consequences of each available alternative. Logic trees and flowcharts are discussed briefly in section 12.3 below.

Systems that permit the user to see the results during the process of assembly, or to examine the assembled text on the terminal screen before printout, make it possible to edit the material before printout.[22] Systems that permit the user to view and change the answers to questions that have already been asked give the user the flexibility to experiment.[23] Ideally, both capabilities should be included in future systems.

Finally, the computer, operating as a word processor, can print out, for example, a draft will or lease. This is a critical moment, because it is tempting at this point to assume that the draft is wholly adequate for the client's purposes. Even with interim editing, it should be carefully scrutinized and revised as needed to get it right. From here on, only the word processing function is needed.

This brief sketch is a gross oversimplification of a complicated area of development that needs further refinement and

[21]Sprowl & Staudt, *supra* note 1 at 708-710.
[22]Saxon, *supra* note 1 at 701, 709.
[23]Sprowl says that this has been shown by the work of Lawrence Farmer at Brigham Young University.

testing,[24] because workable approaches will not satisfactorily jell until there is a better understanding not only of what is technically possible but of what incidence of use can be expected at the anticipated cost. That is why this chapter will obsolesce faster than its fellows.

Presumably, a delivery system should pay for itself.[25] Unfortunately, there have been many instances in which the capabilities of the equipment used far outran general need, thus reducing the economic feasibility of much computer use by needlessly inflating the costs of equipment and operating time. What works is not necessarily cost efficient. Incidence of use and unit cost are the critical factors.[26]

From this, it should be plain that in the hierarchy of drafting problems the systems described relate mostly to efficiency and, except for reducing typographical errors and substantive omissions, only modestly to the quality of the end product. Improvement of quality from the use of computers is most likely to result from a closer attention to internal arrangement and completeness through the use of logic trees and flowcharts to organize interrelated networks of contingencies. Allen's approach to this problem will be discussed more fully later in this chapter.

Sprowl suggests that one of the benefits of computerized boilerplate is that, with the availability of telephone coupling

[24]That this will continue is strongly suggested in Sprowl, Developing Computerized Practice Aids for Tomorrow's Law Office, 131 Chi. Daily L. Bull., April 27, 1985, at 8, 14:

> We now have a simplified personal computer version. . . .
> We are [also] constructing a more sophisticated version that will be able to perform complex mathematical and logical functions as well as document assembly. The new version will include an outliner as an integral component. It will create multiple "windows" on the screen of the computer. Through a first window, you will be able to view and revise the draft. Questions will appear in a second window, and you will type your answers into [a] third window. This new version can be set up to draw legal conclusions (using math and symbolic logic), and it can then use those conclusions to select which language is [to be] included in any given form legal document.

[25]See Sprowl & Staudt, *supra* note 1 at 727-729.

[26]"Our system used in the legal services area worked very well because of the high volume of routine cases. However, the price-performance curve in computing power improved so rapidly that even relatively low volume uses in law offices are now practical, in my opinion." Chatterton letter, *supra* note 17.

arrangements with a central computer, even small firms with text-editing computers (word processors) can use them as "front ends" for the ABF processor.[27] Alternatively, such firms may "phone into a central computer and have an up-to-date copy of the forms transmitted via telephone to their in-house processors to be sure their legal advice reflects possible recent changes in the law." He believes that this capability will enhance the professional position of the general practitioner, because it will make it possible to serve "clients efficiently and competently without the need for a referral to a specialist."[28]

One risk here is that the general practitioner may be referring to forms so broadly gauged that they are inadequately geared to local or more sharply focused considerations. The Office of Price Administration's intensive experience with boilerplate regulations during World War II showed that the wider and more detailed a piece of boilerplate's coverage the less likely it was that it would fit the varying specifics.[29] It is easy to be over-optimistic here. At any rate, current transmission media, with their capacity for quick communication, shorten turn-around time.[30]

The best reason for computerizing boilerplate delivery systems is that it makes possible faster and cheaper delivery of relatively uncomplicated documents such as wills, leases, and

[27]See Sprowl, *supra* note 1 at 79.

[28]*Id.* at 80. "Of course such a system would depend upon the competency of the people developing the flow charts and drafting the documents in question, and whether the system was properly supported so that it was kept up to date." Chatterton letter, *supra* note 17.

[29]See §5.7 *supra* and appendix C *infra;* Dickerson, FPR No 1: An Experiment in Standardized and Prefabricated Law, 13 U. Chi. L. Rev. 90 (1945); Chatterton letter, *supra* note 17:

> The Legal Services people operated in all states so that a general divorce system would not be very useful. By the same token, a strictly Illinois divorce system would not be very useful in Texas or California. We, therefore, first had to develop a problem-oriented flow chart, perhaps similar to your logic trees. The analysis was similar to comparative law techniques. Each state has the same problems but solve[s] them in different ways. We could then have a node covering grounds, support, custody, etc. Texas, Illinois, or California procedures could then be substituted interchangeably for each such node. We even tried it with English divorce law and German automobile accident law, and it worked fine.

[30]Saxon, *supra* note 1 at 689.

divorce settlements for clients of limited means.[31] How to keep such services from producing superficially adequate but substantively shoddy materials is a problem that calls for the best resources of the drafting art. Incorporation of material in electronic or mechanized systems that receive wide use could justify the time and money needed to achieve elegantly drafted material.

In the meantime, the computer is not yet fully domesticated for routine use by lawyers in every area in which it is potentially helpful and should be approached warily for wide use to assemble legal boilerplate. But a solid potential exists.

§12.2. SYMBOLIC LOGIC; A "LOGIC MACHINE"

Another point at which the computer might be useful in preparing a legal instrument is in testing its logical structure and measuring its impact on documents that it is intended to supplement, change, or replace. The system about to be described is apparently more of a potentiality than an actuality. For this reason, it will be described in the sparest language possible. This can best be done in terms of a statute, for which it is more likely to be helpful. Even so, it could be helpful also for highly complicated private instruments.

Recent developments in the field of symbolic logic and electronics suggest the feasibility of using these disciplines to test the internal coherence of statutes and to determine the extent to which a proposed statute would be inconsistent with current statutory law and thus require its amendment.

One development has been the conception, if not birth, of a "logic machine."[1] The capabilities of the propositional calculus for solving logical problems is well established. Experiments in the field of military strategy, for example, have already suggested the feasibility of using the propositional calculus to test the logical coherence of military texts. The same approach could make it possible to test the logical coherence of an existing or

---

[31]Sprowl, *supra* note 1 at 74.

§12.2.   [1]The Logic-Machine and Its Applications, AFC Electronics (Alexandria, Va. 1954).

a proposed statute. The only new elements are (1) the capability of translating the complicated language of legal instruments into the unambiguous and consistent language of formal logic, and (2) the possibility of computerizing the process of logical testing.

The possibility of such a logic machine rests on the fact that the logic of classes (Boolean algebra) and the propositional calculus involve the use of expressions that can be digitized by the assignment of binary numbers, which in turn permit the use of computers. The use of binary numbers is possible because in the discipline of legal drafting all legal materials can be translated into statements that are either true or false.

This would also make it possible to determine which provisions of an existing statute would need to be amended to give effect to a proposed statute. Under such an approach, statements of existing law needing amendment would appear as statements with which the proposed statements of law were inconsistent. Inconsistencies could be brought to light by forming the logical product of the numbers representing the statements involved. Both the underlying logical process and its electronic version are capable not only of detecting the existence of a logical inconsistency, but of ascertaining the specific provisions of existing law that created the inconsistency. The latter would be the provisions that needed amending or repealing. Critical tacit assumptions would have to be taken into account and, presumably, expressed.

Similar applications could, of course, arise for complicated private instruments. Indeed, in 1937 Edmund Berkeley was using Boolean algebra to improve the substantive coverage of insurance policies.[2] Thirteen years later, John E. Pfeiffer reported in Scientific American that:

> Symbolic logic has since been used in many other insurance problems. Mathematicians at Equitable, Metropolitan, Aetna and other companies have applied it to the analysis of war clauses and

[2]Berkeley, Boolean Algebra (the Technique for Manipulating "and," "or," "not," and Conditions) and Applications to Insurance, 26 Record of the American Institute of Actuaries 373 (1937). A discussion of this paper appears in vol. 27, at 167.

employment eligibility under group contracts. And other corporations have found symbolic logic very helpful in analyzing their contracts. . . . Are there holes or inconsistencies? A symbolic analysis can readily answer such questions and lawyers have begun to call on mathematicians to go over their contracts.[3]

On the basis of Berkeley's revelations and Pfeiffer's popularization, I surmise that the activities they described were largely sporadic and limited to particular aspects of insurance without coalescing into a full-blown effort to exhaust the structural aspects of a complete insurance policy or program. In any event, it remains doubtful that computer technology has developed to the point where it could handle so widely ranging an effort.

In the meantime, Layman E. Allen has developed, as a by-product of his efforts to disclose (if not wholly eliminate) the uncertainties of syntactic ambiguity, some promising ways to analyze and improve the internal structure of complicated sentences, paragraphs, and sections by examining and testing their internal syntax through the use of flowcharts, symbolic logic, and even computers.[4] For the most part, these devices accomplish this by making it easier for draftsmen to spot mistakes or uncertainties of modification and, even more important, gaps or omissions.

Allen's approach is enhanced by an updating and refinement of Hohfeldian analysis to identify more precisely the basic legal relations (such as right, duty, power, privilege, and immunity, and their opposites or negations) that are involved in the drafting of legal documents. It is intended mainly to test, in "normalized" form, the coherence of the conceptual relation-

[3]Pfeiffer, Symbolic Logic, 183 (No. 6) Scientific American 22, 23 (1950). See also R. Dick, Legal Drafting 218-223 (2d ed. 1985).
[4]Allen, A Language-Normalization Approach to Information Retrieval in Law, 9 Jurimetrics J. 41 (1968); Allen & Engholm, *supra* §12.1 note 17; Allen & Engholm, Need for Clear Structure in "Plain Language" Legal Drafting 13 U. Mich. J.L. Ref. 455 (1980); Allen & Ohta, Better Organization of Legal Knowledge, 1 U. Toledo L. Rev. 491 (1969). See also Edwards & Barber, A Computer Method for Legal Drafting Using Propositional Logic, 53 Tex. L. Rev. 965 (1975); Engholm, Logic and Laws: Relief from Statutory Obfuscation, 9 J. of Law Reform 322 (1976).

ships among the elements constituting the particular provision. Built as it is by symbolizing the pathways defining the logical flow of ideas, the approach is essentially the same as tabulation, except that the wide use of symbolic logic, including its computerization, makes it possible to deal more adequately with extremely complicated provisions such as those rampant in the Internal Revenue Code. For more modest provisions, however, the approach seems unnecessarily elaborate.

In the revision of instruments drafted by others, the approach faces a problem in the case of provisions so badly drafted that their intended syntax is not reflected in the syntax actually created. In such cases it is risky to symbolize or computerize the provision until the more obvious errors of drafting have been removed. Certainly, it is more useful to test the syntax that the original author more probably intended than the syntax that he in fact created.

How can we revise what we do not understand? This is not as hard as it may seem, and Allen's methods do not hesitate to adjust syntax preparatory to his main effort to portray the conceptual linkages[5] that define the structure of the provision.

The danger here is that, because clarity and readability do not depend wholly on syntax, disproportionate attention to syn-

---

[5]Allen & Engholm, Normalized Legal Drafting and the Query Method, 29 J. Legal Educ. 380, 392, 397 et seq.

Persons who remain skeptical are invited to see whether they can test the syntax of the following without revising it:

Someone recently sent me a manuscript that had been solicited for publication. I couldn't understand it, so I rewrote it as well as I could. I still couldn't understand it, so I rewrote it again. The third time I rewrote it, I began to understand it. Later, the author accepted my draft just as I had rewritten it.

19. A person who is nominated for public office at a primary election, with or without balloting, and whenever required accepts such nomination, may decline such nomination if such person is thereafter nominated for another office by such party; or any such person thereafter nominated to fill a vacancy caused by such nomination by such party may decline the nomination made at the primary election not later than September twenty-first preceding the general election, but such a declination shall not be effective if such nomination by such party is duly declined, or if the person nominated to fill such vacancy duly declines the nomination made at the primary election, as aforesaid.

tax at this stage may lead the draftsman to overlook semantic or contextual considerations that could help forestall a defective clustering of elements resulting in faulty structure.

The point is illustrated by Allen and Engholm's analysis of Louisiana's statute on obscene telephone calls,[6] in which the authors concentrate on a troublesome "and," as litigated in a Louisiana case.[7] Unfortunately, focusing on a unique factual situation, while appropriate to a court, is not enough for a draftsman, who is necessarily concerned almost exclusively with generalities. As a result, their analysis produced a draft that solved only one of the problems that should concern a draftsman. The broader draftsman's approach would have not only produced a better redraft but made it easier to support the reading of the Louisiana court.[8]

§12.3   LOGIC TREES AND FLOWCHARTS

Lawyers as a whole are inept in drafting because they don't know how to analyze and design systems. Here are at least two devices for meeting this lack. In chapter 5 on arrangement and section 6.3 on tabulation, we saw the advantages of taxonomic divisions into classes and subclasses, sometimes to the third or fourth degree (but rarely beyond). This improves not only understandability by the ultimate users of the document but the draftsman's own understanding of the relevant substantive considerations and their interrelationships.

---

[6]Id. at 384-387, 399.

[7]*State v. Hill,* 245 La. 119, 157 So. 2d 462 (1963). The statute (La. Rev. Stat. Ann. §14-285 (Act No. 54 of 1963)) read as follows:

> No person shall engage in or institute a local telephone call, conversation or conference of an anonymous nature and therein use obscene, profane, vulgar, lewd, lascivious or indecent language, suggestions or proposals of an obscene nature and threats of any kind whatsoever.

[8]Dickerson, Obscene Telephone Calls: An Introduction to the Reading of Statutes, 22 Harv. L. Legis. 173, 183-186 (1985). Lack of adequate attention to context can be a serious threat to the efficacy of Allen's otherwise impressive methods.

In the preceding section, we saw that a logic tree or flow-chart might be useful in selecting and arranging intricately inter-related boilerplate.

A logic tree is a proliferation device that shows the significant contingencies starting with a trunk, moving to branches, and ending in a number of small branches or twigs. As a branching technique, it is similar to tabulation, except that, in addition to showing the pathways to success, it shows explicitly the pathways to failure. In legal drafting, the potential usefulness of logic trees is limited for the most part to instances in which alternative situations lead to different legal results not inferrable from the main provisions. An example of a logic tree in the form of a visual graph appears on below.[1]

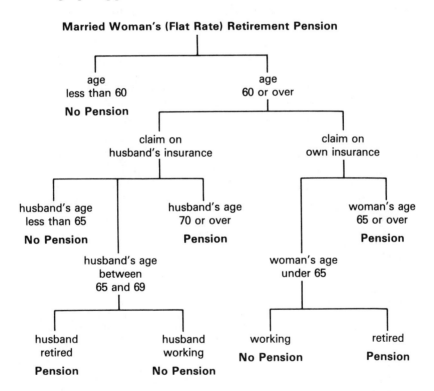

Married Woman's (Flat Rate) Retirement Pension

§12.3 [1]Wason, The Drafting of Rules, 118 New L.J. 548 (1968). See also, W. Twining & D. Miers, Algorithms and the Structure of Complex Rules, in How to Do Things with Rules (1976), ch. 9; Benson, Up a Statute

There are only occasional uses for logic trees in situations not involving boilerplate. Like other logic trees, this example shows not only the pathways to the main legal affirmation (or denial) but the pathways to its opposite. Although they may be useful to the draftsman in fully understanding substance, in legal instruments opposites are normally left to implication (unless they carry a special legal consequence), allowing a highly desirable economy of expression.

The flowchart is the more useful device for showing the pathways through the intended conditions (conjunctive or disjunctive) leading to the intended legal consequence. Following is how the complicated military disability retirement provision[2] looks, first as tabulated and segmented and then on p. 274 in flowchart form ("C" stands for condition and "R" for legal result).[3]

Title 10, United States Code (70A Stat. 91)[4]
§1201. Regulars and members on active duty for more than 30 days: retirement

If the Secretary concerned determines [C_1] that a member of a regular component of the armed forces entitled to basic pay [C_2], or any other member of the armed forces entitled to basic pay [C_3] who has been called or ordered to active duty (other than for training) for a period of more than 30 days [C_4], is unfit to perform the duties of his office, grade, rank, or rating [C_5] because of physical disability [C_6] incurred while entitled to basic pay [C_7], the Secretary may retire the member [R_1], with retired

---

with Gun and Camera: Isolating Linguistic and Logical Structures in the Analysis of Legalative Language, 8 Seton Hall Legis. J. 279, 296-300 (1984); and *infra* note 6. A more general reference on trees and discrete structures is Grimaldi, Discrete and Combinational Mathematics (1985). See also MLD 325-326.

[2]See §6.3, *supra.*

[3]Compare Allen & Engholm, *supra* §12.1 note 17 at 393.

[4]Slightly edited. The untabulated original appears in 63 Stat. 816, 817, 820.

pay computed under section 1401 of this title [R_2], if the Secretary also determines that:

(1) according to accepted medical principles, the disability is permanent [C_8];

(2) the disability is not the result of the member's intentional misconduct or wilful neglect [$-C_9$], and was not incurred during an unauthorized absence [$-C_{10}$]; and

(3) either —

    (A) the member has at least 20 years of service computed under section 1208 of this title [C_{11}]; or

    (B) the disability is at least 30 percent under the standard schedule of rating disabilities in use by the Veterans' Administration at the time of the determination [C_{12}]; and

        (i) the member has at least 8 years of service computed under section 1208 of this title [C_{13}];

        (ii) the disability is the proximate result of performing active duty [C_{14}], or

        (iii) the disability was incurred in line of duty in time of war or national emergency [C_{15}].

See Figure 1 on the next page for a flowchart representation of this provision.

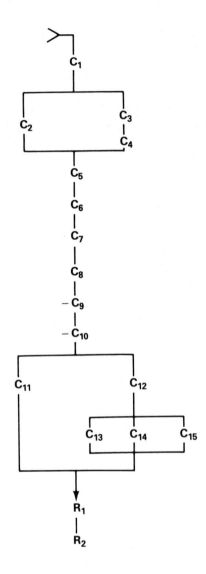

Figure 1

Let's see how a flowchart can help clarify an innocent-looking but defective provision. Here is the original from the Rules of Procedure of the House of Delegates, American Bar Association:

> *§42.3 Presiding Officer.* The Chairman of the House of Delegates shall preside at the meetings of the House. If the Chairman vacates the chair during a meeting, he may, if there is no objection from the House, appoint a temporary chairman. If the Chairman is absent from a meeting of the House or if there is an objection to the appointment, the Secretary of the Association or his designee shall preside pending the selection by voice vote of a temporary chairman. The office of temporary chairman terminates when the Chairman assumes the chair.

Look at the flowchart (Figure 2) for this provision on p. 276. It shows that, although the general thrust of the provision is clear (including the strongly implied element of presence), one important contingency has been left wholly to extrapolation: What happens if the chairman is present and vacates the chair, but does *not* appoint a temporary chairman? The most plausible remedy, of course, is to insert as an alternative to C_3 a new contingency $(-C_3)$ and tie it to temporary chairmanship by the Secretary (R_2).

How concepts are segmented is left to the discretion of the draftsman. The more minutely segmented concepts are more helpful in sorting out details but more cumbersome to deal with. It may be useful to do first a general one and later a more particularized one.

The importance of flowcharting, at least for handling boilerplate, is underscored by Thomas Chatterton's comment that he is "often appalled at the use that even large law firms make of computer-assisted document generation in that they do not seem to get beyond the paper doll stage. Flowcharting makes for a much more efficient use of such systems."[5]

There are many kinds of flowcharts.[6] A more recent ver-

[5]Chatterton letter, *supra* §12.1 note 17.

[6]See, e.g., R. Elliott, Problem Solving and Flowcharting (1972); M. Bohl, Flowcharting Techniques (1971); M. Farina, Flowcharting (1970) (for computer use).

275

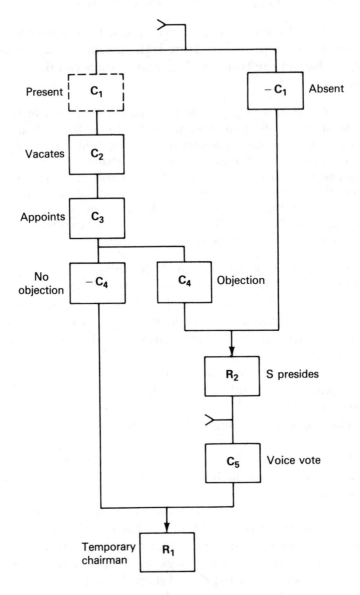

Figure 2

sion, for example, is the "Petri net," named for its German creator. As described by Jeffrey A. Meldman and Sanford J. Fox, Petri nets have been found useful "for modeling the complex activities performed by . . . modern computer systems . . . " and for describing rules of law, including those in complex statutes. It illuminates interrelationships especially involving successive and interrelated activities.[7] Petri nets can thus "represent a sequential ordering of events legally required to reach a decision."[8] Meldman and Fox recently used simplified Petri nets to analyze the complicated structure of the Social Work (Scotland) Act 1968.[9]

Flowcharts have lost some of their scientific glamor in the past decade, because in computer programming greater attention is being paid to the structural programming in such systems as PASCAL, which nevertheless is built on subroutines that reflect less visible flowcharting. The legal draftsman, whose challenges in this respect are less awesome, will still find flowcharting highly useful.

---

[7] Meldman & Fox, Concise Petri Nets and Their Use in Modeling the Social Work (Scotland) Act 1968, 30 Emory L.J. 583-584 (1981).

[8] *Id.* a* ;29.

[9] *Id.* See also Meldman & Holt, Petri Nets and Legal Systems, 1971 Jurimetrics J. 65 (1971).

XIII

Problems Peculiar to Statutes

§13.1. CONSTITUTIONAL CONSIDERATIONS

Both federal and state constitutions contain provisions that affect the substance of legislation. Naturally, the legislative draftsman needs to be aware of requirements of "due process" and "equal protection" and more specific guarantees against legislative abuses such as the enactment of *ex post facto* laws and bills of attainder. There are many others.

The draftsman of state law must be familiar with constitutional provisions unknown to his federal counterpart. Besides imposing substantive limitations, the state constitutions include provisions directed at the mechanics of the legislative process.[1] Forty-two prescribe the form of the enacting clause.[2] Forty-two provide that a bill may cover only one subject and that the subject must be expressed in its title.[3] (Mississippi's constitution

---

§13.1. [1]See H. Walker The Legislative Process 340 (1948).

[2]See appendix D. On this subject generally, see J. Sutherland, Statutes and Statutory Construction ch. 19 (4th ed. 1985); Anderson, Drafting a Legislative Act in Arkansas, 2 Ark. L. Rev. 382, 386 (1948); Lazarus, Legislative Bill Drafting in Louisiana, 1 West's Louisiana Stat. Anno. 191, 196.

[3]See appendix D. Among other things, this kind of constitutional requirement has the salutary effect of preventing the attachment of riders. On the difficult problems of meeting the requirement, see E. Crawford, The Construction of Statutes ch. 10; Sutherland, *supra* note 2, ch. 18; Anderson, *supra* note 2 at 382; Everstine, Titles of Legislative Acts, 9 Md. L. Rev. 197 (1948); Lazarus, *supra* note 2 at 195; Manson, The Drafting of Statute Titles, 10 Ind.

imposes only the latter requirement.)[4] Those of Idaho, Indiana, and Oregon provide that laws must be plainly worded, avoiding as far as practicable the use of technical terms.[5] Alabama's constitution requires that bills be divided into sections "according to substance."[6] Forty-two forbid various kinds of special legislation.[7] Fourteen require that general laws be uniform.[8] Colorado's has a similar requirement applicable only to "laws relating to courts."[9] Thirty-three include provisions relating to effective dates.[10]

Thirty-two state constitutions provide that amendatory legislation must set forth the amended or revised provisions in full.[11] (Those of Kansas, Nebraska, and Ohio also require that the material so displaced be expressly repealed.)[12] Georgia's constitution provides that an act that amends or repeals must describe the law affected and the change made.[13] Tennessee's constitution provides that "All acts which repeal, revive or amend former laws, shall recite in their caption, or otherwise, the title or substance of the law repealed, revived or amended."[14] The constitutions of New Jersey and New York forbid incorporation by reference.[15] Louisiana's forbids the incorporation by reference of "any system or code."[16]

L.J. 155 (1934); Mason, Legislative Bill Drafting, 14 Calif. L. Rev. 298, 305, 379, 383 (1926); Note 37 Ky. L.J. 192 (1949).

[4] Art. IV, §71.

[5] Idaho, Art. III, §17; Indiana, Art. IV, §20; Oregon, Art. IV, §21.

[6] Art. IV, §45.

[7] See appendix D. The problems of special legislation are considered in Crawford, *supra* note 3, ch. VIII; Sutherland, *supra* note 3, ch. 40; Cloe & Marcus, Special and Local Legislation, 24 Ky. L.J. 351 (1936); Mason, *supra* note 3 at 299.

[8] See appendix D.

[9] Art. VI, §19.

[10] See appendix D. On this subject generally, see Crawford *supra* note 3, ch. 11; Sutherland, *supra* note 3, ch. 33; Anderson, *supra* note 2 at 401; Lazarus, *supra* note 2 at 198.

[11] See appendix D. "Blind amendments" are discussed in §11.1 *supra*.

[12] Kansas, Art. 2, §16; Nebraska, Art. II, §14; Ohio, Art. 11, §15.

[13] Art. III, §5, par. IV.

[14] Art. II, §17.

[15] New Jersey, Art. IV, §VII, 5; New York, Art. III, §16.

[16] Art. III, §15.

Seventeen state constitutions provide that the state's general appropriation bill may cover only the ordinary expenses of the legislative, executive, and judicial departments and other named purposes, and that each other appropriation must be made by separate bill.[17] There are also constitutional provisions that a bill authorizing the borrowing of money,[18] appropriating money,[19] or imposing a tax[20] must state the relevant purpose or amount, or both. The constitutions of New Mexico, Oklahoma, and Wisconsin require bills authorizing the borrowing of money to provide for a sufficient annual tax.[21] About a half dozen constitutions forbid the inclusion of other materials in appropriation bills for state salaries,[22] other named appropriation bills,[23] or revenue bills.[24]

Florida's constitution provides that any law creating or consolidating county offices must prescribe the powers, duties, and compensation of the incumbents.[25]

According to Professor Millard H. Ruud,[26] all states except North Carolina and the New England states have some form of one-subject rule in their constitutions. The Minnesota provision is typical: "No law shall embrace more than one subject, which shall be expressed in its title."

Thirty-seven states have adopted substantially the same general requirement of unity of subject matter. Thirty-two of these states declare that no law shall embrace more than one *subject,* while five announce the rule in terms of *object.* Two additional states, New York and Wisconsin, have a constitutional one-subject rule that is applicable only to private and local

---

[17]See appendix D.
[18]See appendix D.
[19]See appendix D.
[20]See appendix D.
[21]New Mexico, Art. IX, §8; Oklahoma Art. 10, §25; Wisconsin, Art. VIII, §6.
[22]Florida, Art. III, §12; Nebraska, Art. III, §22; Oregon, Art. IX, §7.
[23]New York, Art. VII, §6.
[24]Delaware, Art. VIII, §2.
[25]Art. II, §5.
[26]Ruud, No Law Shall Embrace More Than One Subject, 42 Minn. L. Rev. 389, 390 (1958).

laws. Arkansas and Mississippi have constitutional one-subject provisions applicable only to appropriation bills.[27]

§13.2.   LONG TITLES

Every statute carries an official title, called a "long title," that precedes the enacting clause and describes very generally what the statute is about.[1] Here is the long title for a federal act:

An Act

To provide equitable tax treatment for foreign investment in the United States, to establish a Presidential Election Campaign Fund to assist in financing the costs of presidential election campaigns, and for other purposes.

Standards for the content of federal legislative titles are not prescribed by the federal constitution, but are left to the good judgment of the draftsman. On the other hand, most state constitutions expressly regulate the use of titles. The typical requirement is that the subject of the Act must be expressed in the title. Noncompliance results in invalidating either the act or the parts that deal with the unexpressed subject.

The state draftsman should examine the local constitution to see what, if anything, it says about the titles of acts (see appendix D).

Technically speaking, nothing that precedes the enacting clause is part of the statute. If so, how appropriate is section 10(b) of Public Law 88-269?

[27]These numbers appear to be still accurate.

§13.2.   [1]E. Driedger, The Composition of Legislation — Legislative Forms and Precedents 153-154 (2d ed., revised 1976); G. Thornton, Legislative Drafting 143-146 (2d ed. 1979); Everstine, Titles of Legislative Acts, 9 Md. L. Rev. 197 (1948); Kirk, Legal Drafting: How Should a Document Begin?, 3 Texas Tech. U.L. Rev. 233, 238-243 (1972); Manson, The Drafting of Statute Titles, 10 Ind. L.J. 155 (1934); Menard, Legislative Bill Drafting, 26 Rocky M.L. Rev. 368, 382 (1954).

(b) The title of such Act is amended to read "To promote the further development of public library services."[2]

§13.3. ENACTING CLAUSES

The formal launching platform for a statute is the enacting clause. What precedes the enacting clause is technically no part of the statute; what follows is. In most states the form of the enacting clause is fixed by the state constitution. The same is not true of federal legislation. Here, the form is fixed in section 101 of title 1, United States Code, as follows: *Be it enacted by the Senate and House of Representatives of the United States of America in Congress assembled,* [That . . .].[1]

The draftsman should examine the constitution of his state to see what, if anything, it says about the form of the enacting clause. If it says nothing, he should examine the form used in a recent volume of the state's session laws. In any event, the accepted form should be followed exactly.

§13.4. SHORT TITLES

In long acts, a short title is often included in addition to the long title. Generally, it appears in the first section of the act or near the end. Unlike the long title, which precedes rather than follows the enacting clause, it is part of the act. Unlike the long title, it is not constitutionally required. Its main purpose is to provide a short, handy name for the act. Short titles that have been used in federal legislation include the following:

[2]"Section 10(b) is not only inappropriate but can cause problems. My approach in the rare case when it arose was to use devices that permitted me to ignore the so-called amendment." Edward O. Craft, letter to author, July 15, 1985.

§**13.3.** [1]Section 102 fixes the form for joint resolutions.

That this Act may be cited as the "Narcotic Addicts Treatment Act of 1974."

Section 1. This Act may be cited as the "Intervention on the High Seas Act."

Section 1. This Act may be cited as the "Energy Supply and Environment Coordination Act of 1974."

Some acts set up permanent frameworks for continuing programs. Others merely amend such acts. Although short titles are often useful for the former, they are ordinarily inappropriate for the latter, mainly because for citation purposes new provisions, having been incorporated into the parent act, ordinarily need not be treated as having an independent status. There was little point, for example, in calling Public Law 88-489 the "Private Ownership of Special Nuclear Materials Act" when it did no more than amend the Atomic Energy Act of 1954. But if such a title is used, it should show its amendatory character, as in the following example:

Section 101. This Act may be cited as the "National Cancer Act Amendments of 1974."

The matter is discussed in greater detail in section 11.2.6.

§13.5. PURPOSE OR POLICY CLAUSES

It is generally assumed that if the interpreter of a statute knows its ulterior legislative purpose, he may more easily discover the statute's meaning. Assuming this to be generally true, should the draftsman include a statement of purpose at the beginning of the act? Professor Karl N. Llewellyn once wrote that *"sound recitals of situation and purpose constitute one of the great drafting devices and one of the vital drafting arts,"* but he may have been over-enthusiastic.

If the purpose clause is intended to compensate for the draftsman's own mistakes or inadequacies in drafting, he can obviate much of the need for it simply by addressing himself more intensively to the working provisions of his text. For this reason, a purpose clause should not be routinely included. On the other hand, if the draftsman believes that circumstances have prevented him from achieving his specific goals and that he can draft a purpose clause that will help future readers, he should include it.

A purpose clause may help the reader in interpreting the enactment if there is a pervasive uncertainty that cannot be removed in the specific directions, authorizations, and prohibitions of the bill. Thus, in a codification bill intended to restate existing law without substantive change, it is appropriate to include a statement that "in this Act it is the legislative purpose to restate, without substantive change, the law replaced by the Act on its effective date."[1] This rebuts the normal presumption that a change in language implies a change in substance.

A statement of purpose may also serve as a useful guideline in cases where the legislature wishes to give the administrator wide discretion in applying the law to concrete cases. Here the statement of purpose is a statement of legislative policy and is

§13.5. [1]This purpose clause was used in the statute that recodified titles 10, 32, and 34 of the United States Code (§49(a) of the Act of August 10, 1956, ch. 1041, 70A Stat. 640). Shortly after enactment, it was discovered that, owing to a faulty cross reference, some classes of military personnel had been deprived of service credit that they had otherwise earned toward retirement. The question then arose whether the purpose clause shielded these people from the unintended result. The old law, the new law, and the purpose clause were each clear. Fortunately, the Comptroller General ruled that the offending reference prevailed over the general, but not wholly realized, aspiration voiced by the purpose clause, thus requiring an amendment.

Why "fortunately"? Had the decision gone the other way, the new title 10 would have been destroyed as a reliable restatement of current military law; no provision, however clear, could be relied on.

When the original United States Code was enacted in 1926, it suffered just such a fate because a last-minute change reduced it to a "prima facie" status (see appendix E, par. 2 *infra*). One wonders whether a similar fate was intended for sections 1 and 2 of the Act of January 12, 1983, P.L. 97-452 (96 Stat. 2467), which, after declaring as its legislative purpose that those sections restated, without substantive change, the laws that they replaced, added this sentence (§3a, 96 Stat. 2479): "Sections 1 and 2 may not be construed as making a substantive change in the laws replaced." If this means what it says, it effectively prevented *any* of the laws "replaced" from being reliably replaced.

It is tempting to call such limitations "suicide clauses."

285

often so designated. The following statement appears in the Farm Credit Act of 1953:

Declaration of Policy

Sec. 2. It is declared to be the policy of the Congress to encourage and facilitate increased borrower participation in the management, control, and ultimate ownership of the permanent system of agricultural credit made available through institutions operating under the supervision of the Farm Credit Administration.[2]

In practice, unfortunately, the statement of purpose or policy has not been an unmitigated blessing. Too heavy reliance on such a clause leads to sloppy drafting elsewhere in the bill. The feeling that the court or administrator will somehow work out the tedious details and uncertainties tends to laziness and fuzzy thinking. Such a statement, therefore, should be relied on only so far as its objectives cannot otherwise be achieved as a clear by-product of the concrete, working sections of the bill. In strict logic, it should be among the last sections drafted. If the rest of the bill is properly drafted, the need for a statement of purpose or policy usually disappears.

Most general purpose clauses wind up as pious incantations of little practical value because what little information they contain is usually inferable from the working text. Indeed, the draftsmen who consolidated title 49 (part only) of the United States Code, in their bill restating federal transportation laws,[3] dropped most existing purpose clauses as superfluous, and, I am informed, no one complained.

Statements of legislative purpose are more helpful when fragmented and focused on specific uncertainties. For example, the draftsman might well write, "To reduce security risks, the Secretary of Defense shall . . ." The same statute might contain a number of such guides.[4]

[2] 12 U.S.C. 636a, 67 Stat. 390.
[3] H.R. 14028, 91st Cong. 1st Sess. Sept. 25, 1969.
[4] The Preparation of Legislation, report of the Renton Committee para. 11.6 HMSO Cmnd. 6053 (London 1975).

Suggestions that legislatures extend their highly generalized public policy pronouncements beyond shedding purposive light on their specific mandates (as in purpose clauses), and beyond providing guidelines for delegated legislation, raise questions of political theory and practical feasibility, but few questions of draftsmanship.[5]

My own tentative assessment of such suggestions is that the political realities of the legislative process, which focus almost exclusively on immediate concerns, permit only passing attention to broad policy utterances. Indeed, most legislators treat them as background music. What does this portend for the great bulk of judges who have only a minimal grasp of the legislative process and a minimal opportunity to integrate the better social insights of our times? However hungry for statutory guidance, they will not be significantly helped by expanding the kind of legislative ineptitudes that unfocused and loosely conceived policy announcements inevitably constitute. Who can make jurisprudential capital, for example, out of a 329-word "Declaration of National Environmental Policy"[6] that, in Charles B. Nutting's apt translation, says no more than "Hurrah for Nature"?

If the client insists on a general purpose or policy clause, the draftsman should aim for the most conservative statement that the client will accept.

What about a formal recital of facts? This is appropriate only where they express assumptions that are needed to understand the statute and are not otherwise generally shared with the legislative audience. They should not be left to legislative history.[7]

---

[5]See, e.g., Hammond, Embedding Policy Statements in Statutes: A Comparative Perspective on the Genesis of a New Public Law Jurisprudence, 5 Hast. Int. & Comp. L. Rev. 323 (1982).

[6]See 42 U.S.C. §4331.

The probably useful six-fold "finding" in section 1(b) of the Orphan Drug Act, P.L. 97-414 (96 Stat. 2049) might have been simply stated: "The purpose of this Act is to encourage the development of adequate drugs for rare diseases and conditions for which commercially feasible drugs are inadequate."

[7]R. Dickerson, The Interpretation and Application of Statutes ch. 10 (1975). Cf. the comparable problem that arose in a contract, §14.8 *infra.*

§13.6.   ARRANGEMENT: SECTIONAL SEQUENCE

The problems of legislative architecture are for the most part the problems of legal architecture generally (see chapter 5). Even so, it may be useful to set forth a generally acceptable sequence of statutory sections (so far as they apply).

(1)   Short title, if any
(2)   Statement of purpose, if any
(3)   Application
(4)   Definitions
(5)   Main working provisions
(6)   Subordinate provisions, and special provisions broad and important enough to be stated as separate sections
(7)   Administrative and procedural provisions
(8)   Sanctions and enforcement
(9)   Authority to implement statute by regulation
(10) Transitional provisions
(11) Amendments of other laws
(12) Specific repeals
(13) Savings clause, if any
(14) Severability clause, if any
(15) Expiration date, if any
(16) Effective date, if different from date of enactment or date otherwise fixed by the applicable constitution.

This order may be changed to fit the needs of particular enactments.

§13.7.   INTERPRETATION ACTS

Most states have interpretation acts that purport to control the reading of even future statutes.[1] To what extent, if any, should

§13.7. [1]See R. Dickerson, The Interpretation and Application of Statutes 277-278 (1975). Persons interested in drafting or evaluating interpretation acts will probably benefit from reading chapter 10.

the draftsman take the local interpretation act into consideration? Technically, he is free to ignore it, if he pleases, because no legislature can tie the hands of future legislatures. Practically, he will do well to take into account, and if necessary compensate for, any instances in which the courts of the state have been induced by the act to deviate from normal meanings or from accepted principles of communication.

More important, the draftsman may find it useful to adopt from the interpretation act specific standardized provisions ("boilerplate") that he considers appropriate to the bill he is drafting. But if he does, he should take the wise (though rare) precaution of expressly incorporating those provisions in the new statute and not rely on the target-seeking capability that the typical interpretation act purports to build into its own provisions. Such a precaution makes clear that the authors of the act have specifically adverted to the earlier provisions and it removes the doubt that often arises whether and to what extent the later act in fact took the earlier into account. The device for so transferring the adoptive force from the existing interpretation act to the later statute being drafted is illustrated by the introductory clause of section 101 of title 10, United States Code: *"In addition to the definitions in sections 1-5 of title 1* [the federal counterpart of the state interpretation act], *the following definitions apply in this title: . . . ."* (emphasis added). This made clear that the authors of title 10 affirmatively approved and adopted the existing general definitions in sections 1-5 of title 1 of the United States Code, which currently read as follows:

§1. Words denoting number, gender, and so forth

In determining the meaning of any Act of Congress, unless the context indicates otherwise —

words importing the singular include and apply to several persons, parties, or things;

words importing the plural include the singular;

words importing the masculine gender include the feminine as well;

words used in the present tense include the future as well as the present;

the words "insane" and "insane person" and "lunatic" shall include every idiot, lunatic, insane person, and person non compos mentis;

the words "person" and "whoever" include corporations, companies, associations, firms, partnerships, societies, and joint stock companies, as well as individuals;

"officer" includes any person authorized by law to perform the duties of the office;

"signature" or "subscription" includes a mark when the person making the same intended it as such;

"oath" includes affirmation, and "sworn" includes affirmed;

"writing" includes printing and typewriting and reproductions of visual symbols by photographing, multigraphing, mimeographing, manifolding, or otherwise.

§2.   "County" as including "parish," and so forth

The word "county" includes a parish, or any other equivalent subdivision of a State or Territory of the United States.

§3.   "Vessel" as including all means of water transportation

The word "vessel" includes every description of watercraft or other artificial contrivance used, or capable of being used, as a means of transportation on water.

§4.   "Vehicle" as including all means of land transportation

The word "vehicle" includes every description of carriage or other artificial contrivance used, or capable of being used, as a means of transportation on land.

§5.   "Company" or "association" as including successors and assigns

The word "company" or "association", when used in reference to a corporation, shall be deemed to embrace the words "successors and assigns of such company or association," in like manner as if these last-named words, or words of similar import, were expressed.

§13.8. ISSUANCE OF REGULATIONS

Should the draftsman include a provision authorizing or directing the appropriate administrative official to issue regulations implementing the statutory program?

The question is complicated by the ambiguity in the word "regulation." In its procedural sense it means a mechanical device by which an administrative official expresses a general principle of action in carrying out his statutory functions. In this sense, it is unnecessary to authorize the use of this device since it is normally implied. In exceptional instances, however, it may still be desirable to phrase duties or powers in terms of procedure.

Example:

The superintendent of the school shall issue regulations:
(1) defining hazing;
(2) designed to end that practice; and
(3) prescribing dismissal, suspension, or other adequate punishment for violations.

Even in the example given it is not necessary to refer to the mechanics of regulation.

Example:

The superintendent of the school shall prescribe:
(1) what constitutes hazing;
(2) measures designed to end that practice;
(3) dismissal, suspension, or other adequate punishment for violations.

The word "regulation" also means a rule of conduct prescribed by an official of the executive branch of the government, as distinct from the mere mechanics of formalizing and issuing the rule. Here, a grant of regulation-making authority is a grant of the authority to make substantive rules. These rules may be addressed either to employees of the government subject to the jurisdiction of the official issuing the regulation or to members of the public.

Even here it is not always necessary to prescribe the power to issue regulations. So far as the first group is concerned, the power to direct the activities of subordinates is necessarily implied from the basic authority to carry on the particular legislative program. Within the field of his legitimate activity the supervisor is presumed to have full control of his subordinates.

Where the legislature wishes to grant the power to regulate members of the public, it must, in addition to meeting constitutional limitations on the delegation of legislative authority, make clear in the statute that such a power to regulate is conferred. This should not be left to inference. However, the grant need not be couched in terms of the power to issue regulations. In general it is probably preferable, in the absence of special considerations, to grant the authority without using the ambiguous word "regulations."

§13.9.   PROVISIONS RELATING TO APPROPRIATIONS

In a bill setting up a federal program it is unnecessary to include a provision that expressly authorizes Congress to appropriate money for the purpose, unless the provision is to name a specific amount or there is another special reason for including it. As an authorization, the provision is unnecessary because by prescribing or authorizing an action Congress impliedly authorizes the necessary appropriation. If such a provision has any effect, it can only be restrictive. Thus, if an existing provision authorizes a specific amount, the appropriation of a larger amount would be subject to a point of order.

If it is desirable in a special case that Congress keep a year-to-year check on the expenditures for a particular program, the draftsman may include a watch-dog provision. With a provision that action must be "within funds specifically appropriated for the purpose," no money may be spent for the named purpose unless it has been so earmarked by Congress in the appropriations for that fiscal year.

As already shown,[1] many state constitutions provide what general and special appropriation bills may cover or what they must specify.[2] These provisions are tabulated in appendix D.

§13.10. EVASION

Occasionally draftsmen include clauses forbidding persons subject to the prohibitions of the bill to evade them. Some are elaborate sections banning a list of specific subterfuges. Other clauses hit generally at "artifices, subterfuges, devices, and tricks." Others forbid the doing of specified acts "either directly or indirectly."

Language directed at "evasion" either is useless[1] or represents bad arrangement. So far as it strikes directly at the evasion of prohibitions already spelled out, it is superfluous since forbidden acts are forbidden even when done under the pretense of legality. (The courts do not need to be told they can penetrate sham.) So far as it strikes at specific practices not otherwise included in the general prohibitions of the bill, it merely finishes the job of naming or clarifying the proscribed acts. "Evasion" here is a misnomer and the substantive prohibitions are better moved to where they can accompany their related prohibitions.

§13.9. [1]See §8.1 *supra.*
[2]Appropriation bills are too specialized for detailed coverage here.
§13.10. [1]Cullen, The Mechanics of Statutory Revision, 24 Ore. L. Rev. 1, 18 (1944).

§13.11.   REPEALS AND COMPARABLE AMENDMENTS[1]

Before he can consider his job done, the draftsman must survey the field his bill will occupy to see what specific statutes and parts of statutes should be repealed if it is enacted. These he should specifically name in a special repeal section ("The following laws and parts of laws are repealed: . . . ").[2] If he does nothing or expresses the repeals inadequately, he passes the buck to the courts and creates uncertainty in the minds of those affected by the enactment. The courts' interpretation may not be what Congress or the state legislature intended.

Where the existing law is complex and located in many statutes, identifying the pieces to be displaced is hard and takes time. It is not surprising that draftsmen often fall back on the flimsy expedient of a general repeal clause. ("All laws and parts of laws in conflict herewith are hereby repealed.") Although such a clause has an air of legislative respectability, it is at best a waste of time and print, since it only says what would necessarily be so without it.[3] At worst it pretends to solve a problem that it does not touch, and in some cases it may even boomerang. Thus, if the bill is meant to preempt the whole legislative field that it will invade, even to displacing compatible provisions, merely enacting a general repeal clause such as the one above

---

§13.11   [1]"A Benthamite once complained that Parliament passes statutes by wagonloads and repeals them by cartloads. . . . Lord Halsbury said that the best Act was a Repealing Act." A. Russell, Legislative Drafting and Forms 50 (1890). On this subject generally, see E. Crawford, The Construction of Statutes §93 (1940); C. Jones, Statute Law Making in the United States ch. X (1912); J. Sutherland, Statutes and Statutory Construction ch. 23 (4th ed. 1985); J. Thornton, Legislative Drafting 305-308 (2d ed. 1979); A. Willard, A Legislative Handbook 47-57 (1890); Anderson, Drafting a Legislative Act in Arkansas, 2 Ark. L. Rev. 382, 390 (1948); Van der Zee, Form and Language of Statutes in Iowa, Vol. III of Applied History 337-342 (1916).

[2]Sutherland, *supra* note 1 at §23.07; H. Walker, The Legislative Process 352 (1948); Mason, Legislative Bill Drafting, 14 Calif. L. Rev. 379, 387 (1926); Note, 45 Harv. L. Rev. 364 (1931).

[3]Jones, *supra* note 1 at 150; Walker, *supra* note 2 at 353; Poldervaardt, Legislative Drafting in New Mexico, New Mexico Tax Bulletin XXVIII 593, 598 (1949).

will imply that only the incompatible provisions are displaced. Here it is better to say nothing.[4] Even better is to say specifically what is intended.

In many cases, the draftsman cannot, by simple repeal, neatly excise the law to be killed without leaving jagged wounds in the law that is intended to remain alive. In these cases he should amend the affected law, by naming the deletions and insertions or by fully restating it.

Substantively, there is no difference between an act that amends the whole by striking out a part ("the Act of April 27, 1983, ch. 25 (41 U.S.C. 501-518), is amended by striking out section 104") and an act that repeals the part ("section 104 of the Act of April 27, 1983, ch. 25 (41 U.S.C. 503), is repealed").[5] Federal draftsmen customarily use the repeal approach to kill an entire act or an entire part carrying a number or letter ("title IV," "section 104," "section 104(a)(2)") and the amendment approach to kill undesignated fragments ("section 104(a)(2) is amended by striking out the second sentence and the third through the tenth words of the last sentence" or "section 104(a)(2) is amended to read as follows: . . . "). For draftsmen in states whose constitutions require that amended provisions be set forth in full,[6] use of the repeal approach even for undesignated sentences and paragraphs avoids the constitutional requirement[7] except where the requirement expressly extends to repeals.[8]

§13.12. SEVERABILITY CLAUSES.[1]

Removing a brick from a building will not make it collapse. Removing a keystone may. The same thing happens when a

---

[4]But see Sutherland, *supra* note 1 at §23.08.

[5]*Id.* at §§22.22, 22.23.

[6]See §13.01 *supra* and appendix D.

[7]Sutherland, *supra* note 1 at §22.23.

[8]E.g., Georgia, Art. III, §5, par. 4.

§**13.12.** [1]See E. Crawford, The Construction of Statutes §§144-145 (1940); J. Sutherland, Statutes and Statutory Construction ch. 44, esp. §44.08

court finds a statutory provision invalid. The problem here is that, to determine whether the rest of the building has fallen down, the court must determine whether it has removed a brick or keystone. This depends upon what Congress or the state legislature made it. It is often hard to tell.

To help the courts decide such questions consistently with its own objectives, the legislature often includes a "severability clause," to the effect that the valid provisions stand even after any invalid ones have fallen. These clauses usually do little more than declare a principle the courts will often apply anyway: The invalidity of a provision does not affect the validity of other provisions that are severable from it. Besides, they do not ordinarily show what provisions were intended to be severable from what others.

On the other hand, because some courts presume the inseverability of the statute as a whole, the inclusion of a severability clause will at least rebut the presumption. Such a clause has further use in the federal courts and some state courts, where in the absence of a severability clause they will not find the valid applications of a provision severable from the invalid applications of the same provision.[2]

Where a severability clause seems appropriate, the following form is suggested:

> SEC._____. If a part of this Act is invalid, all valid parts that are severable from the invalid part remain in effect. If a part of this Act is invalid in one or more of its applications, the part remains in effect in all valid applications that are severable from the invalid applications.

A clause that went on to name the specific provisions that were to be considered "severable" would be correspondingly

---

(4th ed. 1973); Anderson, Drafting a Legislative Act in Arkansas, 2 Ark. L. Rev. 3892, 398 (1948); Menard, Legislative Bill Drafting, 23 Rocky Mt. L. Rev. 127, 139 (1950); Stern, Separability and Separability Clauses in the Supreme Court, 51 Harv. L. Rev. 76 (1937).

[2] Sutherland, *supra* note 1 at §44.16, says that the federal rule is limited to federal acts.

more helpful to the courts.[3] At the same time it might be correspondingly more dangerous for what it implied in case a problem of severability were to arise within a named area. Thus if the legislature were to name certain large segments as severable from each other, the provision might be interpreted as indicating that the invalidity of any significant aspect of one of those parts destroyed all of that part.

§13.13. SAVINGS CLAUSES[1]

It is normally presumed that changes in the law are intended to be in full force from the effective date of their enactment. Since many statutes deal with situations that have existed for a substantial time, this presumption would often disrupt transactions already in progress. Accordingly, it is common to soften the effect of a new law, or the amendment or repeal of an old one, by including a savings clause. In some states, this result is written into general law,[2] and in the absence of conflicting language in the particular statute it is assumed that the statute was enacted in the light of that general law.

The usual savings clause preserves rights and duties that have already matured and proceedings that have already been begun. The following form is suggested:

> SEC._____. This Act [or "title," "part," or "section"] does not affect rights and duties that matured, penalties that were incurred, and proceedings that were begun, before its effective date.

In a special situation it may be desirable to preserve rights, duties, or proceedings that have not reached these stages. Here

[3]E.g., *Hubbell Bank v. Bryan*, 124 Neb. 51, 245 N.W. 20 (1932).

§13.13. [1]See E. Crawford, The Construction of Statutes §93 (1940); J. Sutherland, Statutes and Statutory Construction §§20.22, 21.12 (4th ed. 1985); Ruud, The Savings Clause — Some Problems in Construction and Drafting, 33 Tex. L. Rev. 285 (1955).

[2]See, e.g., Ark. Stat. (1947) §§1-103, 1-104.

the savings clause must be tailored to the needs of the particular case.

§13.14. TIME OF TAKING EFFECT[1]

If it does not provide otherwise, a federal act takes effect at the moment of enactment, which is usually when it is signed by the President. If the statute specifies a day on which it is to become effective, it takes effect at the beginning of that day. The effective date of a statute is often an important substantive consideration, because (together with any savings clause) it is a means of controlling the statute's impact on proceedings and transactions not yet completed by the time of enactment. This gives people a better chance to adjust to the new law.

At common law, a statute was considered to have been effective from the first day of the session at which it was enacted. Today, the effective dates of statutes are variously regulated by the constitutions of more than 40 states. In Wisconsin, for example, Article IV, section 17(2), provides, "No law shall be in force until published." More typical is Article IV, section 28 of the Oregon Constitution, which provides:

> No act shall take effect, until ninety days from the end of the session at which the same shall have been passed, except in case of emergency; which emergency shall be declared in the preamble, or in the body of the law.

This means that, in fixing an effective date other than that otherwise prescribed by the state constitution, a draftsman may establish a later effective date simply by naming it, but he may set an earlier one only if he includes an appropriate recital of emergency.

The draftsman should examine the constitution of his state to see what, if anything, it says about effective dates. He should

---

§13.14.　　[1] See J. Thornton, Legislative Drafting 155-158 (2d ed. 1979); E. Driedger, The Composition of Legislation — Legislative Forms and Precedents 109-110, 173-176 (2d ed., revised 1976).

also examine the state's interpretation act. A general Wisconsin statute provides: "Every act and every portion of an act enacted by the legislature over the governor's partial veto which does not expressly prescribe the time when it takes effect shall take effect on the day after the publication. . . ."[2]

[2]Wis. Stats. Ann. §991.11.

XIV

Some Specific Results

§14.1. SUBSTANTIVE BENEFITS OF GOOD DRAFTING

This book began with the recommendation that the draftsman pay adequate attention to matters of substantive policy and avoid being preoccupied with matters of form.[1] It now ends by underlining the assurance that a thoroughgoing attention to architecture, arrangement, consistency, clarity, brevity, and style, all of which are significant aspects of legal form, almost always produces important benefits.

One benefit is that, even while the draftsman is preoccupied with such formal matters as logical arrangement or verbal consistency, the putting of substantive elements into the most favorable juxtapositions, or stating similar ideas similarly, is almost certain to bring into view important substantive considerations that the draftsman would otherwise overlook. A valuable by-product of a wholesome attention to form, therefore, is the clarification and improvement of substantive policy itself.[2]

§14.2. FORMAL BENEFITS OF GOOD DRAFTING

More obvious as benefits of good drafting are greater clarity, readability, and usability. The degree to which traditional

§14.1. [1]See §§1.2, 2.1, and 2.2 *supra.*
[2]See §§2.2 and 2.3 *supra.*

methods of legal expression can be improved in these respects can best be seen by examining specific instances in which modern drafting principles have been applied. Accordingly, examples from several legal fields are set forth below. The inclusion of suggested revisions, however, is not meant to imply that they are perfect examples of drafting, the best possible alternatives to the original, or even adequate in all factual situations. As with form books, no provision that is viewed out of the specific environment in which it is to be used can be more than tentatively evaluated. Even with these reservations, the following examples may be helpful in suggesting some of the benefits that the application of sound drafting principles may be expected to produce.

§14.3. ILLUSTRATIVE REDRAFT: AN INDENTURE

Original (the article on "Subordination of Debentures"):

The Company, for itself, its successors and assigns, covenants and agrees, and each holder of Debentures or any coupon, by his acceptance thereof, likewise covenants and agrees, that the payment of the principal of, and the premium, if any, and interest on, each and all of the Debentures is hereby expressly subordinated, to the extent and in the manner hereinafter set forth, in right of payment to the prior payment in full of all Senior Indebtedness.

As redrafted:

By holding a debenture or coupon, a holder agrees with the Company that payment of principal and interest, and of any premium, is subordinated to the payment in full of all senior indebtedness.[1]

§14.3. [1]"Company" is defined elsewhere in the indenture to include "successors and assigns." "Payment in full" and "senior indebtedness" are also defined.

§14.4.   ILLUSTRATIVE REDRAFT: A WILL

Original:

All the rest, residue and remainder of my said estate whatsoever, real, personal, or mixed, of every kind and character, wherever the same may be situated, excluding any property over which I may have a power of appointment, of which I shall be seized or entitled to at the time of my death, not hereby or by any codicil hereto otherwise specifically disposed of, after payment of my debts, funeral and testamentary expenses and the legacies bequeathed hereby or by any codicil hereto, I give, devise and bequeath unto my beloved son, to have and to hold the same in trust as Trustee, for the use and purposes and with the powers and duties following, that is to say: etc.

As redrafted:

I give the rest of my estate as it exists at the time of my death, except for property under power of appointment by me, to my son [insert name], in trust as follows:[1]

§14.5.   ILLUSTRATIVE REDRAFTS: TWO STATUTES

a.   Original (Revised Statutes (1875)):

Section 5298. Whenever, by reason of unlawful obstructions, combinations, or assemblages of persons, or rebellion against the authority of the Government of the United States, it shall become impracticable, in the judgment of the President, to enforce, by the ordinary course of judicial proceedings, the laws of the United States within any State or Territory, it shall be lawful for the President to call forth the militia of any or all the States, and to employ such parts of the land and naval forces of the United States as he may deem necessary to enforce the

§14.4.   [1]Reference to the payment of debts and funeral and testamentary expenses is unnecessary because their payment is required by statute.

faithful execution of the laws of the United States, or to suppress such rebellion, in whatever State or Territory thereof the laws of the United States may be forcibly opposed, or the execution thereof forcibly obstructed.

As redrafted (Title 10, United States Code (70A Stat. 15)):

§332. Use of militia and armed forces to enforce federal authority

Whenever the President considers that unlawful obstructions, combinations, or assemblages, or rebellion against the authority of the United States, make it impracticable to enforce the laws of the United States in any State or Territory by the ordinary course of judicial proceedings, he may call into Federal service such of the militia of any State, and use such of the armed forces, as he considers necessary to enforce those laws or to suppress the rebellion.

b. Original (Act of September 16, 1942, ch. 561, §204(b) (60 Stat. 97)):

(b) It is recommended, in order to minimize the possibility of physical adhesion of State balloting material, that the gummed flap of the State envelope supplied for the return of the ballot be separated by a wax paper or other appropriate protective insert from the remaining balloting material, and, because such inserts may not prove completely effective, that there also be included in State voting instructions a procedure to be followed by absentee voters in instances of such adhesion of the balloting material, such as a notation of the facts on the back of any such envelope, duly signed by the voter and witnessing officer.

As redrafted (Title 10, United States Code, §1080(b) (70 A Stat. 86)):

(b) It is further recommended —
(1) that the gummed flap of the return envelope for the

ballot be separated from the balloting material by waxed paper or other protective insert to minimize the possibility that the balloting material will stick together;

(2) that the voting instructions include a procedure to be followed by the voter if the balloting material does stick together, such as a notation of the facts on the back of the envelope, signed by the voter and the witness; . . .

§14.6. Illustrative redraft: An ordinance

Original:

Section 1. There is hereby levied and imposed a tax at the rate of two cents (2¢) on each twenty (20) cigarettes, or fractional part thereof, on all cigarettes possessed or held within Washington County by any person for sale on and after July 1, 1984. It is the intent of this section that a package of twenty (20) cigarettes, or less, shall be taxed two cents (2¢); provided however, that a package of cigarettes retailing at a price of one dollar ($1) or less, shall be taxed one cent (1¢); that a package containing more than twenty (20) cigarettes shall be taxed, in addition to the tax of two cents (2¢) on twenty (20) cigarettes, in proportion to the number of cigarettes contained in each package, a tax of one cent (1¢) for each additional ten (10) cigarettes, or fractional part thereof, with the tax computed so as to include the next full cent for any fractional part of said additional ten (10) cigarettes and in no event shall the amounts or denominations of the tax be less than one cent (1¢).

Section 2. The tax herein levied and imposed shall be collected and paid upon only one sale of the same cigarettes, and after the tax shall have been paid, as provided by this Ordinance or by regulations established pursuant thereto, it shall not be necessary for any subsequent vendor to pay any further tax.

Section 3. It shall be presumed that all sales of cigarettes within the County are subject to the tax herein levied unless and until the contrary is established, and the burden of proof that a sale is not taxable, or that the tax has been paid, shall be upon the vendor.

As redrafted:

(*Note:* The following draft assumes that the rule relating to cigarettes retailing for one dollar or less is intended to apply to packages containing any number of cigarettes.)

Section 1. A person who sells cigarettes in Washington County after June 30, 1984, shall pay a tax on each package so sold, unless a tax has been paid under this section on an earlier sale of the same package. If the package retails for more than one dollar, the tax is:

(1)　2 cents, if the package contains 20 cigarettes or less; and

(2)　1 cent for each 10 cigarettes, or fraction of 10 cigarettes, if the package contains more than 20 cigarettes.

If the package retails for one dollar or less, the tax is 1 cent.

Section 2. The burden of proof that a sale is not taxable under section 1, or that the tax has been paid, is on the seller.

(*Note:* The following draft assumes that the rule relating to cigarettes retailing for one dollar or less is intended to apply only to packages containing 20 cigarettes or less.)

Section 1. A person who sells cigarettes in Washington County after June 30, 1984, shall pay a tax on each package so sold, unless a tax has been paid under this section on an earlier sale of the same package. If the package contains 20 cigarettes or less, the tax is:

(1)　2 cents, if the package retails for more than one dollar; and

(2)　1 cent, if the package retails for one dollar or less.

If the package contains more than 20 cigarettes, the tax is 1 cent for each 10 cigarettes and, if the package does not contain an even multiple of 10, it shall be treated as containing the next higher multiple of 10.

Section 2. The burden of proof that a sale is not taxable

under section 1, or that the tax has been paid, is on the seller.

§14.7. ILLUSTRATIVE REDRAFT (WITH SUBSTANTIVE CHANGES): A LEASE

Original:

LEASE — INDIANA UNIVERSITY

I accept this contract for (address)_____ at a monthly rental of $____ from _____ to _____ unless sooner terminated as herein specified, having made the required deposit of $____ and having knowledge of the following Terms and Conditions of this contract which are a part of this contract. I agree to assume the financial responsibility of this agreement, with the understanding that my staff appointment or student status qualifies me for University housing, and to be bound by this contract for the period specified. I sign this contract with the understanding that should I become ineligible to live in University housing during the term of this contract it shall be cancelled and I may be requested to vacate without prior notice, and unless I am eligible and I contract for another period immediately following the term for which contract is signed, I will vacate my space by 5:00 P.M., on the last day of the contract period. I understand that any resident whose actions are found by the Administration of the University to be detrimental to the welfare of the dwelling unit, neighborhood, or the University may be requested to withdraw from the housing covered by this contract.

Signature_____ Date_____

TERMS AND CONDITIONS

(1) This contract is binding, and the student or staff or faculty member shall be responsible for the full amount of charges. (2) This contract may be cancelled without forfeiture upon 60 days notice to the Real Estate office *providing* the date of vacating

is not prior to December 1, April 1 or July 1, whichever is the nearest future date.

(3) The tenant shall pay said rent promptly as it becomes due at the Real Estate office, room 315, Administration Building, and it shall be considered delinquent after the 10th day following the day due.

(4) The tenant shall use said premises well and keep the same in good condition and repair at all times, reasonable wear and tear and damage by fire or other unavoidable casualty only excepted. The tenant shall be held liable for damages beyond normal wear and tear, including the responsibility of any frozen plumbing caused by his negligence.

(5) The tenant shall, at his own expense, keep the lawns, trees, vines, bushes and hedges of the demised premises cut, watered and trimmed during the term of this lease.

(6) The duly authorized agents and representatives of the University shall have the right at any time to enter upon and in said premises for the purpose of inspecting the same, or with notice and at a reasonable hour, for the purpose of showing the premises to persons who may wish to lease.

(7) The tenant expressly assumes all risk of accident, injury or damage to persons or property in or about said premises and shall hold the University harmless from any and all liability therefor. This condition shall not operate to prevent provisions of Workmen's Compensation laws, when otherwise operative, from applying in event of accident or injuries involving University workmen engaged in performing their authorized duties.

(8) The tenant shall use said premises only as a residence and in accordance with the laws, regulations and ordinances of the United States of America, the State of Indiana and the City of Bloomington, Indiana.

(9) The tenant shall furnish heat and all utilities for said premises, and shall promptly pay all gas, oil, coal, electric, water and sewer, and telephone rates and charges which may become due and payable during the term thereof, unless otherwise stated herein as follows: _____

_____

(10) The tenant shall not injure, overload or deface or suffer to be injured, overloaded or defaced the said premises or any part thereof.

(11) The tenant shall not make alterations, additions or improvements without the written consent of the University, but after such consent has been given, unless otherwise agreed upon in writing, all alterations, additions or improvements made by the tenant upon said premises shall be at the tenant's own expense and, at the option of the University, shall remain upon the premises at the expiration of this lease and become the property of the University as a further consideration for this lease.

(12) The tenant shall not assign, sublet or part with the possession of the whole or any part of the leased premises without first obtaining the written consent of the University.

(13) At the expiration of the term herein before specified, or upon termination of this lease in advance of such time as provided for herein, the tenant shall deliver up the demised premises peaceably to the University; and neither the terms of this indenture nor the fact of possession of said premises hereunder shall in any way serve as an option for the renewal thereof.

(14) The University shall place the building in reasonably good condition considering age and present condition and the use to which it is to be put.

(15) It is agreed between the University and the tenant that if any default be made in the payment of rent, or any part thereof as herein specified, and such default shall continue for a period of ten (10) days, the University may exercise the rights granted it herein by reason of said default.

(16) The University shall prorate rental on a day rate based on a 30-day month when occupancy is less than a full month.

(17) The tenant shall agree to leave premises free of all trash and in a sanitary and clean condition. A representative of the Real Estate office shall inspect the property the day the premises are vacated to estimate the amount of damages or loss, if any, as outlined in this lease.

Policy Changes:

POLICY STATEMENT

(1)   Provision should be made for the signatures of the tenant and the University representative and for the date on which each signs the lease.

(2)   Rent is to be paid in advance on the first of each month. However, rent will be treated as delinquent only if not paid before the eleventh of the month.

(3)   The University is to have the power to cancel the lease after 60 days' notice if the land is needed to make way for University construction that is imminent.

(4)   The University wants the right to enter the premises at any time for purposes of maintenance and will give reasonable notice. The notice under clause 6 is also to be reasonable.

(5)   The University wants to cancel the lease after 10 days' notice if the tenant violates clauses 3, 4, 5, 8, 10, 11, and 12; the fourth sentence of the preamble; or the tenant's duty to repair.

(6)   The University wants to be compensated for damage to the premises resulting from violations of clauses 4, 5, 8, 10, 11, and 12; the fourth sentence of the preamble; and the tenant's duty to repair.

(7)   Proration is intended to cover the right to possession rather than mere physical occupancy. No proration will be made, in cases of cancellation, if the tenant fails to cancel the lease in accordance with clause 2 or if the University cancels the lease because of a violation of clauses 3, 4, 5, 8, 10, 11, and 12; the fourth sentence of the preamble; or the tenant's duty to repair.

(8)   In clause 16 the phrase "less than a full month" is not intended to refer to total occupancy but to the right to possession during the initial or terminal calendar month.

(9)   The lease should provide for a return of the deposit subject to deductions for damage unless, in cases of

cancellation, tenant fails to cancel the lease in accordance with clause 2 or the University cancels the lease because of a violation of clauses 3, 4, 5, 8, 10, 11, and 12; the fourth sentence of the preamble; or the tenant's duty to repair. The deposit will be returned not too long after the tenant leaves the premises.

(10) The University does not intend that compensation for damage be limited to the amount of the deposit.

(11) The University will make major repairs, such as repair of the roof and replacement of doors and windows. The tenant will make minor repairs, such as repair of leaky faucets and faulty electrical outlets.

(12) If the tenant loses his eligibility, he is subject to having to vacate immediately and without notice.

(13) Under clause 5 the tenant is to keep the lawns, trees, vines, bushes, and hedges in a reasonably good condition. The tenant is also to keep the sidewalks, drives, and steps free from obstructions.

(14) Clauses 4, 8, 10, 11, and 12 and the fourth sentence of the preamble are intended to apply to the tenant, his family, or guests.

(15) Under clause 6 the phrase "persons who may wish to lease" should be limited to those who may want to lease the premises which are the subject of the lease.

(16) Under clause 8 the premises are to be used also in accordance with County ordinances.

(17) The option of clause 11 is to be taken out. The University's rights will depend on the agreement referred to in line 1 of clause 11.

(18) Clause 14 should more clearly state that the University's obligation exists only before the tenant moves in.

(19) Clause 14 is to turn only on "age and present condition." It is intended to cover the entire property.

(20) Under clause 12 the "part with possession" provision is intended to keep out all occupants (other than guests and members of the immediate family) unless they are approved by the University, where the "assign or sublet" provision is not applicable.

(21)   The tenant must take out a public liability policy within a reasonable time after his occupancy begins.

(22)   Under clause 7 the phrase "assume all risk" is intended to put all landlord or tenant liability with respect to third parties on the tenant. The phrase "hold harmless" is intended to be limited to cases where the tenant's wrongdoing was a cause of the injury or damage.

(23)   Under clause 11 alterations, additions, or improvements the tenant, his family, or guests permit to be made are also prohibited unless the University consents.

(24)   If the premises are destroyed by fire or other unavoidable casualty the tenant may cancel the lease.

(25)   A space for exceptions should be provided in clauses 5 and 9.

(26)   The "dwelling unit" concept of the fourth sentence of the preamble should be made to turn on the existence of a duplex or apartment building.

(27)   In clause 11 the phrase "unless otherwise agreed upon" does not modify the phrase "at the tenant's own expense."

As redrafted:

INDIANA UNIVERSITY HOUSING LEASE

SECTION 1.   *Basic agreement*

Beginning _____ and ending _____, Indiana University agrees to lease to the tenant the premises located at _____. For this period and for any other period of actual occupancy by the tenant, the tenant agrees to pay rent at the monthly rate of $____, and the parties agree to comply with sections 2-11, as applicable. The tenant agrees to deposit $____.

Date _____

_____
University Representative

Date _____

_____
Tenant

SEC. 2.   *Rent*

(a) Rent is due on the first day of the calendar month whose occupancy it covers. It shall be paid at the Bursar's Office, Room 100, Bryan Hall. (If rent remains unpaid after the 10th day of the month, this lease is subject to termination[1] under section 9(2)).

(b) If the period during which rent is payable begins after the first day, or ends before the last day, of the calendar month, the rent shall be prorated at a daily rate based on a 30-day month. However, if the University terminates the lease under section 9(2), or if the tenant's occupancy at the end of that period is unauthorized, rent is due for the entire month in which the period ends.

SEC. 3.   *Restrictions on use*

(a) No person other than the tenant, his/her spouse, his/her children, and temporary guests may occupy the premises without the written consent of the Real Estate Director.

(b) The tenant, the members of his/her household, and his/her guests may use the premises only as a residence and only in compliance with applicable laws, regulations, and ordinances.

(c) The tenant, the members of his/her household, and his/her guests may not:

    (1)   make alterations or additions to the premises without the written consent of the Real Estate Director;

    (2)   beyond normal wear, intentionally or negligently damage the premises or permit them to be damaged; or

    (3)   use the premises in a way that is detrimental to the welfare of the neighborhood or the University or, if the premises are an apartment or a duplex, to the welfare of the dwelling unit.

---

§**14.7.** [1]See §8.14 note 3 *supra.*

SEC. 4.   *Maintenance*

(a) The tenant shall, at his/her expense, in a workmanlike manner, and within a reasonable time after the need is discovered, make minor repairs and perform other minor maintenance. For example, he/she shall:

(1) repair leaky or stopped-up plumbing; any defective dishwasher, garbage disposal, or room air conditioner; defective electrical switches or outlets; and malfunctioning doors and windows;

(2) service furnace, filters, fans, and water heater;

(3) do any needed housecleaning;

(4) except in the case of an apartment, maintain the yard; and

(5) except in the case of an apartment, keep the sidewalks, driveways, and steps free of snow, ice, and obstructions.

(b) The University shall, at its expense and within a reasonable time after it is informed of the need, make major repairs and perform other major maintenance necessary to keep the premises livable. For example, it shall:

(1) repair or replace defective plumbing or electrical fixtures, pipes, heating system elements, gutters and downspouts, storm sashes, and screens;

(2) clean and pump septic tanks;

(3) repair defective chimneys;

(4) repair or replace defective driveways, walks, and steps;

(5) do necessary exterior painting; and

(6) repair or replace leaky roofs.

The tenant shall promptly notify the University of any need, covered by this subsection, of which he/she has knowledge.

SEC 5.   *Utilities*

The tenant shall promptly pay for heat, light, cooking fuel, water, and any other utilities that he/she uses.

SEC. 6.   *Right to enter*

Authorized representatives of the University may enter the premises:
   (1) at a reasonable time with reasonable notice, to show them to a prospective tenant of the premises;
   (2) at any time with reasonable notice, to perform maintenance prescribed by section 4(b); and
   (3) at any time without notice, to inspect the premises.

SEC. 7.   *Legal responsibility of the tenant*

(a) The tenant assumes any legal responsibility of the University, and shall hold it harmless from any liability, that arises because of injury to persons or property on the premises not resulting from the misconduct of a representative of the University. (As soon as possible after this lease is executed, the tenant should make sure that he/she is adequately covered by public liability insurance.)

(b) The tenant shall reimburse the University for any cost to it resulting from a violation of section 3, 4(a), or 5.

(c) This section is not intended to affect the operation of workmen's compensation laws as they apply to employees of the University.

SEC. 8.   *Termination by the tenant*

(a) By giving notice to the University, the tenant may at any time terminate this lease effective no sooner than 60 days and on a date that falls within the earliest of the following periods: December 1 — last day of the first semester final examinations; April 1 -- last day of the second semester final examinations; and July 15–August 31.

(b) By giving notice to the University, the tenant may terminate the lease, effective immediately, if through no fault of his the premises become unlivable or are declared unsafe by authorized officials.

SEC. 9.   *Termination by the university*

By giving notice to the tenant, the University may at any time terminate this lease:

(1)   effective immediately, if the tenant becomes ineligible to live in University housing;

(2)   effective no sooner than 10 days, if the tenant fails to pay a monthly installment of rent before the 10th day after it becomes due, or if there is a violation of section 3, 4(a), or 5; and

(3)   effective no sooner than 60 days, if the premises will be needed for University construction purposes within a reasonable time after the termination takes effect.

SEC. 10.   *Moving out*

(a) The tenant shall vacate the premises by 5 P.M. on the last day of the period during which he/she is authorized to occupy them. This lease does not authorize renewal or occupation of the premises beyond the lease period.

(b) When he/she moves out, the tenant shall leave the premises clean and sanitary. (They will be inspected on moving day for compliance with this subsection and sections 3 and 4.)

(c) When he/she moves out, the tenant may remove only those alternations or additions to whose removal the Real Estate Director has consented in writing.

SEC. 11.   *Return of deposit*

Unless the University has terminated this lease under section 9(2), the tenant is entitled to return of his/her deposit within a reasonable time after he/she moves out, subject to deduction for unpaid obligations under the lease.

§14.8.   ILLUSTRATIVE DRAFT: A CONTRACT

AGREEMENT

A.   PURPOSE

This agreement is made by the legatees, next-of-kin, and creditors of Carole E. Oliver and of her husband, Robin G. Oliver, both dead, to pay the debts of the decedents and distribute their remaining personal effects without undue effort or expense. The parties believe that the agreement will carry out the wishes of Carole E. Oliver, as expressed in her will, and will fully protect the interests of the creditors.

Carole E. Oliver died in Washington, D.C., on August 19, 1980, leaving a will (copy attached) and an estate consisting of only tangible personal property, most of which is stored at Mantell Transfer and Storage Company, Washington, D.C., together with property owned by Robin G. Oliver, who died on March 25, 1982, likewise leaving only tangible personal property. Each of the decedents was domiciled in the District of Columbia at the time of death.

This agreement is made because of the difficulty of segregating the assets of the two estates and because neither estate appears to be large enough to warrant the expense of formal administration.

Besides unpaid storage for property held by Mantell Transfer and Storage Company ($851.51 as of August 1, 1983), the unpaid debts are the funeral ($1,342.60) and medical ($1,500) expenses of Carole E. Oliver (copies of bills attached), for which Robin G. Oliver was also obligated, and two notes totaling $2,400 (copies attached), which were jointly executed by them on October 17, 1976, in favor of Harmon L. Foules to cover a loan made by him. By signing this agreement, each party represents that he knows of no other creditor of, or claimant against, either decedent.

B.   PARTIES

The parties to this agreement are:

(1)   The next of kin and legatees under the will of Carole E. Oliver:

Harmon L. Foules formerly "Fowles" (son)
Donald Randel Foules (son of Harmon)
Eugene Harmon Foules (minor son of Harmon)
Georgia S. (Mrs. Boyd) Paxton (daughter)
Ellen (Mrs. Powell) Oldham (daughter of Georgia)
Jane Quincy (Mrs. James) Bilder (daughter of Georgia)

(2)   The next of kin of Robin G. Oliver:
Richard H. Oliver (brother)
Donald N. Oliver (brother)
May Fears (half-sister)

(3)   The creditors of Carole E. Oliver and Robin G. Oliver:
Mantell Transfer and Storage Company
James Lawlere's Sons, Inc.
Dr. Karl Birgin
Harmon L. Foules (see paragraph 1)

C.   TERMS OF AGREEMENT

For the reasons given in paragraph A, the parties named in paragraph B agree as follows:

(1)   The will of Carole E. Oliver shall be filed with the appropriate court, but not probated.

(2)   Mantell Transfer and Storage Company shall exercise its storage lien by public auction sale. All property held by it for the account of "Mr. or Mrs. R. G. Oliver" shall be put up for sale.

(3)   Any legatee of Carole E. Oliver and any of the next of kin of Robin G. Oliver may bid at the sale in open competition with members of the public.

(4)   After the proceeds of the sale have been used to pay the storage lien, the remainder of the proceeds shall be paid to the other creditors in the following order:

James Lawlere's Sons, Inc. ($1,342.60)
Dr. Karl Birgin ($1,500)
Harmon L. Foules ($2,400)

(5)   (a) If the proceeds of the sale are insufficient to pay the creditors in full, any property of Carole E. Oliver or Robin G. Oliver remaining unsold at the end of the

sale, including property not stored with Mantell Transfer and Storage Company, shall be applied first to the payment of the balance of the claim of James Lawlere's Sons, Inc., and then to the payment of the balances of the other creditors in the following order:

> Dr. Karl Birgin
> Mantell Transfer and Storage Company
> Harmon L. Foules

(b)   A creditor entitled to property under clause (a) may, subject to clause (c), either keep it in full satisfaction of his claim or sell it.

(c)   Each of the following persons has the right to buy from the creditor concerned the property listed opposite his name at the price listed opposite his name (prices are based on rough estimates because professional appraisal is impracticable):

Buyer	Property	Price
Harmon L. Foules	Duncan Phyfe dining room table	$800
	Portrait of Carole E. Oliver by Eleanor Parsons	550
	Maple desk	300
	Oriental rugs (each)	400
	Flat silver (all)	1,500
Georgia S. Paxton	Portrait of Carole E. Oliver by Major Lacey	400
	Portrait of Carole E. Oliver's maternal aunt by Jules Randel Sneed	400
	Mahogany drop leaf table	250
	Gold watch	100

Each right must be exercised within 30 days after the creditor concerned has notified the person entitled that the property has been received by the creditor under this term of agreement.

(d)   If a creditor sells any of the property, he shall release for distribution in accordance with this agreement all proceeds of the sale that are not needed to pay the balance of his claim.

(6) Any property of Carole E. Oliver remaining after the execution of the preceding terms of agreement shall be distributed among her legatees in accordance with the will. Any property of Robin G. Oliver remaining after the execution of those terms of agreement shall be distributed among his next of kin. Any proceeds of sales remaining after the execution of those terms of agreement shall be divided equally among each of the legatees of Carole E. Oliver and the next of kin of Robin G. Oliver.

(7) All property now held by Mantell Transfer and Storage Company shall be held by it until disposed of under this agreement, subject to its storage lien.

(8) Any distribution of property or money required by term of agreement (4), (5), or (6) shall be made by Mantell Transfer and Storage Company, with respect to property of the decedents now held by it, and by Donald N. Oliver with respect to all other property of the decedents.

D.   EFFECTIVE DATE

This agreement takes effect as soon as all the parties named in paragraph B have signed the agreement.

Date signed

_____

for Mantell Transfer and Storage Company

_____

for James Lawlere's Sons, Inc.

_____

Dr. Karl Birgin

_____

Harmon M. Foules

Donald Randel Foules

for Eugene Harmon Foules

Georgia S. Paxton

Ellen Oldham

Jane Quincy Bilder

Richard H. Oliver

Donald N. Oliver

Mary C. Fears

§ 14.9.   ILLUSTRATIVE FORM: AN INSURANCE POLICY

Introduction

1

This insurance policy is a legal contract between the policy-owner (you) and the company (we or us). It insures you and your auto for the period shown on the Coverage Selections page.

As long as you pay your premium and any Merit Rating surcharges when due, we agree to provide you or others the benefits to which you or they are entitled. The exact terms and conditions are explained in the following pages.

There are two basic categories of insurance described in this policy, Compulsory Insurance and Optional Insurance.

Compulsory Insurance

There are four Parts to Compulsory Insurance. They are all required by law. Every auto registered in Massachusetts must have them.

Optional Insurance

There are eight Parts to Optional Insurance. Some of them extend the coverage or the amounts of protection provided by Compulsory Insurance. Some of them provide protection not found in Compulsory Insurance. You do not have to buy any of these eight Parts if you do not want to.

Auto insurance claims arise in hundreds of different ways. Autos are sometimes stolen or damaged. Accidents may injure people in your auto, people in other autos or pedestrians. You may be responsible for an accident or someone else may be. An accident may happen in Massachusetts or out of state. Different situations require different kinds of insurance.

Please read the whole policy to see what kinds of insurance are available to cover these different situations. At the same time, you should check the Coverage Selections page to make sure it correctly indicates the coverages you purchased. Each coverage you purchased will show a premium charge next to it. If no premium charge is shown, you do not have that coverage.

Sometimes you and we will agree to change this policy. The only way that can be done is by an "Endorsement" added to the basic policy form. All endorsements must be in writing. They then become part of this policy.

We are pleased to have you as a customer and hope you have a safe and accident-free year. But if you need us, we are here to help you. If you have an accident or loss, or if some-one sues you, contact your agent or us.

Do the same if you have any questions or complaints. If you think we have treated you unfairly at any time, you may contact the Division of Insurance. In Boston call (617) 727-3341. In Springfield call (413) 736-8340.

General Provisions And Exclusions **19**

This section of the policy contains general provisions which, unless otherwise noted, apply to all of your coverages. It also describes some situations in which policy benefits will *not* be paid.

1. Where You Are Covered

Compulsory Bodily Injury To Others (Part 1) only covers accidents in Massachusetts. All the other Parts provide coverage for accidents and losses which happen in the United States or Canada. We consider United States territories and possessions and Puerto Rico to be part of the United States. We will pay for accidents and losses which happen while your auto is being transported between ports of the United States and Canada. Your auto is *not* covered in any other country.

2. Our Duty To Defend You And Our Right To Settle

We have the right and duty to defend any lawsuit brought against anyone covered under this policy for damages which might be payable under this policy. We will defend the lawsuit even if it is without merit. We have the right to settle any claim or lawsuit as we see fit. Our duty to settle or defend ends when we have paid the maximum limits of coverage under this policy. If any person covered under this policy settles a claim without our consent, we will not be bound by that settlement.

3. Additional Costs We Will Pay

We will pay, in addition to the limits shown for Compulsory and Optional Bodily Injury To Others (Parts 1 and 5) and Damage To Someone Else's Property (Part 4):

A. Premiums on appeal bonds and premiums on bonds to release attachments for an amount up to the applicable limits you selected in any suit we defend.

B. Interest that accrues after judgment is entered in any suit we defend. We will not pay interest that accrues after we have offered to pay up to the limits you selected.

C. Up to $40 a day for loss of earnings, but not for loss of other income to any person covered under this policy who attends hearings or trials at our request.

D. Other reasonable expenses incurred at our request.

4. What Happens If You Die

If you die, we will continue coverage for the period of this policy for:

A. Your spouse if a resident of your household at your death.

B. Any legal representative to the extent he or she is responsible for maintenance or use of your auto.

C. Any person having proper temporary custody of your auto.

323

§14.10. ILLUSTRATIVE REDRAFT: A PLEADING

(*Note:* Although a pleading is not a definitive legal instrument, this example is included to show that many of the drafting principles set forth in this book are also helpful in preparing other legal documents.)

Original:

That the occurrences described hereinabove resulted without any negligence on the part of the plaintiff but solely by reason of the negligence on the part of the defendants, their agents, servants and employees in preparing said spaghetti together with the sauce commonly served therewith, and that the said defendants were otherwise careless, reckless and negligent in preparing and cooking said spaghetti and its accessories and in selling the same with the glass therein contained, when the same was unfit for human consumption and in failing to exercise care knowing the spaghetti, sauce and appurtenances, commonly served with spaghetti was to be distributed to patrons of the restaurant for human consumption.

As redrafted:

The defendants and their employees caused the plaintiff's injury by negligently preparing and selling spaghetti and sauce with glass in it when they knew it would be served to patrons of their restaurant. The plaintiff was not negligent.

Postscript

A CAVEAT AND SEVERAL WORDS TO THE WISE

Circumstances have made it impossible to do adequate justice, even on a very general plane, to the full range of matters comprising the main concerns of legal drafting. The best I can do in completing this edition is to invite attention to several important areas of neglect and suggest sources where interested draftsmen can begin self-education. Several of these matters involve legal drafting on the grand scale.

Persons concerned with the codification of statutory or regulatory law (without substantive change), which the British call "consolidation" and which is exemplified by the enactment of 21 titles of the United States Code into "positive law," can well begin with the textual materials compiled as chapter 15 of my coursebook, Materials on Legal Drafting (West Pub. Co. 1981),[1] cited throughout this book as "MLD." (Large-scale substantive revision involves the same drafting problems.)

The most neglected aspect of legal drafting is the organizational and management arrangements most conducive to success. The biggest need here is in the legislatively active executive agencies of the federal government. Potentially, it is of concern also to large law firms. So far as I know, the only readily available sources of information on the problem are

[1]See also Cullen, The Mechanics of Statutory Revision, 24 Ore. 1 (1944).

found in chapter 14 of Materials on Legal Drafting or in the ABA's published proceedings of the conference held at Catholic University in 1971: Dickerson (ed.), Professionalizing Legislative Drafting — The Federal Experience (1973).

Another matter deserving attention is the improvement of the legislative process so as to enhance the opportunity for qualified draftsmen to participate even in the final phases of enactment "where, all too often, the draftsman has lost effective touch with the proposed bill." (This could even include changes in form after passage.)[2]

As for the stylistic bog in which the legal profession is still deeply mired, the quickest way to extricate it is to reform the bar-approved forms and the commercial form books. Here is the greatest unexploited opportunity to improve the language of legal instruments.

The biggest need of all is to improve the teaching of legal drafting in the law schools. One way to start is to read appendix F.

Although there are other matters worthy of serious attention, this is a good place to call a halt to the current effort.

[2]Dickerson, The Environment Needed for Legal Drafting, talk at Annual Meeting, Canadian Bar Association, August 24, 1974, MLD 389.

Appendix A

A Select Bibliography

For reasons explained in section 1.2, this book concentrates on the general principles common to legal drafting. Accordingly, it gives less than full consideration to the substantive and terminological aspects peculiar to particular kinds of instruments, such as statutes, leases, contracts, wills, and indentures. For these, the draftsman can profitably turn to treatises and articles such as those listed below. Because many of the works listed, however long on substance, are short on the subjects of conceptual clarity, organization, form, and style, this book can readily serve as a supplement.

The following bibliography is suggestive rather than definitive. The omission of a work does not imply that the work is generally inadequate, nor does its inclusion imply that it has been wholeheartedly approved. Whether such a work deals adequately with particular substantive problems or specialized terminology in the particular instance must be judged by specialists. No final evaluation has been attempted here.

LANGUAGE AND LEGAL DRAFTING GENERALLY

Biskind, Writing Right! 43 N.Y.S.B.J. 185, 269, 426 (1971).
Cook, Legal Drafting, Foundation Press (rev. ed. 1951).
Cooper, Writing in Law Practice, Bobbs-Merrill (1963).
Dick, Comparisons in Legal Drafting, 4 Estates & Trusts Q. 195 (1978).

Dick, Legal Drafting, Carswell Co., Ltd. (2d ed. 1985) (Canada).

Dickerson, Materials on Legal Drafting, West (1981).

Freeman, The Grammatical Lawyer, ALI (1979).

Goldfarb & Raymond, Clear Understandings, Random House (1982).

Gopen, Writing from a Legal Perspective, West (1981).

Gowers, The Complete Plain Words HMSO (1954).

Mellinkoff, The Language of the Law, Little, Brown & Co. (1963).

Mellinkoff, Sense and Nonsense, West (1981).

Piesse, The Elements of Drafting, The Law Book Co. (5th ed. Aitken 1976) (Australia).

Squires & Rombauer, Legal Writing in a Nutshell, West (1982).

Thomas, Problems in Drafting Legal Instruments, 39 Ill. B.J. 51 (1950).

Weihofen, Legal Writing Style, West (2d ed, 1980).

Wydick, Plain English for Lawyers, Academic Press (1979).

Bibliography of Materials on Legislative and Other Legal Drafting and the Interpretation of Statutes, Commonwealth Secretariat, London (rev. ed. 1985).

LEGISLATION

Cullen, Mechanics of Statutory Revision — A Revisor's Manual, 24 Ore. L. Rev. 1 (1944).

Dickerson, Professionalizing Legislative Drafting — The Federal Experience, ABA (1973).

Driedger, A Manual of Instructions for Legislative and Legal Writing, Department of Justice, Canada (1982).

Driedger, The Composition of Legislation — Legislative Forms and Precedents, Department of Justice, Canada (2d ed. 1976).

Hirsch, Drafting Federal Law, Department of Health and Human Services (1980).

Matthews, Drafting Municipal Ordinances, Callaghan (1956).

Menard, Legislative Bill Drafting, 23 Rocky Mt. L. Rev. 127 (1950).

Peacock, Drafting a Proposed Statute, 1 Prac. Law. 19 (November 1955).

Peacock, Notes on Legislative Drafting, REC Foundation, Inc. (1961).

Statsky, Legislative Analysis and Drafting, West (1984).

Thornton, Legislative Drafting, Butterworths (2d ed. 1979) (Australia).

Van Alstyne, Aids to Drafting Local Ordinances, 16 La. L. Rev. 639 (1956).

CONTRACTS

Bicks, Contracts for the Sale of Realty, Practising Law Institute (6th ed. Glassner & Kufeld 1978).

Fabyanske, How to Draft an Arbitration Agreement, 17 Forum 491 (1981).

Farnsworth, Some Considerations in the Drafting of Agreements, 39 Okla. B.A.J. 917 (1968).

Felsenfeld & Siegel, Writing Contracts in Plain English, West (1981).

Fendler, Drafting Instruments for Purchase and Conveyancing of Land, 13 Ark. L. Rev. 26 (1958).

Friedman, Buying and Selling a House — Some Considerations in the Drafting of the Contract of Sale, 14 Prac. Law. 13 (November 1968).

Friedman, Contracts and Conveyances of Real Property, Practising Law Institute (3d ed. 1978).

Friedman, Preparation of Leases, Practising Law Institute (rev. ed. 1962).

Jones, Drafting the Installment Contract, 62 Chicago Bar Rev. 97 (September/October 1980).

Keaton, Drafting the Collective Bargaining Agreement, Part 1, 7 Prac. Law. 66 (February 1961); Part 2, 7 Prac. Law. 41 (March 1961).

Landis, Problems in Drafting Percentage Leases, 36 Bost. U.L. Rev. 190 (1956).

Mandel, The Preparation of Commercial Agreements, Practising Law Institute (rev. ed. 1978).

Marceau, Drafting a Union Contract, Little, Brown & Co. (1965).

Mayers, Drafting Patent License Agreements, Bureau of National Affairs (1971).

Richards, Drafting and Enforcing Restrictive Covenants Not to Compete, 55 Marq. L.R. 241 (1972).

Sack, How to Draft a Nuclear Fuel Reprocessing Contract, 18 Prac. Law. 51 (January 1972).

Thompson, Drafting the Formal Parts of a Commercial Lease, 15 Prac. Law. 79 (October 1969).

Volz & Berger, The Drafting of Partnership Agreements, American Law Institute (6th ed. 1976).

Waddleton, Some Observations on the Problems of Drafting a Labor Contract, 1960 Wis. L. Rev. 265.

Wincor, Contracts in Plain English, McGraw-Hill (1976).

CORPORATE CHARTERS AND BY-LAWS

Pantzer & Deer, The Drafting of Corporate Charters and By-Laws, ALI-ABA (2d ed. 1968).

CREDIT INSTRUMENTS

Felsenfeld & Siegel, Simplified Consumer Credit Forms, Warren, Gorham & Lamont (1981).

LEASES

Drafting Shopping Center Leases, 2 Real Property & Trusts J. 222 (1967).

Kemph, Drafting Commercial Leases, 10 Real Estate L.J. 99 (1981).

ORDERS

McMahon, How to Draft an Order, 13 Clearinghouse Rev. 858 (1980).

WILLS AND TRUSTS

Abel, Drafting of Wills, 31 Idaho S.B.J. 5 (1957).

Blank, Problem Areas in Will Drafting Under New York Law, 56 St. Johns L. Rev. 459 (1982).

Bowe, Problems in Drafting Wills and Trusts, 37 Neb. L. Rev. 127 (1958).

Corcoran, Drafting a Modern Will, 16 Prac. Law. 13 (January 1970).

Durand, Draftsmanship: Wills and Trusts, 96 Trusts & Estates 871 (1957).

Endacott, Problems in Drafting and Administering Discretionary Trusts, 46 Neb. L. Rev. 110 (1967).

Grutzner, Tips on Will Drafting the Modern Way, 44 Wis. Bar Bull. 27 (December 1971).

Huff, The Irrevocable Life Insurance Trust, 38 Ark. L. Rev. 139 (1984).

Johnson, A Draftsman's Handbook for Wills and Trusts, Little, Brown & Co. (1961).

Klipstein, Drafting New York Wills — Laws & Forms, Matthew Bender & Co. (2d ed. 1969).

Lyman, Practical Aspects of Drafting Wills, Prentice Hall, Inc. (1962).

Schwarzberg & Stocker, Drawing Wills, Practising Law Institute (8th ed. 1973).

Shaffer, The Planning and Drafting of Wills and Trusts, Foundation Press (1972).

Squires & Mucklestone, The Simple "Simple" Will, 57 Wash. L. Rev. 461 (1982).

Weinberger & Others, Advanced Will Drafting, Practising Law Institute (1977).

Appendix B

Complete Tabulation of Postal Statute

A complete tabulation of the postal statute set forth in section 6.3 may be made as follows:

Any
- (1) key;
- (2) identification
    - (A) card;
    - (B) tag; *or*
    - (C) device that is similar; *or*
- (3) other small article that the Postmaster General may by regulation designate;

that
- (1) bears;
- (2) contains; *or*
- (3) has attached securely thereto;

both
- (1) a post office address that is
    - (A) complete;
    - (B) definite; *and*
    - (C) legible;
    including (if such exists) any
    - (A) street address; *or*
    - (B) number of
        - (i) box; *or*
        - (ii) route; *and*

    (2)   a notice
        (A)   directing that the
             (i)   key;
            (ii)   card;
          (iii)   tag;
          (iv)   device; *or*
           (v)   small article
          be returned to that address; *and*
        (B)   guaranteeing the payment, on delivery, of the postage due;

may be sent through the mails to that address at the rate of 5 cents for

    (1)   each two ounces; and
    (2)   any remaining fraction of two ounces.

Appendix C

Excerpts from Food Products Regulation No. 1[1] and Supplement No. 3[2]

The following excerpts are selected to give the general flavor of the instruments. However, they do not show their relative size. FPR No. 1, which standardized 46 commonly used provisions, covered about ten pages of the Federal Register; whereas Supplement No. 3, setting forth eight provisions peculiar to macaroni and noodle products, covered about two pages.

A. FOOD PRODUCTS REGULATION 1 — GENERAL PRICING PROVISIONS FOR CERTAIN FOOD PRODUCTS (GROUP I).

ARTICLE I — GENERAL DEFINITIONS

Section 1.1 *Meaning of "person."* "Person" means an individual, corporation, partnership, association, any other organized group of persons, and their legal successors or representatives. The term includes the United States, its agencies, other governments, their political subdivisions and their agencies.

Sec. 1.2 *Meaning of "processor."* "Processor" means a person who processes any part of what he sells of the kind and brand of product being priced. The term includes a person who has the goods "custom-packed" or "toll-packed" by another. . . .

Appendix C [1]9 Fed. Reg. 6711 (1944).
[2]9 Fed. Reg. 6724 (1944).

Appendix C

Sec. 1.8 *Meaning of "item."* "Item" means a kind, variety, grade, brand, style of pack, container type and size of product. . . .

ARTICLE II — PRICING PROVISIONS

Section 2.1 *Processors who have two seasonal packs.* This section applies only to processors.

Any processor who has two seasonal packs of a food product during the calendar year may, if he wishes, figure maximum prices for it as if each pack were a separate commodity. If the maximum prices so figured for the two packs are different, the processor shall plainly indicate on the invoice in each case, and on each consumer package, whether the product is the "spring pack" or the "fall pack." . . .

Sec. 2.10 *Maximum prices for sales by distributors who are not primary distributors, wholesalers or retailers.* The maximum price, f.o.b. shipping point, of a distributor who is not a primary distributor, wholesaler, or retailer shall be the maximum price of his supplier, f.o.b. shipping point, plus incoming freight paid by him. . . .

Sec. 2.16 *Maintenance of customary discounts and allowances.* When this section applies to a supplement, it applies to all sellers covered by the supplement.

No person shall change any customary allowance, discount or other price differential to a purchaser or class of purchasers, if the change results in a higher net price to that purchaser or class. However, in the case of sales to government procurement agencies, the seller is not required to give a discount for prompt payment.

ARTICLE III — MISCELLANEOUS PROVISIONS

Section 3.2 *Weights.* Where labels weights are used, prices figured by weight shall be based on the weights named on the label and not on actual fill.

Sec. 3.3 *Storage.* Storage costs incurred by the seller on goods owned by him shall not be added to his maximum prices. Storage by the seller of goods owned by the buyer may be charged for in accordance with the maximum price regulation applicable to such services. . . .

Sec. 3.8 *Sales slips and receipts.* Any seller who has customarily given a purchaser a sales slip, receipt, or similar evidence of purchase, shall continue to do so. Upon request, any seller, regardless of previous custom, shall give the purchaser a receipt showing the date, the name and address of the seller, the name and quantity of each item sold, and the price received for it. . . .

B. Supplement 3 to Food Products Regulation 1 — Prepared Flour Mixes.

ARTICLE I — EXPLANATION OF THE SUPPLEMENT

Section 1. *Explanation of the supplement.* (a) This supplement establishes maximum prices for the kinds of prepared flour mixes designated below, and processors shall figure their maximum prices in accordance with the provisions of the respective section listed for each kind. Further kinds may be added from time to time. The maximum prices take into consideration such factors as variety, brand, container type and size, unit of sale and class of purchasers. Additional factors may be specified for some kinds of items.

Kind	Section
Pancake mix	4
Waffle mix	4

(b) This supplement applies to sales . . . by all persons except wholesalers and retailers (wagon wholesalers, however, are included).

(c) This supplement applies in the 48 states of the United States and the District of Columbia. . . .

(d) This supplement becomes effective on June 21, 1944.

Sec. 2. *Applicability of Food Products Regulation No. 1.* Important: Not all of the provisions affecting the maximum prices of the designated prepared flour mixes are stated in this supplement. Those which are not specifically set forth here are stated in Food Products Regulation No. 1, and they are just as much a part of this supplement as if they were printed here . . .

Sec. 3. *Definitions.* (a) When used in this supplement, the term:

"Class of purchasers" refers to the practice followed by the seller in setting different prices for sales to different purchasers or kinds of purchasers.

"Flour" means the flour and the combinations of flour produced from wheat, rye, buckwheat, rice, corn, oats, barley, soy beans and potatoes. Included in this term are those flours and combinations which are bleached, bromated, enriched, phosphated and rendered self-rising.

"Kind" means a type of prepared mix such as pancake mix, waffle mix, etc.

"Mix," where used alone, means a finished collection of ingredients prior to and ready for packaging. . . .

(b) The definitions of the following terms, set forth in the designated sections of Food Products Regulation No. 1, are applicable to this supplement:

"Person" (section 1.1 of FPR 1).
"Processor" (section 1.2 of FPR 1).
"Distributor" (section 1.3 of FPR 1).
"Primary distributor" (section 1.5 of FPR 1).
"Wholesaler" and "retailer" (section 1.6 of FPR 1).
"Ultimate consumer" (section 1.7 of FPR 1).
"Item" (section 1.8 of FPR 1).
"Container type" (section 1.9 of FPR 1).
"Sale" (section 1.10 of FPR 1).
"Price" (section 1.11 of FPR 1).
"Net delivered cost" (section 1.12 of FPR 1).
"Records" (section 1.14 of FPR 1).

ARTICLE II — PRICING PROVISIONS

Section 4. *Maximum prices for sales of pancake mix and waffle mix by processors.* The pricing method of this section applies to all of the processor's sales of pancake mix or waffle mix, except those in which he is selling branded pancake mix or branded waffle mix no part of which he processes himself.

(a) *General pricing method.* The processor shall figure his maximum price per sale unit for each item of pancake mix or waffle mix, f.o.b. shipping point, to each class of purchasers, by adding together (1) the weighted average price, figured f.o.b. shipping point, which he charged for that item to the particular class of purchasers during the base period June 1, 1941, through August 31, 1941, and (2) the increase in cost of ingredients and packaging materials provided for in paragraph (c), below. . . .

Sec. 6. *Provisions of Article II of Food Products Regulation No. 1 applicable to this supplement.* The following provisions of Food Products Regulation No. 1 are applicable to this supplement:

(a) Maximum prices for products in new container types or sizes (section 2.2 of FPR 1).

(b) Elective pricing method for processors (section 2.4 of FPR 1). The "markup percentage" figure is 165%.

(c) Individual authorization of maximum prices (section 2.5 of FPR 1).

(d) When a seller must figure a delivered price (section 2.6 of FPR 1).

(e) Uniform prices where the processor or packer has more than one factory (section 2.7 of FPR 1).

(f) Uniform delivered prices where the seller has customarily been selling on an f.o.b. shipping point basis (section 2.8 of FPR 1).

(g) Maximum prices for sales by primary distributors (section 2.9 of FPR 1).

(h) Maximum prices for sales by distributors who are not primary distributors, wholesalers or retailers (section 2.10 of FPR 1).

(i) Payment of brokers (section 2.11 of FPR 1).

(j) Special packing expenses which may be reflected in maximum prices for sales to Government procurement agencies (section 2.13 of FPR 1).

(k) Treatment of federal and state taxes (section 2.14 of FPR 1).

(l) Units of sale and fractions of a cent (section 2.15 of FPR 1).

(m) Maintenance of customary discounts and allowances (section 2.16 of FPR 1).

ARTICLE III — MISCELLANEOUS PROVISIONS

Section 7. *Reports which sellers must file.* Every processor who determines a maximum price under section 4 or 6 (a) of this supplement shall, on or before July 12, 1944, or within twenty days after the maximum price has been established in the manner explained in section 8 (j) below, file with the district office of the Office of Price Administration for the area in which he is located a true copy of the calculations showing his determination of such maximum price. However, if a processor reported a lawful maximum price under any provision of Maximum Price Regulation No. 462 and his maximum price is not changed by this supplement, he is not required to report that maximum price again under this section.

Sec. 8. *Provisions of Article III of Food Products Regulation No. 1 applicable to this supplement.* The following provisions of Food Products Regulation No. 1 are applicable to this supplement:

(a) Restrictions on sales to primary distributors (section 3.1 of FPR 1).

(b) Weights (section 3.2 of FPR 1).

(c) Storage (section 3.3 of FPR 1).

(d) Export sales (section 3.4 of FPR 1).

(e) Notification of new maximum price (section 3.4 of FPR 1).

(f) Records which must be kept (section 3.6 of FPR 1).

(g) Authority of regional and district offices to audit reports (section 3.7 of FPR 1).

(h) Sales slips and receipts (section 3.8 of FPR 1).

(i) Transfers of business of stock in trade (section 3.9 of FPR 1).

(j) How a figured maximum price is established and how an established maximum price may be changed (section 3.10 of FPR 1).

(k) Adjustable pricing (section 3.11 of FPR 1).

Appendix C

(l) Compliance with the applicable supplement (section 3.12 of FPR 1).

(m) Adjustment of maximum prices of food products under "Government contracts" or subcontracts (section 3.13 of FPR 1).

(n) Application for adjustment by sellers who have been found to have violated the Robinson-Patman Act (section 3.14 of FPR 1).

(o) Application for adjustment and petitions for amendment based on wage or salary increases requiring approval of the National War Labor Board (section 3.15 of FPR 1).

(p) Petitions for amendment (section 3.16 of FPR 1).

Appendix D

Table of State Constitutional Provisions

Note: This table is intended to give a general overview of the state constitutional provisions relating to the drafting of statutes. However, it includes only those that appear in the constitutions of six or more states. Other state constitutional provisions are cited in the appropriate footnotes.

State	Enacting clause	One subject, expressed in title	General laws uniform	Special laws forbidden	Amend., etc., set forth in full	Borrowing law must specify purpose	What tax law must specify	What appropriation law may cover	What appropriation law must specify	Effective date
Alabama	Art IV §45	Art IV §45		Art IV §104	Art IV §45			Art IV §71		
Alaska	Art II §13	Art II §13		Art II §19						Art II §18
Arizona	Art IV(2) §24	Art IV(2) §13		Art IV(2) §19	Art IV(2) §14		Art IX §§3,9	Art IV(2) §20		Art IV(1) §1(3)
Arkansas	Art 5 §19			Amend. 14	Art 5 §23		Art 16 §11	Art 5 §30	Art 5 §29	Amend. 7
California		Art IV §9	Art IV §16	Art IV §16	Art IV §9	Art XVI §1			Art IV §12(c)	Art IV §1
Colorado	Art V §18	Art V §21		Art V §25	Art V §24	Art XI §4		Art V §32		Art V §19
Connecticut	Art 3d §1									
Delaware		Art II §16		Art II §19		Art VIII §3	Art VIII §1			
Florida	Art III §6	Art III §6		Art III §11	Art III §6			Art III §12		Art III §18
Georgia		Art III §V Par III	Art III §VI Par IV	Art II §II Par IV	Art III §V Par IV	Art VII §IV Par VII		Art III §IX Par III	Art III §IX Par VI (a)	
Hawaii	Art III §15	Art III §15				Art VIII §1	Art VII §2			
Idaho	Art III §1	Art III §16		Art III §19	Art III §18	Art IX §9				Art III §22
Illinois	Art IV §8	Art IV §8		Art IV §13	Art IV §8			Art VIII §2 Art IV §8		Art IV §10

State										
Indiana	Art 4 §1	Art 4 §19	Art 4 §23	Art 4 §22						Art 4 §28
Iowa	Art III Leg Dep §1	Art III §29	Art I §6, Art III §30	Art III §30			Art VII §7			Art III §26
Kansas	Art 2 §20, §62	Art 2 §16, §51	Art 2 §17	Art 2 §17, §§59,60	Art 2 §16, §51	Art 11 §6, §178	Art 11 §5			Art 2 §19, §55
Kentucky										
Louisiana	Art III §14	Art III §15			Art III §15			Art III §16	Art III §16	Art III §19, Art IV Part 3d §16
Maine	Art IV Part 1st §1			Art IV[1] Part 3d §13						
Maryland	Art III §29	Art III §29		Art III §33	Art III §29				Art III §32	Art III §31, Art XVI §2
Massachusetts	Part 2d Ch VI Art VIII									Art XLVIII Ref 1
Michigan	Art IV §23	Art IV §24		Art IV §29	Art IV §25	Art IX §15			Art IV §31	Art IV §27
Minnesota	Art IV §22	Art IV §17		Art XII §1						
Mississippi	Art 4 §56	Art 4 §71		Art 4 §§87, 89	Art 4 §61				Art 4 §63	Art 4 §75
Missouri	Art III §21	Art III §23		Art III §§40, 41	Art III §28				Art IV §23	Art III §29

State	Enacting clause	One subject, expressed in title	General laws uniform	Special laws forbidden	Amend., etc., set forth in full	Borrowing law must specify purpose	What tax law must specify	What appropriation law may cover	What appropriation law must specify	Effective date
Montana		Art V §11		Art V §12		Art VIII §11		Art V §11		
Nebraska	Art III §13	Art III §14		Art III §18	Art III §14			Art III §22		Art III §27
Nevada	Art IV §23	Art IV §17	Art IV §21	Art IV §20	Art IV §17	Art IX §3				
New Hampshire	Part 2d Art 92									
New Jersey	Art IV §VII (6)	Art IV §VII (4)	Art IV §VII (7)	Art IV §VII (7,9)	Art IV §VII (5)	Art VIII §II (3)		Art VIII §II (2)		
New Mexico	Art IV §15	Art IV §16		Art IV §24	Art IV §18	Art IX §8		Art IV §16		Art IV §23
New York	Art III §13	Art III §15		Art III §17		Art VII §§11,17	Art III §22	Art VII §6	Art VII §7	
North Carolina	Art II §21			Art II §24						
North Dakota	Art IV §34	Art IV §33	Art IV §44	Art IV §43	Art IV §38	Art X §13	Art X §3	Art IV §36		Art IV §41
Ohio	Art II §15	Art II §15	Art II §26		Art II §15		Art XII §5		Art II §22	Art II §§1c,1d
Oklahoma	Art V §3	Art V §57	Art V §59	Art V §§46,59	Art V §57	Art X §§16,25	Art X §19	Art V §56		Art V §58
Oregon	Art IV §20	Art IV §20		Art IV §23	Art IV §22		Art IV §3	Art IX §7		Art IV §28
Pennsylvania	Art III §3	Art III §3		Art III §7	Art III §6			Art IV §11		
Rhode Island	Art IV §2									Art XV §1

State										
South Carolina	Art III §16	Art III §17	Art III §34 (X)	Art III §34						Art III §22
South Dakota	Art III §18	Art III §21		Art III §23				Art XII §2		Art II §20
Tennessee	Art II §20	Art II §17		Art XI §§4,5,8						
Texas	Art III §29	Art III §35		Art III §56	Art III §36					Art III §39
Utah		Art VI §22	Art I §24	Art VI §26		Art XIV §5				Art VI §25
Vermont	Ch. II §10									
Virginia	Art II §18	Art IV §12		Art IV §14	Art IV §12	Art X §9 (c)				Art IV §13
Washington		Art II §19		Art II §28	Art II §37	Art VIII §3	Art VII §5		Art VIII §4	Art II §31
West Virginia	Art VI §1	Art VI §30		Art VI §39	Art VI §30					Art VI §30
Wisconsin	Art IV §17	Art IV §18	Art IV §32	Art IV §31		Art VIII §6				
Wyoming	Art III §21	Art III §24	Art I §34	Art III §27	Art II §26		Art XV §13	Art III §§34, 36		

Appendix E

Where the Federal Statute Law Is

1. THE STATUTES AT LARGE[1]

The most reliable way for a draftsman to find what an existing federal law says is to look at the enrolled bill itself. Because there is only one copy of this, and because it is in the custody of the General Services Administration, it is ordinarily beyond convenient reach. The next most reliable source is the Statutes at Large. This chronological presentation of successive enactments is much more widely available and has been declared by Congress[2] to be "legal evidence" of the law (rebuttable by the respective enrolled bills).

Before Volume 64, the Statutes at Large were a separate printing of the law. As such, they were subject to occasional printing errors and in this respect yield to the superior authority of the enrolled bills. Beginning with Volume 64, the Statutes at Large have been a representation, by the photo-offset process, of a proof of the enrolled bills. Although they remain "legal evidence" of the law, rather than the law itself, the possibility of error is now almost zero. For most practical purposes, these volumes of the Statutes at Large are, therefore, as fully "the law" as the enrolled bills themselves.[3]

Appendix E [1]See generally J. Sutherland, Statutes and Statutory Construction, §36.18 (4th ed. 1972).

[2]1 U.S.C. 112.

[3]On the persuasiveness of the enrolled bill, and the "journal entry rule" (followed in some states), see E. Crawford, The Construction of Statutes §§139-142 (1940); Sutherland, *supra* note 1, ch. 15.

Volumes 1-17 of the Statutes at Large have little more than historical interest, since the laws they contain were replaced by the Revised Statutes, enacted June 22, 1874, as a codification of the permanent laws in force on December 1, 1873. The Revised Statutes are discussed in section 3 below.

2. THE UNITED STATES CODE[4]

Except for titles that have been enacted into law, the United States Code is an official editorial compilation of the general and permanent laws of the United States arranged by subject.

The Act of June 30, 1926,[5] enacted the text of the original United States Code, which it set forth in full, into "prima facie evidence" of the law. It had the anomalous effect of enacting specific statutory language without giving it full effect as law. The act also provided that the text as printed by the Government Printing Office was to be conclusive evidence of what was in the enrolled bill. So doing, it gave unique standing to the book containing Part I of Volume 44 of the Statutes at Large. While other volumes of the Statutes at Large are "legal evidence" of the law this book was made "conclusive evidence" of the law.

Under examination, however, this nominally superior status dissolves because the book is "conclusive" evidence of what is only "prima facie" evidence of the law! Consequently, the volume appears to have about the same standing as the unenacted parts of the "United States Code," parts which as "prima facie" evidence of the law hold an evidentiary position that is inferior, rather than superior, to the Statutes at Large.

The situation is clouded by unfortunate terminology. The term "United States Code" is at the same time (1) the configuration of ideas set forth under that designation in the Act of June 30, 1926 (as modified by later legislation), and (2) a set of dark red books published by the Committee on the Judiciary of the House of Representatives.

[4]See, generally, Sutherland, *supra* note 1, §36.20.
[5]44 Stat., part 1.

Since 1946, that Committee has been sponsoring the enactment into "positive law" of the 50 titles of the United States Code. Because all general and permanent law is, in the special sense used by the Committee, "positive law," this is a program to enact the laws represented by each of the 50 titles in such form that the new text can be included without editorial change in the books called "the United States Code" and that when it is so included the pages on which it appears have the same evidentiary weight as the corresponding pages of the Statutes at Large. This program perpetuates the dual use of the term "United States Code" as a basic law and as a set of books evidencing what that law is. The practical difference between these two ideas lies in the fact that the books contain editorial materials not found in the law as enacted and that so far as they remain a reprint of what appears in the enrolled bills there is always the possibility of discrepancies between what is enacted and what is separately printed.

3. THE REVISED STATUTES[6]

Doubt sometimes arises as to the legal status of the "Revised Statutes." On the one hand they are said to be the law itself. On the other, the Act of March 9, 1878 (20 Stat. 27), says of the second edition (1878) what the Act of June 20, 1874 (18 Stat. 113), said of the first (1874): that it is "legal," but not "conclusive," evidence of the law. In short, the Revised Statutes are the law and they are not the law.

Fortunately the contradiction is only verbal. The term "Revised Statutes" is traditionally used in two concurrent senses: (1) as the short title for the Act of June 22, 1874, which codified most of the laws then in effect, and (2) as the title of the two volumes (first and second editions) in which that restatement physically appears. Thus, in the first sense the term "Revised Statutes" refers to the law itself; in the second, it refers to a book that is not the law, but evidence of it. The two acts mentioned in the first paragraph merely gave the printed volumes the same

[6]See generally Sutherland, *supra* note 1, §36.19.

evidentiary status that is enjoyed by the volumes of the Statutes at Large; they did not affect the law reflected in those printed volumes.

The second edition (1878) is a special hybrid. It is like the first edition (1874) and all the volumes of the Statutes at Large in that it is "legal evidence" of the law (i.e., stronger than "prima facie" evidence). But it is unlike them, and like the unenacted titles of the United States Code, in that it sets forth an official, but unenacted, compilation of laws. Briefly, it is an editorial compilation of (1) the Act of June 22, 1874, and (2) the specific amendments to that act which had been enacted in the meantime to remove errors from it. It did not include laws, enacted in the interim, that did not specifically amend that act.

Appendix F

On Teaching Legal Writing, Particularly Legal Drafting

Although this is not a book on pedagogy, it seems appropriate to suggest a way in which an adequate drafting discipline can be taught.[1]

In 1979, the Association of American Law Schools conducted a legal writing panel discussion on what law schools can do to solve the problems of instructor turnover, inadequate transitional guidance, administrative inefficiency, low evaluation of the task, low salaries, lack of prestige, and student discontent. Some of the solutions suggested for discussion were providing more money, rotating responsibilities among experienced faculty, and attaching small sections to substantive courses. Unfortunately, such suggestions deal with symptoms rather than causes. None relates to the root causes of the law schools' general lack of success. Here are some of them:

(1) We have trivialized legal writing by calling it a "skill," when expository writing, of which legal drafting is one kind,[2] is a basic discipline, perhaps the most basic of all

Appendix F   [1]This appendix is drawn for the most part from Dickerson, Teaching Legal Writing in the Law Schools (With a Special Nod to Legal Drafting), 16 Idaho L. Rev. 85 (1979), which in turn was an expanded, edited version of remarks made at Scribes' Teaching of Legal Writing Institute, held at New York Law School, April 28, 1979. The other materials drawn on are Dickerson, Legislative Process and Drafting in U.S. Law Schools — A Close Look at the Lammers Report, 31 J. Legal Ed. 30 (1981); Foreword to MLD and its Teacher's Manual (Part A, 1981).
[2]See §1.2 *supra*.

disciplines. ("Skill" is the academician's semantic put-down.)

(2)   We have demeaned legal writing by treating it as mainly a matter of language, thus playing down one of its most important functions: the improvement of substantive ideas. Expository writing not only reflects thought, but helps shape it.[3] Preoccupation with merely putting words together tends to obscure, for example, the fact that as a planner, the draftsman is also a sculptor of ideas, an engineer, and an architect.

(3)   We have further demeaned legal writing by trying to crowd too much into single, elementary courses.

(4)   The growing practice of importing English teachers and other language experts into law schools (and even law firms) tends to confuse the need for special instruction in forensic legal writing, or in legal drafting, with the need for remedial general writing.

(5)   Misreading the need to join form with substance, we have needlessly diluted writing courses by requiring the student to do the kind of time-consuming legal research traditional to courses on law library research, term papers, or law review assignments. Unfortunately, we cannot make a concentrated attack on the legal writing problem if we continue to combine it with a comparable attack on legal bibliography or with one on legal or factual research. No course aptly called "Legal Research and Writing" can provide adequate training in legal writing (or, for that matter, in legal research).

The first thing, therefore, is to stop teaching courses with this kind of blurred emphasis. They slight both emphases in-

[3]See H. Martin & R. Ohmann, The Logic and Rhetoric of Exposition 1-2 (rev. ed. 1963) (MLD 97-98); Wason, On Writing Scientific Papers, in The Psychology of Written Communication 248-249 (Hartley ed., 1980); Dickerson, Legal Drafting: Writing as Thinking, or Talk-Back from Your Draft and How to Exploit It, 29 J. Legal Ed. 373 (1978) (MLD 99-105); and §§2.2, 2.3, 10.1 *supra.*

volved and mislead students into believing that they are receiving adequate instruction in either.

Does separating the two necessarily disembody the writing discipline by divorcing form from substance? Not at all. Although a factual and legal background is necessary, a course in legal writing should permit only such research as is compatible with an adequate attack on the relevant conceptual, architectural, and verbal problems. One way to handle this is to select topics that enable the students to write on the basis of substantive considerations that are already in their heads or have already been developed in large part by others. I have found several beautiful drafting problems in which most of the basic data can be taken for granted and in which the policy research consists mainly of thinking about the problem and organizing the information that is already in hand or quickly available.[4]

In legal drafting courses, the best insurance against sacrificing precious writing time to the needs of substantive research is to revise existing instruments. In this way, it is possible to meet both the need to learn how to compose and the need to show how good writing is integrated with the ascertainment and improvement of substantive policy.

To do justice to legal research (and to legal writing), on the other hand, some integration of research strategy with writing strategy is desirable to show how the two can be most profitably dovetailed. In my assigned drafting exercises, I permit only very general research before the student puts his tentative thoughts in writing. He thus defers the more detailed research until he has prepared a coherent draft whose unsubstantiated assumptions are plain enough to indicate where the remaining research needs exist. By thus providing specific research foci, the approach saves valuable time and, by encouraging substantive "talk-back,"[5] it enhances the quality of the end product. Imparting this valuable insight does not require heavy doses of factual or legal research.

The draftsman's research obligation is ordinarily not to dig

[4]See, e.g., the exercise on regulating babysitting, MLD 122, 151, and corresponding pages of its Teacher's Manual.

[5]Dickerson, *supra* note 3.

out the basic facts but, by the quickest trustworthy means available, to ascertain (and help develop, if necessary) the specific policies that the client wants to implement.[6] Here, satisfactory initial policy research can often be done mainly by explicating an existing instrument. The conceptual structure is then built and, where necessary, gaps are filled with compatible tentative assumptions, which follow-up research will verify or refute. This moves the draftsman quickly into the essentials of drafting and illustrates the benefits of substantive talk-back that this approach inevitably produces.[7]

Even if freed from conventional legal research, legal writing is too important to be confined to one course. If the case method deserves attention in many courses, legal writing, which is a more basic discipline, certainly deserves something better than a single shot. For one thing, the nonemotive expository writing that we call "legal drafting" should be separated from forensic legal writing. The disciplines differ in rigor and approach, and each is important enough to deserve separate treatment. It is ironic that current courses in legal writing are severely tilted in favor of litigation, when in the real world of modern lawyering dependence on the drafting discipline is far more pervasive than is dependence on litigation skills. Incidentally, except for jury instructions and court orders, the litigation process involves almost no legal drafting.

In turn, training in legal drafting is appropriately distributed between a large-class course in the basics of legal drafting for lawyers generally and an advanced seminar in legislative

---

[6] *Supra,* at §4.2.

[7] I would think it desirable to separate courses or seminars that are heavily oriented toward legal research from the mechanics of library research and the modest ancillary writing exercises necessary to direct library searches. As with their self-proclaimed writing ability, lawyers tend to take for granted their facility with both doctrinal research and nondoctrinal research. Because our immediate preoccupation lies with legal writing and only secondarily with legal research, I merely point out here that each is important enough to receive special consideration in the legal curriculum. Relief from acute academic congestion can be achieved in almost any curriculum by dropping several of what some wit has called "Law and the Elephant" courses. Peter Nycom has described legal research as "the unrecognized legal discipline." Nycom, Legal Research — The Unrecognized Legal Discipline, in Sense and Systems in Automated Law Research 81 (1973).

drafting for those interested in becoming specialists in that field.

Another reason for including core courses in legal writing or drafting is that the "pervasive" method of teaching (distributing a discipline widely within the substantive curriculum), which has succeeded beautifully for the case discipline and only mildly for such across-the-board concerns as professional responsibility, has yet to be satisfactorily adapted to legal drafting. The specifics are simply not there. I tried the pervasive approach of injecting drafting exercises into substantive courses such as Sales and Legislation, but I found that I was spending too much time accomplishing too little. From then on, I limited my drafting efforts in such courses to commenting, as the occasion arose, on the deficiencies of particular litigated instruments. As a buttressing operation, it was no substitute for a core course in drafting.

In the meantime, either we are relegated to the status quo, which is intolerable, or we can break up this congeries of problems and give each element the attention it deserves. Unfortunately, the venerable case method has little to offer preventive law, where we deal only with kinds of situations, dissociated from the specifics of particular controversies.

A pedagogical strategy that has proved ineffective is a variant of the thoroughly discredited apprentice method. Under the fashionable rubric of "clinical education," law students are released to outside legal offices to perform designated drafting tasks, theoretically under the specific supervision of those offices and under the general supervision of the responsible law professor. Ironically, the drafting standards of the participating offices, more often than not, have suffered from the very malaise that the clinical program is intended to cure, and the general supervision supplied by the law schools has been inevitably loose.

There is an important difference here between placing student interns in such offices (which has been generally unsuccessful) and having them work within the law schools and under professorial supervision on assignments made by such offices (which has, on occasion, been quite successful). This difference, of course, relates to the law schools' opportunity for close supervision, the general need for which needs no stating. Even when it is otherwise successful, the latter approach is inhibited by the same limited reach as narrow-gauged seminars.

Today's main problem is to adopt and perfect a pedagogy for teaching elementary legal drafting to large classes. It is not enough to conduct an occasional and reasonably successful project seminar for a mere 8 to 12 students. The course must be not only equipped to handle substantially larger numbers but made acceptable to faculty members other than intimidated recent recruits.

The most baffling pedagogical problem is to handle the chronic student requests for personal attention. This requires developing a method of sharing with the students the specific benefits of completing their assignments. The classic method is to have the instructor or a teaching associate prepare a detailed critique of each student paper. Although this is not as effective as the idealized master-apprentice approach, the latter is beyond the practical reach of educational institutions. As the theoretically next-best alternative, personal attention to individual student papers has been routinely accepted as a *sine qua non* of instruction in expository writing.

Wherever adopted, this assumption has effectively aborted large-class instruction in legal drafting in the law schools. Almost no senior professor will touch such a course because, in the absence of enough affordable teaching assistants, he is unwilling to suffer the numbing burden of analyzing and discussing individual student drafts, which are much more demanding than ordinary expository exercises.[8] Putting that burden on junior instructors has failed because they are only rarely trained in the drafting discipline, and the traditional editorial tedium has resulted in high turnover. Worst of all, the intellectual challenge of most classroom writing projects (as traditionally conducted) is relatively low. This is unlikely to intrigue the better legal minds.

The only solution seems to be to provide a communicable pedagogy by which the instructor can learn as he teaches. This

[8]The problem of academic burn-out is serious. See Cavers, Signs of Progress: Legal Education, 1982, 33 J. Legal Ed. 33, 37 (1983).

can be done only by providing (1) carefully programmed student materials and (2) an adequate teacher's manual.

The heart of the problem is to extend the instructor's academic reach without overwhelming him with the analysis and evaluation of individual papers, without diluting the drafting effort with unnecessary forays into conventional legal research, and without relying substantially on teaching associates. On the positive side, the main problem is to broaden the perspective of both the student and the professor to give them an adequate appreciation of the relation of drafting to the improvement of substantive policy and its impact on jurisprudence and, indeed, on thinking itself.

Here is how we have tried to solve the problem of teaching legal drafting at the Indiana University School of Law. My sample is the class of 78 students who took my course in Legal Drafting in the spring of 1980. This was taught without pedagogical help, my part-time student assistant having only kept track of student assignments and done miscellaneous research.[9]

The keystone of the approach is the decision, announced at the outset of the course, that the student will get *no* outside-of-class individual attention. Assignments are collected and their receipt recorded. The professor samples the papers and from them selects for class discussion the most typical or significant drafting errors or contributions, most of which are predictable. The relevant parts of the text involved are put on transparencies that can be marked up while projected on a screen, making it possible for all members of the class to observe and participate with the professor in developing an improved draft.

At the beginning of the course, each student acquires a course book of materials exemplifying almost all of the many dimensions of drafting.[10] Although the materials are too voluminous to be discussed in their entirety, the student is required to read all of them to enlarge his perspective, particularly to emancipate him from the confining notion, still widely shared,

[9]Once the pattern has been set, even this kind of help can be dispensed with, depending on the size of the class.
[10]MLD.

that legal drafting requires only wordsmiths and that legal drafting, far from being a hard-nosed basic intellectual discipline, is a pedestrian skill, worthy only of paraprofessionals or eccentric pedants.

Among the topics covered by the course materials are the nature of legal drafting, some basics about language and communication (especially in their interaction with thought), relations between the draftsman and his client, the basic elements of communication, the role of external context, the relation between legal drafting and research, the concepts of legal audience and editorial attitude, the problem of conceptualizing the elements implicit in the particular problem, some rudiments of epistemology, the architecture of legal instruments, the elements of drafting style, the role of definitions, the hierarchical aspects of legal rules, the simplification of legal instruments (especially consumer documents), scientific aids to drafting (such as logic trees, flow charts, "language normalization," and computers), amendments, the organizational and procedural environment necessary to effective drafting, and the codification of statutes or regulations.

Although most of the material is unconventional for law schools, it is intellectually stimulating and much of it illumines other courses. My own experience is that the discipline helps to root out many of the verbal and logical fallacies that plague, not only the law, but intellectual disciplines generally. The total effort is likely to be as much of an eye opener for the instructor as it is for the student. Indeed, there is some justification for dissociating legal drafting from other legal writing courses and, as suggested in section 1.3, teaching it as legal dialectic and thus as a component of jurisprudence.

During the course, the student is given a series of assignments, each designed to represent a significant aspect of the drafting process. One is to explicate an existing or proposed document for the purpose of preparing the student to interrogate the client. Another is to prepare a set of questions to ask the client before embarking on a first draft. Another is an exercise in de-gobbledygooking an existing contract preliminary to a thoroughgoing effort to revise it without changing substance.

Others involve specialized exercises in arrangement, tabulation, definition making, and simplification.

To fit the untrained instructor for this job requires a more detailed teacher's manual than is ordinarily necessary in conventional law courses. On the other hand, burdening him with too many teacher aids can be as frightening as providing him with inadequate ones. It is best to steer a middle course.[11]

Three teaching methods are used: (1) Students are required to read the entire course book, regardless of what materials are discussed in class. (2) Substantial amounts of material are handled by lecture. (3) With the help of an overhead projector, a number of legal provisions are redrafted, through joint effort, in class.

The new instructor educates himself through reading the course book and its manual and through the normal interaction of teacher and student.

Many of the specific points are illustrated by projecting transparencies. In most cases, the students have been given hard copy on which they can post the changes made in class and which they can then keep as a record.

As the first part of the final examination, the students are assigned a take-home project of revising (without substantive change) a complicated one-page legal document that contains typical drafting inadequacies. They are also invited to append such comments on the redraft as they think appropriate.

The second part, which is given in the conventional way, is designed for the most part to let the students show how adequate a grasp they have of the assigned reading materials. It also includes a short drafting exercise to help verify that they have not obtained outside help on the take-home part.

Viewed as a whole, these materials may look formidable to a person teaching the course for the first time. Closer study will show that, taken step by step, the job is clearly manageable.

Although drafting cannot be taught in a substantive vacuum, its rudiments can be effectively taught at any time after the first year and even after the first semester. A plausible reason for

[11]As in the Teacher's Manual for MLD.

postponing it is that student attrition helps alleviate the heavy pedagogical burden that today's scarcity of law teachers who are adequately trained in drafting would otherwise impose. But with adequate materials now available, there is a better reason. Properly presented, these materials offer not only a stimulating intellectual challenge but a pedagogical change of pace that can be a welcome escape from the repetitions and now traditional tedium associated with the third year of modern legal education.

A person teaching legal drafting for the first time, however experienced in teaching substantive law by the case method, should not expect the level of performance that he might expect were he teaching a new substantive course by the case method.

Anonymous student evaluations made at the end of the 1980 effort showed a general satisfaction with the course, with several important reservations. The most prevalent comment was that the student would have liked personal attention, a seemingly reasonable suggestion that for any large class must, nevertheless, be rejected out of hand. To comply with it would mean early death for the course (and perhaps for the professor!).

In general, the approach is sound because it works. Even so, there may be lingering doubts. The new approach has worked well for me, but will it work acceptably for others, especially the untrained and inexperienced?[12] The answer seems to be yes.

A highly expert legislative draftsman with considerable teaching experience wrote that, armed with the teacher's manual, even a chimpanzee could teach the course! This hyperbolic reassurance does not necessarily reflect the reactions of the generally competent, dedicated, but inexperienced law teacher who might be prone to panic at his first encounter with the materials in the course book.

The teachers of that description with whom I am most familiar who are now using the new approach not only have had no difficulty in adjusting to the materials but have expressed great satisfaction with their intellectual content. An important

[12]See, e.g., Johnstone, Some Thoughts on Legislation in Legal Education, 35 Mercer L. Rev. 845, 846 (1984).

psychological boost was provided by the teacher's manual's inclusion of much explanatory "connective tissue" that was withheld from the course book to help the conscientious teacher look good, even during his first effort. The supportive strength of the teacher's manual is strongly suggested by the fact that in the four years since publication I have received only one call for help on a specific problem. To ease the transition to proficiency, the manual recommends limiting the initial course to two hours (instead of the preferred three) and a maximum of 20 students. After that, the ceiling can be lifted.

We have here a professional problem that cannot be solved outside the law schools and cannot be solved in any significant way inside the law schools until the nature of the drafting problem is better understood by academics and an adequate pedagogy is adopted to deal with it. It can be solved only through required courses in legal drafting that adequately reflect the fact that legal drafting is a special kind of writing that concerns all lawyers and constitutes a basic part of their education.

Index of Words and Phrases

References are to sections.

a, 9.4, 9.6
a day, 9.3
a foot, 9.3
a year, 9.3
about, 9.3
above, 9.1
above-mentioned, 9.1
accorded, 9.3
act (in the sense of "statute"),
    11.2.6
actor, 10.4, 10.6
actual, 6.11
adequate number of, 9.3
admit of, 9.3
afforded, 9.3
afore-granted, 9.1
aforementioned, 9.1
aforesaid, 9.1
after, 9.3
after this . . . takes effect, 9.3
all, 9.5
all and every, 9.2
all of the, 9.3
all the, 9.3
allow, 9.3
already, 6.8
alter or change, 9.2
and, 6.2, 6.3, 9.9
and/or, 6.2
any, 9.5
any and all, 9.2
applies (in the sense of having
    applicability), 8.20

apply (in the sense of "make an
    application"), 8.20
appoint, 8.20
approximately, 9.3
as, 9.6
as amended, 11.2(6)
as if, 7.3
as the case may be, 9.7
ask, 9.3
assist, assistance, 9.3
assumes and agrees, 9.2
at his request, 9.3
at the time, 9.2
attains the age of, 9.3
attempt, 9.3
attends, 8.20
attorney, 10.4 n.3
authorize and direct, 9.2
authorize and empower, 9.2
authorize and require, 9.2

because, 9.3
becomes . . . years old, 9.3
before, 9.3
before-mentioned, 9.1
before or after this . . . takes effect,
    8.17, 9.3
before this . . . takes effect, 6.8
begin, 6.8
bind and obligate, 9.2
binds, 9.3
bitch, 10.8

Index of Words and Phrases

Index of Words and Phrases

one, 10.5
or, 6.2, 6.3, 9.9
or, in the alternative, 9.3
order and direct, 9.2
over and above, 9.2

paragraph . . . of subsection . . . of
  section . . . , 9.3
part, 9.3
Party of the First Part, 9.3
pay, 8.20
per annum, 9.3
percent, 9.3
per centum, 9.3
per day, 9.3
per foot, 9.3
perform and discharge, 9.2
perform or observe, 9.2
period, 9.3
period of time, 9.3
permit, 9.3
place, 9.3
policeman, 9.3
portion, 9.3
possess, 9.3
possible, 9.3
power and authority, 9.2
premises (in the sense of matters
  already referred to), 9.1
present, 6.8
preserve, 9.3
prior, 9.3
prior to, 9.3
proceed, 9.3
procure, 9.3
properly, 6.11
prosecute its business, 9.3
provide for, 8.20
provision of law, 9.3
purchase (as a verb), 9.3
pursuant to, 9.3

question, 9.3

real, 6.11
recognize, 8.20
refers to, 7.5

relieve and discharge, 9.2
remainder, 9.3
remise, release, and forever
  quitclaim, 9.2
render, 9.3
request and demand, 9.2
require (in the sense of "need"),
  9.3
residence, 3.4
respectively, 9.7
rest, 9.3
result, 9.3
retain, 9.3

said (as a substitute for "the,"
  "that," or "those"), 9.1
same (as a substitute for "it," "he,"
  "him," etc.), 9.1
sections . . . - . . . , 9.3
sections . . . to . . . , inclusive, 9.3
send, 9.3
send for, 9.3
shall, 6.7, 9.3, 9.4
shall and will, 9.2
shall be considered (or "deemed")
  to be, 9.2
shall be construed to mean, 9.2
shall have and exercise (the power),
  9.2
shall have and may exercise (the
  power), 9.2
shall not, 6.7, 9.4
she, 10.5
show, 9.3
smallest, 9.3
sole and exclusive, 9.2
some, 9.5
specified (in the sense of "expressly
  mentioned" or "listed"), 9.3
speed up, 9.3
spend, 9.3
spokeswoman, 10.7
stand and be in full force, 9.2
start, 9.3
state (in the sense of "utter"), 9.3
State of . . . , 9.3
stop, 9.3
subject to section . . . , 5.7
subsequent to, 9.3

369

Index of Words and Phrases

Index of Names

References are to sections.

Abel, Brent M., app. A
Abrahamson, Shirley S., 11.4; 11.4
   nn.1, 2, 4, 6, 10, 11, 13, 16
Allen, Layman E., 3.4 nn.5, 7, 11;
   6.3; 6.3 n.10; ch. 12 n.1; 12.1
   n.17; 12.2; 12.2 n.4; 12.3 n.3
Alston, William P., 10.3 n.7
Anderson, Robert M., 13.1 nn.2, 3,
   10; 13.11 n.1; 13.12 n.1
Attneave, Fred, 3.4 n.1
Ausness, Richard, 10.5 n.7

Bacon, Francis, 8.2 n.1
Barber, James P., 12.2 n.4
Beaman, Middleton, 2.1; 4.2 nn.13,
   14; 4.7 n.1; 8.4 n.1; 8.12
Beardsley, Charles A., 4.11 nn.1, 6
Becker, Benjamin Max & David M.,
   4.2 n.10
Benjamin, Robert M., 3.4 n.10
Benson, Robert W., 12.3 n.1
Bentham, Jeremy, 1.2 n.5; 2.4 n.1;
   8.2; 8.4; 8.20 n.1
Berenson, Bernard, 3.2 nn.2, 3; 7.3
Berger, Arthur L., app. A
Berkeley, Edmund, 12.2
Bernanos, Georges, 4.14 n.4
Bernstein, Theodore M., 10.5; 10.5
   nn.8, 13
Bertrand, Gerard, 11.2 n.13
Bhatia, V. K., 8.26 n.4
Bicks, Alexander, app. A
Bird, Frank B., 5.7 n.2

Biskind, Elliot L., app. A
Black, Bernard, 8.10 n.10
Black, Max, 2.1 n.8; 3.2 nn.1, 4; 3.5
   n.3; 3.6 n.2; 10.3 n.3
Blake, R. H., 5.3 n.1
Blank, Philip B., app. A
Block, Gertrude, 10.5 nn.3, 16
Bohl, Marilyn, 12.3 n.6
Bonapart, Alan D., 12.1 n.10
Bosanquet, Bernard, 6.2 n.3
Bowe, William J., app. A
Boyd, William E., 12.1 n.20
Brabner-Smith, J., 6.12 nn.1, 5, 7
Bracton, Henry de, 8.7 n.4
Bradley, F. H., 6.2 n.3
Burtt, Edwin Arthur, 6.2 n.3

Caldwell, Mary Ellen, 4.2 nn.4, 8
Cantwell, William P., 12.1 n.10
Cardozo, Benjamin, 1.3 n.3
Carman, Fred J., 4.2 nn.2, 10
Carroll, Lewis, 2.3; 7.3
Carter, Jimmy, 8.3; 8.11; 10.1
Cavers, David, F., 1.2 n.1; 8.2; 8.2
   n.7; 8.12; app. F n.8
Charrow, Robert P., 8.9
Charrow, Veda R., 8.9, 8.9 nn.2, 5;
   10.5 n.21
Chatterton, Thomas A., 12.1 nn.17,
   26, 28; 12.3; 12.3 n.5
Cherry, Colin, 3.2 nn.2, 3, 7; 3.7
   n.1; 7.3
Christie, G. C., 3.5 nn.1, 2

Index of Names

Cloe, Lyman H., 13.1 n.7
Clubb, Jr., Merrel D., 10.3 n.1
Cohen, Morris R., 2.4 n.4; 3.5 n.3; 5.4; 5.5 n.1
Coke, Edward, 8.2 n.2
Collins, Ronald K. L., 10.7 n.1
Conard, Alfred F., 3.8; 8.2
Coode, George, 8.14 n.2; 8.17 n.2
Cook, Robert N., 2.1 n.2; 7.1 nn.2, 4; app. A
Cooper, Frank E., 4.2; 4.5 n.2; 4.7 n.1; 7.3 n.6; app. A
Corcoran, James M., app. A
Craft, Edward O., 8.26 n.3; 13.2 n.2
Craies, W. F., 8.4; 8.4 nn.2, 5
Crawford, Earl T., 13.1 nn.3, 7, 10; 13.11 n.1; 13.12 n.1; 13.13 n.1; app. E
Cullen, Robert K., 6.12 n.1; 13.10 n.1; 15.1 n.1; app. A; app. E n.3
Curtis, Charles P., 1.2; 3.3 n.3; 3.5 nn.2, 7

Dale, William, 8.8 n.5
Dalkey, Norman, 3.5 n.2
Deer, Richard E., 1.1 n.4; 2.1 n.6; 4.2 n.2; 4.3 n.1; 4.4 n.1; 4.10 n.1; app. A
Demeo, J. N., 12.1 n.10
Dennenberg, Walter, 8.3
Dewey, John, 7.3 n.8
Dick, Robert C., 6.2 n.1; 6.9 n.1; 12.2 n.4; app. A
Dickerson, Reed, 2.5 n.2; 3.2 nn.1, 12; 3.4 n.12; 3.5 n.2; 3.9 nn.2, 3, 4, 7; 4.11 n.2; 5.6 n.1; 8.2 nn.1, 7, 8; 8.6 n.2; 10.7 n.6; 11.2 n.6; ch. 12 n.1; 12.1 nn.1, 6, 29; 12.3 n.8; 13.5 n.1; 13.7 n.1; postscript; app. F. nn.1, 3, 5
Dosland, G. L., 6.12 n.1
Driedger, Elmer A., 6.1 n.5; 6.2 nn.2, 4; 6.3 n.1; 6.5 n.1; 6.9 n.1; 6.12 n.1; 7.1 n.1; 8.8 n.2; 8.14 n.2; 8.17 n.2; 9.4 n.2; 10.5; 11.2 n.1; 13.2 n.1; 13.14 n.1; app. A
Durand, Harrison F., app. A

Edwards, Thomas Haines, 12.2 n.4
Eliot, T. S., 4.14
Elliott, Ronald E., 12.3 n.6
Ely, John Hart, 6.3 n.7
Endacott, Richard R., app. A
Engholm, Rudy, ch. 12 n.1 12.1 n.17; 12.2 nn.4, 5; 12.3 n.3
Everstine, Carl N., 13.1 n.3; 13.2 n.1

Fabyanske, Marvin T., app. A
Farina, Mario V., 12.3 n.6
Farmer, Lawrence, 12.1 n.23
Farnsworth, E. A., app. A
Farrand, Max, 4.9 n.3
Felker, Daniel B., 8.29 n.2
Felsenfeld, Carl, 3.2; 3.8; 5.2; 7.5 n.7; 8.7 nn.5, 7; 8.8; 8.9 n.1; 8.10 n.1; 8.10; 8.19; 8.29; app. A
Fendler, Oscar, app. A
Fertig, John H., 6.12 n.1
Flesch, Rudolf, 8.2; 8.9; 8.14 n.1; 8.19; 8.20 n.1; 12.1 n.18
Fowler, H. W., 1.3 n.2; 2.3; 8.10; 9.6 n.1
Fox, Sanford J., 12.3
Frank, Jerome, 3.4 n.3
Freeman, Morton S., app. A
Freund, Ernst, 6.12 n.11
Friedman, Milton R., 4.11 n.2; app. A
Friedman, Wilbur H., 8.5 n.1
Friendly, Alfred, 10.7 n.2
Frye, Albert M., 6.2 nn.2, 3

Galbraith, John Kenneth, 10.5 n.7
Ghardi, James D., 8.10 n.9
Gibson, W. R. Boyce, 6.2 n.3
Givens, Richard A., 8.8 n.6
Glassner, Herbert M., app. A (see "Bicks")
Goldfarb, Ronald, app. A
Goodrich, Peter, 1.3 n.1
Gopen, George D., app. A
Gowers, Ernest, app. A
Grad, Frank P., 8.8

Index of Names

Gray, John Chipman, 3.3 n.3
Grimaldi, Ralph, 12.3 n.1
Grutzner, Edward, app. A

Hall, Edward T., 3.2
Hall, Jerome, 7.3 n.10
Halsbury, Lord, 13.11 n.1
Hammond, R. Grant, 13.5 n.5
Hare, R. M., 1.2 n.5
Harris, J. S., 5.3 n.1
Hart, Jr., Henry M., 3.8 n.5
Hathaway, George H., 8.3 nn.1, 5,
    12
Hawkes, Terence, 2.5 n.2
Hayakawa, S. I., 4.14 n.2
Heller, Joseph, 4.14
Henle, Paul, 2.5 n.3
Hirsch, Donald, 6.2 n.6; 8.24; 10.2
    n.1; 10.5 nn.18, 19; 11.2 nn.8, 9;
    11.2; 11.4; 11.4 n.15; app. A
Hogan, Michael J., 10.1 n.7
Holland, V. Melissa, 8.9 n.2
Holmes, O. W., 3.1 n.1
Holt, Anatol W., 12.3 n.9
Huff, William S., app. A
Huxley, Aldous, 1.2

Ilbert, Courtenay, 1.2 nn.1, 5; 2.4
    n.1; 4.15 nn.1, 2; 6.12 nn.1, 4;
    8.4 n.10; 8.14 n.1

Jacobson, Richard, 10.7 n.6
Jamieson, N. J., 12.1 n.19
Jefferson, Thomas, 8.2
Jevons, W. S., 5.4
Johnson, Flora, 10.7 n.3
Johnson, James P., 1.1 n.4; 1.2 n.6;
    2.3 n.4; 2.4; 2.4 n.5; 3.7; 8.1;
    8.13 n.1; 8.26 n.2; 8.27 n.1; 9.3
    n.1; 11.3; app. A
Johnstone, Quintin, app. F n.12
Jones, Chester Lloyd, 8.4 n.4; 8.15
    n.1; 13.11 n.1
Jones, Harry Willmer, 3.5 n.1; 4.2
    n.14; 4.15
Jones, Michael F., app. A
Jones, Roger S., 2.5 n.2

Joseph, H. W. B., 6.2 n.3

Karlin, Calvin J., 8.10 n.10
Keaton, Harry J., app. A
Kemph, Carleton Richard, app. A
Keynes, J. N., 6.2 nn.3, 4
Kilpatrick, James K., 10.5 n.7
Kirk, Maurice B., 2.1; 2.1 n.3; 4.2;
    4.3 n.2; 6.2 n.6; 6.13; 8.6 n.3; 9.4
    n.3; 13.2 n.1
Klipstein, Harold D., app. A
Kufeld, William M., app. A (see
    "Bicks")

Ladd, Mason, 4.2
Lamb, Sydney M., 2.4 n.3
Landis, Harry, app. A
Lazarus, Carlos E., 13.1 nn.2, 3, 10
Lerner, Max, 4.14 n.5
Leventhal, Harold, 8.6
Levi, Albert W., 6.2 nn.2, 3
Lewis, Clarence M., 4.9 n.1
Lincoln, Abraham, 4.12
Lipson, Ashley S., 12.1 n.10
Littleton, Arthur, 2.2 n.1
Llewellyn, Karl N., 1.2 n.8; 13.5
Locke, John, 5.5 n.1
Lockwood, David G., 2.4 n.3
Luneberg, William V., 3.8 n.5
Lyman, Charles M., 4.2; 4.2 n.12;
    app. A

MacDonald, Duncan A., 8.3
McCall, Raymond J., 6.2 n.4
McCoy, Richard, 12.1 n.17
McFadden, Cyra, 10.1 n.7
MacKaye, James, 2.2 n.1; 3.4 n.6;
    5.4; 5.4 n.3; 7.3
McMahon, David B., app. A
Mace, C. A., 6.2 n.3
Mackay, E. J. G., 1.2 n.3; 3.8 n.2
Makkai, Adam, 2.4 n.3
Mandel, Ludwig, 3.1 n.1; 4.11 n.2;
    app. A
Marceau, LeRoy, app. A
Marcus, Sumner, 13.1 n.7
Manson, Carl H., 13.1 n.3, 13.2 n.2

373

Index of Names

Martin, Harold C., 2.2 n.1; 3.2
n.11; 3.4 n.13; 4.14 n.2; 5.2 n.1;
7.1 n.1; 7.3 n.10; 7.5 n.6; app. F
n.3

Mason, Paul, 13.1 nn.3, 7; 13.11
n.2

Matthews, Thomas Alexander, app.
A

Maverick, Maury, 8.2

Mayer, Martin, 4.14 n.6

Mayers, Harry R., app. A

Meldman, Jeffrey A., 12.3

Mellinkoff, David, 8.4 nn.6, 10; 8.5
n.4; 8.7; 8.7 nn.3, 6; 10.4; 10.4
n.4; 10.5 nn.1, 3, 10, 17; app. A

Menard, Jr., Albert R., 13.2 n.1;
13.12 n.1; app. A

Merrell, Floyd, 2.5 n.2

Miers, D., 12.3 n.1

Mill, John Stuart, 5.5 n.1; 7.3

Miller, Arthur S., 3.3 n.2; 3.6
n.6

Miller, Casey, 10.3 n.1; 10.7 n.1

Minor, James B., 8.26 n.1

Mircher, John J., 8.10 n.9

Moynihan, Daniel F., 4.14 n.4

Montrose, J. L., 3.4 n.7; 6.1 n.4;
6.3 nn.9, 11

Morris, Charles, 2.2 n.1

Morris, Gouverneur, 4.9 n.3

Moses, Albert L., 12.1 n.10

Mucklestone, Robert S., app. A

Nagel, Ernest, 2.4 n.4; 3.5 n.3; 5.4;
5.5 n.1

Newman, Frank C., 3.4 n.5

Nida, Eugene A., 2.2 nn.2, 3

Nutting, Charles B., 10.7 n.6;
13.5

Nycom, Peter, app. F n.7

O'Connor, June, 10.3 n.3

Ogden, C. K., 2.3; 3.2 n.1; 7.3 n.9

Ohmann, Richard M., 2.2 n.1; 3.2
n.11; 4.14 n.2; 5.2 n.1; 7.1 n.1;
7.3 n.10; 7.5; app. F n.3

Ohta, Tomoyuski, 12.2 n.4

Pantzer, Kurt F., 1.1 n.4; 2.1 n.6;
4.2 n.3; 4.3 n.1; 4.4 n.1; 4.10 n.1;
app. A

Partridge, Eric, 10.5

Pasquesi, T. A., 12.1 n.10

Pavlov, I. P., 7.3

Peacock, James Craig, 6.3 n.3; 8.24
nn.1, 11; 8.24; 8.26 n.5; 11.2
n.11; 11.4; 11.4 nn.1, 3, 9, 14;
app. A

Peirce, C. S., 2.2; 3.2 n.1

Pfeiffer, John E., 12.2

Philbrick, Frederick Arthur, 1.2

Piesse, E. L., 2.1 n.1; 2.3 n.3; 3.1
n.1; 4.4 n.1; 4.9 n.1; 6.1 n.3; 6.8
n.1; 7.1 n.1; 8.4 n.9; 8.14 n.1;
8.17 n.1; 8.18 n.1; app. A

Pirsig, Robert M., 2.5 nn.4, 5; 5.3
n.1

Plato, 1.3 n.1; 7.3

Poldervaardt, A., 6.12 nn.1, 3, 5, 6,
7, 8, 10, 12; 13.11 n.3

Pollock, Frederick, 4.15

Quine, Willard Van Orman, 6.2 n.3

Rabkin, Jacob, 4.7 n.1; 4.11 n.5

Radin, Max, 3.6 n.1

Ray, Dixy Lee, 10.1

Raymond, James C., app. A

Read, Horace E., 6.12 nn.1, 4, 5, 7,
8, 10

Redish, Janice C., 8.7, 8.9 nn.2, 3,
8, 9

Redman, Ben Ray, 7.6.3

Richards, George A., app. A

Richards, I. A., 2.3; 3.2 n.1; 7.3
n.9

Richie, Leroy C., 8.3 n.12

Robinson, Richard, 2.4 n.7; 7.1 n.1;
7.2 nn.1-8; 7.3; 7.3 n.10; 7.4;
7.6.3; 7.6 n.17

Rodell, Fred, 8.2

Rombauer, Marjorie Dick, 10.5
nn.6, 20; app. A

Rosser, John Barkley, 6.2 n.1

Russell, Alison, 6.12 n.2; 13.11 n.1

Index of Names

Index of Subjects

References are to sections.

Index of Subjects

Index of Subjects

Index of Subjects

Index of Subjects

Index of Subjects

Over-generality as disease of language, 3.6
Over-particularity
  as disease of language, 3.5
  avoided by using lowest common denominator, 2.4
Over-precision as disease of language, 3.5
Over-vagueness as disease of language, 3.5
Overzealousness, 2.1

Pairs of terms, 4.10, 9.1
Panel as critic of completed work, 4.9
Parentheses, 6.1, 8.21
Parol evidence rule, 4.2
Partial definition, 7.2, 7.4, 7.5
Participation of draftsman in final phases of enactment. See Postscript
Participle less desirable than finite verb, 8.20
Passive approach in boilerplate provisions, 5.7, 13.7
Passive past participle semantically ambiguous, 6.4
Passive voice, 8.18
Past tense, 8.17
Pavlov's dogs, 7.3
Pedagogical problems, app. F
Pentagon's efforts to simplify, 8.2
Perception, creativity in, 2.5
Periodic statutory revision, 8.24
Period to begin in future, 6.8
Person, use of first, second, or third, 8.19
Persuasion in legal instruments, 1.2
Petri nets, 12.3
Placement. See Location
"Plain English." See Plain language
Plain language statutes. See also Readability; Simplification
  existing statutes, 8.3
  good faith defense, 8.3, 8.10
  history of need for, 8.2
  inappropriateness for instruments other than consumer

    instruments, 8.11
  preferability of uniform act, 8.10
  readability formulas, 8.3, 8.9
  specifications for, 8.10
  terms of art, 8.7
Plain language movement, history of, 8.2, 8.3
Planning as core of preventive law, 1.3
Planning, estate, use of computers in, 12.1
Pleading, with illustrative revision, 14.10
Plural
  as less desirable than singular, 6.5
  change from singular to, 6.5
  use of to avoid verbal sexism, 10.5
Point of view
  as affecting arrangement, 5.2
  as affecting basis of division, 5.4
"Policies of clear statement," 3.8 n.5, 8.8 n.5
Policy
  as affected by across-the-board checks, 4.8
  as affected by systematic treatment of form, 2.2, 2.3, 4.8, 4.14, 14.1
  ascertaining and helping to perfect, 1.2, 2.1-2.3, 4.8
  controlled by client, 2.1, 4.2, 4.5
  draftsman's role in making, 2.1, 2.2
  knowledge of important, 2.1
  of interest to draftsman, 1.2, 2.1, 4.2
Policy clauses. See Purpose clauses
Policy maker, draftsman as, 2.1
Policy statements, broad, 13.5
Postal statute, 6.3, app. B
Postal statute tabulated, app. B
Potential ambiguity differentiated from actual ambiguity, 6.3
Powers, conferring of, 8.18, 9.4
Pragmatics, 1.3
Precision
  as requirement of "plain English" statutes, 8.10

Index of Subjects

general repeal clause, avoidance
of, 11.7.1, 13.11
kinds of, 13.8
location of clause, 13.6
state constitutional restrictions on
form of, 13.1, 3.11
when amendment preferred,
13.11
Repetition of provisions, 5.5
Requirement compared with
condition precedent, 6.10
Research
as aided by "write early"
approach, 4.14
by draftsman, 4.2
computerized, 4.3
time needed for, 4.2 n.14
Responsibility for drafting
centralized, 4.9
Retyping of draft desirable, 4.7
Reverse (negative) implication, 3.4,
3.5, 3.9, 8.10
Revised Statutes section, with
illustrative redraft, 14.5
Revised Statutes, nature of, app.
E.3
Revision as step in composition,
4.7
Rewriting as necessary to good
drafting, 4.7
Rhetoric, legal, distinguished from
legal dialectic, 1.3 n.1
Rights, conferring of, 9.4
Right stated as duty to enjoy right,
9.4
Risk. See Danger
Role of modern lawyer, 1.1
Rules of interpretation, 3.9
Rules of Procedure, American Bar
Association, 12.3

Savings clauses, 13.6, 13.12
Scientific aids. See also Computers
algorithmic programming, 12.1
Boolean algebra, 12.2
flowcharts, 12.1 n.18, 12.1, 12.2,
12.3
"logic machine," 12.2
logic trees, 12.1 n.20, 12.1, 12.3

magnetized cards, 12.1
nonmechanized and nonelectronic
systems, 12.1
Petri nets, 12.3
propositional calculus, 12.2
Rules of Procedure, American
Bar Association, flowchart
for, 12.3
symbolic logic, 12.2
title 10, United States Code,
§1201, flowchart for, 12.3
Scriveners as draftsmen, 8.4
Section, separate sheet for each
desirable, 4.6
Sectional sequence
in legal instruments generally,
5.6
in statutes, 13.6
Sections
designation of parts of, 8.25
length of, 6.3
numbering of, 8.24
Segmenting language, as similar to
factoring, 8.1
Selection
of concepts, 2.4
of entities, 2.4
Semantic ambiguity
in false imperative, 6.7
in general, 3.4, 6.2, 6.4-6.9
in passive past participle, 6.4
in provision involving time or
age, 6.8
in provisos, 6.9
Semantic innovation in legal
drafting, 10.2 n.1, 10.5
n.17
Semantic readjustment, minimizing,
10.4 n.7
Semantics, 1.3
Semiotics, 1.3
Sentence form of tabulation 6.3
Sentences, length and form of, 8.9,
8.14
Sentence structure, complexity of,
as threat to clarity, 8.7
Sentry Life Insurance Company,
8.3
Separability clauses. See
Severability clauses

Index of Subjects

Index of Subjects

Titles of Statutes
  long titles, 13.2
  short titles, 13.4
Titles, state constitutional
    requirements for Statutory,
    13.1, app. D
Tone, 8.9, 8.19
Topic headings, 8.23
Training in draftsmanship, 1.1,
  app. F
Truth in Lending Act, 8.4

U.S. Commission on Civil Rights,
  10.1 n.2, 10.3 n.9, 10.4 n.6
Uncertainty
  of modification or reference,
    6.1-6.3
  removal not always necessary, 3.8
Unconscionability, 2.1, 2.5, 8.2,
  8.8
Under-generality as a disease of
  language, 3.6
Under-vagueness as a disease of
  language, 3.5
Undistributed middle to be avoided,
  9.9
Uniform Age of Majority Act
  (proposed), 8.8
Uniform Commercial Code, 6.3,
  8.7
Uniform Determination of Death
  Act, 8.26 n.6
Unitary phrases, 6.1
United States Code, 5.5, 5.7, 7.6.3
  n.12, 13.5, 14.5, Postscript,
  app. E.2
Unnecessary concepts, 2.4
Usability as benefit of good
  drafting, 14.2
Usage. See also Humpty
    Dumptyism
  as basis for implication, 3.4
  as device for avoiding ambiguity,
    6.14
  as device for improving policy,
    2.3.3
  as related to court decisions, 3.9

  as related to simplicity and
    readability, 8.1
  importance of conforming with
    established, 2.3.3, 7.3.
Users of the language, 3.2. See also
  Audience; Speech
  communities
"Utraquistic subterfuge," 2.3.1

Vagueness
  as caused by open texture of
    concepts, 3.5
  compared with ambiguity, 3.5
  compared with generality, 3.6
  in general, 3.5, 8.6
  need to control, 4.5
  often desirable, 3.5
  reduced by definition, 7.2, 7.4
Verbal plane as related to
    conceptual plane, 1.2, 2.2,
    4.14, 7.4
Verbal sexism, ch. 10
Verbal units, 6.1
Verb in definition, 7.5
Verbosity, 3.2, 3.7, 4.10, 8.4, 8.14
Verbs preferred, 8.20
Voice, 8.18

Warranty, consumer product, 2.1,
  8.3
Westlaw computer system, 12.1
Will
  codicils as amendments, 11.3
  policy considerations, 4.2
  with illustrative redraft, 14.4
Wordiness, 3.2, 3.7, 4.10, 8.4, 8.14
Word processor as aid to drafting,
  12.1
"Write early" approach as aid to
    thought and research, 4.14
Writing by conference, 4.9
Written numbers combined with
  arabic, 6.6

Zoning ordinance, 2.4